D1594297

The
Authority
of
Experience

Literature & Philosophy

A. J. Cascardi, General Editor

This series publishes books in a wide range of subjects in philosophy and literature, including studies of the social and historical issues that relate these two fields. Drawing on the resources of the Anglo-American and Continental traditions, the series is open to philosophically informed scholarship covering the entire range of contemporary critical thought.

Already published:

The Authority *of* Experience

Sensationist Theory *in the* French Enlightenment

John C. O'Neal

The Pennsylvania State University Press
University Park, Pennsylvania

Library of Congress Cataloging-in-Publication Data

O'Neal, John C.
The authority of experience : sensationist theory in the French
Enlightenment / John C. O'Neal.

    p.   cm. — (Literature and philosophy)
Includes bibliographical references and index.
ISBN 0-271-01515-2 (alk. paper)
1. Enlightenment—France. 2. Empiricism. 3. Philosophy,
French—18th century. 4. French literature—18th century—History
and criticism. I. Title. II. Series.
B1925.E5054 1996
146'.44—dc20   95-18091
                                             CIP

Copyright © 1996 The Pennsylvania State University
All rights reserved
Printed in the United States of America
Published by The Pennsylvania State University Press,
University Park, PA 16802-1003

It is the policy of The Pennsylvania State University Press to use acid-free paper for
the first printing of all clothbound books. Publications on uncoated stock satisfy the
minimum requirements of American National Standard for Information Sciences—
Permanence of Paper for Printed Library Materials, ANSI Z39.48-1992.

Contents

For Kate and Vaughan

Acknowledgments

The research for this book was supported by a Margaret Bundy Scott Fellowship from Hamilton College in the spring of 1988 and a National Endowment for the Humanities Fellowship for College Teachers and Independent Scholars in 1989–90. Without such support from Hamilton and the Endowment, this work could not have been completed in a timely manner.

For permission to reprint material that appeared earlier in articles and reviews, I am indebted to the editors of *Corpus, Revue de Philosophie* (Chapter 3); *Eighteenth-Century Studies* (a few sentences from Chapters 1 and 8); *L'Esprit Créateur* (Chapter 4); *Philosophiques* (Chapter 2); *Romanic Review* (Chapter 5); and *Studies on Voltaire and the Eighteenth Century* (brief summaries of Chapters 2 and 4).

In its various stages, this project involved many different people, to whom I wish to express my sincere thanks here. Jean Starobinski, Aram Vartanian, and Renée Waldinger gave me initial encouragement and direction. At Hamilton's Burke Library, Joan Wolek in interlibrary loans and Catherine Miller and Julia Abel at the circulation desk made my many visits to the library both enjoyable and productive. For library privileges during my stays in Paris, I am grateful to the Bibliothèque Nationale and the Ecole des Hautes Etudes en Sciences Sociales. Max Grober, Julie Hayes, Marie-Hélène Huet, Regina Kecht, John H. O'Neill, Peter Rabinowitz, English Showalter, Martin Staum, Virginia Swain, Daniel Teysseire, and John Yolton all read portions of the manuscript and offered helpful suggestions. For their assistance with the bibliography, textual references, and the preliminary clerical preparation of the manuscript, I am thankful not only to Christina Bariatti and Ingrid Johnson but especially to Jody Jackson and Amy O'Neill, whose diligence and perseverance I greatly appreciate. In the choice of an appropriate image for the book's cover, I benefited from the sage advice of Charles Wirz, who confirmed my penchant for a painting of a child by either Greuze or Chardin. Pierre Rosenberg from the Louvre generously granted me permission to reproduce Chardin's *L'Enfant au toton* and supplied the photographic print necessary for the cover and the illustration opposite the Introduction. This image serves as a visual aid for many of the ideas I am trying to convey in this book—among others, the increased attention paid to children in the eighteenth century; the centrality of movement in the cognitive process, a process which is informed to a large degree by the senses; and the absorption and fascination that learning can entail in all its positive forms, including play. Last, I want to thank my family: my wife, Nancy, who unfailingly remained my strongest advocate throughout this project, and my children, Kate and Vaughan, from whom I have learned a great deal. At their own level, my children have come to understand the authority of experience and its import for their own lives, which I hope will continue to be wonderful and empowering adventures in learning. This book is dedicated to them.

A Note on the Selection and Translation of Texts

In selecting the editions of French primary sources consulted for this study, I attempted to use those that were readily available or that became available in the course of my research. In this regard, I was enormously helped by the major publishing endeavor at Fayard under Michel Serres's direction entitled "Corpus des oeuvres de philosophie en langue française." To date, the series has published many of the authors studied here. When works were not available in this series, I used as much as possible editions that were currently in print. All translations of French primary works and of unattributed French secondary works in this book are my own. The punctuation of the original passages, however, has been retained.

List of Abbreviations

DE	Claude-Adrien Helvétius, *De l'esprit.*
DH	———, *De l'homme, de ses facultés intellectuelles et de son éducation.*
DSL	Etienne Bonnot de Condillac, *Dissertation sur la liberté.*
EA	Charles Bonnet, *Essai analytique sur les facultés de l'âme.*
EFP	Marie-François-Pierre Gonthier de Biran [Maine de Biran], *Essai sur les fondements de la psychologie et sur ses rapports avec l'étude de la nature.*
EI	Antoine-Louis-Claude Destutt de Tracy, *Elements d'idéologie.*
Em	Jean-Jacques Rousseau, *Emile.*
EOCH	Etienne Bonnot de Condillac, *Essai sur l'origine des connaissances humaines.*
EP	Charles Bonnet, *Essai de psychologie, ou Considérations sur les opérations de l'âme, sur l'habitude et sur l'éducation.*
ER	Etienne Bonnot de Condillac, *Extrait raisonné du "Traité des sensations."*
F	Claude-Adrien Helvétius, *De l'homme, de ses facultés intellectuelles et de son éducation* (Fayard edition).
HM	Julien Offray de la Mettrie, *L'Homme-machine.*
HNA	———, *Histoire naturelle de l'âme.*
J	Donatien-Alphonse-François, comte [marquis] de Sade, *Justine, ou Les Malheurs de la vertu.*
LC	Etienne Bonnot de Condillac, *La Langue des calculs.*
LD	Pierre Choderlos de Laclos, *Les Liaisons dangereuses.*
OC	Jean-Jacques Rousseau, *Oeuvres complètes.*
PB	Donatien-Alphonse-François, comte [marquis] de Sade, *La Philosophie dans le boudoir, ou Les Instituteurs immoraux.*
PP	Charles Bonnet, *Principes philosophiques sur la cause première et sur son effet.*
RA	Denis Diderot, *Le Rêve de d'Alembert.*
RPM	Pierre-Jean Georges Cabanis, *Rapports du physique et du moral de l'homme.*
SN	Paul-Henri Thiry, baron d'Holbach, *Système de la nature, ou Des lois du monde physique & du monde moral.*
TSn	Etienne Bonnot de Condillac, *Traité des sensations.*
TSy	———, *Traité des systêmes.*

Jean-Baptiste Chardin, *L'Enfant au toton,* Louvre
(© Photo Réunion des Musées Nationaux)

Introduction

Т he most widely accepted way of thinking among eighteenth-century French intellectuals, sensationism was both a philosophical and a psychological theory.[1] Its adherents attempted to explain the origin of knowledge even as they strove to reach an understanding of human behavior. Their goal, in sum, was to facilitate progress in as wide a range of human endeavors as possible. Sensationist arguments from the very experience of the body in seeing, hearing, smelling, tasting, and touching enabled all individuals to chal-

---

1. I have used the term *sensationism* (*sensualisme* in French) throughout this work to avoid confusion with the journalistic tendency to hyperbole known as sensationalism. Even in French, the term *sensationniste* is much preferable to *sensualiste* according to Victor Delbos, who nonetheless recognizes the conventionality of the latter term. See Delbos, *La Philosophie française* (Paris: Plon, 1921), p. 252. Sainte-Beuve took a similar position earlier and reproached Victor Cousin for a certain "iniquity" in popularizing the use of the inaccurate word *sensualiste* around 1817. Sainte-Beuve's *Mes Poisons* is quoted in Paul Foulquié, *Dictionnaire de la langue philosophique* (Paris: Presses Universitaires de France, 1962), p. 667. The earliest known reference to this French adjective in its philosophical meaning dates from 1801. See Bernard Quemada, ed., *Matériaux pour l'histoire du vocabulaire français: Datations et documents lexicographiques,* 2d ser., vol. 22 (Paris: Klincksieck, 1983), p. 265.

The word *sensationalism* still has a certain currency in English, having been introduced around the middle of the nineteenth century, although the recent inclusion in the *Oxford English Dictionary* of an entry for *sensationism* suggests the increasing use of the term I have employed here. See the *Oxford English Dictionary,* prepared by J. A. Simpson and E. S. C. Weiner, 2d ed., vol. 14 (Oxford: Oxford University Press, 1989), p. 977. The word *sensualism* or *sensualist* in English suffers from the same inadequate reflection of the theory and negative connotation that Delbos and Sainte-Beuve had noticed in the French word *sensualiste*.

lenge the sometimes arbitrary authority of those in positions of power
and led to the establishment of a new authority, the authority of
experience. As the wisdom that is accumulated over time about what is
hot or cold, good or bad, right or wrong, beautiful or ugly, experience
provides the individual with compelling support for his or her convictions in the face of so-called higher authorities making contrary claims.

Sensationist theory itself rested on two assumptions: that we cannot
know external objects with certainty; all we can know is our relation to
them (i.e., our sensations), and that we can achieve progress only after
coming to a thorough understanding of the nature of humanity, which
was seen as universal. Sensationism's chief claim was, of course, that all
of our ideas come from sensations.[2] But numerous philosophical and
psychological implications flowed from this claim. On the philosophical
level, the belief in the sensory origin of ideas allowed sensationists to
view all of the mind's faculties as nothing more than transformed
sensations. Absolutely everything that occurs at one stage or another in
intellectual development can be traced back to the senses. For some
sensationists more than for others, the soul played a key role in relating

---

2. It was Aristotle's notion of the sensory origin of ideas that first gave sensationism
prominence as a philosophy. His important dictum, rendered usually in Latin by his successors,
was: *"Nihil ist in intellectu quod non prius fuerit in sensu"* (nothing is in the mind that has
not first been in the senses or, translated less literally, all knowledge comes to us through the
senses). See Paul F. Cranefield, "On the Origin of the Phrase *Nihil ist in intellectu quod non
prius fuerit in sensu," Journal of the History of Medicine and Allied Sciences* 25 (1970),
77–80. This was to become the refrain (my term) used time after time by the eighteenth-
century French sensationists for the Aristotelian concept of the sensory origin of ideas, to
which they gave renewed importance, and assumed in the thinking of practically every
philosophe. Aristotle's sensationism was echoed by Plato, then later by Thomas Aquinas,
Francis Bacon, Thomas Hobbes, and John Locke. For works by these authors that reflect basic
sensationist precepts, see Aristotle, *De anima, De memoria et reminiscentia*, and *Metaphysics*;
Plato, *Protagoras, The Republic, Theaetetus*, and *Timaeus*; Thomas Aquinas, *Summa theologica*; Francis Bacon, *Novum Organum*; Thomas Hobbes, *De Corpore, De Homine*, and *Levia-
than*; and John Locke, *An Essay Concerning Human Understanding*. Full references for these
standard works and the ones in the following paragraph can be found in the bibliography.

In the eighteenth century, George Berkeley, David Hume, and David Hartley discussed
questions raised by sensationism. See George Berkeley, *A Treatise Concerning the Principles
of Human Understanding*; David Hume, *A Treatise of Human Nature, An Abstract of "A
Treatise of Human Nature,"* and *Enquiry Concerning Human Understanding*; and David
Hartley, *Observations on Man*. For the history of sensationism, see Edwin G. Boring, *Sensation
and Perception in the History of Experimental Psychology* (New York: Appleton-Century-
Crofts, 1942), pp. 3–7; and *The Encyclopedia of Philosophy*, 8 vols. (New York: Macmillan
and the Free Press, 1967), esp. 7: 415–19. But it was especially Locke's *Essay Concerning
Human Understanding* that directly influenced thinkers across the Channel and inspired them
to develop their own view of experience based on sensation.

the mind to the body. In any case, sensationism constituted a kind of religiously moderate midway point between Cartesian metaphysical dualism (in which the mind and body are viewed as separate entities) and materialism's monism (in which the mind and body are viewed as one substance). Philosophically, sensationism had affinities with idealism, materialism, and *idéologie*.

On the psychological level, sensationism implied that our actions can be explained by the pursuit of pleasure or the avoidance of pain. Human behavior then in this view is essentially determined by self-interest. One's basic pursuit in life is happiness and self-preservation. The plenitude of one's existence depends on the quantity of pleasurable feelings. The more one feels (and feels happily, in the absence of pain), the more fully one exists. The contrary is also true. Few enjoyable moments make for a paltry life. Even pain, though, can play a constructive role, for we learn from those instances in which we experience it. No pain, no gain, as the popular saying would have it. In a transformation of Descartes's "I think, therefore I am," a sensationist might well say "I feel, therefore I am." Feeling is living, and living is feeling. According to the sensationist outlook, life begins and ends with sensibility.

Distinguishing sensationism were a number of characteristics and tendencies, perhaps the most important of which lay in an insistence on method. Above all, the sensationists used analysis as their method of choice. Their form of analysis entailed a genetic approach that began with an origin (in this case, the sensations) and proceeded in an orderly fashion step by step toward an explanation. In so doing, sensationism emphasized continuity and precision. It privileged simplicity over complex abstraction, the particular over the general, analysis over synthesis. True to the overall objective of the *philosophes,* the sensationists endeavored by their method to avoid error and obfuscation as well as to establish positively the light of reason. Consequently, the theory was never far removed from the rationalist tendency of the period.

Previous discussions of sensationism by intellectual historians and others have been marred by three shortcomings: (1) a reluctance to recognize the centrality of sensationism to Enlightenment epistemology that has resulted in a piecemeal treatment of it, (2) the surprising lack of emphasis given to this major cognitive theory in relation to the period's aesthetic thinking and the evolution of the novel, particularly in view of the close connection between psychology and literature at the time, and (3) a failure to take into account the important implications of the polemics surrounding sensationism in the eighteenth century and today. In addressing these shortcomings, I first bring together in one place an analysis of all the leading sensationists. I then offer a new theory of aesthetics for the French Enlightenment based on sensationism.[3] Finally, I discuss various interpretations of sensationism, showing what drew thinkers to this theory and repelled them from it, both then and now. Such an approach yields the corresponding three parts of the book, all of which are organized to a large degree around the central question of the mind-body problem.

The book's three parts thus concentrate on the history of an idea, sensationist aesthetics, and the politics of sensationism. Part I provides a comprehensive background for sensationism by putting it in a historical perspective and following its development through the major adherents of this theory; this sets the stage for later discussions. This part consists of three chapters focusing on Enlightenment thinkers writing in French who can be called sensationists, namely, Condillac, Bonnet, and Helvé-tius, who are frequently mentioned as the central sensationists.[4] It is important to consider sensationists other than Condillac to see the slightly different forms the theory would take on. Particular attention is nonetheless paid to Condillac, widely recognized as the movement's chief spokesman, and to his intertextual sources in Locke. Condillac provides a new definition of experience based on his notions of origin and nature, analysis, order, analogy, and language, all of which give rise to his method in a logical sensationism. Bonnet introduces a physiologi-cal element into sensationism. His own analytic method and sensation-ism are fundamentally intertwined in their reliance on a continuum between the body and the mind. This continuum in turn depends on a number of general assumptions that include the necessity of a soul, humanity's mixed being, the law of union, the predominance of the physical over the metaphysical, and the importance of succession in human cognition. Moving away from the sensationists' spiritualist posi-tion, minimal as it was in Condillac and somewhat eccentric in Bonnet, Helvétius develops both a sanguine and a fatalistic view of physical

3. The French Enlightenment, as it is defined in this book and for the purposes of the works cited from the period in the bibliography, is understood as extending from 1700 to 1815, that is, from the beginning of the century until the time sensationist disciple and *idéologue* leader Destutt de Tracy finished publishing his *Eléments d'idéologie.*

4. See, for example, Martin S. Staum, *Cabanis: Enlightenment and Medical Philosophy in the French Revolution* (Princeton: Princeton University Press, 1980), pp. 34–48. Staum is of course interested in the enormous influence the sensationists exercised on the *idéologues* later in the century.

sensibility. He connects it not just to memory, judgment, and ideas but also—at a fundamental level through pleasure and pain—to the passions, virtue and vice, self-interest, happiness, sociability, and power. It will become apparent from this first part as well as from the rest of the book that sensationism informed to a considerable degree the writings of many other important thinkers during the period. All of the chapters, then, supplement the partial treatments the subject has received to date as the object of biased, polemical discussion,[5] as a topic in a chapter where it is either singled out along with related ideas,[6] subsumed under more general categories and associated primarily with one author, Condillac,[7] or outlined very briefly in its principles and considered only marginally.[8] Needed is a general introduction to what Hippolyte Taine called "the doctrine of the most lucid, methodical, and French minds to have honored France."[9] From this first part emerge an

5. Victor Cousin, *Philosophie sensualiste au dix-huitième siècle,* 3d ed. (Paris: Librairie Nouvelle, 1856). This work summarizes the revised and corrected class lectures Cousin first presented in 1819. It is usually accepted that Cousin set out to deny Condillac any credibility in philosophical circles for posterity. He was intent on ensuring the triumph in French schools of Cartesianism over the Condillacian tradition, associated as it was in part with materialism. As Cousin himself writes: "We proposed firmly to combat and interrupt the tradition of materialism and atheism, of blind hatred for Christianity, of revolutionary violence and servility that it conveyed to us, and which at the beginning of the Restoration, weighed still with a fatal burden on minds and souls, and raised obstacles to the establishment of freedom as well as of true philosophy" (pp. ii–iii; my translation).

Of the French Enlightenment's sensationists, Cousin chooses to write about Condillac, Helvétius, and Saint-Lambert. I have substituted Bonnet for Saint-Lambert, whose work is quite far removed in time from that of the other mainstream sensationists. Could Cousin have omitted Bonnet because of Bonnet's Swiss origins? Saint-Lambert's *Catéchisme universel* was not published until 1798. Although conceived as early as 1755, it appears to fall more into the category of the work of the *idéologues* as disciples of the sensationists than into that of original sensationist theory. Cousin's consciously tendentious approach to the sensationists was more or less unopposed until Hippolyte Taine attempted to rescue the theory around the mid-century. See Taine, *Les Philosophes français du XIXe siècle,* 2d ed. (Paris: Hachette, 1860).

6. J. H. Brumfitt, *The French Enlightenment* (Cambridge, Mass.: Schenkman, 1973), pp. 99–132; and Lester Crocker, *An Age of Crisis: Man and World in Eighteenth-Century French Thought* (Baltimore: Johns Hopkins University Press, 1959), pp. 119–35.

7. Ernst Cassirer, *The Philosophy of the Enlightenment,* trans. F. C. A. Koelln and J. P. Pettegrove (Princeton: Princeton University Press, 1951).

8. Edwin G. Boring, *Sensation and Perception in the History of Experimental Psychology,* pp. 3–7; and Walter J. Moser, "De la signification d'une poésie insignifiante: Examen de la poésie fugitive au XVIIIe siècle et de ses rapports avec la pensée sensualiste en France," *Studies on Voltaire and the Eighteenth Century* 94 (1972), esp. 279–85.

9. Taine, *Les Philosophes français du XIXe siècle,* p. 6. See also p. 16, where Taine calls Condillac's method "one of the masterpieces of the human mind" and where he bemoans the neglect of Condillac's works.

attempt at such a general introduction and an increasingly precise idea of sensationism, as it was understood not just by Condillac but also by his fellow sensationists. A broad grasp of the theory at this point of the book is indispensable for the ensuing discussion of aesthetics.

Part II pursues the ongoing inquiry into the genesis of the novel[10] by pointing out the unexamined contribution sensationism makes to eighteenth-century aesthetics in the light of previous studies on the subject.[11] The eighteenth century, which laid the foundation for modern psychological studies of perception, also witnessed the rise of the novel. If, as Bakhtin assures us, epistemology is the "dominant discipline for the novel," then surely we should look to sensationism for the ways the eighteenth-century novel is structured.[12] Although some observers

10. Of special interest to the present study are Peter Brooks, *The Novel of Worldliness: Crébillon, Marivaux, Laclos, Stendhal* (Princeton: Princeton University Press, 1969), and Thomas M. Kavanagh, *Enlightenment and the Shadows of Chance: The Novel and the Culture of Gambling in Eighteenth-Century France* (Baltimore: Johns Hopkins University Press, 1993), esp. the chap. "Toward a Novel of Experience," pp. 107–22. Brooks's definition of worldliness emphasizes social experience, that is, the individual's interaction with a society that qualifies both as "the whole of organized human existence" and "the self-conscious 'being together' of an élite" (p. 4). Focusing on the elemental origins of human behavior and thought rather than on the human activities in society that occur considerably later, I take, as do the sensationists themselves, what might best be called a phenomenological approach to experience. Social experience is seen from this perspective as an extension, albeit a highly sophisticated one, of certain fundamental early behaviors. Kavanagh calls attention to the importance of experience for the novel but develops this along the lines of probability theory. See also Georges May, *Le Dilemme du roman au XVIIIe siècle: Etude sur les rapports du roman et de la critique, 1715–1761* (New Haven: Yale University Press, 1963); English Showalter, Jr., *The Evolution of the French Novel: 1641–1782* (Princeton: Princeton University Press, 1972); Catherine Lafarge et al., ed., *Dilemmes du roman: Essays in Honor of Georges May* (Saratoga, Calif.: Anma Libri, 1989); and Joan DeJean, *Tender Geographies: Women and the Origins of the Novel in France* (New York: Columbia University Press, 1991).

11. Jacques Chouillet, *L'Esthétique des lumières* (Paris: Presses Universitaires de France, 1974); Isabel F. Knight, *The Geometric Spirit: The Abbé de Condillac and the French Enlightenment* (New Haven: Yale University Press, 1968), pp. 176–97; and Ira O. Wade, *The Structure and Form of the French Enlightenment*, vol. 1, *Esprit philosophique* (Princeton: Princeton University Press, 1977), pp. 279–312.

12. Mikhail Bakhtin, "Epic and Novel: Toward a Methodology for the Study of the Novel," in *The Dialogic Imagination: Four Essays by M. M. Bakhtin*, ed. Michael Holquist, trans. Caryl Emerson and Michael Holquist (Austin: University of Texas Press, 1981), p. 15. This key passage from Bakhtin is worth quoting in its context: "In ancient literature it is memory, and not knowledge, that serves as the source and power for the creative impulse. . . . The novel, by contrast, is determined by experience, knowledge and practice (the future). . . . When the novel becomes the dominant genre, epistemology becomes the dominant discipline." I am grateful to Irene Tayler and Rita Goldberg for the bibliographical reference to this section of Bakhtin's work where he makes the association between epistemology and the novel.

acknowledge the important nexus between psychology and aesthetics, they have not explored, for instance, the major implications of Condillac's chief psychological work, the *Traité des sensations*, or the psychological writings of Bonnet and Helvétius for literary aesthetics—the subject of Chapter 4 in this part.[13] Simply put, a contemporary theory of the mind, my study shows, can be seen as a theory of the novel. This is not to say that all authors consciously followed a sensationist aesthetics in the period. Aesthetics was of course beginning to take hold as a branch of philosophy only with Baumgarten at the mid-century. But a study of sensationism and eighteenth-century French literature can and indeed does reflect the fertile interconnections between literature and philosophy at the time. Sensationism directly suggests useful ways in which authors might develop their characters, plots, and narratives as well as shape the attitude of their readers. Moreover, the age's literary productions can be understood in the century's own terms according to a general philosophical view current at the time and not limited exclusively to one theorist. The chapter also explores the possibility of a gender bias in Enlightenment epistemology as formulated through sensationist theory. Does the mind in the writings of these theorists refer to man, and the body and sensations to woman? This part includes a practical application of this aesthetics to many literary works from the period and a detailed discussion of its pertinence to one work, Graffigny's *Lettres d'une Péruvienne*. This epistolary novel provides in many ways a textbook example of such an aesthetics and serves to underline the interplay between sensationism and the century's most persistent literary theme—sensibility, which gave primacy to feeling as a *modus operandi*. A close analysis of this particular book indicates the ways in which a work by a woman author can both use and subvert novelistic conventions issuing from a sensationist aesthetics. For this theory is shown to generate contemporary subgenres such as the *Bildungsroman*, the critique of mores, the love novel, the novel of sensibility and of seduction as well as popular *topoi* like persecuted innocence, the problem of evil, libertinism, exoticism, and cultural relativism. All of these are blended in an original but unstable way characteristic of the emerging French novel. Works from the late Enlightenment by Laclos and Sade attempt to turn around this aesthetics in a perverse fashion. Perversion is carried out on the level of character, plot, and narrative as

13. Cassirer, *The Philosophy of the Enlightenment*, p. 298; Knight, *The Geometric Spirit*, p. 181.

these two authors attack the implications from sensationists' discussions of the mind. Those discussions had typically centered on clear language, sensibility, experience, and the soul.

Part III complements the general introduction to sensationism in Part I. Any introduction of this nature must take into account sensationism's significant implications for education as well as for materialism and for *idéologie*—two other eighteenth-century philosophies with which sensationism is often compared for good reasons, as the last two chapters make clear. Additionally, this part treats the politics surrounding the topic of sensationism especially in the eighteenth century but also in our own times. The two previous parts bear fruit at this point as the mind-body problem comes prominently to the fore. A number of significant questions are raised by the implications of sensationist theory. Is the mind merely a passive mechanism? If so, how can human beings exercise their free will? What is the relationship between sensation and sentiment or feeling? How does sensationism distinguish itself from and contribute to the views taken by the materialists and *idéologues?* Can the senses be developed to improve man's moral character or do they lead inevitably to self-interest and evil? What are the limits of personal pleasure and sensualism? Does sensationism provide a realistic view of humanity's position in the Chain of Being that can explain both rational and irrational or even brutish behavior? These questions allow for a coherent appraisal of the mind-body problem and other important issues such as the problem of free will, the problem of evil, and the conflict between private, individual desires and a public sense of duty to the community—a conflict that has given rise to the phenomenon of narcissism, identified by twentieth-century sociologists as one of the principal ills of modern Western society.[14] These issues were all fervently contested in the eighteenth century and still spark animated debate today.

The chapters in Part III deal specifically with education, materialism, and *idéologie.* All of them demonstrate the ways in which thinkers can make different uses of the same philosophy. Although general ideas from sensationism may be shared between two distinct writers or theories, the results produced by these writers and theories are sometimes different. In Chapter 7, which is on education, Helvétius and Rousseau are shown to share similar sensationist views to effect moral

14. On the emergence of narcissism, see Christopher Lasch, *The Culture of Narcissism: American Life in an Age of Diminishing Expectations* (New York: Norton, 1978).

and intellectual progress. But their respective attitudes about progress differ markedly. The history of two other Enlightenment theories, materialism and *idéologie,* are for their part too closely related to that of sensationism to be omitted from a book on this subject. A comparative study of these other movements provides a critical analysis of sensationism from two different perspectives and deepens our understanding of this theory. In a study of the transition from sensationism to materialism, Chapter 8 addresses questions of epistemology and of origin, the mind-body problem, the immateriality of the soul, movement, causality, passivity, and determinism. Although the *idéologues* themselves used sensationist tenets, they also reacted critically to some of them, especially sensationism's exclusive focus on the sensations as the sole cause for our ideas. They came to extend the notion of experience to embrace both external and internal phenomena.

The Conclusion summarizes some of the main observations from the chapters and opens a discussion of the lessons of the French Enlightenment for our own times. Ultimately, this investigation aims to reveal our abiding human strengths and weaknesses as beings endowed with sensibility, our concern for others and preoccupation with ourselves. A sustained analysis of the enormously influential mind-body problem during the critical period that definitively shaped modern consciousness provides an exemplary point of departure for doing so and helps bring a new focus to some of our most pressing debates about late twentieth-century society.

PART I

THE EIGHTEENTH-CENTURY
FRENCH HISTORY OF AN IDEA

1

Condillac and the Meaning of Experience

When the *Essai sur l'origine des connaissances humaines* by Etienne Bonnot de Condillac appeared in print in 1746, fifty-six years had elapsed since the publication of John Locke's monumental *Essay Concerning Human Understanding*. For a variety of reasons, the abbé de Condillac could assume his readers' familiarity with Locke's writings. The French *Abrégé* (1688) of Locke's *Essay* written by Leclerc for the *Bibliothèque universelle* two years before the publication of Locke's work, Coste's translation (1700) of the *Essay,* Voltaire's popularization of the British empiricist's philosophy in his *Lettres philosophiques* or *Lettres anglaises* (1734), and the numerous reviews of Locke's *magnum opus* as well as books inspired by it in the eighteenth century all made Locke one of the most influential thinkers for the French Enlightenment.[1] In order to affirm his own importance, Condillac had at once to establish the connections between Locke's philosophy and his own related theory of sensationism as well

---

1. For a discussion of the propagation of Locke's ideas in France, see Gabriel Bonno, "The Diffusion of Locke's *Essay Concerning Human Understanding* in France Before Voltaire's *Lettres Philosophiques,*" *Proceedings of the American Philosophical Society* 91 (1947), 421–25; the same author's *La Culture et la civilisation britanniques devant l'opinion française de la paix d'Utrecht aux "Lettres Philosophiques"* (Philadelphia: American Philosophical Society, 1948), esp. pp. 83–96; Jørn Schøsler, *La Bibliothèque raisonnée (1728–1753): Les Réactions d'un périodique français à la philosophie de Locke au XVIIIe siècle* (Odense: Odense University Press, 1985); and John W. Yolton, *Locke and French Materialism* (Oxford: Oxford University Press, 1991).

as to distinguish between the two.[2] What emerges from Condillac's work—not just from this early work but from the core of his writings—is a new, different, and more specific definition of experience than that which existed previously. The concept ties together all of Condillac's basic thinking about the origin of human knowledge and the operations of the mind.

Like the word *nature* in the eighteenth-century parlance of the Republic of Letters, the term *experience* is coded. Both words are among the most frequently used expressions in the period and invariably confer a certain amount of authority on the point of view of any author using them to bolster an argument. Used as broadly as they were, the terms came to have multiple contextualized associations. This first chapter aims to show what Condillac means by experience, and how, why, when, and where he uses or alludes to the concept in relation to others such as nature, analysis, order, analogy, and language. These other concepts gain coherence and force from their association with experience. Theoretically, at least, if not perhaps altogether in practice, its polar opposites are arbitrariness and empty abstraction. To create a theory based on experience is to remain humbly within the confines of the world in which we live and to avoid extravagant, poorly founded explanations. In experience, Condillac finds as much a positive method for attaining the Enlightenment goals of truth and knowledge as a way of rooting out prejudice and mysticism. Experience for Condillac is intimately associated with sensory perception. The well-nigh exclusive connection between experience and sensation in Condillac's writings differentiates him from Locke, who emphasized both sensation and reflection as the sources for our ideas. An initial discussion of Condillac's divergence from Locke gradually unpacks the French author's radical definition of experience, grounded as it was in his notions of origin and nature, analysis, order, analogy, and language, all of which give rise to his sensationist method and progressive rationalism based on logic.[3]

2. In addition to Locke's influence, that of Isaac Newton should also be mentioned. According to Georges Le Roy, Condillac "borrowed from Locke the idea of a descriptive analysis of the understanding; from Newton, that of a single principle, explaining all nature." The sensations were to be the metaphysical counterpart for the force of gravity in the physical world that Newton discovered. See Le Roy, "Introduction à l'oeuvre philosophique de Condillac," in *Oeuvres philosophiques de Condillac* (Paris: Presses Universitaires de France, 1947), 1: xiv, xvii.

3. The definition of experience initiated here stresses the interrelation of many key Condillacian concepts and the unity of Condillac's writing. François Duchesneau offers the following definition: "In all likelihood, a mode of specific joining of the elements or materials

Condillac's praise and criticism of Locke in a number of his works provide an outline of the very path Condillac charts for himself in developing his theory of sensationism. Two of Locke's conclusions caught Condillac's attention: the sensory origin of ideas and the inability of metaphysical abstractions to explain knowledge, both of which were central parts of Locke's argument against innatism.[4] Inextricably tied to each other, these conclusions strongly influenced Condillac. But it was the former of the two on which Condillac focused his utmost attention and which no doubt led him, and consequently many other French thinkers because of his position as *chef de file* of the sensationists, to give less importance to some of Locke's other major propositions, such as the controversial suggestion that matter could think.[5] Nearly every *philosophe* thoroughly exploited the considerable potential of the sensory origin of ideas. It represented the veritable cornerstone of the edifice they were attempting to construct in order to achieve progress in a multitude of different ways. After centuries of the idea's neglect, Locke at last, following Bacon, not only sees the truth of Aristotle's dictum and what the Peripatetics used as a "principle" without understanding its real value—the powerful principle "that all our knowledge comes from the senses"—but goes on to "prove" it.[6]

Condillac invariably reproaches Locke, however, practically in the same breath for not having gone far enough. Presumably, Condillac himself will properly extrapolate Locke's thinking on the sensory origin of ideas. According to Condillac, Locke does not make it his main concern; nor does he adequately study "the origin of our knowledge" (*EOCH* 102). In point of fact, Condillac describes his own goal in terms of what Locke has not done:

---

of knowledge, that is, a connection of ideas among themselves or with signs such that it can gain credence as the fundamental law of the operations of the mind." See Duchesneau, "Condillac critique de Locke," *Studi internazionali di filosofia* 6 (1974), 77–98, esp. 78, 81. Duchesneau also notes Locke's definition of experience as the combination of sensation and reflection: "[For Locke] experience consists in sensory activity itself and corresponds either to the perception of impressions that have come from the outside world through the channel of the senses or to the consciousness the mind has of its own operations."

4. In the early eighteenth century, French discussions of Locke's *Essay* focused on three areas: the critique of innatism, the thinking-matter controversy, and the relation between reason and faith. See Bonno, *La Culture et la civilisation britanniques*, pp. 86, 89.

5. For a full discussion of this thinking-matter suggestion and the French response to it, see Yolton, *Locke and French Materialism.*

6. See Etienne Bonnot de Condillac, *Essai sur l'origine des connaissances humaines*, ed. Charles Porset (Paris: Editions Galilée, 1973), p. 102; hereafter cited as *(EOCH)*.

> The Scholastics and the Cartesians knew neither the origin, nor the generation of our knowledge: it is because the principle of innate ideas and the vague notion of understanding they used as a point of departure have nothing to do with this discovery. Locke succeeded better, because he started with the senses; and he left imperfect things in his work only because he did not develop the first advancements of the soul's operations. I have tried to do what this philosopher forgot; I have gone back to the first operation of the soul, and I have, it seems to me, not only given a complete analysis of understanding, but I have also discovered the absolute necessity of signs and the principle of the connection of ideas. (*EOCH* 283)

Condillac again praises Locke for beginning with the senses in explaining the origin of knowledge but criticizes him for not taking his idea far enough. Condillac pushes for a genetic, analytic explanation of knowledge, one that begins in the beginning and shows step by step how the soul develops its operations. For him, the beginning of experience and of the knowledge that comes from it is in the senses. While proceeding in this way, Condillac comes to discover language as the critical transitional stage between sensation and thought that Locke had overlooked.

In his *Traité des systèmes* (1749) and *Traité des sensations* (1754), Condillac reiterates and strengthens his position. "Locke," he writes in the earlier of these two pieces, "knew about the origin of our knowledge, but he does not develop its progress in sufficiently comprehensive and clear detail."[7] By the time of the publication of the *Traité des sensations,* Condillac finds the self-confidence to assert: "It is not enough to repeat, after Locke, that all our knowledge comes from the senses: if I do not know how they come from them, I shall believe that as soon as objects make impressions on us, we have all the ideas that our sensations can contain, and I shall be mistaken."[8] Although Locke may have "thrown much light" on the sensory origin of ideas, he also leaves a certain amount of "obscurity" on the subject and "does not suspect that they [the faculties of the soul] could derive their origin

---

7. Condillac, *Traité des systèmes,* ed. Francine Markovits and Michel Authier (Paris: Fayard, 1991), p. 82; hereafter cited as *(TSy)*.

8. Condillac, *Traité des sensations* (Paris: Fayard, 1984), p. 170. Hereafter cited as *(TSn)*.

from sensation itself."[9] While acknowledging his indebtedness to Locke, Condillac also distances himself from him and underlines the originality of his own work. Condillac thus grows in stature, as it were, at Locke's expense. There is unquestionably a transition that occurs in Condillac's attitude toward Locke. The passages quoted above clearly illustrate Condillac's increased independence vis-à-vis Locke on the question of the sensory origin of ideas, ideas which in turn contribute to one's knowledge. Moreover, the passages reinforce those that trace his mounting differences with Locke on the faculty of reflection.

Whereas Condillac forthrightly states that Locke passes somewhat precipitously over the first few steps in the acquisition of knowledge and that he will correct Locke's oversight, he is slow to come to terms with his differences with Locke about the crucial mental operation of reflection. After all, Locke had claimed that all knowledge comes from sensation or reflection; alongside of sensation, he places reflection.[10] In his earlier work, Condillac pays lip service to this coupling of the two operations. His own *Essai sur l'origine des connaissances humaines* is indeed quite Lockean in this regard. It should be remembered, however, that in the metaphysical vocabulary of the eighteenth century, reflection essentially denoted introspection, that is, the mind reflecting on its own activities. Reflection, then, is not synonymous with the faculty or the power of the mind known as reason, although it may of course enhance one's reasoning abilities. In its attempt to explain various mental phenomena, faculty psychology traditionally made a distinction between mental powers such as reason, memory, and the imagination and their operations.[11] In the initial moments of human experience, Condillac distinguishes man's "first thoughts," which are "different sensations," and "his second thoughts," which consist in acts of perceiving or

9. This quotation (p. 287) comes from an appendix to the *Traité des sensations* entitled *Extrait raisonné du "Traité des sensations"* in Condillac, *Traité des sensations* (Paris: Fayard, 1984); hereafter cited as *(ER)*. This work was first published with Condillac's *Traité des animaux* in 1755.

10. John Locke, *An Essay Concerning Human Understanding,* ed. Peter H. Nidditch (Oxford: Oxford University Press, 1975), bk. 2, chap. 1, esp. § 1–5, pp. 104–6 passim.

11. For a succinct statement on eighteenth-century faculty psychology and its importance for understanding the Enlightenment rhetoric of universal human nature, see Daniel W. Howe, "The Political Psychology of *The Federalist,*" *William and Mary Quarterly* 44 (1987), 485–509. Despite the distinction between the faculties and their operations, however, there was at times a tendency to conflate the terms. Reflection is thus sometimes referred to as a faculty or an operation.

imagining and which arise from man's "reflecting on what the sensations occasion in him" (*EOCH* 107). What makes possible the smooth transition from sensation to reflection is, as will be clarified subsequently, the invention of signs.[12] Although this passage at the very beginning of the *Essai* puts sensation first and reflection second, Condillac refers to them both at the same time elsewhere in this work as the sources for our first ideas. He does not insist on an important temporal nuance, as he will later. Moreover, he implies that sensations without reflection are "only sensations" and that they need reflection, which "has them considered as images of something" in order to become ideas (*EOCH* 169, 172). Through language, reflection turns sensations into ideas or produces ideas from them. Conversely, though, reflection depends on sensations, since "the mind is incapable of reflecting on nothing" (*EOCH* 176). There is indeed some ambiguity whether Condillac initially relates experience to sensation or to reflection. At times, he pairs experience and reflection as ways of understanding, while at others, he uses reflection alone in the sense of perceiving within oneself as a criterion for truth (*EOCH* 180, 190). One might best describe Condillac's sensationism as tentative in the *Essai.* When he does state that "all knowledge comes from senses," he precedes the statement with a hypothetical "if" (*EOCH* 288). Such an approach makes his claim that "the senses are the source of our knowledge" (*EOCH* 289) on the last page all the more surprising.

From the very beginning of the *Traité des sensations,* one detects the true emergence of Condillac's sensationism. No longer does he put reflection or any other operation of the mind on a par with sensation,

---

12. Careful not to use any arguments from innatism to explain the workings of the mind, Condillac resorts to the invention of language to "awaken" reflection. See Le Roy, "Introduction à l'oeuvre philosophique de Condillac," p. xv. Cf. André Rauch, "Le Souci du corps chez Condillac," *Stadion* 3 (1977), 65. For Rauch, "sensation comes to vivify the human mind" in Condillac's *Essai sur l'origine des connaissances humaines.*

Ellen McNiven Hine calls language the "bridge" between reflection and sensation in Condillac's metaphysics. See her "Condillac and the Problem of Language," *Studies on Voltaire and the Eighteenth Century* 106 (1973), 23. Elsewhere, Le Roy speaks of language as a kind of missing "link." See his *La Psychologie de Condillac* (Paris: Boivin, 1937), p. 75. He sees Condillac as "overthrowing Locke's classical thesis, which placed thought before language, [by] finding the origin of intellectual faculties in the use of conventional signs." See also Julie Andresen, "Langage naturel et artifice linguistique," in *Condillac et les problèmes du langage,* ed. Jean Sgard (Geneva: Slatkine, 1982), pp. 280–84. Andresen sees continuity in the development of language as Condillac portrays it. Her argument seems to point to a proportion—nature is to art as experience is to language—in which nature and sensory experience would be closely related if not equated.

but subordinates them to sensation: "Judgment, reflection, desires, passions, etc., are only sensation itself which is transformed differently" (*TSn* 11). Condillac uses the pleasure principle or the notion of self-interest, which involves the choice of more agreeable sensations over less agreeable ones, to explain how the faculties of the soul can be derived from sensation. The *desire* for a cold drink on a hot day can be explained by the pleasing *sensation* it has given us in the past. Likewise, judgment, reflection, and the passions correspond at some point to sensations. To appreciate just how far he has come from Locke, one need only consult his summary remarks: "Locke distinguishes two sources of our ideas, the senses and reflection. It would be more exact to recognize only one of them, either because reflection is in its principle but sensation itself, or because it is less the source of ideas, than the canal through which they flow from the senses" (*ER* 290).

The profound distinction from Locke at which Condillac only hints earlier has now been refined and fully formulated. Sensationism thus emerges from British empiricism as it had evolved through the writings of Bacon, Hobbes, and Locke. The sensory origin of ideas, which constituted a major but not all-encompassing part of Locke's philosophy, becomes central to Condillac's sensationist theory. One can retrospectively read Condillac's *Essai* and find—both in his plan to reduce all human understanding to a single principle as well as in his wish to find "a constant experience" on which he can rely for truth—early, masked allusions to sensation itself (*EOCH* 101). For sensation, seen as an actual and not an imaginary experience, fills the void Condillac saw in abstract, metaphysical explanations of knowledge.

Ironically, though, even as Condillac refines his sensationist theory and distances himself from Locke in the *Traité des sensations,* he also moves closer to him on the question of the physical influence of the body on the mind. As John Yolton has pointed out, there were in the eighteenth century three hypotheses explaining the relation of the mind to the body: physical influence, occasionalism, and preestablished harmony.[13] The systems are respectively associated with the Scholastics

13. Yolton, *Locke and French Materialism,* pp. 10–37. Following the *Journal helvétique* writer N. Beguelin, Yolton indicates that each system arises from the different ways in which perceptions themselves can be considered: either they " 'are carried to the mind by a *physical influence* on sense organs; or . . . God excites them in the soul each moment, on the *occasion* of changes made in sense organs; or . . . the soul is equipped from its creation with faculties for representing the universe' " (p. 10, my emphasis). The key words appear here in all but the last hypothetical explanation for perceptions, which is for the system of preestablished harmony. The system of physical influence attempts to establish a causal theory of perception

and the materialists; Descartes and Malebranche; and Leibniz. Locke subscribed to the system of physical influence, which established a direct connection between the body and the mind and which identified him with the materialist school of thought. Condillac, despite the alleged fact that as an abbot he only said one Mass in his life, had religious convictions that made him avoid any alignment with atheistic materialism.[14] His approach to the mind-body problem relies largely on the system of occasional causes, as the *Essai* makes clear: "The soul being distinct and different from the body, the body can be only the occasional cause of what it seems to produce in the soul. Hence one must conclude that our senses are only occasionally the source of our knowledge. . . . The soul is therefore absolutely able, without the help of the senses, to acquire knowledge" (109).[15] The constant cause, as opposed to the occasional cause, in this theory as well as in that of preestablished harmony, is God or some omnipotent being who for the most part lets the senses act as a means of transmitting knowledge to human beings.

Whereas Condillac's *Essai* fluctuates back and forth in its use of occasionalism,[16] the *Traité des sensations* introduces even further ambiguity in his thinking on the mind-body relation. Written, as it is generally viewed, as a reaction to the criticism leveled by Diderot in his *Lettre sur les aveugles* (1749), this treatise had to address the problem of Berkeley's idealism.[17] The *Essai* left some serious questions for Diderot about the possibility in Condillac's way of thinking for human beings to

---

not only from the mind to the body but also—and the rub came here—from the body (i.e., sense organs) to the mind.

14. For a discussion of Condillac's religious beliefs, see Knight, *The Geometric Spirit*, pp. 137–43.

15. In *Locke and French Materialism* (p. 72), Yolton uses a portion of the same passage from Condillac's *Essai*. For Yolton, Condillac is and remains essentially an occasionalist. For concise accounts of Malebranche and occasionalism, see Jean A. Perkins, *The Concept of the Self in the French Enlightenment* (Geneva: Droz, 1969), pp. 16–19; and the articles "Cartesianism" and "Mind-Body Problem" in *The Encyclopedia of Philosophy*, vol. 2, esp. pp. 41–42, and vol. 5, esp. pp. 342–43.

16. Yolton rightly points out that Condillac does not always use occasionalist language in the *Essai*. See *Locke and French Materialism*, p. 72; and Gianni Paganini, "Psychologie et physiologie de l'entendement chez Condillac," *Dix-Huitième Siècle* 24 (1992), 167–69. Paganini finds examples of physical causality in the *Essai*.

17. On the importance of Diderot's *Lettre sur les aveugles* for the composition of Condillac's *Traité des sensations*, see Emile Bréhier, *The Eighteenth Century*, in *The History of Philosophy*, trans. Wade Baskin, vol. 5 (Chicago: University of Chicago Press, 1967), pp. 80–86; Knight, *The Geometric Spirit*, pp. 79–83; and Le Roy, "Introduction," pp. xvii–xxi.

exist in a real, external world and not remain cut off from it in some ideal universe whose only reality consists in the various states of the mind.[18] Condillac's *Traité des sensations,* especially its passages on the sense of touch, ultimately proves the existence of such a real world that the hypothetical statue-man, ironically an abstract invention for Condillac, discovers through this sense.[19] But in the process there seems to be a shifting away from occasionalism and toward the theory of physical influence espoused by Locke. The movement of the statue-man toward the external world entails certain risks, not the least of which is recognition of the material nature of that world and the concomitant recognition of the body as another form of material substance interacting closely with it. The step from occasionalism to materialism can be but a small one, once emphasis is increasingly placed on the interaction of matter.

Although there are of course passages from the *Traité des sensations* that one could adduce to show Condillac's occasionalism, there are some others that are irreducibly problematic and point to an incipient turn to the theory of physical influence on his part.[20] Typical of these is

18. See Diderot, *Lettre sur les aveugles à l'usage de ceux qui voient,* in *Oeuvres philosophiques,* ed. Paul Vernière (Paris: Garnier, 1964), pp. 81–146, esp. pp. 114–15. In asking for some explanation of exteriority, could Diderot possibly have been disingenuously setting a materialist trap for Condillac?

19. By their very titles, the second and third parts of the *Traité des sensations* clearly underline the key role of touch in having one relate to the physical world. Respectively, they are entitled "Of Touch, or Of the Only Sense that Judges External Objects by Itself" and "How Touch Teaches the Other Senses to Judge External Objects."

In this *Traité,* the statue-man, which will be discussed later in the chapter on sensationist aesthetics, is Condillac's hypothetical construction of a marble statue whose senses come to life one by one. Condillac uses it to show how all of the mind's faculties are nothing more than transformed sensations. It is ironic, though, that someone so opposed to abstract and deductive thinking as was Condillac chose such an artificial statue to represent the evolution of the mind from sensation. Contrary to his professed method of starting with nothing mysterious, Condillac presents the statue as a given that he expects his reader to accept as such. Moreover, the statue's senses are unrealistically separated from one another. Although an ingenious and honest attempt on Condillac's part to focus on the earliest stages of intellectual development, the statue indeed hardly resembles a live human being.

20. Paganini, "Psychologie et physiologie," 168–71. Paganini detects Condillac's cautious approach to the theory of physical influence in the *Traité des sensations* and *Traité des systèmes* but does see evidence of the theory in Condillac's description of the neurophysiological functioning of memory and the causes of forgetfulness. Paganini argues persuasively against the view of Condillac as an entirely psychological writer who makes human beings into pure abstractions.

Phillip P. Hallie, however, believes that Condillac could not use the theory of physical influence for logical reasons and writes that the *Traité des sensations* "required a new

the passage in Part III, Chapter 2, in which the statue-man is shaking an object that produces a sound (a child's rattle comes to mind). By alternately shaking and not shaking the object (the senses of touch and hearing are combined here), the statue judges that the sound comes not from itself but from the object outside of itself. Such a sound is no longer perceived as being located exclusively in the soul but exists in the external world as well. The statue hears the sounds "in this [other] body" (*TSn* 164) and not just in itself. It may confuse these sounds with the sensation in itself but realizes that they come from without. A physical object acting on the senses thus appears here to be the direct cause, and not merely the occasional cause, of perceptions. In attempting to prove the statue's grasp of a real external world, Condillac finds himself in a difficult position. That he felt compelled to write the *Traité des animaux* (1755), to which was appended the overtly occasionalist *Extrait raisonné du "Traité des sensations"* (see 285, 293, 303, 307) as a defense against Buffon's charges of materialism, attests to an undeniable slippage on Condillac's part toward a materialistically oriented causal theory of perception. In so doing, he corrects the so-called misunderstanding. But his unconscious actions are not surprising for an age in which even traditional thinkers could slip into sympathetic support for the radical system of materialism.[21]

Related to Condillac's acceptance of the sensory origin of ideas is also his rejection of nonexperiential abstraction, whereby he demonstrates his other affinity to Locke. There is of course an apparent contradiction in Condillac's abstracting of ideas from sensation through a sensory theory of knowledge and his opposition to abstraction. Let us clarify from the outset that Condillac is by no means opposed to all abstractions; his very book constitutes an exercise in abstraction. He is, however, opposed to those abstractions that have no basis in experience. An overview of the times proves helpful here. Abstract philosophical formulations in the seventeenth and eighteenth centuries took many

---

approach, the rejection of the assumption that sensations or impressions are images occasioned by external material things. Condillac could not assume what he had to prove. By means of purely mental sensations he had to prove the existence of a material world external to the mind." See his entry on Condillac in *The Encyclopedia of Philosophy*, 2: 181.

21. Witness, for example, the denunciation of the abbé de Prades's Sorbonne thesis as heretical or the ambiguous writing of David Boullier. Discussion of these writers and their tendencies toward materialism can be found in Yolton, *Locke and French Materialism*, pp. 88–101, 110–35. My chapter on materialism will scrutinize the fine line between this theory and sensationism.

forms. But one of the most notorious was that of innate ideas, insofar as they tended to be accepted *a priori* by a kind of leap of faith and were not derived from experience. When Condillac decries the excesses of abstraction, he typically equates it with moving away from the senses.[22] Like Locke, Condillac strives to make metaphysics more scientific than it had been with its Cartesian notion of innate ideas. If Condillac can address other abstractions, it is only because Locke had discredited innate ideas in his *Essay Concerning Human Understanding*. Despite his chiding Locke for having "given much honor to the opinion of innate ideas by the number and the soundness of the critiques he brought against it" (*TSy* 60), Condillac could not have forgone Locke's thorough bashing of this concept. Innate ideas were the very epitome of the kind of speculative metaphysical abstraction that Condillac, in the footsteps of Locke, wanted to dispel once and for all. One cannot abstract them from or trace them back to some lived experience. Hence, they have no real content or meaning and are merely empty abstractions. Locke is the only thinker Condillac exempts from the charge of not being able to penetrate "the chaos in which the abstract sciences find themselves" (*EOCH* 166). He further credits Locke for having "known that abstract maxims are not the source of our knowledge" (*TSy* 10). Locke's ingenious metaphor of the *tabula rasa*, or an empty white sheet of paper, for the mind effectively excludes any preexisting ideas and legitimizes only those ideas that are acquired through experience.

Although Locke finds in experience the basis of all our knowledge and a safeguard against meaningless abstractions, he does not define it as precisely as does Condillac, who will refine his definition of it so as to mean essentially sensory experience.[23] Nor does Locke adequately integrate the understanding into his otherwise admirable explanation of the mind but grants it an independent, abstract, and quasi-mystical status that Condillac in his "rigorous sensationism" finds intolerable.[24] For Condillac's particular method entailed not just the sensory origin of ideas but also the sensory origin of the faculties and operations of the

---

22. See below, pages 31–32.

23. For this passage and the justly famous section on the mind as a *tabula rasa* or a "white Paper, void of all Characters, without any *Ideas*," see Locke's *An Essay Concerning Human Understanding*, bk. 2, chap. 1, § 2, p. 104.

24. Le Roy, *La Psychologie de Condillac*, pp. 52, 58, 83, 87, 89; and Andresen, "Langage naturel et artifice linguistique," p. 278.

mind, including understanding.[25] Such an opinion of Locke's vagueness is of course Condillac's own. At the cost of a certain indiscrimination on his part, the notion of precision and clarity, as will be demonstrated subsequently, becomes the putative hallmark of Condillac's presentation.[26] Typically, when Condillac criticizes Locke, he adduces the image of "obscurity," as he does in the passage where he states that Locke makes the soul's faculties "innate qualities" (*ER* 287, see also 290, 307). Hindering Locke in a clear definition of experience is his "inexactness" (*ER* 290), a shortcoming for which Condillac will compensate by a careful analysis of all the faculties. Condillac's other cavils with Locke primarily concern blurred distinctions among the soul's faculties or its operations: consciousness and perception (*EOCH* 116), memory and imagination (*EOCH* 122), judgment and consciousness (*EOCH* 182–84), and vision and judgment (*TSn* 191–92). All of these metaphysical distinctions as well as many others Condillac hoped to clarify through a precise, methodical language. That would be his lasting contribution to the progress of humanity.

This brief introduction to the similarities and differences between Condillac and Locke illustrates the preoccupations that would cause Condillac to elaborate his distinct theory of sensationism and his new definition of experience. Condillac's chief concerns bear repeating, since taken together, they form the basis of sensationism as he envisioned it. In an adequately clear-minded metaphysics, one must take into account the close association between experience and its related concepts of origin and nature, analysis, order, analogy, and language. Now that I have sketched out the preponderant influence of the precursor, it is time to look closely at the disciple.

Questions of origin fascinated eighteenth-century thinkers.[27] They

25. Herbert Dieckmann, "Condillac's Philosophical Works," *Review of Metaphysics* 7 (1953–54), 256.

26. Condillac's theory of transformed sensations, for instance, tends to make sensations and faculties practically interchangeable. His search for unity (the one principle that would explain all) and continuity can eventually blur important distinctions.

27. Cf. Pierre Saint-Amand, "Original Vengeance: Politics, Anthropology, and the French Enlightenment," *Eighteenth-Century Studies* 26 (1993), 399–417, esp. 399. Saint-Amand cites Cassirer as the one to have called attention to the Enlightenment's paradoxical interest in the question of origins. "Haunted by its origins," writes Saint-Amand, echoing Cassirer, "the Enlightenment is condemned to a process of continual regression with respect to itself . . . [which] runs counter to the central project of the Enlightenment, that is, the development of rationalism with a view to progress."

wrote a plethora of works studying the origins of language, society, the arts and sciences. Such a list would include, to mention only a few of these works, Dubos's *Réflexions critiques sur la poésie et la peinture*, Montesquieu's *L'Esprit des lois*, Voltaire's *Essai sur les moeurs*, both Rousseau's *Discours* and his *Essai sur l'origine des langues*, Diderot's *Lettre sur les sourds et les muets*, and many of the articles written for the *Encyclopédie*.[28] In their anthropological discourse tracing the transition from nature to culture, Enlightenment writers invariably identified nature with an original experience whose truth was authentic and not based on anything that might be considered artificial or abstract. What was valid as an approach for practically every discipline was no less valid for metaphysics. Its inquiry into the nature of man's being inevitably led metaphysicians to focus on the origin of human existence. Differentiating men and women from the animals were their ideas and a host of faculties that allowed them to think and to reason. In concentrating his efforts on the origin of human knowledge, Condillac then was exemplary of an entire age's aspirations to pursue questions to a primeval beginning and to their most fundamental, elementary aspects.[29]

Condillac's language about origins is nothing less than moralistic. They represent what is pure and good, whereas a start at any other point leads to evil results. Simply put, "everything is bad after a poor start."[30] One must begin at the beginning or, if need be, "go back"

28. See the Bibliography for the full references to the individual titles or to the complete works.

29. Yet as the example of Condillac himself will demonstrate (see pages 57–59), the concept of origin and nature can be problematic in the eighteenth century. In his attempt to reveal an original or prerational human being, Condillac creates an abstraction with the statue-man, as does Rousseau with his state of nature. Even as these and other eighteenth-century authors sought to recover an original experience, an uncontaminated state of the body in nature, elements from the rational world of culture tend to insinuate themselves into their discussions, raising obstacles to the very accessibility of experience and ultimately making the body as an original or natural state irretrievable without the mind. The debates in our own century between Habermas and Derrida have called further attention to the problematic relationship between nature and culture, language and writing, and the body and the mind. See esp. Jacques Derrida, *De la grammatologie* (Paris: Editions de Minuit, 1967).

30. Condillac, *La Langue des calculs*, ed. Anne-Marie Chouillet and Sylvain Auroux (Lille: Presses Universitaires de Lille, 1981), p. 40; hereafter cited as *(LC)*. In this unfinished work, published posthumously in 1798, Condillac develops further a number of ideas from his *Grammaire* (1775) and *Logique* (1780)—in particular, the idea from the first of these works that any language is an analytic method and the idea from *La Logique* that any analytic method is a language. See Auroux's introductory essay, "Condillac, ou La Vertu des signes," pp. ix–x.

(*remonter* [*EOCH* 99, 281–82]) to the cause or origin of an effect. Otherwise, one's method is either doomed to failure or produces pernicious results. By "going back further" than Locke to the origin of our knowledge in sensations (*ER* 289), Condillac gains a kind of moral ascendancy over his predecessor. Experience itself will "teach the dangers there are in beginning poorly" (*TSy* 56), that is, in not using an origin as a point of departure for a system. Recognizing an origin can have a healing effect. Ignoring it can do actual harm or damage. To cure a sick man, one finds the "source" or origin of the illness and treats it (*EOCH* 269). In this case, an origin is associated with a sickness. But Condillac typically is speaking of the origin of errors in someone whose ideas are "poorly defined," whereas truth is associated with a good beginning and "well-defined areas" (*EOCH* 270). The kind of evil Condillac has in mind usually takes the form of speculative metaphysical abstractions or prejudices such as innate ideas that cannot be traced to an origin in experience. They are "bad," from Condillac's moralistic standpoint, because they entangle thinkers in error.

In becoming more and more removed from the origin of ideas, which Condillac and all the sensationists found to reside in the senses, one slides unwittingly into error. The prejudice of innate ideas blinds philosophers to the true origin of ideas and wrongly justifies their invention of meaningless and abstract expressions such as being, substance, essence, or property (*TSy* 61). Condillac can, for example, speak of the "vice" of the logic used by Spinoza, who substitutes imaginary abstractions for actual things and thereby loses track of reality (*TSy* 160). What we experience in the real world must not be confused with mere linguistic representations. Things are not words; nor are objects abstract ideas. By keeping an eye, as it were, on the origin of anything, one avoids falling into abstraction. Origins serve as a safeguard against error. The proper logical argument moves from the particular to the general. Without the former, it is impossible to explain the origin of the latter (*EOCH* 180). Systems become confused precisely because abstract principles are taken as facts. But sound principles and origins should not necessarily be opposed, as Condillac points out: "in any system, there is a first fact, a fact that is the beginning of the system, and that, by this reason, would be called *principle:* because *principle* and *beginning* are two words that originally meant the same thing" (*TSy* 7). Problems arise, however, in moving further and further away from original facts or principles toward ill-conceived abstractions. Twisted philosophies thus can even claim abstract principles such as innate ideas, which have no basis in fact or in experience, as the origin of our knowledge (*TSy* 9). Thinkers sometimes mistake definitions and axioms for principles and thereby "harm" their works which will "poorly guide" anyone seeking helpful instruction (*TSy* 264).

The signal advantage of an origin is that it is not abstract and therefore has, in Condillac's eyes, a greater claim to truth than do abstract principles. Hence, his attraction to sensations as a nonabstract origin for knowledge is grounded in experience. Either Condillac begins with an origin, as he does in the *Traité des sensations,* in which he attempts to demonstrate the full implications of the sensory origin of ideas. (Likewise, in the *Langue des calculs,* he "begins with the beginning" [65] by showing the way all calculations have their basis in the fingers, which are our first sensible representations of mathematical units.) Or else Condillac illustrates the necessity for beginning with an origin, as he does in the *Traité des systèmes,* in order to point out the numerous serious errors that befall those who do not do so. Or finally, he works his way back to an origin, as he does in the *Essai sur l'origine des connaissances humaines.* Such a process reveals the importance of language and signs, which I shall discuss later on.

But his immediate method for going back to an origin lies in analysis, which is by definition at once regressive and reductive. For all Condillac's intents and purposes, analysis is a positive form of abstraction. As such, it abstracts from actual experience in the everyday world and is what Condillac opposes to empty metaphysical abstractions without reference to concrete reality.[31] In constantly going back as it does to the origin of ideas in sensory experience, analysis shores up the foundations of knowledge even as it builds on them. When analysis is used to create a system, "it begins with the principle, with the beginning" (*TSy* 267). The beginning and end results of analysis, however, are the same. Analysis ultimately uncovers an origin that Condillac inextricably associates with truth or its visible counterpart in eighteenth-century culture, nature.

Condillac's analysis of anything, human knowledge or even the sup-

---

31. The ensuing pages elaborate on Condillac's positive form of abstraction. His opposition to metaphysical abstraction is clarified in my discussion of the imagination on pages 32–34.

For all his insistence on analysis and positive abstraction from nature and our lived experience in it, Condillac chooses an artificial marble statue to represent human experience and thereby seriously undermines the coherence of his theory. Bonnet's statue suffers from the same inconsistency, but his introduction of a physiological vocabulary including nerve fibers enhances somewhat the claims his statue may have as a representation of human reality.

posedly indivisible soul, begins by breaking the subject down or separating it into its component parts. For him, any analysis depends on an orderly succession of the parts of an argument that allows one to return to an origin. It results in a rational discourse that underscores once again the importance of language and signs. The process of decomposition or separation, with which analysis begins, is fundamental to Condillac's method. In his *Essai sur l'origine des connaissances humaines*, he gives the following definition of analysis:

> analyzing is, according to me, only an operation that results from the combination of the preceding operations. It consists only in setting up and breaking down ideas in order to make different comparisons of them, and to discover, by this means, the relations they have between them, and the new ideas they can produce. This analysis is the true secret of discoveries, because it has us always go back to the origin of things. It has the advantage of never offering but a few ideas at the same time, and always in the simplest gradation. (139)

In order to build or compose an analysis, one must paradoxically break down or decompose the ideas in question. By the time he writes his *Langue des calculs*, Condillac has simplified his definition: "To what are all the processes of analysis reduced? To setting up and breaking down. One makes in order to unmake; and one unmakes in order to remake. That is the only clever trick: it is simple" (272–73). Analysis manages to consider only a few ideas at once by separating them.

The code word for analysis in Condillac's writings is *démêler*, which can mean to distinguish something from something else, or to untangle or sort out a problem, and literally "to unmix."[32] Although he does not use it conspicuously in the *Essai*, it already figures in the subtitle of the *Traité des systèmes, où l'on en démelle des inconvénients et les avantages*, three years later. It becomes the watchword of the *Traité des sensations*, where he uses it some fifty times in the treatise itself, including the additional appearances of the expression in the *Extrait raisonné* of that work. What is being decomposed, broken down, or separated, and therefore clarified, takes on many different forms: objects, sensations, numbers, paintings, colors, bodies, differences, depth, reasons, ideas, properties, space, and so forth. Analysis is a corrective

---

32. The positive and negative uses of the imagination are discussed on pages 32–34.

process. It sorts out data and corrects the excesses or errors of some of the soul's other operations, like imagination. As Condillac puts it, analysis "breaks things down, and untangles *[démêle]* everything that the imagination assumes without any basis to be in them" (*TSy* 239).[33] He associates it with the emergence of consciousness and the development of personal identity. The fictional words of the statue-man reflect just such an association: "In the first moment of my existence, I did not know at all what was happening in me; I sorted out *[démêlais]* nothing yet in myself; I had no consciousness of myself; I existed, but without desires, without fear, I hardly enjoyed myself: and if I had continued to exist in this way I would never have suspected that my existence could embrace two instants" (*TSn* 258).

Analysis begins only when the circumstances that make it possible are in place. In order to analyze, one must have an awareness of more than one feeling. For Condillac as well as for Bonnet, that awareness arises from the succession of two or more sensations.[34] However fleeting or prolonged the moment of undifferentiated sensation may be, it ultimately gives way to differentiated sensation with the inevitable changes in one's environment. Sooner or later, a succession of sensations shakes one from the stasis of the primary narcissistic state. From that point on, the changes become all the more perceptible and set into motion the inner mechanism of analysis that the statue-man has to give meaning to itself and its external world. As is readily apparent even in this brief sketch of the sensationist view of existence, the meaning or content of experience—the knowledge human beings gradually amass over time and that they use subsequently to form judgments, opinions, and all manner of decisions—is based to a large degree on the sensations. And it is their succession or temporal quality that makes analysis possible.

The process itself is seen as an entirely natural one. The statue's judgment, which results from a sequence or succession of observations,

---

33. According to Derrida, the two key words in the *Essai* are "retracing" *(retracer)* and "making up for a lack or supplementing" *(suppléer),* both of which also center on the question of origins. He writes: "Supplementing is, after having noticed and 'retraced' the origin of what is missing, adding what *is needed.*" In a deconstructive turn, Derrida transforms what is needed in language into its opposite, what is superfluous or frivolous. See *L'Archéologie du frivole* (Paris: Denoël/Gonthier, 1976), pp. 12–14, 84. This essay also serves as the introduction to Charles Porset's 1973 edition of Condillac's *Essai.* I have used this separate edition to avoid confusion in the references.

34. See the chapter on Bonnet, page 66f.

allows it to "analyze naturally: and that confirms . . . we learn analysis from nature itself" (*TSn* 125). It is necessary both to look at things separately as well as to maintain the sequence and order of events. Condillac distinguishes between seeing and observing, the latter being the operation that gives us ideas through analysis:[35] "In a word, our eyes must analyze: because they will not seize the whole of even the least composite figure, if they have not observed all its parts, separately, one after the other, and in the order the parts have among themselves" (*TSn* 170). Looking at the parts separately gives one an idea of the whole figure (*TSn* 175).

Analysis, the decomposition or unmixing of the whole object of inquiry into its separate parts, which are studied in succession, constitutes the central method Condillac uses time and again. The entire first part of the *Essai sur l'origine des connaissances humaines* examines, as the title of that part indicates, the "materials of our knowledge and especially the operations of the soul." Knowledge is not regarded as a monolithic entity but is immediately divided into its component parts. So, too, the soul—viewed as it was in the eighteenth century as the seat of knowledge, sometimes out of innocence and sometimes out of necessity to avoid censure—is broken down into its various faculties. Since Condillac views language as an analytic method, as he would put it later in his *Grammaire,* the second part of the *Essai* is naturally about language and method itself. The analytical process of decomposition here results in a return to the origin of language. The *Traité des systêmes* exposes by turns the excesses of a number of metaphysical systems by analyzing the wrong use these systems make of language. Condillac's form of analysis, it will be remembered, starts in the beginning. Many systems erroneously start with definitions and abstract principles, which may have a perfectly logical relation among themselves but do not have any relation to any actual origin in experience. Experience in fact has been superseded by abstract metaphysical speculation in these systems. In a gesture of artificial abstraction for which Condillac would be criticized for his bad faith, the *Traité des sensations* removes the five senses from their normal combined state, analyzing them separately, one after the other. In so doing, Condillac demonstrates through this

---

35. See my *Seeing and Observing: Rousseau's Rhetoric of Perception,* Stanford French and Italian Studies, 41 (Saratoga, Calif.: Anma Libri, 1985). Rousseau differentiates himself from the *philosophes* by his virtual but not complete rejection of analysis in favor of a more intuitive mode of perception based on feeling and sensation.

work the centrality of the sensations and sensibility to knowledge. In the last piece he wrote, *La Langue des calculs,* Condillac insists no less than he had in his previous writings on the necessity of an analytic method. Despite the differences between metaphysics and mathematics, their respective forms of analysis are the same (*LC* 218). This, his last work and published after his death, shows with remarkable clarity and simplicity the sensory origin of some of the most complex mathematical calculations, which Condillac traces first to our fingers then to visible numbers. It represents in many ways, as we shall see presently, a valiant effort on his part to make his form of analysis the only credible scientific method.

Condillac insisted as much as he did on analysis because he felt that it would add a much-needed orderly and rational element to philosophical discourse.[36] As long as our ideas naturally follow one another in succession, there is little or no room for error, according to Condillac, and we can be reasonably sure of attaining truth in an argument (*EOCH* 278f.). Condillac prefers to build his own system of analysis by starting with what is simple and proceeding toward the more complex. He carefully avoids, as much as possible, beginning with definitions and abstract principles, which reverse the true order for the generation of ideas, as he points out: "It is up to the easier ideas to prepare the mind for ideas that are less easy to grasp. Now everyone can know, from his or her own experience, that ideas are proportionately easier as they are less abstract and draw nearer the senses; that on the contrary they are proportionately more difficult as they move away from the senses, and become more abstract. The reason for this experience is that all our knowledge comes from the senses. An abstract idea thus needs to be explained by a less abstract idea, and so on in succession, until one arrives at a particular and sensible idea" (*TSy* 10).[37] If he must begin with an abstract idea, Condillac returns to its

36. Analysis also stands diametrically opposed to synthesis and its tendency to generalize abstractly. For the opposition between analysis and synthesis, see Auroux, "Condillac, ou La Vertu des signes," p. iv. See also Delbos, *La Philosophie française* (Paris: Plon, 1921), pp. 261, 273. According to Delbos, Condillac uses deductive "composition" (the procedure of synthesis) only as "a second test for decomposition" (the method of choice for analysis).

37. The French word *sensible* literally means, "in reference to objects or phenomena, capable of being apprehended by the senses." This first definition of the word in English is sometimes obscured by its association with the synonym *reasonable.* For lack of a more frequently used word in English, one that would adequately emphasize its relation to any or all of the senses, I have for the most part left it simply as "sensible." In addition to its meaning of "sensitive" in French, there are other translations of *sensible* such as "tangible" or

origin rather than advancing any further into the obscurity he perceives in this kind of thinking. Abstractions are permissible only once their origins have been clearly delineated. Condillac ensures clear thinking by tracing the continuous, uninterrupted steps from abstract ideas to their sensory origins in experience.

In the strong interdependence he prescribes for the parts of any art or science (*TSy* 245), Condillac establishes a new notion of order. The highest form of order he envisages comes to resemble that of experience, whose basic structural unit is sensation. The beginning of a system, like the beginning of knowledge, lies in the "facts" or *évidence* provided by sense perception (e.g., the sensations of one's fingers used by children to count and perform mathematical operations). An ideal system's order functions essentially as does that of the sensations, which are interrelated and continuous and which build on one another. In order to learn to count, one must first begin with the sensation of a unit, which is usually represented by a finger that a child senses on his or her hand and that lies in close proximity to other fingers. The next finger over represents a second unit or the number two and so on. Like the relation between the fingers, the relation between the units of knowledge is contiguous in the sensationist perspective. Knowledge of experience arises from the fundamental basis of the sensations, increasing in a linear fashion. Condillac affirms the centrality of experience for an orderly method as follows in the *Essai:* "to expound truth in the most perfect order, one must have noticed the order in which it could naturally be found; because the best way to teach others is to lead them by the path that one had to stay on to teach oneself" (*EOCH* 288). Given Condillac's sensationist bent, it is not difficult to read between the lines here. We learn from the uninterrupted experience the senses give us, just as children learn arithmetic from the connected fingers on their hands. In short, Condillac's ideal order is the natural order of experience itself.

When metaphysics or any science or system does not rely on a step-by-step analytical approach, it makes unjustifiable leaps of the imagination. This faculty has two meanings in Condillac's writing. It is both "the operation that awakens perceptions in the absence of objects" and "the effects of this operation" (*EOCH* 143). Taken in either sense,

---

"perceptible," although they do not emphasize the relation to any or all of the senses. It is a key word in the vocabulary of sensationism. See the debate between Locke, Berkeley, and Hume over abstract ideas.

the imagination has advantages and disadvantages. But preoccupying Condillac most are the imagination's disadvantages, which are perhaps best elucidated in this faculty's contradistinction from memory. Whereas the latter faculty recalls things from the past and keeps track of their actual temporality in the past, imagination makes objects or events experienced in the past seem as though they are present or happening once again (*TSn* 29). Its powers obviously become problematic when past events are mistaken for current reality. What the pernicious effects of the imagination do for Condillac is to throw into glaring opposition sensations and empty abstractions such as innate ideas. Sensations can be attached, so to speak, to the apparent or real qualities of actual objects in the present, whereas the imagination and some of its excessive abstractions cannot. The odor of a rose indeed comes from a rose. Even when the sensations perceived do not correspond exactly to the true characteristics of an object—as in the case of the straight stick half-immersed in water and which appears bent—the sensations are nonetheless occasioned by some real object. Such a claim cannot always be made for the imagination. The sensations can in fact act as a kind of antidote for the imagination. There is an inverse relationship between the sensations and the imagination, as Condillac shows: "the easier it is to come by sensations themselves, the less one practices imagining them" (*TSn* 213). Condillac traces to the excesses of the imagination some of the most extravagant systems, such as astrology, magic, the interpretation of dreams, augury, and haruspex (*TSy* 54). As not just bankrupt abstract principles but entire abstract systems, these superstitions have no more credibility for Condillac than do innate ideas. He practically makes the imagination the seat of all those ill-founded abstractions he held in contempt when they are not solidly based in experience.[38] In Condillac's eyes, the imagination certainly misleads Spinoza, who uses it to give a sense of reality to his abstract ideas (*TSy* 160, 165).

The imagination and analysis seem to be two diametrically opposed operations. Condillac himself does not diminish their differences or their frequent exclusion of each other. The imagination's "empire" or authority "ends where that for analysis begins" (*EOCH* 148). Condillac associates for the most part the former with beauty and the latter with

---

38. The misuse of the imagination for validating empty abstractions, which Condillac condemns, should not be confused with its positive use in language for representing sensory experience by signs.

truth. The beauty that imagination can add to objects or language (as in poetry) is acceptable, however, only insofar as it does not contravene the truth and lead one into error or decadence (*EOCH* 149, 265–66). Whereas imagination can veer from the truth and lose its authority, analysis always gains its authority and validity from its close association with experience. Despite their apparent differences, though, these two operations can and should complement each other, as Condillac suggests: "Imagination ought to provide the philosopher with attractive features, without taking anything away from accuracy; and analysis ought to give accuracy to the poet, without taking anything away from pleasure" (*TSy* 240). When the two are not mutually reinforcing, analysis serves to counterbalance the excesses of the imagination by virtue of its capacity to "sort out" baseless assumptions (*TSy* 239). It simply goes back to the origin of an idea or of an image from the imagination to verify its firm grounding in sensory experience.

By basing as he does analysis on experience, Condillac associates his own system with reasoning and clear language, which in fact become virtually indistinguishable in his writing. His *Logique* serves to prove "that *the art of reasoning is reduced to a well-made language*" (*TSy* 28). And the rest of his writing, especially that toward the end of his life in the *Langue des calculs,* reinforces this point, which Condillac must have considered one of his major contributions to Western thought.[39] Progress, that ultimate ideal of all of the *philosophes,* can be attained only through reason, which turns out to be the proper use of language in Condillac's scheme of things. It should be clear, simple, precise, and exact. Language is indeed the mother of thought. From the sensationist standpoint, its constitutive function and intermediary role ensure that no thinking is possible without it.[40] Following the seventeenth-century tradition of Descartes and of Port-Royal, Condillac intimately relates language and thought. The universality of reason for

---

39. Laromiguière considered the language Condillac developed in this work the only language of reasoning to meet his three criteria of analogy, simplicity, and a rigorous determination of signs. See Pierre Laromiguière, *Paradoxes de Condillac* (1805; rpt. Paris: Brunot-Labbé, 1825), pp. 84–85.

40. Bernhard Henschel, "Les Conceptions rationaliste et sensualiste du langage au siècle des lumières dans l'interprétation moderne," in *Actele celui de-al XII-lea congres internaţional de lingvistică şi filologie romanică,* vol. I (Bucharest: Editura Academiei Republicii Socialiste România, 1970), p. 916. Henschel distinguishes between the rationalist perspective on language, where it is merely an instrument of thought, and the sensationist perspective, where it is indispensable to thought.

human beings implies the universality of language for them.[41] Like Maupertuis and many other Enlightenment *philosophes,* Condillac was interested in the study of the origin of languages as a way of probing the initial workings of the human mind and clarifying its thinking.[42] Incoherence in language leads to imprecision in thinking and error-ridden reasoning. Not surprisingly, Condillac ties language, just as he does the ideas of reasoned thinking, to a sensory origin. His sensationism thus becomes a form of both nominalism and rationalism.[43] This is another way of saying that language precedes thought (i.e., ideas can be reduced to names) and that language serves to advance reason. To maintain the purity and precision of both language and thought, one must understand and be able to follow as much as possible the continuous relations that exist between sensory experience and ideas on the one hand, and signs and words on the other.[44] Condillac's great efforts to do so reveal much about his profoundly sensationist method.

41. Ronald Grimsley, "Some Aspects of 'Nature' and 'Language' in the French Enlightenment," *Studies on Voltaire and the Eighteenth Century* 56 (1967), 661.

42. Cf. Pierre-Louis Moreau de Maupertuis, *Réflexions philosophiques sur l'origine des langues et la signification des mots* (Paris: n. p., 1748), pp. 5–6.

43. According to Auroux, "sensationism is a nominalism on two accounts: its theory of arbitrariness (or better, the first such Condillacian theory, set out in the *Essai*) and the thesis according to which general ideas are only names." For Auroux, "the basis of nominalist doctrine is the affirmation of the necessity of language for thought." See "Condillac, ou La Vertu des signes," p. vii; and Chantal Hasnaoui, "Condillac, chemins du sensualisme," in *Langue et langage de Leibniz à l' "Encyclopédie,"* ed. Michèle Duchet and Michèle Jalley (Paris: Union Générale d'Editions, 1977), pp. 101, 116–17.

Knight echoes this association of the two theories: "the interest in language reflects the inherent nominalism of the empirical philosophy. What the realist had believed to be things, the nominalist thought were only names." See *The Geometric Spirit*, p. 146. She also points out the rational as well as antirational characteristics of Condillac's writing about language. It is rationalist in method but antirational in content. Condillac uses logical analysis to uncover the impulse to speech "which was expressive, not communicative, emotive, not logical." Language evolved, furthermore, in an "almost accidental" way through the association of ideas. But once past the primitive stage, "man's acquisition of language precisely paralleled his acquisition of reason," and Condillac's treatment of it takes on a decidedly rationalist character. The search for a universal grammar and a perfect language were both rationalist ideals. Yet as Knight points out, "Condillac did not share the dream of a single perfect language, because his criteria of perfection were both rational and empirical, both universal and particular." He admitted the possibility of several languages depending on the individual needs of the various peoples. See pp. 147–48, 159–63, 168, 175.

44. See Nicolas Rousseau, *Connaissance et langage chez Condillac* (Geneva: Droz, 1986), p. 412. For Rousseau, Condillac was "more interested in examining the way ideas progressed and were linked together than in what they actually represented, since their reality value ultimately proved itself to be no more in question than that of the sensations from which they originated."

The connecting link between language and thought lies in experience. If all of our ideas come from the sensations, as Condillac claims, then in order to express those ideas we must have recourse once again to the sensations experience provides. The idea of the odor of a rose comes originally from the sensation of a rose's smell. Similarly, words being one of the primary ways we connect ideas, the word for rose must be related to the idea of a rose, which in turn is related to the sensation of a rose. What relates a sign to a sensation is the context. The meaning of a sign is thereby contextualized and defined by physical circumstances.[45] The word *rose* is uttered and accompanied by a gesture pointing out this particular flower. Ronald Grimsley highlights and aptly explains the sensationist basis for Condillac's theory of language, by which sensory experience assures continuity throughout all the various mental faculties:

> Even though language had ultimately to be related to thought, the first problem was to trace its gradual development. This genetic approach meant that the study of language had to begin with an analysis of sensation rather than abstract thought. Condillac treated the language of "signs" as a means of enabling man to pass from "sensations" to "ideas." Reflection, he insisted, was not some unique faculty, because, far from involving a sudden break in the continuity of the psychological chain, it resulted from the "natural progress of the human mind" and especially the activity of "imagination, memory and reminiscence"; it was through its power to use signs and associate ideas that reflection became identified with higher forms of mental activity. The history of language, in Condillac's opinion, fully supported the idea that reflection had developed naturally from sensation.[46]

When Condillac states that he aims to reduce all human understanding to a single principle, it is ultimately to the ever-present experience of the senses that all of the faculties lead and not entirely to the connection of ideas with signs or other ideas, as he at first directly states. Although it takes Condillac the entirety of his *Essai* to affirm forthrightly his sensationism, the work's opening pages already offer

---

45. G. A. Wells, "Condillac, Rousseau, and Herder on the Origin of Language," *Studies on Voltaire and the Eighteenth Century* 230 (1985), 237.

46. Grimsley, "Some Aspects of 'Nature' and 'Language,'" 665–66.

some telling clues about his solution: "One sees that my design is to recall everything in human understanding to a single principle, and that this principle will be neither a vague proposition, nor an abstract maxim, nor an unwanted assumption; but a constant experience, whose consequences will be confirmed by new experiments" (*EOCH* 101). The very way in which he describes the kind of experience he is looking for—namely, "an initial experiment [whose validity] no one can question and which suffices to explain all others" (101)—points already to that of the senses. Condillac plays in this passage on the word *expérience*, which in French means both experience and experiment. Both meanings usually entail "observations" of one kind or another through the senses, as experience or experiment ideally "shows perceptibly" what one is seeking. Repeated experiments serve to reinforce one another. No one will question the outcome of an experience involving a flame applied to an unprotected finger. There is no need to question experience. Once one has felt the heat of a flame, there is little use in continually recreating the sensation of one's burning flesh to understand any better the idea of a flame's heat. Condillac may well claim to have discovered the "solution" to a number of metaphysical questions in "the connection of ideas, either with signs, or with other ideas" (101). But ideas themselves, as he forcefully points out in this work's conclusion, have their origin in the senses. Once and only once one begins to have more than a single idea—a moment that Condillac in his *Traité des sensations* will later elucidate at length with the arrival of a second sensation in the statue-man—do the various mental faculties come into play. As a solution to the metaphysical questions he was raising, Condillac insisted in the *Essai* more on the connection of ideas than on the sensory origin of ideas. That he did so reflects perhaps a certain reticence on his part in the face of possible censure for materialism. However the case may be, his later works belie somewhat his conviction about the primacy of the connection of ideas even as they increasingly reinforce his firm belief in sensationism as a powerful theory of knowledge.[47] What does not change, though, is his recognition of the funda-

47. Similarly, Bréhier approaches this apparent contradiction in Condillac by pointing out a critical difference between the *Essai* and the *Traité des sensations*. As Bréhier writes, "if each sensation contains every faculty, then it is not true, as [Condillac] said in the *Essay* of 1746, that intelligence depends on the linking of ideas and signs. That all mental faculties are prior to the use of signs was one of the most important conclusions of the *Treatise.* . . . The role of signs is to make possible the extension of these faculties. Thus in a sense his *Treatise on Sensations* provides the differentials of the faculties whose integration is made possible by signs. The problem of the mind is resolved, as economically as possible, through *sensations*

mental importance of language. For language plays a pivotal role not only in the acquisition of knowledge but also in its propagation. As a sensationist and a progressive *philosophe,* Condillac was interested in both.

---

and signs" (my emphasis). See *The Eighteenth Century,* pp. 81–82.

Derrida also recognizes Condillac's change of mind regarding signs, to which he apparently had "given too much" (Condillac's words in a letter to Maupertuis). For Derrida, "the sign, as will be seen, is in sum the name the *Essai* probably gave to the detour in general, to experience itself as a detour, the generation of the supplemental replacement [*suppléance*] to be retraced." He goes on to point out: "Condillac probably never affirmed that the sign is first in experience in general. The chain of signs rises *above* perceptions. . . . In the order of experience and the operations of the soul, the sign is thus never *(put)* in the beginning." See *L'Archéologie du frivole,* pp. 74–77. Clearly, what does lie "below" and "before" signs is sensory experience or perception.

The seeming ambivalence of Condillac's writing is sometimes misleading. Hans Aarsleff, who at first is convinced that the single principle Condillac speaks of is sensation, later changes his mind. Taking the *Essai* as Condillac's last word on the question, he asserts rather dogmatically that this principle is the connection of ideas. In his second reading, he rejects passive sensation as a single principle and takes reflection to be an innate faculty that voluntarily creates arbitrary signs. Aarsleff disparages some of the commonplace views of Condillac's sensationism but fails to notice the problematic nature of his own position. Condillac scholars see sensation, and not the connection of ideas, as his single principle for human understanding because it does not put Condillac in contradiction with himself. See, for example, R. Carré, "Sur la sensation condillacienne," in *Proceedings of the Tenth International Congress of Philosophy* (Amsterdam: North-Holland, 1949), p. 1157. Carré affirms that the sensations are indeed the traditional answer to the frequent question about the identity of Condillac's one organizing principle for the mind. Carré sees the sensations as an active, albeit primitive, sensory consciousness. Aarsleff's position disassociates Condillac from an essential portion of the *philosophe's* thinking about experience and the analytic method and analogy he strove to derive from it, while associating Condillac with much that he loathed (e.g., arbitrariness, empty abstractions, and innate principles). Although Condillac may not be entirely innocent of any internal inconsistencies, it is difficult to imagine his arguing for what he was trying to avoid as much as possible. Reflection may play a central role in language formation for Condillac after its evolution, but he does not make it or any other mental operation innate. Moreover, he wishes to rid language of some of its abstract arbitrariness. Aarsleff does make an important distinction between the voluntary connection of ideas *(la liaison des idées),* which leads to increased knowledge, and the association of ideas *(l'association des idées),* which, being out of our control, Locke considered as madness. He also points out that Condillac's statue would be speechless. See Aarsleff, *From Locke to Saussure: Essays on the Study of Language and Intellectual History* (Minneapolis: University of Minnesota Press, 1982), esp. pp. 11–12, 29, 155, 170, 173, 195, 214–23. Noam Chomsky of course takes the opposite view of language development (contrary to Condillac's position), claiming that the kind of knowledge necessary to produce language is innate and not acquired. See Chomsky, "Recent Contributions to the Theory of Innate Ideas" and "Some Empirical Assumptions in Modern Philosophy of Language," in *Challenges to Empiricism,* ed. Harold Morick (Indianapolis: Hackett, 1980), pp. 23, 230–39, 287–318. This collection of essays demonstrates that the debate on the origin of language is far from being resolved.

Time and again, Condillac calls for greater precision in the language used by metaphysicians, for he saw a number of severe shortcomings in that used in his day. He focuses primarily on the misapprehensions that can arise over the relationship between words and other categories such as things, ideas, or definitions. The most notorious misuse of words generally stems from their confusion with things. Words for Condillac always lack the ontological solidity of things, which themselves as well as their qualities can be directly perceived through the senses and which therefore may lay claim to a greater truth. The process for determining accurate meanings for words takes "time, experience and reflection" without which one might be led "to confuse them with . . . [things] and conclude that they perfectly explain their nature" (*EOCH* 180). When Condillac wants to belittle a philosophical system, he points to the emptiness or hollowness of its words. Following Locke, he compares words to mere tokens in currency exchange like the *louis,* the pound, or the *écu,* which as such will never be, even in large sums, anything but tokens. Likewise, a philosopher's "conclusions are never but words" (*TSy* 24). Such is the case especially with Spinoza, whom Condillac chastises for his imprecise language that gives rise to a confusing abstract system. When words lose touch with concrete reality, they can also lose their meaning. In a sense, all words lose touch with the natural world as language becomes increasingly the result of conventions. Condillac, however, downgrades the arbitrariness of linguistic convention and emphasizes the continuity between the first language and subsequent languages. To be meaningful, the latter must incorporate some elements of the former or at least maintain a traceable continuity with it. There may be arbitrariness in the process, but it is combined with previously experienced natural signs in a specific, concrete setting. As one observer of Condillac puts it: "The meaning of the first words was settled not only by accompanying them with gestures (i.e., arbitrary sounds were accompanied by signs of known meaning) but also by the fact that these words were pronounced in situations which betrayed their meaning."[48] Indeed, the intelligibility of institutional signs requires that they be "not totally arbitrary."[49]

48. Wells, "Condillac, Rousseau, and Herder on the Origin of Language," 237. Earlier in this article (234–35), Wells explains through the notion of "curtailed gesture" the way in which "self-explanatory gestures become conventionalised."

49. R. H. Robins, "Condillac et l'origine du langage," in *Condillac et les problèmes du langage,* ed. Jean Sgard (Geneva: Slatkine, 1982), p. 99. In the same collection of essays, see also Auroux, "Empirisme et théorie linguistique chez Condillac," pp. 177–210, esp.

Simply put, meaning lies in experience. It comes from familiarity, the kind of familiarity attained by seeing, touching, or somehow sensing a physical object like a car or by having had an experience that demonstrates an abstract concept such as speed by riding in a fast car, feeling one's body being pressed back into the seat, and seeing objects outside the car go by very quickly. If one has not experienced what a term means, then that word is devoid of meaning. Typically for Condillac, the experience (or experiment) of which he speaks—a word he uses countless times throughout all his writings—entails initially sense perception. As one becomes further and further removed from the sensible universe one is trying to represent through linguistic signs, one can wrongly substitute increasingly meaningless abstractions for an authentic, real experience. Words like essence and substance, which for Condillac are without referents and without any relation to a lived experience, can crop up in one's vocabulary. Spinoza typifies this departure from the *évidence* of sensation into the abstract world of circular definitions, whose only validity consists in their coherent references to other definitions. Like any abstract system, Spinoza's fails to begin in the beginning with original or first principles, namely, those that can be established by sensory experience. His definitions start at a certain level of abstraction that has already lost contact with the reality of physical objects and their qualities. Thus cut off from the real world, they take on chimerical qualities. Building on themselves and not on any solid ground, his words only refer to one another (*TSy* 183; also *TSy* 210–11). His very assumption that "his definitions of words have become definitions of things" (*TSy* 161) is faulty and leads him to create what may well be a marvelously self-contained system but one without exterior referents. True to the spirit of his fellow *philosophes*, Condillac in effect demands of Spinoza a natural system, that is, one that has its origin in nature, which, to repeat, is explored and explained only by experience. Words simply do not exist in nature. Condillac insists on ideas of things that do exist in nature. He criticizes Spinoza's inability to

---

pp. 181–86. "A well-made language," Auroux writes, reinforcing Robins, "cannot be constructed at random and out of capriciousness; it is not arbitrary. Beginning with the *Grammaire,* Condillac changes his conception of arbitrariness; the word becomes the antonym of 'analogous' " (p. 181). Like Condillac, Auroux wants to banish the notion of a language without constraints, which would give rise to what he calls an "instrumental" arbitrariness. This notion, which not even classical grammarians supported, is clearly distinguishable from the commonly accepted conventionality of signs. He states finally that "languages are not unmotivated . . . otherwise there would be no general grammar, nor even any grammatical categories" (p. 186).

formulate a natural religion as follows: "How can he propose to me conceiving whether God exists or not, if in his entire system he has not taught me to conceive the ideas, not of these words, but of these things, *substance, infinity, attribute, essence, God?*" (*TSy* 173–74). Teetering on the brink of materialism in his demand for a quasi-material God, Condillac nonetheless retreats in his attack when a critique of Spinoza's excessive abstraction begins to sound like a call for a materialist's system of nature. After first stating that "the idea of God in thought" and other ideas are "things which are too abstract," he checks himself by saying: "rather these are words from which I confess understanding nothing" (*TSy* 191). It is Condillac's subtle distinction between words and things that saves this text from being censored here. God is not merely a word, Condillac implies, but much more. Condillac can understand God while claiming to fail to understand the words used to describe Him. Concrete examples are worth more than words linked no matter how carefully in useless definitions.

The morass of terms that metaphysics mixes therefore produces worthless definitions, which Condillac never ceases repudiating. One gathers in reading his works that what he finds objectionable in them is their massive accumulation of words with little or no connection to experience. If individual words already deceive us into believing a mistaken representation of reality, then definitions, which group words together, accelerate the process of deception and deserve our utmost scrutiny. By "sorting out" the various parts or words of a system, analysis is of course the method Condillac uses to scrutinize definitions. Although he speaks of the "uselessness" of some definitions in his *Essai* (158), it is not until his *Traité des systêmes* that he attacks them with vehemence. In general, definitions for Condillac serve as forewarnings of further imprecisions to come. Thus, when he mentions from the first part of Spinoza's *Ethics* this author's eight definitions and seven axioms, all of which are "not very exact and highly equivocal" (*TSy* 156), one can be sure that Condillac will soon proceed to take apart or "unmix" all of the wrong-headed assumptions he finds in Spinoza's work. After he clears away all of the various confusing parts of a metaphysical argument, it is not unusual for him to find an entire proof "based only on a definition of a word" (*TSy* 181).

Along with empty words and abstractions, definitions constitute some of the major causes for error and obfuscation. Innate ideas, the bane of the progressive *philosophes,* seem to spawn all of these evils. Philosophers who have "imbibed this prejudice . . . have infinitely multiplied vague definitions, abstract principles; and, thanks to the terms *being, substance, essence, property,* etc., they have encountered nothing that in their view they have not already explained" (*TSy* 61). The insidiousness of innate ideas lies in their substituting a false sense of clarity for the true clarity that comes only from ideas derived through the senses. The definitions that arise from innate ideas therefore have an alluring but factitious quality about them.

Words, whether alone or in definitions, ultimately are no more equal to things than they are to ideas. They are of course always representations of things or ideas. But there are varying degrees of accuracy in representation. Hence, Condillac can mock Spinoza for never having furnished "accurate ideas" for the "big words" he uses (*TSy* 203). Words should take the place of ideas no more than they should take the place of things. And yet the language of conversation and indeed of many systems seems to have just such an implicit convention (*TSy* 268). Condillac would have all language and ideas closely connected to experience. Like things, ideas are first presented to us by the senses. Experience is indeed a process of presentation and representation, that is, it presents and re-presents sensible objects to our senses. We seize the same meaning from objects we have previously experienced and new meaning from new objects. The ideas that arise from these experiences are ultimately expressed as words. Words constitute therefore a linguistic (and hence mental) representation of some lived experience, whereas the senses provide a physiological representation that results in ideas. The language we use to express things or ideas should thus be simple and devoid of abstract complexity. Condillac wants nothing less than to redo language, giving it the highest degree of precision possible in order to obtain the highest clarity in his ideas. To achieve this, Condillac resorts to sensible images, signs, analogy, and reason.

Condillac's solution for language as for practically everything else consists in an analytic return to the origin of knowledge in sensory experience. The body and its senses are intimately involved in the production of language and the acquisition of knowledge. Sylvain Auroux has rightly seized the importance of sensory and bodily engagement in the world for Condillac's linguistic and epistemological theory when he writes: "For the sensationist, it is not actually the question of generality that is important, it is that one must *pronounce,* say *I,* which is to engage oneself in the world by a corporeal action. Without the body, there would be no language, that is to say speech act, and without this latter, there would be no affirmation, no true or false, thus no knowledge."[50]

The two parts of Condillac's *Essai* constantly reinforce each other in their sensationist approach to knowledge and language, which are interrelated. Part I, "Of the Materials of Our Knowledge and Especially of the Operations of the Soul," constitutes the necessary prelude to Part II, "Of Language and Method." In this regard, Condillac reflects a basic preoccupation of his age, which gave primacy to epistemology in any discussion. It comes therefore as no surprise when Condillac states that he was "led to believe that, in order to give clarity and precision to language, it was necessary to take up again the materials of our knowledge, and to make new combinations out of them without regard for those that happen to have been made already" (*EOCH* 272). Specifically, the materials of our knowledge Condillac has in mind are "the different sensations, perception, consciousness, reminiscence, attention, and imagination" (*EOCH* 289). He goes back to them and their sources, the senses, when he attempts to improve language. In an important passage, Condillac outlines his proposed way to do so and to minimize the role chance plays in determining the meaning of words:

> There is no other way always to give precision to language than that way which has produced it every time in the past. One must first place oneself in sensible circumstances, so as to make signs to express the first ideas one would acquire by sensation and reflection; and, while reflecting on these one would acquire new ones, one would make new names whose meaning would be determined by placing other people in the same circumstances, and by having them make the same reflections. Then expressions would always follow ideas; they would thus be clear and precise, since they would render only what everyone else would have experienced through the senses. (*EOCH* 272)

Language thus arises from experience. The more similar the sensory environment to which people can be exposed, the more precise the language will be. Condillac's ideal goal would be to have identical circumstances for everyone in developing a language. But given the major role played by chance in the circumstances that befall individuals,

50. Auroux, "Condillac, inventeur d'un nouveau matérialisme," *Dix-Huitième Siècle* 24 (1992), 162.

such a goal is practically impossible. Condillac nonetheless insists on as much similarity as possible in language—similarity not only in the physical circumstances in which language is created but also in the mental and physiological experience of those creating language. A word or idea must have some basis in experience. When we speak of the color red, there must have previously been some simultaneous experience (say, the sensation of a red rose accompanied by the utterance of the word *red*) shared by a number of different people to confirm the existence of this color so that it does not become a meaningless term or concept. Meaning comes from similar experiments. And the degree of similarity is determined above all by the experience of the senses.

Sensory experience informs language at every step of its evolution, from its earliest beginnings to some of its most sophisticated forms. The factors that come together to produce language in the first place—the so-called language of action, the language of articulated sounds, and sensible images (*EOCH* 256)—all have in common a necessary reliance upon the senses. For its effectiveness, the first language, which Condillac calls the "language of action," depends largely on sense data to communicate a message. Primitive people *saw* and hence understood the "contortions" and "violent movements" (*EOCH* 195) of their fellow men and women. When cries were added to these gestures, they *heard* and *saw* signs that had meaning for them. The more they were able to sense through different senses signs expressing the same idea, the clearer the idea. For Condillac, the clarity of language and thought is thus firmly grounded in sensory experience.

Combined with some gesticulation, articulated sounds, with which early humans very gradually named things (*EOCH* 196), themselves have a perceptually distinguishable component beyond mere pointing. They can be either long or short. The length or brevity of sounds must, however, be *sensible* or noticeably different to the senses, in this case, hearing. With its easily distinguishable syllables, the language of the ancients thus had a markedly inflected character to it and resembled singing (*EOCH* 208–10). Because it exaggerated auditory signs in the same way it sometimes concurrently did visual ones, such a language had tremendous power and could be communicated over large public spaces (*EOCH* 210, 214). The force of this language lay in its sensory effectiveness.

Likewise, when Condillac notes the sensible images of early language, he further underlines the close connection between language and sensations. Subscribing to the classical notion of *ut pictura poesis*,

Condillac sees a complementary relationship between the sister arts of painting and poetry.[51] As he puts it, "If, in the origin of languages, prosody [or the art of versification] resembled singing, then style, in order to copy the sensible images of the language of action, adopted all manner of figures and metaphors, and was a true painting. . . . Style, in its origin, was poetic, since it began by painting ideas with the most sensible images" (*EOCH* 227). Only later did it become more like prose, but even then authors could use the utility of ancient language, which was "more lively and capable of being etched in one's memory" (*EOCH* 228). It derives its lively and unforgettable qualities from its proximity to the rich, vibrant, and spontaneous world of experience itself. By using a highly figurative language that conjures up sensible (in this case, visual) images, a writer can both delight and instruct his audience. Even as it does today in televised newscasts that incorporate the anchor person's face and voice with a photographic or other image of what is being reported, the figure served then as a kind of cognitive support, helping keep the listener/viewer interested in and aware of the subject at hand. Mere words, unless they can be attached to a sensible image, are easily forgotten.

Not only are the sensations important in supporting language, they also determine, according to Condillac, what comes first and last in the genesis of a language. The first words are precisely the ones for "sensible objects"; "sensible qualities" of these same objects receive names next (*EOCH* 232–33). One might think in studying Condillac's theory of language that the importance he grants to the senses in the formation of language would diminish as words take on increasingly abstract meanings. To the contrary, Condillac stresses the continuity of sensory experience as a basis for all language, simple or complex. Even abstract words should follow the same path as those for concrete objects. Condillac describes the identical development for both as follows: "if it is certain that the most general notions come from ideas we hold immediately from the senses, it is equally certain that the most abstract terms derive from the first names that were given to sensible objects" (*EOCH* 238–40). For example, if our general notion of a tree, an abstraction from experience, comes from ideas obtained from numerous observations of many different trees, then highly abstract terms like goodness or evil derive from the first names given to sensible objects.

---

51. A clear and concise summary of this idea can be found in Rensselaer W. Lee, *Ut Pictura Poesis: The Humanistic Theory of Painting* (New York: Norton, 1967).

All sensationists in fact associate these abstract terms at some point with physical reactions: goodness initially corresponds to what we find physically attractive, and evil to what we find repellent. Self-interest, which attracts us to and repels us from certain objects, helps us gradually define abstract concepts. Sensory experience thus provides the key to understanding language at both ends of the spectrum, from the very simple to the most complex.[52]

Following Warburton's work on Egyptian hieroglyphics in *The Divine Legation of Moses Demonstrated*, Condillac also traces the origin of written language to sensible images, which gather their evocative power primarily through analogy. Analogy in turn is made possible by experience. It involves an ability to find two things that resemble each other. Relationships of resemblance are determined largely by comparisons from visual inspection. One validates a sign over another sign for a given referent on the basis of the closeness of the analogy. The closer the resemblance, the better the sign. Primitive people sometimes call forked lightning a serpent because it physically resembles either the reptile itself or its forked tongue.[53] The word for forked lightning and serpent is the same in their language because the sensory appearance of each referent is similar. Primitive people make a connection between two analogous figures and the same word. Their language is thereby extended by similar sensory experiences (i.e., the sight of forked lightning and the sight of a snake), and another referent in their natural world receives a name. In point of fact, the highly complex human activities of abstract thought and analysis are made possible through analogical vocabulary, which "was created from sensible details."[54] In his interpretation of Condillac's *Logique*, Nicolas Rousseau discerns that words only mean anything from their first or original meaning in experience, which can be rediscovered through analysis; other meanings come from analogy.[55] As Rousseau felicitously puts it, there must be a "uniform perceptual resonance" in any Condillacian representation of thought, which in its turn constantly renews its contact with experience through analysis.[56] Language, like knowledge,

52. Condillac says as much about mathematical language in *La Langue des calculs*. Computations at all levels of difficulty are similarly based on experience.

53. The example comes from Cassirer, *Language and Myth*, trans. Suzanne K. Langer (New York: Harper, 1946), p. 96. See his analysis of the "equivalence" principle, pp. 95–99.

54. Robins, "Condillac et l'origine du langage," p. 99.

55. Rousseau, *Connaissance et langage chez Condillac*, pp. 263–64.

56. Rousseau, *Connaissance*, pp. 413, 422. There is thus a kind of circular or reciprocal relation between language and experience. In Rousseau's words, "language depends upon

has its origin in the senses. Hence, in Condillac's sensationist theory of language, the first language is figurative precisely because figures are accessible to the senses. The figurative nature of language is not a haphazard characteristic of language but a necessary precondition for being understood by human beings endowed with sensibility. Condillac affirms the centrality of the senses to language in the following words: "it is obvious that in the origin of languages, it was a necessity for men to join the language of action to that of articulated sounds, and to speak only with sensible images. Besides, today's most common knowledge was so subtle for them that it could fall within their reach only inasmuch as it came close to the senses" (*EOCH* 256). Condillac thus explains the importance of fables as forms of instruction. He considers metaphors, too, not originally as mere linguistic ornaments but as part of the natural development of language. Even when serving as ornaments, figures in general do not necessarily "harm the clarity" of language as long as they are "used with discretion" (*EOCH* 259). They both lose their utility when they become difficult to understand in parables, enigmas, or metaphysical systems.

Abstruse, mysterious, imprecise metaphorical language receives some of Condillac's harshest criticism. It is a decadent form of the positive sensible images Condillac sees in man's first language. Although he does not mention it specifically, it is one of the languages Condillac has in mind when speaking of the two sorts of metaphysics at the beginning of the *Essai.* Its words are "vague" and have "no sense" because they have lost all touch with the sensible universe. Whether it be for language or ideas, meaning comes from the senses. Condillac's thesis is not that a meaningful word or idea must always have a direct sensory referent. It is not that restrictive. It does imply, however, that experience must be part and parcel of the creation of language. A clear, precise word or idea must at some point have arisen from sensory perception, even though it may not currently have a sensory referent. One may not readily find a referent for the word *beautiful* in one's immediate environment. But one can sift through layer upon layer of sensory experiences and recall sooner or later some one object or event that would qualify as beautiful. The antithesis of metaphorical language, the scientific language that Condillac is promoting maintains clarity even as it maintains connections with sensory experience. The one leads to

---

sensory experience as much as it generates from it, or more precisely language can (re)produce sensory experience to the same extent that it depends on it" (p. 423).

truth, the other to error. Any metaphysics in Condillac's eyes is no better than the language it uses. Hence, Condillac mocks Leibniz's "vague" language, because it is metaphorical (*TSy* 117). The two words "vague" and "metaphorical" are practically synonymous for Condillac when he speaks of later stages in the evolution of language. They also indicate an undesirable distance from the images that come directly from the senses. The language evoked by these epithets comes not from experience but from an overactive imagination (*TSy* 239). It does not have the moderating effects that Condillac finds only in the judicious use of analogy, which gives rise to what he considers the most exact, clear, and precise language possible.

   Condillac's theory of language leads me to claim that he is essentially working out two kinds of metaphor: one that tends toward abstraction or arbitrariness and another that tends toward sensory experience or analogy. But whereas the one foments obfuscation, the other encourages enlightenment. The one has a magical or supernatural quality to it; the other, a scientific character. The two sorts of metaphor correspond in point of fact to the two sorts of metaphysics Condillac mentions at the outset of his *Essai:* "The first makes all nature an enchantment of sorts that wears off; the second, seeking to see things only as they are in fact, is as simple as truth itself. With the former countless errors accumulate, and the mind makes do with vague notions and words without meaning: with the latter not much knowledge is attained, but error is avoided: the mind becomes sound and always forms clear ideas" (*EOCH* 99). Condillac may outline two kinds of metaphysics or metaphorical languages early on in his life as a writer, but he does not fully develop his ideal language until the *Langue des calculs.* Signs of it are apparent throughout his writings, as he sincerely hopes it can be achieved one day. He believes such an ideal language possible and would indeed like "to reason in metaphysics and in moral doctrine with as much accuracy as in geometry" (99). But it will take him a lifetime to perfect a method of doing so. Analysis may be the general method Condillac uses throughout his work. But it is analogy, of which one catches brief glimpses here and there in his writing, that comes to the fore in his last thoughts on scientific language. It reinforces once again the crucial connection between knowledge and language, on the one hand, and sensory experience, on the other.

   Condillac's ultimate means to attain perfection in language thus lies in analogy, for it presumably assures continuity between sensation and reflection by its particular way of inventing signs. As I pointed out earlier and as Condillac defines the term, analogy is "a relation of resemblance" (*LC* 2–3). It is structured in much the same way as is metaphor. That is, like is substituted for like. And the likeness or resemblance is determined primarily by the senses. Condillac uses analogy as a way of justifying his assumptions in *La Logique,* a way that is outdone only by experience itself: "It is a system in which I reason on the basis of assumptions; but they are all advisable by analogy. Phenomena are naturally developed in it, they are explained in a very simple manner, and yet I recognize that assumptions like mine, when they are advisable only by analogy, do not have the same degree of obviousness as the assumptions that experience itself recommends and confirms; because, if analogy cannot allow one to doubt an assumption, experience alone can make it obvious" (*TSy* 232). A system based on analogy is the next best thing, so to speak, to one based on experience. Analogy and experience have in common a reliance on the senses and a rejection of the wholly arbitrary. In order to validate an analogy or some empirical evidence, one must use one's senses to determine if the two entities being compared bear any resemblance to each other or not. Such verification is just as warranted for words and things as it is for numbers and numerical concepts. Because of the verifiable nature of his assumptions, Condillac claims greater veracity for them than for the mere imaginary conjectures of many metaphysicians that have no solid grounding. But his choice of an algebraic language undermines somewhat his claims to avoid abstraction. Not all substitutions in language have the same logical pattern that mathematical proofs can follow.

Condillac nonetheless insists on distinguishing between his analytic method and the haphazard ways of abstract speculative metaphysics by his refusal of arbitrariness. Moreover, it is analogy in language that "sets the law" and "does not allow an absolutely arbitrary choice" of words (*LC* 2). By opting for analogy over random chance as the determining factor in language, Condillac hopes to give a scientific character to the language he is fashioning in a novel way. He wants to reverse the tendency he perceived in his day to make the arbitrariness of signs the pretext for linguistic abuses. Conventions may give rise to word usage, but the conventions themselves "presuppose a reason that has each word adopted" (*LC* 2). For all of the *philosophes* and especially for the sensationist Condillac, reason was an objective attainable by systematic observation or sensory experimentation. Although as a faculty it may seem far removed from some of the other, more mundane mental operations, reason ultimately is inextricably linked to the senses. As the sensationist refrain expresses it time after time, all of our ideas come to us from the senses. If we claim to have an idea that does not come from the senses or that lacks any sensory referent whatsoever in the immediate environment or in our memory, according to Condillac that idea is meaningless. It is difficult for us to understand how even our ideas of the content of Condillac's book can come from the senses. True, the ideas that come to mind while reading Condillac's sentences are not just the shapes of letters and words we see with our eyes. More important, they are what the words mean. But we easily forget how we came to derive meaning from words. First, our eyes had to be trained to follow the shapes of letters, which when put together in certain configurations with other letters produce meaningful words. Even before that stage, though, we had to learn what the words themselves meant through countless experiments with sounds and gestures. For a child to understand what *water* means, he or she must have seen or touched it innumerable times in the presence of an older person repeating the word "water." All of these instances are necessary before one can read and understand *water.* In a word, meaning comes from experience. One cannot have meaning without it. However lofty it may appear, reason or the ability to think and generate ideas logically is supported by the "lowly" senses.[57] They provide the verifiable basis or foothold in experience from which the higher faculties can advance. The mind quite simply needs the body. Such a need does not diminish the hegemony of the *cogito.* But it does make, as the sensationists hoped it would, philosophers more responsible in attributing extravagant powers to the mind. The yoking of reason to the senses constitutes one of the Enlightenment's most subtle paradoxes. Hence, when Condillac mentions the need for a reason behind a linguistic convention, one can rest assured that he is thinking of some sensory experience that originally establishes an analogy between a word and a thing and that authorizes the adoption of one particular word over another. In adopting, for instance, the particular sound of a wolf's howl for the name of that animal, one maintains continuity between sensory experience and linguistic representation, between the physical and the mental worlds.

---

57. Rauch supports such a notion of sensationism's tendency toward hierarchy inversion when he states "the idea is not only not first, . . . but it is also generated from down below, according to the very hierarchy of these systems, that is from the sensory body." See "Le Souci du corps chez Condillac," 85.

Having greater analogy with the sensible universe, the language that arises from such naming can lay claim to greater precision than can a language based on the purely arbitrary selection of signs.

By rejecting arbitrariness in favor of analogy, Condillac takes the first step in laying out a precise, mathematical language. He models his ideal language after algebra. He has a number of reasons for doing so: "Algebra is a well-made language, and it is the only one: nothing seems arbitrary in it. Analogy, which never escapes detection, leads perceptibly from one expression to the next. Usage here has no authority. It is not a question of speaking as others do. One must speak with the greatest analogy to achieve the greatest precision; and those who have produced this language have felt that simplicity of style gives it all its elegance: a truth that is rarely known in our vulgar languages" (*LC* 6–7). Although the terms that algebra compares are abstract, the analogy used in it can proceed "perceptibly." That is, one must be able to seize through the senses (in this case, sight) a conspicuous resemblance between expressions as they are substituted for one another. Rules of usage or linguistic conventions based on a number of people who agree to use a certain expression for a thing do not apply here and are devoid of power. One cannot simply imitate the speech patterns of a limited group of people but must strive for an analogy observable by anyone. The meaning of mathematical operations is much easier to follow if the signs used keep as much resemblance among themselves as possible. Condillac might rewrite $6 - 4$, as he does many other mathematical problems, by substituting like numbers for the two figures. As signs, 6 and 4 do not physically resemble each other. But a Condillacian rendition of them would increase the visual resemblance of the signs themselves. Meaning is not only associated with the ideas of numbers but also with their shapes and sounds. 6 thus might become $2 + 2 + 2$ (or three twos), while 4 becomes $2 + 2$ (or two twos). Three twos $(2 + 2 + 2)$ minus two twos $(2 + 2)$ is one two or 2. The analogy or similarity in the series of twos facilitates comprehension.

Algebraic analogy for Condillac achieves virtual identity by approximating—without ever quite reproducing—wholly identical statements, and it uses analysis to do so. Two of the chief components of Condillac's method, analogy and analysis, thus mutually reinforce each other. The precision sought is not one consisting in the substitution of absolutely identical propositions, for such a language would be circular and meaningless. Without one's falling into a frivolous exercise, the number 4, for instance, cannot be substituted for itself, whereas $2 + 2$ as an equal sum can; the identity is in the ideas not the words (*LC* 60–62).[58] Condillac creates a language that makes analogy more readily apparent to the senses by "decomposing" or breaking down numbers. What the process of "sorting out" or *démêler* is to the analysis of the origin of knowledge, decomposing is to the analysis of numbers. Along similar lines, Victor Delbos points out that Condillac's theory of transformed sensations can be seen as a specific application of the philosopher's "logical formalism" insofar as Condillac "considers the transformations of sensation as simple algebraic transformations, which are intelligible only if they are identities, but which become intelligible as soon as they are reduced to the law of identity."[59] In this way, one can view, as Condillac did, the mental faculties as various permutations of sensations (e.g., attention as "exclusive sensation," comparison as "double attention," judgment as compared sensations, memory as recalled sensations, etc.).[60] Condillac associates analysis with decomposing just as he had associated it with the process of sorting out. Analysis performs both of these functions (*TSy* 239). It is especially effective with numbers because of its simplicity.[61] Yet faculties of the mind, unlike numbers, are often greater than the sum of their parts.

Some other concrete examples are in order here to show "perceptibly" how Condillac uses analogy and analysis in tandem with each other, first with words then with algebraic symbols. One of the first significant examples Condillac uses presents a proportion, five . eight : nine . twelve, which he breaks down as follows: five . five plus three : nine . nine plus three, which can be further formulated as "five is to five plus three, in the same proportion as nine is to nine plus three" (*LC* 112). The two operations of analysis and analogy unfold at once. Condillac "untangles" or decomposes the numbers eight and twelve into sums of their parts. But he chooses not just any addition but an addition that contains the same addend, namely three. Moreover, he repeats the first number to which three is being added each time. Such repetition of terms may seem belabored and tedious. But it makes the identity between the sides of the proportion all the more "perceptible,"

---

58. For a discussion of frivolity in language, see Derrida, *L'Archéologie du frivole,* pp. 101–21. In Derrida's view, Condillac's definition of frivolity, which the author thought could be diminished by method, is based on the lack of a need (esp. pp. 101, 111–12).

59. Delbos, *La Philosophie française,* p. 273.

60. I have borrowed some of these designations from Le Roy. See his *La Psychologie de Condillac,* p. 222.

61. For a summary of the processes of analysis, see the passage quoted above (*LC* 272–73).

just as it does that for the sums of the outside and middle numbers (five plus nine plus three and five plus three plus nine), since identity "is shown even in the words" (*LC* 112). One cannot underestimate the importance Condillac grants the physical, perceptible resemblance between the elements that are being substituted for one another (e.g., the series of twos), whether the elements are signs in the form of verbal or written words taking the place of things or whether they are numbers taking the place of other numbers. In each case, he seeks a resemblance that can be seen, heard, or sensed in some way. The obviousness of the resemblance, and hence the clarity of a language, is thus proven by sensory experience. All one need do to realize the validity of a mathematical proof is to "inspect" (i.e., to look at with one's eyes) its "terms" (*LC* 136). Any such inspection allows one to "see appreciably that you have gone from the known to the unknown, only because what you did not know is the same as what you did know" (*LC* 122; see also 39). The passage from the known to the unknown, across what may have seemed unbridgeable distances, is made possible and enormously facilitated by the senses. For they ultimately establish the analogy necessary to proceed in an analytic, scientific manner.

In Condillac's *La Langue des calculs,* experience plays at least as important a role as it had in his study of the evolution of ideas and language. Nature gives us our "first lessons in arithmetic" by providing us with hands with fingers that allow us "to represent collections perceptibly" (*LC* 32, see also 49–50). Our first ideas of numbers are thus directly connected to sensations of the fingers as numerical units. Condillac's conception of the origin of mathematical knowledge, tied as it is to the sensory origin of all human knowledge in general, could hardly be more sensationist. One must see or sense, as it were, numbers in fingers or in signs to know them and to follow their various combinations. Our ideas of numbers do not of course refer just to the fingers themselves or to the shapes and sounds of numbers. Mental understanding of numbers lies beyond physical apprehension of our fingers and of the shapes and sounds of numbers. But apart from enormously facilitating the mental assimilation of numerical concepts, fingers and other physical aids constitute a necessary precondition for the cognitive process. We do not learn to count in the mind but in the physical world of sensory experience. Moreover, the connection with the senses is never quite lost in all of Condillac's musings on mathematics, no matter how complex the operation. The ulterior substitution of signs such as pebbles *(cailloux)*—which Condillac claims as the etymological derivation for the word *arithmetic (le calcul)*—for fingers changes nothing in the sensationist explanation of mathematical origins, because even these are "under one's eyes" (*LC* 178). Like fingers, they, too, can be sensed and therefore serve as a means of attaining accurate calculations.

Condillac's direct or indirect references to the hands, fingers, and eyes are not gratuitous. They call attention to the author's deeply rooted sensationism. It is no coincidence, for instance, that Condillac states he will toddle about childlike by holding onto something or "walk, if need be, with my hands," as he puts it, to maintain his deceptively simple but ingenious approach to the sciences (*LC* 202). Condillac not only emphasizes here the general need anyone has for some physical, basic, down-to-earth support in order to learn. He also alludes indirectly to the specific role played by the hands in counting and many mathematical operations. Additions and subtractions are performed by opening and closing the hands (*LC* 254). One "gropes" for the right answer in long division (*LC* 267–68), just as one counted originally on one's fingers. The kind of language Condillac hopes to devise should be ideally patterned after finger counting (*LC* 36–37), because it shows or makes readily perceptible its steps and its origin. In the best of all possible mathematical languages, we should always be able to trace our steps back to the beginning. Such a return to the origin of things is facilitated by sensory evidence along the way. Hence, Condillac insists constantly on the need for signs, whether they be fingers, pebbles, or algebraic letters, to be "under one's eyes" or under continual scrutiny at all times. The very expression for this in French, *sous les yeux,* occurs repeatedly in *La Langue des calculs* (89, 112, 181, 227, 335, 412) and reinforces the need Condillac felt for keeping a visible trace of analogy in language. As visual representations, signs help one follow the progression of logical argument and to remember it clearly. Although Condillac may sometimes give the impression that he is speaking of signs as nothing more than visual or auditory representations, he nonetheless assumes that any sign embraces both signifier and signified. Signs are seen or heard on the physical level, but they are also understood for the meaning they convey. The connection of ideas through signs follows the connection of sensations among themselves. By connecting sensations, Condillac also hopes to connect signs and ideas, since presumably ideas come from the sensations. Returning to Condillac's metaphor of the toddler child as learner, we can work our way slowly through any maze of difficult problems, including logarithms, as long as we have something tangible to hold on to or something visible to follow. Condillac's language, especially in mathematics, is thus nothing less than a visible language. It "speaks to the eyes rather than the ears" (*LC* 196, 426) "directing the eyes" (*LC* 469) so that they can easily follow the orderly continuity that flows from a judicious use of analogy. By continually showing through visual means the sequence of steps used to derive any current state, such a language points both back to its own past or origin and forward to a future teeming with countless unknown discoveries. For Condillac, it was simply a question of developing a language precise enough, that is, perceptible enough, to move from the known to the unknown.

Even when numerals and algebraic letters have replaced names for numbers, sensationist principles still apply. Let us "inspect" another one of Condillac's examples, this time one involving variables:

$$\frac{a^1}{a^2} = a^{1-2} = a^{-1} = \frac{1}{a}.$$ And by following the analogy $a^{1-1} = \frac{a^1}{a^1} = \frac{a}{a} = 1.$ But $a^{1-1} = a^0$: thus $a^0, a^{1-1}, \frac{a}{a}$ are just so many examples of oneness. Finally, from $a^{-1} = \frac{1}{a}$, we infer $a^{-2} = \frac{1}{a^2}, a^{-3} = \frac{1}{a^3}, a^{-4} = \frac{1}{a^4},$ etc. (*LC* 291).

The substitution of identical (that is, equivalent) formulations determined by analogy and analysis leads to new mathematical discoveries. Although the terms may be different, the procedure is the same. Moving from the known to the unknown, algebra is no different from any language, insofar as it involves the artful substitution of "identical expressions for identical expressions" (*LC* 292–93). Condillac no doubt consciously repeats the words "identical expressions" here just as he repeats identical words, terms, or formulae elsewhere to underline the continuity of his method.

Like analysis, analogy entails for Condillac continuous, orderly, and logical movement from one step to the next. A careful method or language based on analogy takes no "perilous leaps" (*LC* 257; see also 223) that might possibly appear to gain time in the short term but usually lead to ruinous errors.[62] Condillac reinforces a sense of continu-

---

62. Cf. Bonnet's insistence on continuity in his method and his connection of the concept with the Chain of Being. See Chapter 2, pages 64–66, 81–82.

ity in his language by numerous repetitions. His own method follows that of nature itself, which "instructs only because it repeats the same things in many ways" (*LC* 143). While substituting identical propositions, mathematical analogy also modifies them slightly each time to express the same idea in a different way. Continuity (the known) is maintained and repeated even while the unknown reveals itself. By using new ways to express something we already know, mathematics constitutes a language (*LC* 390–91). Although perhaps not a language in the same way that ordinary language is a language, mathematics has a precision that Condillac would like to extend to all intelligent discourse so as to rid language of some of its egregious errors and to achieve ever increasing discoveries in the name of reason and enlightenment.

Just as mathematics constitutes a language, so, too, does language constitute the very basis of Condillac's method. And Condillac's approach to any subject is nothing if not methodical. In fact, Condillac tends to orient the discussion of any topic to the same parameters of language. Unless we can express ourselves clearly and precisely, we will never be able to make progress in any area, whether it is science, mathematics, or metaphysics. The same rules apply to any discipline. I have dwelled as long as I have on Condillac's conception of language, because it is central to his entire method. Echoing his *Grammaire* and *Logique,* he virtually identifies language and method from the beginning of *La Langue des calculs:* "Any language is an analytic method, and any analytic method is a language" (*LC* 1); and later on in the work: "In order to invent the best methods, it is therefore necessary that the language spoken be a good method itself" (*LC* 208–9; see also 202, 228, 387). A method can be a language in the sense that it ideally allows one to discover meaning just as a good language does. When operating optimally, a language, like an analytic method, makes connections between ideas. Each proceeds in an orderly fashion from the known to the unknown, making the new sorts of associations that will expand knowledge. Despite a certain confusion between a language and its use, Condillac's linking of language and method ultimately underlines their common purpose in enlightenment. Moreover, language serves as a means of analyzing or decomposing our thoughts and ideas successively to see whether they are well founded.[63]

63. Hine, "Condillac and the Problem of Language," 28; and Guy Harnois, *Les Théories du langage en France de 1660 à 1821* (Paris: Les Belles Lettres, 1928), pp. 47–48. According to Lorin Anderson, the reason so many eighteenth-century thinkers, including Condillac and

One might well ask what Condillac hopes to accomplish with a well-crafted language or a "good" method. The answer to that question lies, as I have suggested from time to time in this chapter and as might be expected from Condillac the exemplary *philosophe*, in the cultivation of reason itself. For the projects are one and the same: *"the art of reasoning is reduced to a well-made language"* (*TSy* 28; Condillac's italics). This "great truth" from Condillac's *Logique* serves as an important backdrop to much of his thinking. I have left the somewhat awkward translation of *langue bien faite* as "well-made language," because it calls attention to the labor involved in forging or crafting a language from nothing other than our own experience. Like his fellow *philosophes*, Condillac seeks to dispel any *a priori* notion of anything (in this case, any such notion of language). The French Enlightenment's formulation of reason stood not on questionable abstractions like innate ideas but on the firm bulwarks of verifiable sensory experience. There is no easy formula for making an ideal language such as Condillac envisages it. It requires much hard work and experience. But we can use that experience to advantage by having it confirm by analogy the choices we make of linguistic, mathematical, or metaphysical terms. Condillac's injunction for a clear, precise language "to take up again the materials of our knowledge, and to make new combinations of them without regard for those that happen to have been made already" (*EOCH* 272) should not be taken too lightly. Knowledge of the genesis of ideas helps preclude the intervention of presupposed abstractions. Condillac's method of returning to the origin of things ultimately attests to his profound belief in the authenticity and authority of experience. It is experience, as opposed to complete arbitrariness, that should according to Condillac represent the highest authority in language. Representative of many an eighteenth-century thinker but contrary to the modern view of language as almost entirely arbitrary, Condillac affirms the authority of experience in the important domain of language. Others would fully exploit the rich implications of this authority in domains as diverse as politics, religion, education, the arts, and the sciences.

While at once following Locke and diverging from his way of thinking, Condillac thus makes, as stated earlier, the sensory origin of ideas

---

Bonnet, were interested in associating language and analysis was that they saw analysis as "derived directly from the conception of language and its functions." See *Charles Bonnet and the Order of the Known* (Dordrecht: Reidel, 1982), p. 78.

central to his new theory. He essentially defines experience, which forms the basis for reason and the progress the *philosophes* hoped to attain from it, in terms of the sensations.[64] Although such a definition may at first seem reductionist, Condillac amplifies it specifically with the related concepts of origin and nature, analysis, order, analogy, and language. From the sensationist viewpoint, sensory activity provides an original or first experience from which all subsequent mental operations flow. The sensations are, as Condillac concludes in the *Traité des sensations,* "the sole source of our enlightenment and our feelings" (265). Condillac associates the sensations with his notion of origin and nature. Like nature, analysis works in an ordered, continuous fashion but backwards toward the origin of knowledge in sensory experience at the same time that it builds on it. In conjunction with analogy, which confirms perceptible resemblances between new signs or ideas and old ones, analysis allows one to construct a clear and precise rational language that is grounded in experience. But by experience Condillac also means generally the method whereby one understands anything. By informing all the various mental faculties and Condillac's central concepts, the sensations play a crucial role in the elaboration of his own method. They are used by Condillac to explain the generation of ideas even as they are used to show their decomposition and thereby have epistemological as well as methodological value. Ultimately, it can be said that they both give meaning to experience and allow one to experience meaning.

Condillac's definition of experience was thus at once more and less empirical than Locke's. By subjecting all the faculties of the mind to analysis, which takes him back to an original experience in the senses, Condillac leaves no room for exceptions like the understanding Locke neglected to scrutinize with his usual thoroughness. Whatever limitations the sensations may have sometimes in their deceiving appearances, they at least have, unlike several metaphysical explanations, some relation to a real world that actually exists. Condillac uses sensory experience to support all of his major concepts of analysis, order, analogy, and language—the key components of his method. By his definition of experience as an understandable and verifiable chain of events, he strives to ban arbitrariness and speculative abstraction from metaphysics.

---

64. As the final chapter of the book makes clear, the *idéologues,* especially Maine de Biran, will attack some of the shortcomings of such a limited view of experience.

And yet in so doing, he himself falls into the trap of abstract, deductive reasoning by creating a statue-man lacking the language, self-consciousness, active will, and complexity of a living human being. His logical reduction of human mental life to elemental sensations, although a useful contribution to the progressive thinking of his time, does not fully represent the human condition. Empiricism typically accentuates the confusing diversity of experience. Condillac lets us glimpse its initial confusion but immediately imposes on experience a logical reduction that simplifies and unifies it.[65] His thinking resembles at times that of the rationalist without the rationalist's stipulation of preexisting sophisticated notions or conditions. Condillac follows as rigorously as he can the empirical directive to begin in the beginning without recourse to mystical innate ideas. His preoccupation with logical thinking, however, interferes with his otherwise purely sensationist method. His analogies sometimes curiously slip into claims for identity.[66]

The picture of Condillac's theory that emerges from this study is ultimately one of a "logical sensationism" that simultaneously embraces various aspects of empirical, rational, and logical thinking.[67] I use this term, intentionally leaving aside the word *rational*, to underline, as I have repeatedly throughout this chapter, the centrality of sensory experience to Condillac's theory. For it had a profound resonance not only for the two other major sensationist thinkers, Bonnet and Helvétius, but for the entire French Enlightenment.

65. Delbos, *La Philosophie française*, p. 274; Le Roy, *La Psychologie de Condillac*, pp. 224–28. Hegel had noticed the contrary forces operative in empiricism, which calls attention on the one hand to the multiplicity of experience yet is constrained on the other hand to give it some sense of unity. See Auroux, "Le Rationalisme empiriste," *Dialogue* 13 (1974), 496, 502. According to Auroux, "empiricism welcomes [the notion of] multiplicity not because it cannot overcome it, but because it believes that unity is contained within multiplicity and that the universality of reason is given in the indefinitely compounded unity that makes up the totality of human culture."

66. Duchesneau, "Condillac critique de Locke," 94.

67. Delbos, *La Philosophie française*, p. 273; Le Roy, *La Psychologie de Condillac*, p. 226; Dieckmann, "Condillac's Philosophical Works," 259; and Auroux, "Empirisme et théorie linguistique chez Condillac," pp. 197–98. Respectively, these critics have used the expressions "logical formalism," "panlogism," "logical radicalism," and "metalinguistic empiricism" to characterize Condillac's theory. While each of these terms captures the essence of a certain portion of Condillac's thought, none, with the exception of Auroux's, takes account of the very basic commitment the *philosophe* had—regardless of his failings—to an empirical method grounded in the senses. See also Paganini, "Psychologie et physiologie," 177–78. Paganini calls attention to Condillac's physiological discussions that complement and are never completely divorced from his psychological concerns.

2

Bonnet's Mind-Body Continuum in the Economy of Our Being

Shortly after he began writing his *Essai analytique sur les facultés de l'âme* (ultimately published in 1760), using a fictional statue to explain the genesis of human knowledge, Charles Bonnet discovered that Condillac had already exploited this mental construct in his *Traité des sensations*.[1] Rather than abandoning his project after having perused Condillac's *Traité*, however, Bonnet decided to pursue it, feeling he had a qualitatively different use of the statue and consequently a significant contribution of his own to make to eighteenth-century epistemology. His originality lay, he believed, in a new form of analytic method, the lack of which he had noticed in Condillac's work (*EA* 11, 539). Although he had established his sensationist perspective in an earlier piece entitled *Essai de psychologie* (1754),[2] Bonnet did not entirely develop his own ideas on the subject until the *Essai analytique*.

1. Charles Bonnet, *Essai analytique sur les facultés de l'âme* (Copenhagen, 1760; rpt. Hildesheim: Olms, 1973), pp. 10–11. Unless otherwise indicated, all page references are to this work; hereafter cited as *(EA)*. Italics in the quotations are Bonnet's, as are the punctuation and capitalization. For a comparative study of Condillac's and Bonnet's statues, see Albert Lemoine, *Charles Bonnet de Genève: Philosophe et naturaliste* (Paris: Durand, 1850), pp. 116–47. Lemoine praises Bonnet for his slow and careful method but faults him for not bringing his statue, as Condillac does, to the point of a human being with all senses operative.
2. Bonnet, *Essai de psychologie, ou Considérations sur les opérations de l'âme, sur l'habitude et sur l'éducation* (London, 1755; Hildesheim: Olms, 1978), see esp. pp. 153–54;

In composing this later work, Bonnet takes as the object of his research, in his own words, "the Economy of our Being" (*EA* v, xiii, xxi). By these evocative terms, Bonnet means essentially the study of positive and negative changes in the body, brain, and soul. The concept, however prominently it may be mentioned in the preface, does not take on full meaning, nor is it even frequently repeated verbatim, until quite late in the essay (*EA* 355–56, 370, 473) and at its end (538). The point at which Bonnet mentions in any significant way the economy of our being coincides not surprisingly with increased attention to a critical moment that occurs earlier in his analysis of the soul's operations, a moment in which sensations are either lost or gained for the first time. In retrospect, it is a critical point both textually and intertextually, for it not only gives unity and coherence to Bonnet's work but also allows him to distinguish it clearly from Condillac's. Whereas Condillac has the statue pass by turns from one sense to another and through many different sensations, Bonnet focuses primarily on the very first two sensations his statue will experience from the one sense of smell. This crucial period will explain the functioning of the faculties and the evolution of ideas as well as ultimately reveal the depth of both Bonnet's analytic method and his sensationism, which are fundamentally intertwined in their reliance on a continuum between the body and mind. But before turning his attention to it, he makes a number of claims about the body and soul, as well as several general assumptions that let him build his particular argument. These include the necessity of a soul, man's mixed being, the law of union, the predominance of the physical over the metaphysical, and the importance of succession in human cognition.

As he concludes the preface to his *Essai analytique,* Bonnet gives his reason for the necessity of a soul: "It is not at all because I believe the Soul a Being more excellent than Matter, that I attribute a Soul to Man: it is only because I cannot attribute to Matter all the Phenomena of Man" (*EA* xxiv). It is the immaterial nature of the soul that leads Bonnet to create a place for it in his ontology. Its existence is further "founded on the opposition between the simplicity of feeling and the compound

---

hereafter cited as *(EP).* Written in a very tentative style, the *Essai de psychologie* paraphrases the arguments of other philosophers and makes many conjectures and hypothetical propositions. Apparently, Bonnet had not yet found his own authentic voice and method. Contrasting sharply with the rhythm of the *Essai analytique,* most of the pages of which Bonnet devoted to two sensations, this work moves rapidly from the moment of the fetus's conception to ideas of good and evil in a mere twenty-seven pages (pp. 5–32).

nature of matter" (*EA* 3). The soul explains this simplicity of feeling better than anything else: "It is to satisfy this Feeling of the *Self*, always *one*, always *simple*, always *indivisible*, that we have recourse to the existence of that *immaterial* Substance we call the *Soul*" (297). It also provides an active internal motive force for the body and helps Bonnet conveniently avoid any association with materialism, with which his respectful religious views would put him in conflict (*EA* 86, 296; *EP* viif.).[3]

While Bonnet's addition of the soul to the epistemological equation answers some questions, it raises others. Not the least of these is that of its nature. In the *Essai de psychologie*, Bonnet tries to dodge the question, claiming absolute ignorance in this regard (*EP* 2). It is a position he takes in response to others, too, namely, the way in which a fiber's movement arouses an idea in the soul as well as the nature of movement and of other forces in matter (*EP* 105, 118). Nor does Bonnet attempt to situate or identify the seat of the soul but resorts to mechanical metaphors for it like the harpsichord, organ, or watch (*EP* 13).

But a kind of relative definition of the soul does eventually emerge from Bonnet's writings, stemming from what he calls man's mixed being and the law of union. In the *Essai de psychologie*, he writes of the mixed nature of human beings: "Man is . . . a *mixed* being, a being composed necessarily of two substances, one spiritual, the other corporeal" (*EP* 3). It is not until another work from the same period, *Principes philosophiques sur la cause première et sur son effet*, that Bonnet goes beyond these observations about our mixed being and attempts to unravel its complexity.[4] Although he surrounds the union of the two substances in "thick darkness" and a secret mystery (*EP* 123, 168)—the knots between them are known only to their creator—a law governing the union of body and soul can be formulated: "The *Fundamental* Law of this *Union* is, that on the occasion of *Movements* aroused in the

3. But the frequent references in the *Essai analytique* to fibers and the body's organization made Bonnet's friends and contemporaries in Geneva nervous about the work's potential contribution to the materialist cause. See A. Sayous, *Le Dix-Huitième Siècle à l'étranger: Histoire de la littérature française dans les divers pays de l'Europe depuis la mort de Louis XIV jusqu'à la Révolution française* (Paris: Amyot, 1861), 1: 179–80.

4. Bonnet, *Principes philosophiques sur la cause première et sur son effet* (London, 1755; rpt. Hildesheim: Olms, 1978), pp. 296–98. To the original 1754 edition and to the 1755 edition of the *Essai de psychologie* Bonnet appended this other, separate piece; hereafter cited as *(PP)*.

Body, the Soul is *altered;* & that on the occasion of *Alterations* of the
Soul the Body is *moved*" (*PP* 298–99; *EA* 29). To every bodily movement corresponds a change in the soul, and to every change in the soul
corresponds a bodily movement. Material and immaterial substances
depend on each other; one cannot be defined without the other.

Bonnet's statements about our mixed being and the law of union
reveal a marked preoccupation with the physical world. While his
insistence on human physiology draws him increasingly to a sensationist
viewpoint, it also differentiates him considerably from Condillac and
Helvétius, who normally avoid specific references to anatomical parts
of the nervous system. In a word, he is more of a physician than a
metaphysician. In a single passage from his preface to the *Essai analytique,* he establishes his own status as a researcher into the economy of
our being, echoes the two earlier positions about the body and soul,
and announces a decidedly sensationist approach to his subject:

> I have put in my Book much that is Physical in man, & rather
> little Metaphysics: but in truth, what could I say of the Soul
> considered in itself? We know so little about it. Man is a *mixed*
> Being; he only has Ideas through the intervention of senses, &
> his most abstract Notions still derive from the Senses. It is on his
> Body & by his Body that the Soul acts. One must therefore
> always come back to the *Physical* as to the first origin of all the
> Soul feels. (*EA* xiii)

The physical influences all the operations of the soul (*EA* 12). Notwithstanding a *caveat* to take some of the physical terms he uses in a
figurative sense because of the dearth of suitable terms for the spirit in
any language, Bonnet gives full force to this side of our being (*EA*
85–86). It is used in effect to explain the other side.

To understand Bonnet's method, one must proceed analytically, as he
does, simplifying and decomposing by degrees and successively from
the known to the unknown, from the simple to the composite (*EA* 1–2,
7, 65).[5] In the case of the physical world, such an approach constantly

---

5. Bonnet's method here parallels that which he approves in the *Essai de psychologie*
(244) for the education of the young mechanically minded Architas. The movement from the
known to the unknown is coupled with one from the simple to the complex. The way in
which we learn must be sometimes reversed, however, to explain our current state of being.
In describing his analytic method for the first time, Bonnet may use the expression "from the
composite to the simple" (*EA* 1). But when he expounds on what he means (*EA* 2) and when

connects the body—its sensations, its organs, and its fibers—to higher order faculties. From it there results an epistemological hierarchy. Bonnet himself uses a terminology of mastery in a system presumably governed by the wisdom of the divine author of nature, who has "subordinated the *Activity* of the Soul to its *Sensibility,* its sensibility to the *Play of Fibers;* the Play of Fibers to the *Action* of *Objects*" (*EA* 86–87, 92). It is understood that ideas "in their *first* origin" are "but the movements imprinted by Objects on the Fibers of the *Senses*" (*EA* 40). Freedom will be subordinated to the will, which in turn will be subordinated to the faculty of feeling or knowing and so on (*EA* 116). The order of movement is thus as follows: objects, organs (fibers), sensations or perceptions, will, freedom. Bonnet repeats it as often as he consciously does (*EA* 86–87, 115–16, 258, 287), because this order or hierarchy forms "the Basis of all the Science of our Being" (288).

On several occasions in the *Essai analytique,* Bonnet reiterates the importance of succession in human cognition. The notion is indeed closely tied to that of continuity and gradation in some of Bonnet's other writings.[6] After the statue has smelled its first sensation, the odor of a rose, this sensation disappears only by "degrees" or "gradations" (*EA* 32). Temporality itself is defined in terms of the succession of ideas (*EA* 72). The imagination will reproduce ideas in an order largely influenced by that in which they succeeded each other originally (*EA* 157). The succession of beings allows the mind to grasp the notion of priority and posteriority (*EA* 171). In a word, our very existence is successive (*EA* 234).

As Bonnet proceeds analytically, he establishes nothing less than a cognitive chain of events whose essential defining characteristic is its successive nature. According to Bonnet, the "true sign of an Analysis consists in the truth, distinctness, and concatenation of Ideas" (*EA* xii). The "ideas" linked in Bonnet's analysis represent steps in the cognitive process that ironically lead to the very ideas whose origin he is trying

---

he recapitulates his method (*EA* 65), it is clear that he is proceeding from the simple to the composite.

6. Continuity, gradation, and plenitude constitute the underlying principles of the eighteenth-century view of the universe as a Chain of Being. In his insistence on the continuity of the Chain, Bonnet contributes substantially to this view. See Arthur O. Lovejoy, *The Great Chain of Being: A Study of the History of an Idea* (1936; rpt. Cambridge, Mass.: Harvard University Press, 1978), pp. 183–287, esp. pp. 230–31, 235, 275, 283. Lovejoy quotes from Bonnet's *Contemplation de la nature* (1764–65) and notes the author's promptness in associating humans and apes in the continuous Chain of Being.

to identify in the soul. Nature's way, which is not to proceed "by *Leaps*" but *"by degrees,"* becomes his way of analyzing, too (*EA* 30).

The preceding discussion sets the stage for the crucial moment in which one sensation follows another in the statue. In Chapter XXI—the part that he originally intended as the conclusion to his *Essai analyti-que*—Bonnet finds himself led quite far by his analytic method, to which he willingly submits himself as he recognizes "that two Sensations sufficed to put into play all the Faculties of the Soul of [his] Statue" (355).[7] The surprise that Bonnet, as the author, records in looking back over the distance he has come is of course felt all the more keenly by the reader. It is the reader who must go back and fit together the various pieces of the argument in view of this insight, which is given in the context of a specific reevoking of the economy of our being. In point of fact, the economy of our being, which Bonnet claims to be the object of his research, is intricately tied to the succession of sensations and is largely defined by it in a sensationist vein. Bonnet works it out primarily on the level of the first two sensations in the statue. From them he will explain not only the functioning of a number of important human faculties, attributes, and feelings such as memory, personality, imagination, pleasure and pain, attention, will, freedom, and desire but also the evolution of ideas.[8] A glance at Bonnet's treatment of the statue's initial stages proves useful here.

Bonnet at first considers the statue before it has begun feeling and draws the sensationist conclusion that without sensations, it has no ideas (*EA* 13). Once the statue begins to feel, Bonnet has it start as did Condillac with the sense of smell, since it is the simplest of the senses and most suitable for his analytic method (*EA* 25). He then considers his statue after the first sensation, which of course is the odor of a rose, recognizing that recollection presupposes relationships with other ideas and that therefore a brain with a single idea could not recall it (*EA* 35).

But memory, like the other faculties in Bonnet's work, is linked to the

---

7. Although he goes on in Chapter XXI and beyond to introduce the statue to other olfactory sensations and eventually to "open" its ears (*EA* 507), his method remains essentially the same. His full-fledged analysis of the sense of smell "can easily be applied to the other Senses" (*EA* 538).

8. To the faculties of memory, imagination, will, and freedom I have added the attributes or feelings, personality, pleasure and pain, and desire, because Bonnet either discusses these faculties in terms of them or groups them together.

body, so it has a physiological explanation (*EA* 39). Even before arriving at the second sensation, the statue has already experienced somewhat the economy of its being, which is expressed in the mathematical and tangible terms of loss and gain: "The *primitive* state of the Fibers on which these Corpuscles [those emanating from the object and having an effect on the nose] have acted during a certain time has been *altered,* & this *alteration* is the *physical* expression of the *difference* between the *current* state of our Statue and that which preceded the *Sensation*" (*EA* 43). Only with the succession of one sensation after another, however, does the economy of the statue's being become especially apparent and is its existence reasserted, for feeling is indispensable for a sentient being. Without sensibility or the faculty of sensing or of feeling, it cannot and does not exist (*EA* 44). Bonnet even asks the rhetorical question: "is the *life* of the Soul anything other than the succession of these ideas recalled by one another?" (*EA* 45).

In having one sensation follow another in the statue, Bonnet is interested in answering an important question about memory and the reciprocity of action among fibers of a different kind, namely, "will the odor of the *Carnation* remind our Statue of that of the *Rose?*" (*EA* 54). Although one may be tempted to respond negatively to this question, experience provides us with facts to support reciprocity of action (*EA* 55). The "essential condition" for the recalling of sensations is "that the Fibers on which other Fibers act have been *moved* previously by *Objects*" (*EA* 56). Reminiscence is the impression of feeling again a modification that the soul has already felt (*EA* 59, 346). Its effect is "to instruct the Soul about the *identity,* or the *diversity* of its alterations" (*EA* 62). Bonnet notes that this is "one of the most important points in the Economy of our Being, but that it is not yet time to discuss it" (*EA* 62). He will not actually discuss the economy of our being until later, but one can assert retrospectively that reminiscence lets the soul know whether the change it is undergoing produces a feeling of sameness or difference which results from a loss or gain. Reminiscence further allows the statue to feel "the novelty of its situation," once a second odor is presented to it (*EA* 62). The first sensation of the odor of a rose serves as a kind of index to which any subsequent sensation is compared.

In his approach, which is at once physiological and sensationist, Bonnet explains reminiscence in terms of fibers. It is the body and not the soul that allows for reminiscence: "Memory, by which we retain the Ideas of Things, has been attached to the *Body*" (*EA* 39). The soul may feel, but "it is always the Body that makes Things felt" (*EA* 64). The lines that connect ideas (through reminiscence) to sensations—and the mind to the body—are drawn more tightly: "Because *Ideas* are in their *first* origin but the movements imprinted by Objects on the Fibers of the *Senses,* it follows that the *preservation* of Ideas by Memory depends in the last resort on the *propensity* that the *Senses'* Fibers have to *lend themselves* to these movements & to *repeat* them" (*EA* 40). Bonnet moves from general and indirect allusions to the body (sensations) to ever increasingly specific anatomical and physical ones (fibers, molecules, nutritive juices and atoms [*EA* 64–69]).

Just as there is an economy of our being, so, too, is there an economy of fibers which keep whatever configuration they have received from objects (*EA* 64f.). In one of the rare positive references to—in this case, an actual quotation from—the *Essai de psychologie,* Bonnet states: "'The frequent repetition of the same movement in the same Fiber changes up to a certain point the primitive state of this Fiber'" (*EA* 69–70; *EP* 206). The fibers thus physically retain and can retrace for the soul the remembrance of an impression that an object has left on the senses (*EA* 74, 383–84, 442). Whereas a remembrance of an impression has the same origin (i.e., the fiber) as the original sensation, it is weaker than the sensation (*EA* 366). But there would be no reminiscence in a being that felt the same sensation to the same degree all its life, since reminiscence "assumes in the Soul a change of state, a succession of alterations" (*EA* 71–72).

Such a description of reminiscence may give the impression that the fibers, once arranged in a certain configuration, remain that way all the time. But many forces like "internal movements" and "small impulses foreign to Objects and the Soul" as well as the effects of the circulatory and nutritive systems "conspire all the time to change the current state of the Senses' Fibers" (*EA* 75). In the same way in which fibers are formed to retain a reminiscence, so can they be "erased" either by natural degeneration or wear, as in any animal body, or by foreign disruptive impulses (*EA* 75–76). An economy of growth can give way to one of loss. However the case may be, each economy plays an important part in constituting our being. The total of these various changes by addition or subtraction strongly influences, if it does not actually yield, our personality.

Personality has its basis in memory, which as Bonnet shows, has its own basis in the succession of sensations at the core of the economy of our being. He writes toward the end of Chapter IX (*EA* 59–83), which contains his "Essay of a Theory of Reminiscence": "When the Soul feels therefore the impression of an Object, & remembers at the same time one, or several other impressions, it *identifies* with them all; & this *identification* is the foundation of *Personality"* (*EA* 80). Bonnet distinguishes, however, between two kinds of personality: one which could apply to animals, since it "results simply from the *relationship* that *Reminiscence* places between *earlier* and *later* Sensations, in virtue of which the Soul has the feeling of the changes through which it is passing"; the other being reflexive and "consisting in that return of the Soul onto itself, by which separating somehow its own Sensations from *itself*, it *reflects* that it is *the one* who *feels* them or has *felt* them" (*EA* 80–81). There is of course a difference between reflection and sensation.[9] Reflection presupposes the use of signs (in this case, the word *I*, which the statue cannot say); hence, its lack of any idea of the self (*EA* 81).

Bonnet answers the question of the simultaneous existence of several different sensations or ideas in the soul through his attitude toward reminiscence and personality. Without reminiscence, the same sensation would "appear as new as if it had never been *present"* (*EA* 139–40). Several sensations must be able to coexist in the soul at once. Reminiscence ties together the otherwise confusing succession of disparate sensations into a unified self; without it, there would be no personality (*EA* 140). Consequently, a "total loss of *Memory*, would thus entail the destruction of the *Personality"* (*EA* 458). But the acquisition or loss of ideas, which is a normal process in the economy of our being, does not "denature" a being; either action "only makes its personality more or less composite" (*EA* 460).

In the mechanics of its operations, imagination follows the same path as memory, with which Bonnet practically identifies it (*EA* 134). Like memory, the faculty of imagination represents to the soul ideas from absent objects (*EA* 155). Although he may start with a metaphysical statement, Bonnet moves quickly and invariably to the physical, thereby linking the mental to the sensory and reinforcing his sensationist view. The physiological chain of steps from the body to the soul bears repeating. Ideas correspond to movements of the sensory fibers within an organ, such as that for the sense of smell, which has specialized fibers to detect the play of corpuscles emanating from the object, in this case, a rose or carnation (*EA* 47, 52, 155). Imagination functions by having

---

9. As I shall demonstrate presently, this difference is not a discontinuous division for Bonnet.

the brain repeat the same movements that occurred in the first place. With a compound idea, which arises from the confluence either of two or more orders of fibers from the same sense or of orders from two or more senses affected at the same time, the imagination reproduces it by "a secret *communication* between the *different* Orders of *Fibers* that come together in the production of this *Idea*" (*EA* 152, 156). The initial order of succession of simple or concrete ideas will of course influence and determine the imagination's reproduction of them (*EA* 157). However much the products of imagination and memory can change—we imagine and remember more or less over time in the economy of our being—there nonetheless remains enough continuity in these faculties to give us a feeling of our personality.

Although the statue first gathers a sense of pleasure in the gradual degrees of its first sensation, this phenomenon becomes "more salient" when the statue has felt two different sensations in succession (*EA* 33–34). Both pleasure and pain derive from comparing two different states. To reinforce this comparatively different sense of well-being, Bonnet even uses the neologisms "better-being" *(mieux-être)* and "less-well-being" *(moins-bien-être; EA* 33, 84). Economic and grammatical notions are combined in these terms, which felicitously evoke the changing states of our being. In grammar, it is the comparative, expressed as it is through the words *more* or *less,* that best captures the additions to and subtractions from the economy of our being, whose physical rather than metaphysical nature Bonnet is trying to establish throughout this work. Grammar and especially economics provide for less ephemeral, and hence for Bonnet, more plausible, explanations for our being than does metaphysics.

Bonnet defines pleasure and pain in terms of movement, which also serves as a catalyst for sensation: "We know only that every Sensation comes from a *Movement,* and that a Movement which is more or less strong, more or less accelerated causes Pain or Pleasure to be born" (*EA* 87).[10] The stronger the movement, the greater will be the pleasure derived from it. But there are limits to the amount of movement that can be tolerated. What may begin as a pleasurable experience can become painful. Typically, Bonnet describes the process in physical terms: "the same Fiber that produces Pleasure when its vibrations are

---

10. Not until later in the *Essai* (145) does Bonnet give the particular relationship sensations have with pleasure and pain. Any sensation is always accompanied by a feeling of one or the other. See also page 78 below.

accelerated in a *certain* degree, creates pain when these vibrations are accelerated to the point of *separating* the Fiber's *Molecules* from one another too much" (*EA* 87).

Pleasure and pain play important roles in the statue's economy of being. As its being expands through more and more organs, it comes to appreciate its existence all the more through activities that give it pleasure (*EA* 453–55). The statue enjoys feeling and acting as long as it can do so in a pleasant way (*EA* 453–55). It attains a fuller existence by multiplying successive pleasurable sensations (*EA* 456–57). Whereas, on the one hand, the accumulation of pleasant experiences adds to the sense of self, pain, on the other hand, "warns the Individual of what comes close to destroying his or her Being" (*EA* 89). Pleasure and pain thus reveal themselves as decisive factors not only in expanding but also in preserving the economy of our being. As agents for them, the sensations, although possibly leading humanity at times to perfection, have as their primary function its self-preservation (*EA* 316; *EP* 48).

The reaction of the soul to pleasure, by which it prefers one sensation to another, is called attention (*EA* 33–34, 101–2). In the succession of sensations to which the soul pays attention, one must once again keep in mind the two possible kinds of sensation, which are the same for attention: entirely different sensations or "*different* degrees in the same Sensation" (*EA* 33). But Bonnet strategically defers the "delicate discussion" of attention, as well as that of pleasure and desire, until two different sensations affect the statue and his reader is more "advantageously situated" to grasp the various nuances in the process (*EA* 34).

Bonnet's eventual discussion of attention hinges on the following question: *"what happens in the Soul of our Statue from the greater or lesser amount of Pleasure that two different Sensations make it feel?"* (*EA* 103). The question's simple answer, which comes after some important groundwork, is the notion of preference that is fundamental to attention. The deciding factor for attention consists then in the preference the soul gives to the sensation that affects it *"more pleasantly"* (*EA* 103). The answer Bonnet provides emphasizes, as does the question itself, both the quantity and quality of the two sensations the statue is experiencing: the odor of a rose and that of a carnation. It further reinforces the activity involved in the statue's preference: "This preference the Statue gives to the Sensation that pleases it *the most,* is an *action* that the Statue exercises on this Sensation. *Preferring* is not *sensing,* it is *determining oneself,* it is *acting.* Preference cannot be an *alteration* of the *Faculty of Feeling:* alterations of this Faculty are only

Sensations & *degrees* of Sensations" (*EA* 104, 279). Clearly, attention is not a sensation, but in what order does it occur?[11] Bonnet's discussion points to this very question which, although never actually posed, does receive a reply: "Attention is thus an alteration of the *Activity* of the Soul; or to express myself in other terms, it is a *certain exercise* of the *motive Force* of the Soul on the Fibers of its Brain" (*EA* 105).

On the surface such an explanation appears to contradict Bonnet's earlier sensationist subordination of the soul's activities to its sensibility (*EA* 87, 99). Bonnet seems to imply that in attention the soul acts altogether independently of the faculty of feeling. Yet careful consideration of his argument reveals the consistency of his sensationism. The confusion in Bonnet's analysis of the soul's acting on the body is clarified by his presupposition that "the Soul *alters* the *current* state of its Body" (*EA* 99). But this current state that precedes an action is a perception or sensation of some degree of pleasure or pain: "A *Sentient* Being can be *induced* to act only by virtue of a *Perception*, or of a pleasant or unpleasant *Sensation* by which it is affected" (*EA* 101). When the soul acts, it does so only in response to the sensations already present in the body and does not act separately from it. In this sense, its activity is indeed subordinated to sensibility.

Bonnet at once rescues his sensationism and asserts an active role for the soul. Of the three chief sensationists, he is the only one who seriously addresses the epistemological theory's inherent problem of the mind's passivity. Without relinquishing his fundamentally sensationist position that yokes the mind and body together in an indissoluble union, Bonnet argues against the concept of a human being that merely reflects, as does a mirror, the image of external objects and that feels and recalls sensations on a purely physical basis independently from the soul (*EA* 86, 104). Through attention the soul's active nature becomes especially apparent.[12]

His treatment of such an important cognitive ability as attention is not surprisingly embedded in an analysis of the economy of our being. As I pointed out above, he poses the central question for his discussion of attention in quantitative terms: the statue feels "greater or lesser" amounts of pleasure from the olfactory sensations resulting from its

11. Bonnet contents himself with looking for "facts"—which largely consist in "knowing the *Order* in which Things succeed one another"—rather than for causes, many of which remain unknown to us (*EA* 93–95).

12. Bonnet's thinking about the soul as an active force can be traced to Leibniz. See Georges Bonnet, *Charles Bonnet (1720–1793)* (Paris: M. Lac, 1929), p. 87.

interaction with the rose and carnation. Bonnet solicits even the reader himself to experience the economy of his being by training his eyes on any one object, then removing them.[13] Whereas he "weakens" or decreases the impression of surrounding objects when he removes his eyes from and pays less attention to them, by paying more attention to one object, he "concentrates" or increases his gaze upon it (*EA* 105).

The mechanistic explanation of attention supports and reinforces the notion of a dynamic economy at work in our being. Bonnet's insistence on the physical aspects of attention draws out its "economic" nature even further. In attention, the soul is not acting on the sensation itself, "since that Sensation is but the Soul itself *altered* in a certain way," but on "the Fibers whose *movement* produces the *Sensation*" (*EA* 106).

The reader must acknowledge what anyone learns from the everyday facts of sensory experience: "that Attention increases the *intensity* of movements imprinted by Objects" (*EA* 107). A certain ebb and flow of clarity in perceptions is accompanied by an ebb and flow of the nervous fluid. Bonnet writes: "As the Perception of the Object becomes livelier through Attention Perceptions of neighboring Objects grow weaker" (*EA* 110). Growth in the intensity of one perception causes that of others to recede. On the physiological level, attention accelerates the movement of the respective fibers, which in turn need greater amounts of spirits or fluid that have to be drawn from nearby fibers (*EA* 110–11). Quite literally, one fiber's gain in fluid is another fiber's loss. Bonnet's descriptions of the mental operations and their attendant physical activity conspire to elicit a vibrant image of the economy of our being.

Closely related to the faculty of attention, which establishes the active nature of the soul, are the faculties of the will and freedom. With the second sensation, the statue begins already to exercise them (*EA* 114). Like attention, the will is based on a preference of good over harm to the self: "To will is that act of a *sentient* or intelligent Being; by which it *prefers* among several *manners of being* that which procures for it *the most good,* or *the least harm*" (*EA* 114–15, 278). Since the statue needs to know or feel more than one sensation or manner of being in order to have a preference in the first place, the "Will is thus subordinated to the Faculty of sensing or feeling, or of *knowing*" (*EA* 115). The motive necessary to want to produce an action is "always a *Sensation,* an *Idea*" (*EA* 287).

13. My use here of the masculine pronoun for the reader simply follows Bonnet's own usage of it.

Bonnet expounds on his sensationist approach to the will when he states that the reason needed to will anything can be found "in the *vibration* of the *sensitive* Fibers, from which results that *Alteration* of the *Faculty of Feeling,* that one calls *Sensation, Idea*" (*EA* 299). In both of the quotations given above, Bonnet puts sensations in apposition to ideas, just as he also equated knowing and feeling earlier while speaking of the subordination of the will in the following passage from the same page: "The *Will* assumes therefore the *knowledge* or the *Feeling* of *different* manners of being" (*EA* 115). Clearly, the two are not exactly synonymous, but in the minds of sensationists, and according to them in our own minds, these operations have a contiguous, and hence causal, relationship with each other. The sensationist refrain that all knowledge comes from the senses rings repeatedly in these pages. What is more, the senses and sensibility come to embrace and inform all the faculties.

When Bonnet defines the faculty of liberty or freedom as "the *Faculty* by which the Soul *executes* its *Will*" (*EA* 116) or as "the Power of *executing* its *Will*" (*EA* 287), he submits it each time to the same hierarchy into which will fall all the other faculties. Since there are new elements to it, the order bears repeating: "*Freedom* is *subordinated* to the *Will,* as the *Will* is to the *Faculty of Feeling*" which in turn is subordinated to "the *action of Organs*" which comes from "that of *Objects*" (*EA* 116). The powers of higher faculties are systematically submitted to that of sensibility; action for sentient beings depends on the pleasant or unpleasant qualities of their sensations (*EA* 430). The example Bonnet adduces to prove his sensationist point about the centrality of sensibility to the statue's activities is revealing. Should its soul wish to go directly from sensation *A* to sensation *F* in a series the statue has already learned, all the intervening sensations "must be less agreeable to it" (*EA* 430). In a pithy sentence, Bonnet summarizes the same lesson at an earlier point in the essay: "The *Law* of *Pleasure,* is therefore the *Law* of the *Will*" (*EA* 299). Although he makes an allowance here for the moral pleasures experienced by beings endowed with reflection, the authority of sensibility in determining human actions and wills remains intact.

On the question of freedom, Bonnet differs with the definition Condillac gives to this faculty. Whereas for Condillac, liberty consists in the *"Power of doing what one does not do, or of not doing what one does"* (*DSL* 274), for Bonnet its essence resides in action and in the *"Power of doing what one does"* (*EA* 122–23). Bonnet provides an example from Condillac in the latter's *Dissertation sur la liberté*. In one of his typically more rationalist passages, Condillac insists on deliberation or the ability to deliberate that must precede any free act. Bonnet actually takes a firmer sensationist position on this question than does Condillac, and underlines the free choice involved in doing "what gives one pleasure" (*EA* 125). For Bonnet, an act in accordance with one's will, which is determined primarily by one's sensibility, will always be a free act (*EA* 280–81). Freedom resides in the execution of the will: "One is therefore free every time one does what one wills" (*EA* 284–85). In his conception of freedom, Bonnet thus retains the centrality of the senses.

Desire also becomes easily distinguishable when the statue has two sensations to compare. Sensing only the same odor of a rose, the statue represents the lowest grade on the scale of animality and has no desire, which "assumes *knowledge* of a state *different* from the current state that one *compares* to it" (*EA* 31). A realization of desire thus entails an advancement in the Chain of Being, setting into motion some of the faculties by which human beings come to differentiate themselves from other matter and forms of life. Comparison of different degrees of even the same sensation gives one the sense of a better (or lesser) state of being than that experienced previously. Pleasure, attention, and desire join together in this moment that indeed marks the beginning of a new being: "The knowledge of a better-being *[mieux-être]* is inseparable from the *desire* for the *continuation* of the better-being; & the effect of this desire is *Attention*" (*EA* 33). One is impelled to action and a demonstration of one's own freedom and authority through a desire for increased happiness (defined in terms of the senses), a desire that is derived only from experience. The reader will grasp the import of such a rich convergence of faculties and activities at a similar but later point in the statue's development when it feels two different sensations. But Bonnet cannot resist hinting at the bewildering array of cognitive possibilities that lies in store for the statue: "I could not refrain from indicating all that was enclosed in this first state of our statue" (*EA* 34).

This first state unquestionably constitutes for him a veritably pregnant moment. The primitive state of the statue will in effect give birth to the higher faculties in the same way in which the germs that our bodies contain will give birth to more highly perfected forms of being at the resurrection of the dead in Bonnet's elaborate vision of an afterlife. In it, Bonnet combines elements from Western and Eastern religions; after mentioning the resurrection of the dead, he moves on late in the essay toward a theory of reincarnation: "A Sound Philosophy teaches us to think . . . that there is no true *Generation* in Nature; but, that the Bodies which appear to us to be *engendered,* do nothing but *develop,* because they already existed entirely formed in miniature, in *Germs*" (*EA* 485). What starts as something deceptively simple or small bursts forth at a later stage of development into a potentially glorious form.

As an entomologist, Bonnet was of course familiar with the radical changes that the caterpillar undergoes on its way to becoming a butterfly. He does not hesitate to cite the caterpillar as an example of nature's progressive way (*EA* 481). As he does so, one begins to understand the thrust of his method, which fuses the continuity of the natural world with that in the cognitive process. What Bonnet says about the caterpillar can be applied to his approach to the soul: "Nature's steps are not taken by Leaps. From far away, & in an impenetrable darkness, it makes ready the Productions that it then brings forth in full daylight" (*EA* 130, 481). Like the caterpillar, the statue contains the seeds of its perfection, however invisible they may be to the untrained eye. In his own anticipation over the upcoming activities of the soul, Bonnet himself resembles, as it were, the expectant parent who cannot help imagining and sharing with his friends (here, his readers) what lies ahead.

Through the degradation of movements in the sensory fibers and, by extension, in the economy of our being, Bonnet finally makes the connection between desire, pleasure, and attention that he only suggested earlier in a moment of foresight. By degradation, Bonnet means the gradual diminution or weakening of movements that objects imprint on an organ's sensory fibers (*EA* 32–33, 129). Every sensation has some aftereffect, such as the remarkable one experienced upon closing one's eyes after having looked straight at the sun (*EP* 69–70). After the statue has the sensation of the carnation's smell, which it prefers to that of the rose because of the heightened pleasure this new sensation brings, its attention is engaged. Consequently, it follows and notices all the more keenly the degradation of the movement that originally gave rise to the sensation (*EA* 131–32). Desire thus results from the gradual but noticeable weakening of a sensation that produced pleasure; it increases as the pleasant sensation decreases (*EA* 132). In the economy of our being, the force of desire grows as the difference or gap grows between the current situation and a former preferred moment of well-being that memory recalls to mind (*EA* 132–33). Imagination serves of course only to further desire by recreating a simulacrum of the enjoyable sensation which, however much it may resemble the original desired moment, still maintains a perceptible difference from it (*EA* 134–35). For Bonnet, desire ultimately constitutes the most frequent activity of a sentient being: "the more one [feels and hence] knows, the more one desires" (*EA* 495). In his sensationism, feeling, knowing, and desiring are all closely interrelated, as the analysis of ideas makes clear.

Although Bonnet momentarily "abandons" (*EA* 145) the discussion of his statue when he takes up that of the evolution of ideas, his point of departure remains the same, namely the statue's first two sensations. His analytic method obliges him to "exhaust all that ensues necessarily from" them (*EA* 144). And in the sensationists' logic, little else flows as obviously as do ideas from sensations: "All our ideas derive then originally from the *senses*" (*EA* 13). Bonnet at first broadly defines an idea as "any *manner of being* of the Soul of which it has consciousness or feeling" (*EA* 13–14). In his general theory of ideas, however, he refines his earlier definition, which was for "the Origin of any Idea," by pointing out that:

> the *manners of being* of the Soul change as do the degrees of its Perfection. The word *Idea* receives therefore different determinations according to the *manners of being* the Soul takes on.
>
> Sometimes it expresses only pure *Sensations:* at other times it designates *Notions.* It is thus applied to *Feeling* & to *Reflection.* (*EA* 145)

Bonnet lends to this passage a distinctly Lockean tone that he will echo later when he states in a peculiarly unqualified and offhanded fashion, "they say our ideas have two sources, *Senses & Reflection*" (*EA* 173). What "they say" (they of course being an impersonal reference especially to Locke), however, does not correspond to what Bonnet is saying.[14]

In reading Chapters XIV–XVI, one at first blush gathers the impression that upon abandoning the statue briefly, Bonnet also abandons a sensationist perspective. This break in the continuous discourse about the statue seems to follow a break in Bonnet's otherwise firm adherence to

14. In his thesis, Lemoine notes the distinction Locke and Bonnet make concerning reflection. Bonnet makes of it merely a higher form of sensibility. Whereas for Locke it is "synonymous with consciousness and opposed to sensation; Bonnet's reflection is synonymous with attention and opposed to the involuntary exercise of sensibility and intelligence." See Lemoine, *Charles Bonnet de Genève,* p. 116.

sensationist tenets. True, "the state of a purely Sentient Being [that of the statue] differs greatly from the state of an intelligent Being," as he notes when he later justifies this section of the essay (*EA* 355). But ultimately Bonnet is willing to accept a rupture in the chain of cognitive processes no more than he is willing to accept one in the Chain of Being. Rather, he steadfastly clings to his analytic method that insists on continuity above all else.[15] Bonnet's analytic method ensuring continuity between sensations and ideas naturally gives rise to a sensationist position. The continuum for nature that Bonnet postulates to embrace minerals and man is homologous to that for cognition, which embraces sensations and ideas in an uninterrupted flow. The key transitional points connecting sensations to ideas are called sensory ideas. To understand Bonnet's cognitive chain, one must trace the elements leading up to and issuing from these points.

According to Bonnet, sensory ideas, which are composed of simple and concrete ideas, come from "the *Action* of *Objects* on the *Senses*" (*EA* 152). He contrasts them with "those whose formation is due to some *Operation* of the *Mind*" (*EA* 152).[16] Simple ideas cannot be broken down by the soul into other ideas, "because they *respond* to an *Impression* that is *one & simple*" (*EA* 148). Examples of them are sensations of all perceptible qualities (such as odors, tastes, sounds, colors, cold, and heat); perceptions of extension, solidity, the force of inertia, and movement; and the perception of the effects of irreducible physical and intellectual forces (*EA* 148–50). Bonnet distinguishes sensations from perceptions by the degree of vibration of the sensitive fibers, which is not as great for the latter as it is for the former. A perception, which denotes the *"simple apprehension of the Object,"* can become a sensation, however, through enough increased vibration of the fibers to stimulate the pleasure or pain that always accompanies a sensation (*EA* 145–46).

Concrete or compound ideas differ from simple ideas in the number

15. Despite his considerable experience with plants and animals, Bonnet maintains his notion of an artificial continuum from inorganic to organic matter. See Lorin Anderson, "Charles Bonnet's Taxonomy and Chain of Being," *Journal of the History of Ideas* 37 (1976), 45–58. Anderson explains Bonnet's "zeal" for humanity's closeness to the ape through a perspective that made connections not in time, as did nineteenth-century evolutionism, but in a "static arrangement" (45–46; 54–55).

16. It bears repeating that the operations of the mind, however different they may be from those of the body, are not separate from them according to Bonnet's sensationist viewpoint. Bonnet makes this explicitly clear only later in his essay.

of fiber orders affected. They occur in those instances in which "two or several *Orders* of Fibers from a single *Sense* or Fiber *Orders* from two or several *Senses* are simultaneously shaken by an *Object*" (*EA* 152). All the bodies we perceive in our environment fall into this class of ideas (*EA* 152). By the power of sensory abstraction, which is "an Act of *Attention,*" the soul can decompose these ideas (*EA* 153–54). The soul's activity in this regard might seem to point to an entirely rational process, devoid of any contact with the senses, were it not for Bonnet's subordination of all its activities to sensibility.[17] Indeed, in order to keep the internal consistency of his argument, Bonnet must state that "the *abstract* Idea is but a *sensory* Idea detached by *Attention* from the Whole of which it is a part" (*EA* 154).

As Bonnet moves with his discussion of language progressively toward complex abstractions, also seemingly removed from the sensible universe, he still underlines the ties to the senses: "We endow the Ideas we receive through the senses with *Signs,* or Terms that represent them" (*EA* 158).[18] Although objects may be absent and no longer available to our senses, signs have a physical "presence" that the eye or ear can apprehend and that "awakens the *Idea* attached to them" (*EA* 159). The signs themselves serve, so to speak, as perceptible objects, recalling other objects to mind. In this capacity, they *"multiply* the *Connections* that unite our Ideas" by adding to the *"natural* Relationships that result both from the way in which they [ideas] have been aroused by Objects, & from the *Analogy* of Objects among themselves" (*EA* 160). Moreover, signs facilitate a new form of abstraction which, by breaking down and separating sensory ideas, leads in turn to a greater generalization and classification of ideas (*EA* 161–62). The movement is away from nature and its objects toward an artificial and arbitrary system of signs: "These *Abstractions* by which the Soul *generalizes* its Ideas derive less from what is in Nature, than do *sensory* Abstractions. As *Abstraction* is pushed further by the intervention of *Signs,* the Ideas born from them move further away from purely *sensory* Ideas" (*EA* 163–64).

The sensationist logic that time and again subsides only to reemerge triumphantly encounters one last powerful challenge from intellectual

---

17. See my discussion of attention above on pages 72–73.

18. For a study of Bonnet's ideas on language, which did not differ substantively from Condillac's, see Lorin Anderson, *Charles Bonnet and the Order of the Known*, pp. 59–90, esp. p. 69.

abstractions, which lead to notions and reflection. Intellectual abstractions give rise to general ideas or notions such as that of the "oak tree in general," which of course does not exist in nature (*EA* 165). An apparent rupture begins to form between the soul and mind as Bonnet distinguishes between the interaction of the external world with the senses—one of the principal activities of the soul—on the one hand, and the activity of the mind, on the other: "The *Notion* is thus not a *Perception:* it does not result simply from the *Action* of the Object on the Senses; it assumes further an operation of the Mind on this Action" (*EA* 165). For a sensationist such as Bonnet who is intent on showing the mixed nature or indivisibility of the body, soul, and mind, this represents an extremely delicate point in which union among these constituent elements of our being can be either lost or gained.[19] At this point, Bonnet no longer uses the soul but the mind to denote the inner mechanism responsible for the production of these new ideas or notions. Since Bonnet's hierarchy subordinates only the soul's activity to sensibility, it appears that the mind may be acting independently of the senses to generate the intellectual abstractions called notions.

Not until the following chapter, some eight pages later in the essay, does Bonnet reaffirm his sensationism by clarifying the interdependence of the body, soul, and mind. At the very beginning of that chapter he abruptly (given the eight-page hiatus) and forthrightly states: "It is thus while operating on *sensory* Ideas, that the Mind acquires *Notions.* This operation bears the name Reflection" (*EA* 173). The specific cross-reference in Bonnet's text to the section quoted above allows one to read the earlier passage in a new and different light.[20] The words "not . . . simply" and "further" (*encore,* in the sense of "in addition to" or "still") maintain rather than expunge the role for the senses even in the higher cognitive abilities and indicate a level of activity partly coextensive with the senses rather than separate from them. Reflection or the operation by which the mind acquires notions presupposes the existence of sensory ideas at some previous stage.

Bonnet reverts to the senses through sensory ideas in order to explain

19. With its acquisition and degradation of sensations, the economy of our being closely follows the economy of Bonnet's argument, in which evidence in favor of the ascendancy of the senses in determining ideas is alternately accumulated then dispersed among the various faculties. Content follows form, and vice versa.

20. In the *Essai analytique,* Bonnet has an elaborate system of numbered cross-references based on the various sections of any given chapter. A number is placed at the beginning of each section and subsequently in parentheses to refer to the respective section.

reflection, which results, in his words, "from the Attention that the Mind gives to *sensory* Ideas, that it compares, & that it endows with *Signs,* or Terms that represent them" (*EA* 174). The mind itself does not leap forward from a *tabula rasa* to highly abstract or "reflexive" ideas. The intermediate steps involve the senses at every level up to and including the highest ones. According to Bonnet, we understand even God in terms of the senses: "Our most *abstract* and most *spiritualized,* if I may use this word, ideas derive thus from *sensory* ideas, as from their natural source. The Idea of GOD, for example, the most *spiritualized* of all our *Ideas,* manifestly comes from the *Senses*" (*EA* 174–75).

To resolve then the question about the sources of our ideas, Bonnet does indeed follow Locke by tracing them to the senses and reflection. But in Bonnet's sensationist scheme of things, reflection cannot be wholly separated from the senses. Despite intermittent hesitations on Bonnet's part, the continuity between the two becomes clear as he proceeds with his analysis. Although Bonnet implies a connection between "concrete" and "general" ideas in the sections on the language of signs in Chapter XV, he does not make it explicit until the following chapter. At that time, he not only asserts matters frankly, as when he writes, "We have seen this: the Mind draws its *Notions* from *sensory* Ideas," but he also indicates the cross-references to sections from the preceding chapter that have allowed him to construct his argument (*EA* 184).

By the continuous connection he makes between the senses and ideas, Bonnet also suggests a link between different forms of life, namely, animals and men. Indeed, the two classes of being are extremely close to each other, as Bonnet demonstrates with his statue. The first kind of personality it possesses applies "as well to *Animals,* & even to those that are the least high in the Scale" (*EA* 81). Bonnet even reminds us that the current early state of his statue, albeit a man in its constitution (*EA* 8, 208), "represents that of an Animal which would have but a single Sense, & whose every need & movement would be connected with the exercise of this Sense" (*EA* 500). Whereas the sensibility of animals—who, like us, have sensory ideas—places them above plants in the Chain of Being, man's ability to generalize ideas abstractly through artificial signs distinguishes him from animals (*EA* 180, 500, 523). Bonnet does not, however, exclude the possibility for animals or beings like them to develop their understanding at some future date (*EA* 180–81; *EP* 178). His Chain of Being and concept of "germs" make such movement up the scale possible. With his explanation for the evolution of ideas, Bonnet thus finally traverses the distance separating a purely sentient being from an intelligent being only to show the continuity between them in spite of their major differences.[21]

Simply by using two sensations in his statue, Bonnet calls attention to the dynamic and successive nature of our being. Through them, he not only can explain the faculties of the soul and the generation of ideas but demonstrates his profound commitment to sensationism and analytic method, which are inseparable in his work. In the concatenation of ideas Bonnet strives to attain in analysis, whose central and decisive feature is succession, one idea based on fact leads to another in such a way that a chain of them is formed. Bonnet's professional training as a scientist gives him a distinct bias in favor of the physical world and the reliability of the information it provides. He never really separates the scientific or physical from the metaphysical; hence, his preference to speak of an economy, instead of a metaphysics, of our being: "In a word, the Science of the Soul, like that of Bodies, is based equally upon Observation & Experience" which study nature and not abstractions (*EA* xvii). Like nature, Bonnet's form of analysis neither leaves any links in the chain broken, nor does it take any leaps. It proceeds in uninterrupted fashion from the observable world of sensory experience from which it gathers its authority. His method conflates a continuous view of nature with a similar view of human cognition. The Chain of Being has its epistemological counterpart in the successive steps of the cognitive process. Following "the analytical thread" (*EA* ix) he innocently claims to observe with his eyes, following what experience teaches him, Bonnet naturally traces ideas to the senses. When applied to epistemology, analysis inevitably leads to sensationism for an observer like Bonnet who insists on the primacy of the physical world knowable only through the senses. His method therefore essentially corroborates his message. In the economy of our being, the "reciprocal dependence" (*EA* 355) of the faculties is both assured as well as reinforced by Bonnet's analytic method, as is ultimately the continuity between sensations and ideas, and that between the body and mind.

21. According to Lester G. Crocker, in the concern Bonnet expresses for the mind-body relation, he is following David Hartley's theory of the association of ideas. See his article on Bonnet in *The Encyclopedia of Philosophy,* 1: 345.

3

Helvétius's Seminal Concept
of Physical Sensibility

Among the major thinkers associated with sensationism, Claude-Adrien Helvétius unquestionably presents the most radical form of the theory. Whereas all the sensationists stress the centrality of the senses and sensations in their epistemological schemata, they differ in the way in which they temporalize them. With his teleological bias, Condillac never loses sight of ideas as the final product of sensations.[1] Sensations may be the source of our knowledge, but they eventually give way to the greater faculty of reason. In epistemology and the time frame through which it traces our acquisition of knowledge, they constitute an important but distant past. By his analytic approach, Bonnet emphasizes the continuity of cognition. He keeps track, as it were, of both the beginning and the end of the process. Although he does indeed focus on a very early moment in the life of his statue with its own first sensations, a dialectic comes to govern its movement from sensations to ideas so that it is left neither entirely at one pole or the other. But Helvétius finds in sensation, or more precisely what he calls physical sensibility, an origin from which we never escape. He vacillates between a sanguine and fatalistic view of it. Physical

---

1. It has been suggested that Condillac is ultimately preoccupied more with reason than with sensations and can thus practically be considered a rationalist. See Knight, *The Geometric Spirit*, p. 16 passim; and Wanda Wojciechowska, "Le Sensualisme de Condillac," *Revue philosophique de la France et de l'étranger* 93, no. 3 (1968), 314.

sensibility can lead to enlightenment in a controlled environment, yet at the same time it constantly reminds us of our deeply rooted primitive human nature.

Inasmuch as the other sensationists derive primarily mental faculties from the senses, Helvétius reduces absolutely everything in humanity to physical sensibility. His grandiose kind of sensationism, which converges at times with materialism, extends the theory's implications to a variety of areas.[2] He connects it not just to memory, judgment, and ideas but also at a fundamental level through pleasure and pain to the passions, virtue and vice, self-interest, happiness, sociability, and power. For Helvétius, physical sensibility thus forms the basis of human thought as well as of behavior and consequently supports both an epistemological and a psychological theory.[3] Scholars uniformly recognize Helvétius's sensationist premises, but they do not adequately assess the depth of them. Typically, they consider sensationism a tributary concern rather than grant it the centrality it is accorded in Helvétius's *oeuvre.*[4] In the final pages of *De l'homme* (1772), the book he wished to have published posthumously and in which he gives his definitive statement of his thinking, he writes succinctly in a way that brooks no misunderstanding and that characterizes his purist approach to sensationism: "Physical sensibility is man himself & the principle of all that he is.

2. My chapter on materialism and sensationism will discuss the two theories' similarities and differences. Marx credits Helvétius with broadening the bounds of sensationism to include social relationships. See K. Momdjian, *La Philosophie d'Helvétius,* trans. M. Katsovitch (Moscow: Editions en Langues Etrangères, 1959), p. 4.

3. Aram Vartanian states that Helvétius was more interested in developing "a psychological, rather than epistemological, theory" and diverged from Condillac's Lockeanism in this respect. See his entry on Helvétius in *The Encyclopedia of Philosophy,* 3: 472. I believe the two theories coexist necessarily with each other and are mutually reinforcing. Although Helvétius may give more attention to psychological concerns than to epistemological ones, he nonetheless combines both theories in order to extend the comprehensiveness of his claims.

4. Scholars rightly acknowledge the sensationist principles operating in Helvétius's materialism, his theory of education, and "doctrine of 'environmental behaviorism.' " In so doing, however, they have naturally tended to focus only momentarily on sensationism, then move on to the other topic. See, respectively, D. W. Smith, *Helvétius: A Study in Persecution* (1965; rpt. Westport, Conn.: Greenwood Press, 1982), pp. 103–14; Ian Cummings, *Helvétius: His Life and Place in the History of Educational Thought* (London: Routledge & Kegan Paul, 1955), p. 223; and Vartanian's entry on Helvétius in *The Encyclopedia of Philosophy.* Mordecai Grossman takes Helvétius's sensationism into account for the author's pedagogical thought but leaves aside the central importance this philosophy has for his work as a whole. See *The Philosophy of Helvétius with Special Emphasis on the Educational Implications of Sensationalism* (1926; rpt. New York: AMS Press, 1972).

Hence his knowledge never attains beyond his senses. Anything that is not subject to them is inaccessible to his mind."[5]

In a work published during his lifetime, *De l'esprit* (1758), Helvétius defines physical sensibility simply as "the faculty of receiving the different impressions that external objects make on us" and as one of the causes, along with memory, of our ideas.[6] In a word, it is the capacity to feel or sense. But quickly he subsumes memory under physical sensibility and equates remembering with feeling (*DE* 20). The two contributing factors for ideas fuse into one. Helvétius's discussion of them originates in an attempt to reach a clearer understanding of the mind—which of course is the subject of *De l'esprit*—and its operations. No one can understand the mind, however, without first coming to grips with the concept of physical sensibility, for it explains the mind's activities. By a series of propositions, Helvétius joins them together: "it is in the capacity that we have to perceive the similarities or differences, the affinities or lack thereof that diverse objects have among themselves, that consist all the operations of the Mind. Yet this capacity is but physical sensibility itself: everything is thus reduced to sensing or feeling" (*DE* 21). The entire impact of what Helvétius means by "everything" emerges only as he gradually exhausts practically every possible aspect of human existence.

The implications of his thinking for mental processes, however, are immediately apparent. The mind functions as a passive mechanism

5. Claude-Adrien Helvétius, *De l'homme, de ses facultés intellectuelles et de son éducation* (London: La Société Typographique, 1773), 2: 397. This work appears in two vols., hereafter cited as (*DH* 1) and (*DH* 2). A new edition of *De l'homme* in two volumes with continuous pagination, prepared by Geneviève and Jacques Moutaux, was published in Paris by Fayard in 1989, making this work which was previously difficult to find much more accessible. I have indicated the page references to the Fayard edition as [F]. The corresponding reference here for (*DH* 2: 397) is [F 951].

Despite the clarity of this passage and many others like it, one critic denies Helvétius's pure sensationism. See Irving Louis Horowitz, *Claude Helvétius: Philosopher of Democracy and Enlightenment* (New York: Paine-Whitman, 1954), p. 161. Horowitz finds Helvétius more rationalist than sensationist because of the supposedly "advanced view of the relation of senses to thought" in the passions. These latter may well be a "median point between sensations and reasoning," as Horowitz says, but they are essentially determined by physical sensibility and not by reason.

6. Helvétius, *De l'esprit,* ed. Jacques Moutaux (Paris: Fayard, 1988), p. 15; hereafter cited as (*DE*). The posthumous publication of *De l'homme* is explained in large part by the scandal *De l'esprit* created upon its appearance. The author was later forced to emend a number of controversial passages.

because of the passivity of the two faculties contributing to it, namely, physical sensibility and memory. Since these two faculties are essentially the same for Helvétius, it comes as no surprise that he also equates judging with feeling: "When I judge the size or color of objects that are presented to me, it is obvious that the judgment based on the different impressions that these objects have made on my senses is strictly only a sensation" (*DE* 22).[7] In judgment, he distinguishes no active faculty separate from sensation.

In reading Helvétius's work, both Rousseau and Diderot criticize what they perceive to be a facile identification of physical sensibility with other faculties. At stake in Rousseau's observations is the difference between the terms feeling and sensing, which sensationists tend to render synonymous with each other. Indeed, the French verb *sentir* embraces both meanings. But for Rousseau, who despite a certain sensationist inclination aims to prove the moral superiority of our innately good feelings over possibly suspect sensations in determining our existence, the difference is appreciable.[8] Characterized by their organic nature, sensations have but a local effect, whereas sentiments or feelings take on universal proportions and "affect the entire person."[9] Rousseau apparently overlooks the later passage in which Helvétius endeavors to clarify the ambivalence between sentiment and sensation, both of which he relates to passion. Helvétius distinguishes two kinds of sentiment: sensations, which are associated with natural passions corresponding to physical needs; and a related artificial form of passion like pride or ambition known as sentiments proper (*DE* 434). Rousseau not only questions Helvétius's equating remembering with feeling in the same faculty but also points out their different causes and effects.[10] Likewise, he finds that Helvétius confuses the passive perception of objects (sensation) with the active perception of relationships (judgment).[11]

For his part, Diderot takes a more indulgent attitude than does

7. Helvétius changes somewhat his definition of memory from "a continuous but weakened sensation" (*DE* 15) to "an effect of the faculty of feeling" later in *De l'homme* (1: 88 [F 153]). He thus ceases to identify the two but maintains their close connection.

8. For a de-romanticized account of Rousseau's attitude toward feeling, see my *Seeing and Observing: Rousseau's Rhetoric of Perception*.

9. Jean-Jacques Rousseau, *Notes sur "De l'esprit" d'Helvétius*, in *Oeuvres complètes*, ed. Bernard Gagnebin and Marcel Raymond (Paris: Gallimard, 1969), 4: 1121.

10. Rousseau, *Notes*, 4: 1121–22.

11. Rousseau, *Notes*, 4: 1122–23.

Rousseau toward the identification of feeling and judging. Indeed, Diderot himself, like many of his contemporaries, had been influenced by the renewal of interest in sensationism.[12] Typically, Diderot adduces ironic examples of people who may feel but who do not judge well or even at all, such as the foolish person or the one without any memory whatsoever.[13] Although Helvétius's claim appears to him more suitable for the animal realm than for humanity, Diderot does allow that sensitive and reflective capabilities sometimes come together just as they sometimes remain separate in everyday human actions.[14]

As he argues that all our ideas come from our senses, Helvétius is simply echoing a refrain that across the ages has taken on the authority of truth. He cites Aristotle, Gassendi, and Montaigne as thinkers who recognize the validity of this claim but singles out Locke as the genius who "fathoms this principle, states the truth of it by an infinite number of applications" (*DE* 421–22). Locke alone discovers the full meaning of Aristotle's expression *"Nihil ist in intellectu quod non prius fuerit in sensu"* (*DE* 478–79). In his efforts to extend the ramifications of this fundamental sensationist tenet, Helvétius clearly sees himself as Locke's successor and suggests indirectly that he, too, may quite possibly be a genius. Yet the task that Locke did not accomplish, and that Helvétius gives himself, consists in "reducing all faculties of the mind to the capacity of sensing or feeling" (*DH* 1: 79 [F 142]). By doing so, Helvétius hopes to achieve two goals: to "express how it can be that it is to our

12. Douglas G. Creighton, "Man and Mind in Diderot and Helvétius," *PMLA* 71 (1956), 705–24. Creighton cites Diderot's *Lettres sur les aveugles* as an example of his sensationism and points out that it is only in his later writings around 1770 that Diderot distinguishes himself from this epistemological theory.

13. Diderot, *Réfutation suivie de l'ouvrage d'Helvétius intitulé "L'Homme,"* in *Oeuvres philosophiques,* ed. Paul Vernière (Paris: Garnier, 1964), p. 563.

14. Diderot, *Réfutation,* pp. 564, 567. For a general analysis of Helvétius's epistemology as a movement toward the dialectical materialism of the following century, see Momdjian, *La Philosophie d'Helvétius,* pp. 129–93. According to Momdjian, Helvétius wrongly identifies sensation with thought and, as all pre-Marxian materialists, does not understand the dialectic between them (137). Yet even this Marxist critic, who aims to show some of the philosopher's materialist shortcomings in not adequately accounting for the transition from sensation to thought, recognizes Helvétius's pervasive "tendency to consider as an absolute the sensationist principle not only in [his] theory of knowledge but also in the entirety of his system" (144). As I am trying to demonstrate, Helvétius makes his sensationism explicit, whereas his materialism remains merely implied. Perhaps he did so, as some claim, to avoid being censored during his lifetime. Such a strategy may explain the presence of sensationist principles in *De l'esprit,* but it still does not clarify their continued predominance in *De l'homme,* published as it was after his death.

senses we owe our ideas, & that it is not however, as experience proves, to the extreme perfection of these same senses that we owe the greater or lesser extent of our intelligence" (*DH* 1: 79–80 [F 142]). A practical educational problem about the individual acquisition of knowledge is sometimes intricately but wrongly tied to a general epistemological one about the origin of all knowledge. Helvétius hastens to point out a false conclusion that one might draw from otherwise sound sensationist theory. It is in diverse educations that he ultimately locates the cause for intellectual differences among people. Helvétius's environmental approach to education and his belief in the importance of nurture set him apart from Diderot, who insists on the central role of nature in creating physiological differences in our organization.[15]

The senses indeed lead to ideas, but perfecting the senses does not improve our ideas, as the distinction between the mind and the soul makes clear. If the soul, which Helvétius equates with feeling and sensing, were the same as the mind, then its cultivation would *ipso facto* enhance the mind. The mind may not actually be the soul, but it does not operate independently from it. Proof for the existence of the soul, which we cannot observe but which we can experience, comes from our sensations (*DH* 1: 81–82, 86 [F 146–47, 150]). Unlike the mind and its every ability, all of the soul is innate and necessary to one's existence, being lost only with life itself (*DH* 1: 88 [F 152]). In his connection of ideas with the senses, Helvétius finds that he does not differ fundamentally from Aristotelian theologians either in this regard or in the above-mentioned differences they presumably postulate between the mind and the soul. But in his interpretation of the soul, he makes it identical to sensibility and stops short of separating the mind and soul altogether. Neither are mind and soul equated, nor are they considered as operating independently of each other:

> One must not imagine as a consequence [of Aristotelian theology] that one can look at the mind as entirely independent of the soul. Without the faculty of feeling or sensing, the productive memory of our mind would be without any function: it would be nothing. The existence of our ideas & of our mind assumes that of the faculty of feeling. This faculty is the soul itself. Hence

15. Jean Rostand, "La Conception de l'homme selon Helvétius et selon Diderot," *Revue d'histoire des sciences et de leurs applications* 4 (1951), 213–22; and Creighton, "Man and Mind in Diderot and Helvétius."

I conclude that if the soul is not the mind, the mind is the effect of the soul or the faculty of feeling. (*DH* 1: 88–89 [F 152–53]).

Helvétius thus acquiesces to a soul that is somewhat different from the mind, because it conveniently allows him to reaffirm his sensationism while reinforcing his argument for the origin of intellectual inequalities in education. Ideas still derive from the sensations or the soul; the five senses serve as "the five doors through which ideas go to the soul" (*DH* 1: 128 [F 201]). But one's intellect does not depend on the refinement of any particular sense or even of all the senses. Every people, culture, or sex has the same aptitude to acquire knowledge (*DH* 1: 128–36 [F 201–9]). On the question of education, Helvétius takes a remarkably egalitarian stance. Physical sensibility, which opens the doors on the epistemological level to enlightened ideas, shuts them to no one.

In the psychological realm, Helvétius naturally connects sensibility to pleasure and pain, just as Bonnet does. They seem at times to vie with it for governing all human behavior despite Helvétius's constant reminders that physical sensibility subsumes them. All our relationships with objects in nature are characterized by the pleasant or unpleasant way they affect us, that is, the pleasure or pain they give us (*DH* 1: 90 [F 155]). Helvétius may discover in pleasure and pain "the unknown principle of all human action," but both of them have their "source in physical sensibility" (*DH* 1: 102 [F 170], *DH* 2: 397 [F 951]). These feelings take on the importance they have for us only because we are sentient beings defined entirely, according to Helvétius, by our capacity to sense or feel—our sensibility. They constitute the endless meaningful signals of our human and, by extension, sensible world. Helvétius identifies two kinds of pleasure and pain: physical ones that occur at the time of a sensation and those that we recall from memory or foresee in the future (*DH* 1: 103–4 [F 171]). The radical character of Helvétius's writings stems largely from his reduction of everything not merely to sensibility but to physical sensibility. In other words, what we normally think of as moral or abstract qualities have their basis in physical sensations of pleasure or pain. These are the only true pleasures and pains (*DE* 34, 322). Because he reduces those of the second variety to physical ones, any intellectual, inner pleasure or pain (such as remorse, in the case of a pain) can be linked to physical sensation (*DH* 1: 104–5 [F 172–73]). Simply put, there are no feelings; there are only sensations. In a strongly worded extrapolation of sensationist beliefs, Helvétius explains the passions through the senses:

One principle of life drives man. This principle is physical sensibility. What produces in him this sensibility? a feeling of love for pleasure, & of hatred for pain: it is from both these feelings joined together in man & always present in his mind that is formed what one calls in him the feeling of self-love. This self-love engenders the desire for happiness; the desire for happiness that for power; & it is this latter that in turn brings forth envy, avarice, ambition & generally all the artificial passions, which, under different names, are only a disguised love of power in us & applied to the various means of obtaining it. (*DH* 1: 298 [F 411])

Helvétius's explanation of the passions uses an anthropological model, comparing human beings in a natural state with human beings in society. Nature does not give us passions, which unlike sensations arise as artificial forms of pleasure and pain only with the gradual founding of societies, but it does provide the origin for them in the needs we first have (*DE* 289). Helvétius distinguishes the passions from physical sensibility, culture from nature, even as he derives the passions from the very forces at work in physical sensibility. In a passage that resembles the opening one from Genesis, Helvétius paints a picture of God endowing matter with force and man with sensibility, which unbeknownst to him will guide him according to God's will (*DE* 290). Movement in the physical world has its equivalent in sensibility in the nonphysical, human world. Out of movement will come the ordered universe, just as out of sensibility man will develop. Although not innate, the passions represent a development of the faculty with which we are all born—the faculty of feeling, our sensibility. In order to confirm the origin of the passions in physical sensibility, Helvétius will "follow the metamorphosis of physical pains and pleasures into artificial pains and pleasures, to show that, in passions, such as avarice, ambition, pride, and friendship, whose object appears to belong least to the pleasures of the senses, it is nonetheless always physical pain and pleasure that we flee or seek" (*DE* 292). As he analyzes each passion, Helvétius systematically lowers its status from the intellectual or spiritual sphere to the physical. There results from his study of the passions, which calls for close scrutiny, nothing less than a demystification of the reader, who comes to a new awareness of the human condition.

All passions entail then to some degree the pursuit of pleasure or avoidance of pain. In the case of avarice, greedy people who hoard riches do so less out of a desire to increase pleasure than from a wish to avoid pain. Their minds associate pain with "an excessive and ridiculous fear of indigence" (*DE* 294). Through ambition, one seeks eventually to circumvent the drudgery of hard work over the long term by enduring great hardships and risks in the short term in the hope of obtaining future pleasure (*DE* 302). Pride or the passion for others' esteem stems from a desire for more admirers, who allow us through their greater numbers to take comfort in "the agreeable image of the pleasures they can procure for us" (*DE* 312). Friendship poses the greatest challenge to Helvétius as he attempts to reduce all passions to physical sensibility. The pleasure he does ultimately find in it comes from the pleasure one has in speaking of oneself and one's joys or sorrows to a friend (*DE* 322). Although such a pleasure may not be a physical one itself, coming as it does either from memory or foresight, it assumes another one at some point in the past or in the future (*DE* 322).

In the hierarchy he establishes for physical sensibility, Helvétius also traces to it our vices and virtues, which themselves result from our passions (*DE* 218, 330). Because of our sensibility or sensitive nature, we pursue pleasure that can lead us both to virtuous and depraved actions: "The highest virtue, like the most shameful vice, is in us the effect of the more or less intense pleasure we find in giving ourselves over to it" (*DE* 334). The measure of our virtue or vice depends ultimately on another outgrowth of physical sensibility, the interest in which we act. That interest, which may or may not benefit the public as a whole, is guided entirely by a deeply rooted love of ourselves. Furthermore, it is relative and not absolute.[16] An understanding of Helvétius's representation of virtue and vice entails further discussion of the related concepts of self-love, self-interest, happiness, and sociability.

Self-love, on which everyone's self-interest is based, has its own roots in physical sensibility. In Helvétius's attempt to show that all is acquired in us and that education alone forms the moral man, not even self-love is considered innate (*DH* 1: 326 [F 450]). One might easily misread Helvétius in this regard, but he does in fact indicate a specific time frame for the emergence of self-love, as in the following lines: "What

16. Moutaux suggests the empirical underpinnings of Helvétius's notion of self-interest by associating it with a desire for a relative and not an absolute state. "The search for what is in one's self-interest," writes Moutaux, "is a search not for the absolute good, but for a better condition [*mieux-être*]." See "Helvétius et l'idée de l'humanité," *Corpus, Revue de Philosophie* 7 (1988), 35, 39.

Nature does, it alone can undo. The only feeling that it has engraved in our hearts from *infancy* is the love of ourselves. This love which is founded on physical sensibility is common to all men" (*DH* 1: 230 [F 324–25]; emphasis added). Helvétius distinguishes here between birth and infancy, which of course follows it. Such a distinction is confirmed by an important passage from *De l'esprit* in which Helvétius delineates the steps leading up to complex patterns of human behavior. In order to understand the human heart, one must know "that physical sensibility produces in us love of pleasure and hatred for pain; that pleasure and pain then deposited in all hearts and opened in them the seed of self-love, whose development gave birth to passions, from which issued all vices and virtues" (*DE* 217–18). The only human feature that can be called innate is physical sensibility; we are "*born* sensitive to pain and pleasure" (*DE* 330, my italics here). Not even a predisposition toward pleasure or against pain—from which self-love will only subsequently develop—precedes it. In a very literal and quasi-biblical way, Helvétius's chronology for the causes of human behavior thus constantly reaffirms that in the beginning there was physical sensibility.

Self-interest is the concept Helvétius uses to relate the private life of the individual to the public world of society. The happy coexistence of private interest with the public's interest constitutes virtue. The admixture of the two forms the basis of Helvétius's utilitarianism, which privileges acts useful to the public at large.[17] On the individual level, self-interest corresponds to the pleasure principle inherent in physical sensibility. Its sense for Helvétius extends beyond pecuniary concerns to embrace "everything that can bring us pleasure, or shield us from pains" (*DE* 53). In pages reminiscent of La Rochefoucauld, whose name he actually mentions, Helvétius considers self-love and self-interest the deciding factors in making judgments and meting out esteem (*DE* 45, 53f.). We always prefer that which we can understand with little effort or which we find flattering. Any effort for us can prove tiring, and hence painful, so we content ourselves with ideas similar to our own (*DE* 72).

In his realization of the human tendency toward mediocrity, Helvétius clearly is making an indirect statement about the poor reception new ideas and his own writings had in his lifetime. His work tends to reconcile his own autobiography with moral philosophy. The persecu-

17. In the nineteenth century, a conservative form of Helvétius's utilitarianism developed in England with Jeremy Bentham, James Mill, and John Stuart Mill, whereas on the Continent a liberal form of it evolved with Saint-Simon, Fourier, Marx, and Engels. See Horowitz, *Claude Helvétius*, pp. 170–96.

tion he presciently feels at the probable rejection of his ideas is sublimated into a sensationist account of self-interest, which differs from that of the seventeenth-century moralists in its emphasis on pleasure and pain as the principal causes for it. Later in the posthumously published *De l'homme,* Helvétius can rail without fear of reprisal and does so frequently against the intolerance (especially that of the Catholic Church with its ability to censor books) to which self-interest gives rise. Despite his outrage at obvious displays of self-interest, he is no less convinced of its necessity and the futility of changing this indelible human characteristic (*DE* 217–18; *DH* 1: 281 [F 390]).

By choosing out of self-interest what is most pleasurable or least onerous, humans work toward two objectives: self-preservation and happiness. There is a biological necessity to self-interest. It attracts human beings to warmth, for instance, and repels them from extreme cold, thereby encouraging the search for living conditions conducive to continuous growth and protecting the species from harm. Helvétius does not place any stigma on self-interest and simply acknowledges that "the sentiment of preference that each person feels for himself or herself . . . is attached to the preservation of the species" (*DE* 217–18). Without it, humans might perish, blindly seeking what might prove fatal to them.

Attendant to the preservation of the species that self-interest fosters is the happiness it naturally promotes. Helvétius makes a psychological necessity out of a biological one. In pursuing the one, man is automatically pursuing the other. Everyone shares the common desire to be as happy as possible (*DE* 340, 514). Happiness indeed rivals self-preservation in its importance for our being. Helvétius notes "that all men follow only their own happiness; that they cannot be taken away from this tendency; that it would be useless to undertake doing so, and dangerous to succeed" (*DE* 152). The danger of such an effort to dissuade people from their pursuit of happiness lies in the possible harm to themselves and others. The very notion of normalcy comes from one's anticipated search for pleasure and avoidance of pain. Physical sensibility creates in us a natural inclination toward what brings us happiness. To seek otherwise and injure ourselves intentionally by throwing ourselves into fire or water or out of a window would rightly be recognized as madness, for man, "in all his actions, is necessarily determined by the desire for an apparent or real happiness" (*DH* 2: 154 [F 645]).[18]

---

18. In underlining the rational character of human beings, Helvétius illustrates his adherence to the mainstream thinking of the *philosophes.* At the end of the century, Sade would of

Helvétius devotes a chapter of *De l'homme* to the origin of human sociability, which he necessarily traces to physical sensibility. In joining together to form a society with a set of laws, human beings acknowledge their weak, sensitive nature that has pressing physical needs (*DH* 1: 111–12 [F 181]). Society comes into existence as a whole from individuals following their self-interest in nature. People come together precisely because it is in their best interests to do so. With greater numbers, they can protect themselves better from outside enemies and work more efficiently toward feeding, clothing, and sheltering themselves than they can individually. Quite simply, society enhances the overall pleasure of its members and diminishes the pain they must endure.

Helvétius resolves the origin of society, which itself is part of another question regarding the origin of justice, by going back to physical sensibility. Time and again, he uses physical sensibility to demonstrate our commonality and to argue against those who would claim that our minds differ too much in degrees of attention or anything else to reach general truths. According to Helvétius, "the most sublime discoveries" can potentially be made by all (*DH* 1: 191 [F 272]), and anyone is capable of taking the same mental steps he does in coming to the following conclusion about society and justice:

> Once I have reached this truth [about the social contract], I easily discover the source of human virtues: I see that, without any sensitivity to physical pain and pleasure, men, without desires, without passions, equally indifferent to everything, would not have known any personal interest; that, without personal interest, they would not have gathered into a society, would not have made agreements among themselves, that there would have been no general interest, consequently no just or unjust actions; and that in this way physical sensibility and personal interest have been the authors of all justice. (*DE* 250–51)

To discover profound truths about large, intricate structures such as society, one has only to consult one's physical sensibility and the path it takes in its various permutations. For what applies to one person pertains to an entire society or even many different nations. Helvétius's sensationist explanation of the evolution of ideas or behavior for an

---

course call attention to human irrationality, the fact that men and women can indeed actively pursue what is harmful to them—a perverse but real form of happiness.

individual obtains equally for those social groupings composed of individuals. The self does not differ essentially from society in its workings; the private and public domains are both directed by their interests (*DE* 117). As Jacques Moutaux phrases it: "The horizon of a moral law like Helvétius's, which defines what is good by self-interest, and self-interest by the personal happiness one 'feels,' can only be Humanity, all nations taken together as a whole—what he calls the universe."[19]

The similarities and differences between an individual's interests and those of society define virtues and vices for the society. Helvétius terms society's interests the general interest and makes it synonymous with public happiness. Virtue, whose object is the public good, consists in the desire for public happiness (*DE* 128). Any action worthy of the name virtuous should conform to the general interest and public utility (*DH* 1: 163 [F 240]). Virtue and vice, according to Helvétius's definition of them, sometimes lead to startling behaviors. Different attitudes toward them explain the diversity of cultural practices in the world, make some sense out of several bizarre examples, and allow for renewed understanding of cultural relativism. The general interest or public utility may indeed justify ridiculous or even cruel customs in the name of virtue (*DE* 129). Helvétius mentions a number of examples that may appear strange to the European or Western reader but that corroborate his definition of virtue. The Spartans allow thievery in order to maintain the populace in a salutary courage and vigilance (*DE* 129). The pleasure thieves derive from their acts of cunning emboldens them for future battles. Their victims become all the more alert to painful incursions from the outside and will presumably be ready for any foreign invasion. In certain primitive nations, the slaughter of weak old men before the hunt spares them from a painful death later and is therefore considered in the culture as a humane act for the good of all (*DE* 130). The society itself takes care of the individual's self-interest to avoid pain, a concern that naturally arises from his or her physical sensibility.

Besides promoting tolerance of cultural differences as he does with his diverse examples, Helvétius takes a polemical stance toward the church and state that becomes apparent with his categories of virtues and vices. While he may countenance aberrant behavior far from his

---

19. Moutaux hastens to add, however, that national interests are not always the same. Conflicting interests among nations lead to the idea of a humanity "divided into nations." See Moutaux, "Helvétius et l'idée de l'humanité," 45–46.

home, he proves critical of what he views as unacceptable mores in his own culture. Among virtues, he discerns two types: those of prejudice and "true" ones. The former type makes no contribution to public happiness, indeed is sometimes contrary to it, and causes the suffering of its practitioners (*DE* 135). Helvétius finds no justification for the excruciating penances of Brahmins, the chastity of vestal virgins, or other similarly "sacred" practices that he qualifies as nothing more than superstitious (*DE* 135–36). In his eyes, their behavior furthers neither the society's nor their own interests. In contrast to virtues of prejudice, true virtues, "without which societies could not subsist," constantly "add to public happiness" (*DE* 138).

When turning to vices or moral corruption, Helvétius also distinguishes two kinds, which he names religious corruption and political corruption (*DE* 138). The first kind corresponds to libertinism, which Helvétius does not view as necessarily "incompatible with the happiness of a nation" (*DE* 139). Although it may be criminal in France or anywhere else because it conflicts with the respective country's laws, in many times and places, libertinism has in fact had the protection of laws (*DE* 139). Helvétius mentions the obvious example of the seraglios in the East as well as the numerous temples in which lascivious pursuits form an integral part of the religious ritual. Rather than wholly corrupting a society, libertinism may, to the contrary, sometimes even make its citizens virtuous, as it did in the case of Greeks such as Socrates and Plato, among many others (*DE* 142–43). Political corruption, however, is always degrading and unforgivable. It occurs, as one would expect, when individual interests diverge from those of the public (*DE* 143). In this section of *De l'esprit,* Helvétius bitterly attacks pagan priests, who represent under a thin disguise the priests of his own day opposed to new ideas. Socrates dies at the hands of these corrupt priests whose blatant self-interest in keeping the people in the dark runs counter to the public good that comes from enlightenment (*DE* 144). Montesquieu's *Esprit des lois* cannot be read in certain countries because monks have prevented its circulation (*DE* 144). Clearly, for Helvétius, political corruption constitutes the greatest vice. While claiming not to write as an apologist for debauchery, he does nonetheless to a large degree defend libertinism and differentiate between its uncertain debasing influence and the certain danger of political corruption (*DE* 145–46). The only true virtues, like the only true vices, are political and always entail the fusion or disagreement of interests in the polity. Through his sensationist approach to virtue and vice, Helvétius combats in his turn the two *bêtes noires* of the eighteenth-century *philosophes,* namely, intolerance and fanaticism.

Despotism, the other related evil against which these thinkers also frequently rail, is elucidated in Helvétius's discussion of power. Like many of his fellow French Enlightenment liberal thinkers, Helvétius seeks in reason or experience a basis for law. Without such a basis, a government reflects merely the arbitrariness of its power. Sensationists indeed show the ways in which the ideas of reason evolve from the sensations of everyday experience, which they consider natural and not imposed by some established authority such as the papacy. Laws from reason, based in this way on experience, should be understandable to all. Nature is a legitimate source not only of truth but also of justice. The rights that one has come from nature and cannot be given away to someone else. As the arbitrary exercise of an individual's power, despotism is reprehensible both epistemologically and morally. Neither can we know or understand the reasons for another person's willing a despotic act—since the conditions of that knowledge are impossible to attain—nor can we act virtuously in carrying out the desired wishes—since virtue for Helvétius consists in combining our self-interest with the general interest and not with that of any one individual. Constantly beset with the incomprehensible desires of the despot and forced to pursue someone else's happiness, the inhabitant of a country ruled by such a person withers intellectually and morally. As Helvétius puts it, "The distinctive feature of Despotism is to stifle thought in minds & virtue in souls" (*DH* 1: vi [F 11]). One's own self-interest coincides with that of the despot, because mindlessly pleasing the latter results in greater benefits. This kind of government has a debilitating and corrupting effect on its subjects. As they eventually lose their capacity to think out of fear of punishment and continued mental inactivity, they can no longer formulate any notion of justice (*DE* 347). Despotism encourages only selfishness and does not inculcate in its citizens any sense whatsoever of their duties or of the public good (*DE* 347).

Although Helvétius abhors despotism, he recognizes in it a love of power that is common to all men and women. Power allows one to remove the pain in one's life and to increase its pleasures (*DH* 1: 270 [F 377]). Our physical sensibility naturally urges us to do so. Like the pursuit of happiness, the pursuit of power results directly from human physical sensibility. Without our sensitivity to pleasure and pain, we would be indifferent to sensations that produce them. Because they play such an important part in our happiness, though, we want to control them as much as possible. In order to maximize our control over sensations of pleasure and pain, we not only direct our own efforts to this end but also enlist other people to help us. According to Helvétius, we all have a secret desire to be despots from the innate laziness he perceives in us: "everyone aspires therefore to absolute power, which, sparing him the necessity of any care, study and strain from attention, subjects men in a servile way to his wishes" (*DE* 340). Given the despotic desires of individual members of society, it is little wonder that governments themselves historically have, as Helvétius points out, a tendency toward despotism (*DE* 345). Power thus becomes "the only object of men's search" and in any form of government their "sole driving force" (*DH* 1: 239, 257 [F 338, 361]).

Love of power breeds both civil and religious intolerance, by which terms Helvétius essentially means despotism. Insofar as they all call for uniform beliefs, despots at the helm of the state differ little in his eyes from those in the church who call themselves priests. Indeed, in their abuse of power during the Saint Bartholomew's Day massacre they actively foment, these latter can prove even more dangerous and barbarian than any sultan (*DH* 1: 282–84 [F 393–95]). Despots do not want anyone to challenge their authority by thinking in a way different from theirs (*DH* 1: 270 [F 377]). Rather than tolerate creative or independent thinking, they demand that everyone conform blindly to their viewpoint, even if such conformity leads to the grossest and most absurd errors. The powerful ultimately favor error and adopt it on a widespread basis (*DH* 2: 328 [F 872]).

In popular culture, the tale of the emperor's new clothes raises to the level of common wisdom the alliance of power and error. Duped by flattery into believing he has purchased an exquisite new outfit, which appears invisible and is indeed nonexistent, the emperor proudly parades it in front of his admiring subjects, who submissively refrain from calling attention to the conspicuous point that he is wearing no clothes at all. Although he does not allude directly to this story, Helvétius seems to have its message frequently in mind as he writes about despotic power. This power keeps people from thinking and serves only the pleasure of the present moment for one person (or possibly a small group of people, in the case of priests) and not the future of all (*DH* 1: 273–75 [F 381–83]). The tale, useful as it is in clarifying Helvétius's definition of power, would no doubt constitute an indispensable intertext, were it not for the fact that Helvétius attributes to the people as well as to princes the enjoyment of flattery that comes from the love of power (*DH* 1: 277 [F 387]).

Helvétius adduces the obverse side of flattery, that is, others' contradiction of our ideas, in order to show the actual workings of power and intolerance as well as to show how deeply ingrained they are. Whereas flattery gives one a sense of power and happiness, opposition to one's ideas produces feelings of weakness and misery (*DH* 1: 277–78 [F 387]). Acting entirely in our sensitive character, we avoid painful feelings and consequently reject others' ideas when they do not conform to our own. Helvétius compares the self-absorption of man in his admiration for his own ideas to that of a florist with prejudices for a narrow perspective: "everyone is this florist; if he measures the minds of men only on the knowledge they have of flowers, we similarly measure our esteem for them only on the conformity of their ideas with ours" (*DE* 91). Such behavior results in little or no real progress, as even the ideas of geniuses are rarely greeted warmly. To the contrary, geniuses usually find themselves with more enemies than the common murderer (*DH* 1: 279 [F 388]). Attempting to remedy human intolerance would be unnatural: "Any claim to correct man on this point, is tantamount to willing that he prefer others to himself, and that he change his nature" (*DH* 1: 281 [F 390]).

Intolerance, which comes from the love of power, which in turn results from our physical sensibility, thus ultimately leads to ignorance. And ignorance, for Helvétius as well as for virtually all Enlightenment thinkers with the notable exception of Rousseau, often begets human tragedy. The misery that history depicts across time is due in large part to ignorance "which, even more barbaric than self-interest, has scattered the most calamities across the earth" (*DE* 209). Priests, according to Helvétius, deserve considerable blame for actually encouraging ignorance among the people (*DH* 2: 307 [F 843]). In their intolerance, they do not take into account the diversity of human points of view. Their unnatural wish to impose on everyone the same belief assumes that all people "have the same eyes & the same physiognomy" (*DH* 1: 285 [F 397]). In effect, priests presuppose identical sensory experiences among various people, whereas Helvétius underlines the crucial part that random chance *(le hasard)* plays in our education by constantly subjecting us to different experiential circumstances.[20]

20. For the importance of random chance in education, see esp. *DE* 233; *DH* 1: 14–17 [F 59–62].

Helvétius reserves his harshest criticism for priests, primarily because the ignorance they encourage in their credulous followers ultimately produces the most egregious examples of human cruelty. So-called false religions, which one might dismiss in another set of conditions as laughable and absurd, inevitably concern the serious-minded intellectual when their excesses as a result of their intolerance become "one of the most cruel scourges of humanity" (*DH* 1: 284 [F 395]). In the bloody history of religions, Helvétius has a long list of brutal abuses of power from which to choose. The example he singles out for detailed description is noteworthy for the utter horror it evokes. The story Helvétius offers recounts the treatment that the Christian sect known as the Vaudois or Waldenses received at the hands of soldiers carrying out the orders of the pope. As an eyewitness, the British ambassador in Savoy at the time writes the following account: "Never, he says, have Christians committed so many cruel acts against Christians. The heads of the Bearded Ones (the Pastors of this people) were cut off, boiled, and eaten" (*DH* 1: 319 [F 440]). The list of tortures continues. No one of either sex or of any age elicits any pity. What one finds most disturbing in Helvétius's examination of cruelty and persecution is their inextricable cause, namely, intolerance, which cannot be destroyed, because "men are by their nature intolerant" (*DH* 1: 294 [F 407]).

The unquestionably fatalist side to Helvétius's writings stems largely from his sensationist outlook on human nature.[21] He traces essentially everything that informs our existence to physical sensibility, which constitutes the bedrock of our being. It subtends all that is good and evil in us, our virtues as well as our vices, our happiness and our despair. Whenever Helvétius writes in a categorical and determinist way about the nature of man—that "nothing changes" it (*DH* 1: 243 [F 344]); that "man is & will always be the same" (*DH* 1: 245 [F 346]); that "men are what they must be" (*DE* 112); and that the "ferment of intolerance is indestructible" (*DH* 1: 294 [F 407])—he bases his view of that nature on the seminal concept of physical sensibility, which for him unlocks

21. D. W. Smith traces the Church's condemnation of *De l'esprit* to its determinism and to its materialism, both of which derive in part from sensationism. Doubtless, the passive nature of sensation in the absence of reflection ultimately makes humanity a product of its environment. Smith does not, however, take note of the graver implications of Helvétius's thought that I am trying to draw out here, precisely that humanity is a product of its own nature, which is entirely determined by physical sensibility. With great effort, one might be able to control one's environment optimally, but one surely cannot with any amount of effort change one's nature. See Smith, *Helvétius*, p. 113.

human behavior and thought. For Helvétius, it "explains all manners of being of men, lays bare the causes of their intellect, stupidity, hate, love, errors & contradictions" and becomes nothing less than an axiomatic principle (*DH* 2: 396 [F 950]).

In his radical application of sensationist ideas and by the central importance he gives them in his work, Helvétius thus goes deeper to the roots of the theory and further from them than do Condillac and Bonnet. Unlike some of his contemporaries, Helvétius detects both beneficial and harmful effects from our sensitive nature. In addition to allowing us to attain illustrious goals such as knowledge and happiness, our physical sensibility can on occasion bring about tremendous human suffering. That Helvétius acknowledges the full force of this other proclivity in our nature, clearly increases the urgency with which he writes elsewhere in the same works to support the pressing need for education and laws to counteract it.[22] If in the process, he verges toward materialism, his unvarying adherence to the concept of physical sensibility throughout his work nonetheless not only keeps his sensationism intact but magnifies the epistemological and psychological claims of the theory. By affecting men and women in every aspect of their lives, physical sensibility makes of sensationism, in which it is grounded, an all-inclusive philosophy of life.

---

22. Helvétius uses the concept of physical sensibility itself to encourage enlightenment and desirable behavior, as I shall demonstrate in my chapter on cultivating talent and virtue.

PART II

AESTHETICS

4

The Sensationist Aesthetics of the French Enlightenment

For an age that witnessed the major transition from classicism to empiricism, there were remarkably few all-embracing treatises on aesthetics in eighteenth-century France. French Enlightenment writers resisted any classical formulation of rules for an ideal or beautiful form in works of art. There is no empiricists' version of Du Bellay's *Défense et illustration de la langue française* or Boileau's *L'Art poétique,* although André and Batteux did attempt to write "systematic" books on the subject.[1] The very primacy given to individual sensory experience during the century precluded serious consideration of any *a priori* system of thought. Not even Diderot, who profoundly influenced the aesthetic thinking of his time, wrote a sustained theoretical piece on the topic, with the possible exception of his article "Beau"

1. Rémy G. Saisselin, *Taste in Eighteenth-Century France* (Syracuse: Syracuse University Press, 1965), p. 68; Francis X. J. Coleman, *The Aesthetic Thought of the French Enlightenment* (Pittsburgh: University of Pittsburgh Press, 1971), p. xvii, 135–36, 152; and Annie Becq, *Genèse de l'esthétique moderne: De la raison classique à l'imagination créatrice, 1680–1814,* 2 vols. (Pisa: Pacini, 1984), pp. 5, 14–15, 475. Becq notes that "the modern usage of the term aesthetics appears with Baumgarten's *Meditationes Philosophicae de Nonnullis ad Poema Pertinentibus* in 1735." Baumgarten's *Aesthetica* may have been published in 1750, but Kant's *Critique of Judgment* in 1790 represents the Enlightenment's mature reflection on this nascent discipline. Coleman's very title *Aesthetic Thought* also suggests that there was much thinking on the subject without any one comprehensive treatment of it.

for the *Encyclopédie*.[2] Diderot, the enlightened *philosophe*, recognizing
as he did the relativity of cultures as well as the diversity of languages,
perceived relationships, and judgments, questioned the universality of
any notion of the beautiful.[3]
    The shift from a classical aesthetics in the eighteenth century is
exemplified to a large degree by the blending of the otherwise distinct
relational categories of psychology with aesthetics and of perception
with literature. The person usually credited as the first to have effected
this shift is Dubos in his *Réflexions critiques sur la poésie et la peinture*
(1719). Whereas the Cartesians had sought to reduce the multiplicity
of experience to uniform rules grounded in reason, Dubos denied the
validity of objective rules and posited subjective feeling as the basis by
which to judge beauty.[4]
    This shift also elucidates in part the seeming unwillingness of the
French to compose aesthetic treatises and to follow the example set by
the English, the Scots, and the Germans in the same period. The rise of
subjectivism in taste and its attendant relativism led to an increased
importance being placed on the point of departure in empirical theory
and questions of origin, rather than on the ultimate attainment of those
general rules cherished by classicism. Empirical thinking proceeds from
the particular (in the case of aesthetics, a feeling subject) toward the
general. Perceiving the mind as a veritable *tabula rasa*, empiricists
ruled out such *a priori* notions as innate ideas. In a word, empiricism
constituted a proscriptive way of thinking, in contrast to the prescrip-
tive method of classical doctrine.
    The author who, I believe, has given a notable account of what can
be seen as an aesthetics for literature—my specific concern here—is
Condillac, for whom all the senses, particularly vision and touch, played
a crucial role in the cognitive process.[5] I am, following Condillac,

2. Coleman, *Aesthetic Thought*, p. 135. See also Wladyslaw Folkierski, *Entre le classicisme
et le romantisme: Etude sur l'esthétique et les esthéticiens du XVIIIe siècle* (Krakow, 1925;
rpt. Paris: Champion, 1969), pp. 375–91; and Wade, *Structure and Form of the French
Enlightenment*, vol. 1: *Esprit philosophique*, pp. 291, 297, 312.
3. Diderot, "Recherches philosophiques sur l'origine et la nature du beau," in *Oeuvres
esthétiques*, ed. Paul Vernière (Paris: Garnier, 1968), pp. 426f. This essay by Diderot reproduces his article "Beau" from vol. 2 of the *Encyclopédie*.
4. Cassirer, *The Philosophy of the Enlightenment*, pp. 303f.; Chouillet, *L'Esthétique des
lumières*, p. 45; Knight, *The Geometric Spirit*, p. 181; Saisselin, *Taste in Eighteenth-Century
France*, pp. 69f.
5. Condillac draws a distinction between vision and the other senses. All of my subsequent
references to the senses and sensation—and the characteristics such as movement, astonishment, and curiosity that Condillac uses to describe the effect they produce on the statue in

displacing vision somewhat from its central position in Enlightenment epistemology. Condillac wished to correct the view that grants unwarranted capabilities to vision out of sheer habit and without knowledge of the way in which we learn from the very beginning to use our eyes. First and foremost according to Condillac, the indispensable sense of touch gives vision its power to judge objects. Once and only once such a coordination of the two senses has been perfected does vision become the preferred sense. Condillac pays it his highest compliment by calling the finely tuned eye an organ that has an "infinite number of hands" (*TSn* 167–90).

Scholars generally single out Condillac's *Essai sur l'origine des connaissances humaines* (1746), which traces in its second part the origin of language and the arts in the history of culture, as his primary work with implications for aesthetic theory[6] and occasionally his *Traité de l'art d'écrire* (1775), written as a handbook of style for the Prince of Parma.[7] They have given little attention, however, to Condillac's *Traité des sensations* (1754), which attempts to explain the origin of knowledge through the senses and to derive all the operations of the mind from the one faculty of sensation. Nor have they recognized the aesthetic implications of sensationist philosophy in general.[8] The writings

---

the *Traité des sensations*—include to a large degree the sense of vision. While recognizing the importance of vision, Condillac did not believe that one could judge exterior objects initially through this sense alone. That capacity he attributed exclusively to the sense of touch. Condillac cites Berkeley as the first to have realized that vision by itself could not *a priori* judge qualities of an object in the external world, and states this forcefully himself (*TSn* 193, 73). Like many philosophers of the period including Locke, Condillac replied in the negative to Molyneux's celebrated question about the ability of a man born blind who recovers his sight to distinguish immediately a cube from a sphere without the help of his hands. For an account of the philosophy of perception in the eighteenth century, see Michael J. Morgan, *Molyneux's Question: Vision, Touch, and the Philosophy of Perception* (Cambridge: Cambridge University Press, 1977). For a comparative study of vision and touch as well as for an analysis of the interrelations between sensibility and narrative form in the eighteenth-century English novel, see Ann Jessie Van Sant, *Eighteenth-Century Sensibility and the Novel* (Cambridge: Cambridge University Press, 1993).

Citations to Condillac's and the other sensationists' works are contained parenthetically within the text. An appendix to the Fayard edition of the *Traité des Sensations,* Condillac's *Dissertation sur la liberté* is cited as (*DSL*).

6. Knight, *The Geometric Spirit,* pp. 184f.; Cassirer, *The Philosophy of the Enlightenment,* p. 291; and Wade, *Structure and Form of the French Enlightenment,* 1:281.

7. Knight, *The Geometric Spirit,* p. 176; Saisselin, *Taste in Eighteenth-Century France,* pp. 34–35.

8. In her work on the evolution of modern French aesthetics, Annie Becq does include an important chapter, "Empirisme, sensualisme et imagination." Whereas she aims to show the continuity or "compatibility" between reason and artistic creation through the imagination, I

of Bonnet and Helvétius support and extend those of Condillac in this regard. Although Condillac's *Traité* no doubt provides the most efficient context for discussing the period's sensationist aesthetics, the work of his fellow sensationists also proves illuminating. In his description of the statue-man whose senses are "awakened" one by one, Condillac enumerates some of the fundamental characteristics of human behavior. In this chapter, I argue that these qualities also provide a framework for literature. The activities of the mind become inscribed in the form of many of the century's literary pieces. Simply put, a theory of the mind can be used as a theory of literature. And conversely, although to a lesser extent, a theory of the mind can at times have literary qualities.

Like most of his French contemporaries, Condillac, one of Dubos's successors, did not compose a systematic aesthetics.[9] As author of the *Traité des systèmes* (1749), an attack upon the dogmatism of the preceding century, Condillac could hardly in good conscience himself write in the same manner he was condemning. He, too, had to follow an empirical line of inquiry and eschew the rule-making of the classical systems. When he wrote his *Traité des sensations* five years later, however, he provided a kind of handbook of literary aesthetics for many in his century.[10] That Condillac's works enjoyed immense popularity attests to his ability to reflect the intellectual spirit of the times. His contemporaries could read them and find an acceptable summary of the mind's activities, which mirrored the formal elements of literary works they had read from the first half of the century and those they were currently reading. Isabel Knight describes the probable reception of Condillac's writings as follows: "his readers must have encountered his ideas with a sense of recognition, a feeling that their own thoughts were here stated with new clarity and persuasiveness."[11] In the process of

---

am attempting to show the rich interrelations of philosophy and literature. See *Genèse de l'esthétique française moderne,* pp. 437–86, esp. pp. 437, 454, 458, 462, and 477.

9. Knight, *The Geometric Spirit,* pp. 181, 192.

10. Faced with the absence of a unified text on such an important aspect of the French Enlightenment, scholars have had no choice but to piece together an aesthetics from passages scattered throughout an author's *oeuvre.* Using such a method, Chouillet finds in Hume the aesthetic "conscience of empiricism," despite the fact—acknowledged by Chouillet—that Hume never bothered to codify all of his thoughts in this domain into a doctrine. See Chouillet, *L'Esthétique des lumières,* p. 66. Chouillet does not claim for Hume, however, as I do here for Condillac, that his aesthetics forms the basis for French literary conventions.

11. Knight, *The Geometric Spirit,* pp. 2–3. Although both Knight (p. 181) and Cassirer affirm the virtual identification of psychology with aesthetics during the century, neither of them recognizes the significant implications of Condillac's most important psychological work for aesthetics. Chouillet does mention the *Traité,* but only in his appendix or "Chronology of

unfolding the theory of sensationism, Condillac's *Traité des sensations* also serves, as do the sensationist writings of Bonnet and Helvétius, as an indirect aesthetic treatise and richly suggests useful ways in which novelists might develop their characters, plots, and narratives as well as affect and shape the attitudes of their readers.

Condillac's *Traité des sensations* evidences the interdependence of philosophy and literature in the period. In this work, the statue-man may serve as a metaphorical figure for a literary character. Like such a character, it is a fictional representation. It aims at representing some likeness of our actual behavior. It is at once like and unlike us. It can do more and less than we can in real life. In the operations of its soul, pleasure and pain are the only determining factors (*TSn* 18). Like the countless protagonists of eighteenth-century fiction, it personifies sensitivity, if not sensibility itself. It reacts to the slightest change in environment and initially knows no indifferent states. These will come later only when it has itself undergone the greatest pleasures and pains and has attained the ability to compare them with weaker sensations (*TSn* 26). Its sense of self develops slowly across time as the statue first confuses its very existence with the presented object and the sensation produced by it, namely, the odor of a rose (*TSn* 15).

The statue's self-involvement parallels that of many eighteenth-century characters. They are often egocentric as individuals and ethno-centric as a group—perhaps none more so than the Parisians in Montes-quieu's *Les Lettres persanes* (Letter XXX) who in their inability to recognize another culture ask the ironic question: "Comment peut-on être persan?" The literature of the period charts a voyage in self-discovery. Rousseau developed considerably autobiography, the literary mode of writing most concerned with positive self-awareness. Some of his characters, however, particularly in *Narcisse,* as one would expect, exhibit a selfish attitude that Rousseau severely criticized.

The voyage of self-discovery begins for protagonists, as for the statue-man, with the body and leads sometimes to a certain autoeroticism. In the *Traité des sensations,* a perceived continuity of self arises from the perception of the continuity of the body by the hand through the sense of touch (*TSn* 102–4). In the statue's efforts at self-preservation (*TSn*

Main Works of the Eighteenth Century Concerning Aesthetics," and he gives rather short shrift to Condillac in the body of his book. See Cassirer, *The Philosophy of the Enlightenment,* p. 298 and Chouillet, *L'Esthétique des lumières,* p. 222.

107), its movements are characterized by a "groping" motion not unlike that of Suzanne Simonin in the dark passageways of the convent in Diderot's *La Religieuse* or of Marianne in her struggles in Marivaux's *La Vie de Marianne*. The progress made towards survival, personal identity, and enlightenment has necessarily to include a certain advance in the knowledge of one's own sexuality.[12]

Condillac's treatment of the statue accentuates qualities that are typically female in the male imagination. Its curiosity, defined as the desire for novelty and often the only motive for its actions, "becomes for it a need, which will make it move continuously from one place to another" (*TSn* 115). The characters seeking novelty and exoticism, which of course inform many works from this period, are frequently *ingénues*. Their ultimate preoccupation, like the statue's, consists less in fulfilling desire than in avoiding harm (*TSn* 234). Condillac stresses the vulnerability of the statue and its dependence on "everything that surrounds it" (*TSn* 241; also 45, 83).

That the statue has a markedly female character should not surprise students of the Enlightenment, the literature of which abounds with female protagonists. Such a coincidence of gender does not occur by pure chance. Numerous authors chose female protagonists to portray the world of sensibility and the way in which one acquires knowledge.[13] Women provide in the latter instance a negative example, but one that is not meant to be gender-specific. Their diffused consciousness works to their disadvantage in a world viewed, through the lens of sensationism, as presenting myriad phenomena that demand quick sifting. Their learning process, the lengthiness of which represents the difficulty of learning experienced by all humankind, becomes complicated by their perceived tendency not to differentiate readily between given data. Although some of the *philosophes*, notably Diderot, sought anatomical and physiological explanations for women's supposed intellectual shortcomings, many others attributed them to an unfortunate, indeed an unfair, lack of education.[14] In the literature of those patriarchal times,

12. I have added personal identity and survival to Rita Goldberg's linking of sex and enlightenment. See Goldberg, *Sex and Enlightenment: Women in Richardson and Diderot* (Cambridge: Cambridge University Press, 1984).

13. See my review essay of several books by feminist critics, "Eighteenth-Century Female Protagonists and the Dialectics of Desire," *Eighteenth-Century Life* 10, n.s. 2 (May 1986), 87–97.

14. Elizabeth J. Gardner, "The *Philosophes* and Women: Sensationalism and Sentiment," in *Woman and Society in Eighteenth-Century France: Essays in Honor of John Stephenson Spink* (London: Athlone, 1979), p. 23.

women were often represented as slow learners whose innocence was incessantly persecuted, but who also serve ideally to reflect the arduousness involved in *everyone's* acquisiton of human knowledge.

In his sensationist writings, Helvétius unabashedly uses women as explicit objects of desire. As he endeavors to move men to virtuous acts or stunning inventions for the public good, Helvétius feels that the greatest possible compensation should be offered them. Adherents of the sensationist psychology emerging in the eighteenth century recognized that human beings seek pleasure and avoid pain. Since women according to this logic provide men the greatest possible pleasure, and hence the most powerful motivating factor, Helvétius approves of making them rewards for men's socially useful accomplishments in civilized nations which, unlike primitive or poorer ones concerned with the physical needs of hunger, are driven only by the love of women (*DE* 305; *DH* 1: 121 [F 192]). Helvétius's apparent gender bias against women, whom he exploits as a means of effecting ambitious behavior helpful to the country at large, counters his otherwise enlightened approach to them, especially in their considerable educational needs. The hypothetical intellectual inferiority of women to men stems, Helvétius believes, from their poorer education (*DH* 1: 129 [F 202]). It bears noting, though, that his rationale for better educating women aims ultimately to improve the education of men, who supposedly become frivolous and weak-minded by imitating the women they love. Perfecting women's education presumably would "sow the seeds of intelligence and virtue" in men (*DE* 190).[15] In his utilitarian society, Helvétius thus grants woman a central, albeit subservient, place. She serves at first as a lure for the passions of male characters who pursue her in time and space just as the assumed male reader pursues her, so to speak, in the pages of numerous books from the period celebrating female protagonists. In the end, a woman, although herself still passionate and frequently uneducated, often brings both male hero and reader to virtue and reason in accordance with Helvétius's sensationist master plan for improving society. That she

15. While recognizing Helvétius's "desire to relate all activity to his system of interest and male sexuality" as well as the role he creates for woman as property or "a tool of the state" for shaping virtuous and intelligent men, Gardner ultimately exculpates Helvétius and claims him as a "true" feminist for not making any "*a priori* assumptions about women." One can only assume that Gardner's sympathy towards Helvétius arises from the relatively favorable comparison between him and his contemporaries, whose blatant misogyny enhances his egalitarianism. See Gardner, "The *Philosophes* and Women," pp. 22–23.

sacrifices herself totally to the male culture in the process, as in Prévost's *Manon Lescaut,* concerns the author no more than it apparently does Helvétius. The male novelist uses her as a tool or prop just as the sensationist legislator does to achieve their mutual goal of an enlightened society serving the public interest.

In literature, the so-called female characteristics of Condillac's statue and the depiction of woman in Helvétius's writings call for a heroine or a highly sensitive hero, of which the eighteenth century provided many examples. In Rousseau's *La Nouvelle Héloïse,* both male and female protagonists, Julie and Saint-Preux, exemplify a dependence on their immediate environment for knowledge and happiness. Saint-Preux has to return to Clarens at one point in the novel (Part V, Letter IX) to verify Julie's existence sensorially by the mere sound of her voice in order to dispel a bad dream. Montesquieu's Usbek and the host of characters in real or imaginary travel literature reflect a curiosity that causes them to move about constantly. Suzanne and Marianne also prove instructive in this regard. Their vulnerability, as well as that of all Sade's female victims, illustrates what Chouillet has called a "poetics of misfortune" for the age.[16]

This poetics has its basis, I believe, in the developing sensationist view of sensibility. We may be moved both to seek pleasure and to avoid pain, but fear of pain affects us more than the allure of pleasure. Helvétius suggests our greater sensitivity to pain than to pleasure and finds in misfortune a principle of inventive activity (*DE* 454; *DH* 2: 108 [F 585]). Literary characters ultimately learn more from exposure to misfortune than to bliss, because it forces them to use their intelligence creatively to remove themselves from difficult, unpleasant situations. Helvétius finds adversity beneficial, however, only at a relatively early age and quotes the Scottish proverb according to which misfortune is "healthy for breakfast, indifferent for dinner, & deadly for supper" (*DH* 1: 302–3 [F 415]). To take greatest advantage of hard times, protagonists must encounter them before middle or old age. In choosing the age of their main characters, eighteenth-century French writers seem to have taken note of the sensationist directive for youthful victims.

As the sole driving force behind characters, misfortune proves problematic, however. Its major shortcoming, recognized by Helvétius who wants to exploit it as a pedagogical stimulus, consists in its short-lived

---

16. Chouillet, *L'Esthétique des lumières,* pp. 163–68.

nature, which prompts him to substitute the passions for it (*DH* 1: 303 [F 415]). What spurs on an individual in a system of education also moves literary heroes and heroines. The passions motivate them all the more effectively since they come from within the characters themselves and do not generally depend, as does misfortune, on events outside of us that frequently change. When not confronted by an *auto-da-fé*, a torture chamber, or similarly distressing circumstances, characters can rely on their passions to move them toward a potential pleasure. Although the desire to do so may not be as great as the fear of pain, it is nonetheless constant. In their constancy, the passions thus complement misfortune—no less than pleasure complements pain in sensationist psychology—as defining features of the lives of Enlightenment characters.

In connecting as it does sensations as component parts to ideas as whole entities and vice versa, sensationism functions in much the same way as does synecdoche. Synecdoche constitutes in point of fact the trope *par excellence* of the period's sensationist aesthetics. The egocentrism of Condillac's statue causes it to draw the entire world it experiences into the narrow sphere of its own existence. By defining itself as the odor of a rose, it undergoes a transformation from part to whole and enacts a primary narcissistic state. The statue's world is of course itself limited at this point to this one sensation. Yet even as it evolves, this tendency to relate everything to itself does not totally change. An idea, considered as a whole, can never be entirely disassociated in sensationist epistemology from the particular sensations that compose it. Conversely, individual sensations always lead to abstract ideas. Bonnet makes the dialectic between sensations and ideas, the part and the whole, the particular and the general especially clear by emphasizing the continuity between them. It is of this connectedness that he speaks in part when he says of the increasing abstract powers of language that a single "*Word* suffices to awaken a multitude of ideas" (*EA* 161). In describing self-interest, Helvétius makes little or no distinction between the individual and the society in which he or she lives. The paradigm he establishes for the one serves equally to explain the operations of the other. What applies to the part applies just as well to the whole. Both individuals and societies follow their self-interest, which arises from physical sensibility (*DE* 117).

Synecdoche represents above all an original state of egocentrism and confusion of part and whole that needs to be overcome as much as possible. The statue does not at first differentiate sensations from itself. Bonnet's statue follows Condillac's closely in such an initial tendency.

Its identity or self forms around whatever it may happen to experience at the time, whether that feeling or sensation is one of a carnation, a jasmine, pleasure, pain, and so on (*EA* 534–35). Literary characters ought to move away from this egocentrism, which authors often evoke through the use of synecdoche, and toward reason. But the inevitable process by which they have learned anything by connecting parts to wholes and sensations to ideas, keeps them from doing so completely. As long as they can proceed in one direction toward ideas, progress appears as a logical conclusion to their activities. But as we know, neither the principles of sensationism as it was evolving nor those for synecdoche preclude movement in the other direction from the whole, ideas, society, and progress toward the part, sensation, the self, and decline. The uneasy coexistence of progress and decline as ever-present possibilities for eighteenth-century literary characters establishes the dramatic tension distinctive among the works in which they are portrayed.

As has been suggested above, many of the qualities found in these literary characters hinge upon movement, which belongs properly to the formal domain of plot. The plots for much of the period's literature can be found in the statue's activities which, like its curiosity, necessitate movement. According to Condillac, movement gives children their greatest happiness and most vivid consciousness of their existence, and the statue will derive even more pleasure from its increased mobility (*TSn* 109–10). As I have already indicated, this movement is at first concentrated in the statue so that it can attain an adequate notion of self. Soon, however, the sense of touch pulls the statue away from itself and toward the outside world (*TSn* 111). Movement becomes then the outward sign of an internal desire; "our statue cannot desire a sensation without at the same instant moving in order to seek the object that can procure the sensation for it" (*TSn* 113). It is suspended only when the statue delivers itself entirely to a new pleasurable feeling, when *jouissance* is at once enjoyment and fetishistic orgasm as the statue wishes "to touch with all the parts of its body the object that occasions [the new feeling]" (*TSn* 113). Such passages from the *Traité des sensations* evidence the sheer driving force of desire that literally propels many characters at a frenetic pace throughout the literature of the French Enlightenment. The peripeties of *Manon Lescaut* or a philosophical tale such as Voltaire's *Candide* allow the plots to continue in virtually uninterrupted action.

Bonnet typically defines movement in physiological terms. Human beings are moved emotionally, because their nerve fibers move physically. Bonnet associates movement with feeling. Something as ethereal as a feeling is brought closer to the visible world. One may not be able actually to observe feelings, but one knows from experience that the physical environment has a crucial bearing on them. Its objects, as Bonnet envisages them, constantly emanate corpuscles whose movement is transferred through our organs to fibers and on to the soul. Conversely, sensibility depends on the play of fibers, which in turn depends on the action of objects (*EA* 87). Greater sensibility and pleasure thus result from the greater but not excessive movement to which one exposes oneself (*EA* 90). We increase the movement of our soul and act by paying attention to or comparing different sensations (*EA* 109, 216). The more objects we observe and compare, the more capable we are of distinguishing those that give us pleasure from those that produce pain. As an active mechanism in Bonnet's epistemology, the mind can initiate movement in the fibers by paying attention to objects that memory identifies as having previously produced pleasurable sensations. Movement can thus come from within or without ourselves. Either we can choose in our immediate environment objects that please us or we can move about in the hope of increasing our happiness. Clearly, for all sensationists, the greatest benefits come from our continual movement in the world around us.

Such mobility produces a sense of novelty that is at once enjoyable and necessary. As Bonnet states, "Everything that is *new, unforeseen,* without being painful, brings *Pleasure* to the Soul" (*EA* 204–5). After a while, the same sensations, however delightful they may be at first, become "insipid, & even unbearable" so that we come to value variety (*EA* 209). To escape boredom and to have constant reminders of our existence, reminders that we find pleasurable, we always seek new sensations (*DE* 262–63). Those sensations can come from the same object, but the object itself must constantly change. Helvétius cites the examples of a stream's successive ripples in one spot and a crackling fire that, although stationary, keeps one company (*DE* 262–63). New sensations, even those causing some harm and especially those occurring suddenly, arouse our attention, which when constantly engaged can lead to great ideas helpful to all in society (*DH* 1: 100, 303 [F 168–69, 417]). We need perpetually renewed impressions not only to learn anything well but also to contribute substantively to society and to continue to improve its lot.

Des Grieux's and Manon's interrupted supper in *Manon Lescaut* provides an exemplary scene of the similar need in literature for variety in the plot. In Prévost's novel, this scene echoes others in which the action is broken off suddenly to change the protagonist's feelings of pleasure or pain. The new circumstances, which actually inflict pain on Des Grieux, who is seized by his father's lackeys, and thus separated from his beloved Manon, make the previous situation and its attendant mixed feelings of pleasure and pain, if not melancholy, all the more acute and memorable. By a contextualization of feelings that the sensationists understood well, Des Grieux's initially grieved reaction to Manon's apparent pain is experienced, then remembered vividly as pleasurable.[17] Erich Auerbach calls attention to this scene and its erotic elements but neglects to explore the actual sequence of sensations subtending them and the sequence's ramifications for the plot's form.[18] However perfect or intense they may respectively be, pleasures and pains must be suspended in order for the story to advance, for the characters to learn, and for the readers to enjoy the experience and learn as well. Imperfect, discontinuous pleasures and pains serve them all best. The surprise or astonishment of both the protagonist and the reader at the constantly changing events constitutes one of novelty's principal elements.

Novelty, arising as it does from movement, thus results in turn in a salutary sense of astonishment that makes the statue in the *Traité des sensations* and the various characters in literature "better feel the difference of [their] manners of being" (*TSn* 23). Condillac writes about this reaction in the statue: "The more the passage from one [manner of

17. The admixture of pleasure and pain becomes an integral part of the romantic aesthetics. See Mario Praz, *The Romantic Agony*, trans. Angus Davidson (Oxford: Oxford University Press, 1970). Praz traces this to Sadean sources. I believe its origin can be found in sensationist psychology.

18. Erich Auerbach, *Mimesis: The Representation of Reality in Western Literature*, trans. Willard R. Trask (1953; rpt. Princeton: Princeton University Press, 1974), pp. 395–401. Although he entitles his chapter on eighteenth-century French literature "The Interrupted Supper," Auerbach does not focus on what is novel or noteworthy about an interruption in the plot. It does much more than reveal Manon's disorderly and erotic appearance. For Milan Kundera, who singles out Sterne's *Tristram Shandy*, the interruption of action and digression infuse the novel with "the poetry of existence." See his acceptance speech for the Jerusalem Prize for Literature on the Freedom of Man in Society, "Man Thinks, God Laughs," *New York Review of Books*, June 13, 1985, pp. 11–12.

Georges Poulet recognizes in Prévost a pattern that he calls the *instant-passage*, an abrupt transition from one extreme sensation to another. But he does not attribute this, as I do here, to a particular aesthetics for the century. See Poulet, *Etudes sur le temps humain* (1952; rpt. Paris: Editions du Rocher, 1976), 1:191f.

being] to another is brusk, the greater its astonishment, and the more it is also struck by the contrast of the pleasures and pains that accompany them" (*TSn* 23). Astonishment, which in eighteenth-century literature stems in large part from the rapid series of adventures to which the characters are subjected, heightens the activities of the operations of the soul (*TSn* 23). This state of mind arises primarily from sudden movement. In describing surprise, Bonnet uses the example of a meteor (*EA* 203) to emphasize both the sudden and total break that occurs between the current sensation and those immediately preceding it as well as its bewildering movement. According to Helvétius—who in sensationist fashion wants to communicate with people's minds by speaking to their eyes—large, new images arouse surprise and leave a deeper impression, particularly when characterized by movement (*DE* 455).

The movement sensationists encourage as an indispensable way to learn takes the form of travel in literature. Literature involving travel thus assumes new meaning as an attempt to educate protagonists by engaging them in large-scale versions of the basic means by which knowledge is acquired most effectively. The entire world in a geographical sense represents but a classroom for these new learners. In *Manon Lescaut,* Des Grieux's *amour-passion* for Manon takes him across the high seas to the New World. Like Candide, he is continuously moving from one place to the next in pursuit of the object of his desire. Those rare moments of tranquility in the two works attest not only to the evanescence of ecstasy but also to the intensity of human desire and the necessity of movement in realizing it.

If living consists in enjoying oneself and "life is longer for whoever can maximize the objects of his or her enjoyment," as Condillac states in his *Traité des sensations* (266), then there are seemingly no limits to libertine behavior. The novel of seduction springs from just such a rationale. Its plots parallel somewhat the activities of the statue as it experiments with different degrees of pleasure and pain. The statue discovers, as do some of Sade's characters, that pleasure can lead to pain, which in its turn can, by diminishing, lead to pleasure (*TSn* 25). Fictional libertines such as Valmont and Merteuil in Laclos's *Les Liaisons dangereuses* exhibit an uncanny awareness of sensationist psychology's emphasis on our dependence on our environment and do everything to control that of their victims, who, like the statue, "do not know that a being outside itself solely disposes of its sensations" (*TSn* 45). These latter fall prey to rakes because of their lack of experience, which eventually enslaves them. Freedom, for them as for the statue, assumes a certain amount of knowledge and worldliness (*DSL* 274–75).[19]

Although the statue's activities suggest its significant preoccupation with pleasures (*TSn* 230, 234, 241; *DSL* 271), fear and repentance check its hedonism so that it can ultimately represent progress of a positive kind. Condillac sees his entire treatise as a contribution to the progress of the art of reasoning (*ER* 285). The plots of many literary works in the period advance, as does the statue, toward reason. Indeed an entire subgenre, the *Bildungsroman*, accentuates a process of growth and maturation. Des Grieux finally returns to the rational universe of the seminary after his profligate adventures have ultimately instructed him in the same way the statue has been instructed, namely, through numerous exposures to pleasure and pain (*TSn* 119). Since the extent of one's knowledge depends on individual circumstances that vary in quantity and quality (*TSn* 64), one has all the more justification for multiplying those circumstances as much as possible through travels. These travels can be real or even highly imaginary ones, such as that of a giant from the star Sirius in Voltaire's *Micromégas*. In traveling, one refines one's sensibilities and taste, acquires greater experiences, and loses the intolerance for cultural relativism that sometimes circumscribes one's world view.

In addition to the movement and the progressive nature characteristic of many eighteenth-century literary plots and of the statue's activities, one discerns a marked tendency toward repetition. Although characteristic of any narrative, repetition has particular significance for sensationist theory and for the texts from the period. The statue's very learning process is based on repetition; experience comes from incessant experiments of a similar nature. Several times the statue draws the same flower near and takes it away in order to differentiate itself from the odor of the flower (*TSn* 158–59). Bonnet explains habit by the frequent repetition of movements in the same sense (*EA* 390–91). Fibers tend to shake one another in a given order proportionately more and to resist their reciprocal movement proportionately less as the sensations themselves follow one another more closely and are repeated often (*EA* 391). The moment immediately after the fibers vibrate—and a certain order of movement is established among them—provides the best time to reinforce a lesson. This need for repetition in cognition

19. For a discussion of worldliness as social experience, see Brooks, *The Novel of Worldliness*.

calls for the same or similar scenes in literature that will reproduce a series of sensations imprinted on the main character in previous episodes. The more these two parallel scenes occur in proximity to each other, the more effectively the protagonist presumably acquires knowledge. One can link, as Freud did, the desire for repetition, which has as its object the simple reproduction of a pleasurable sensation, to instinct and the forms of life associated with it. For the Enlightenment, however, the desire for repetition illuminates man's duality, his lower and higher natures. It does not merely reflect an instinctive, mechanical, and circular search for knowledge in which the mind's active qualities receive, as they did with astonishment, positive recognition (*ER* 295). Like the statue, the characters of the period's literature must repeat many of the same or similar operations before they can learn. The epic adventures of Suzanne Simonin, Marianne, and Des Grieux, just to evoke a few names from previously mentioned works, attest to the difficulty of the task.

For the narratives of eighteenth-century literature, the statue provides a model through the sequentiality and succession of its activities. It proceeds one step, indeed often, one sensation, at a time—freezing time, as it were, allowing for an adequate representation of the complexity of each new sensation presented alternately (*TSn* 35). The statue's pleasures derive from a succession of sounds rather than a continuous noise (*TSn* 63). Moreover, only as the sounds and smells are presented successively will it be able to separate them from one another (*TSn* 65, 69; see also *EOCH* 176). Increased knowledge by differentiation comes from the separation or succession of the presented sensations. Clarity of thinking results from an order that is discontinuous.

Of all the sensationists, Bonnet is the one who insists the most upon the importance of succession in the cognitive process. The succession of sensations serves to establish order among them and plays an indispensable role in helping the soul remember them (*EA* 201). More important, one can appreciate the newness of a different sensation only if one has other preceding sensations with which to compare it (*EA* 357). A sense of novelty thus presupposes the presence of a sequence of sensations. Ultimately, Bonnet's statue derives enormous pleasure from the succession of seemingly endless aromas, because such a sequence extends the feeling of its existence (*EA* 456–57).

There are several implications for literature that one can draw from these epistemological considerations about succession. In the telling of any story, the effect of new voices and events depends to a large degree on the pattern established by the succession of previous ones. New voices and events become all the more memorable when they break the pattern of the old sequence and start a new one. The epistolary novel, which enjoyed much success in the eighteenth century, follows this sensationist format of discontinuity and continuity, as one narrator creates a relatively invariant structure only to have it broken in the following letter whose story is told by someone else. In many ways and especially in their narrative structures, the authors of the period want to incorporate endless novelty into their works. As one narrative ends and another begins, the readers experience both pleasure and relief from this novelty. They sense pleasure from the same impression Bonnet's statue has, namely, the plenitude of a worldly existence. Their presumed relief, which is also pleasurable, comes from the sensationist belief that no sensation (and by extension, no narrative) should be continuous. If so, the one, like the other, would ultimately prove both disagreeable and unenlightening, contrary to the French Enlightenment's aesthetic goal of combining the *agréable* with the *utile.*

An interruption or change thus comes to characterize an ideal succession of sensations just as it does an exemplary narrative. There must be intervals between different sensations or degrees of difference in the same sensation—degrees whose passing Bonnet calls degradation—in order to demarcate experience. These intervals or degrees, which indeed define succession, give the statue a feeling of passage from one sensation to the next and of the order in which they occur (*EA* 200–201). Moreover, they allow it to apprehend the relative pleasure or pain involved. Especially in the case of the latter, passages allow the fibers to relax (*EA* 453). Since in Bonnet's view of the mind particular sensations and ideas have their own fibers or combinations thereof, a change in objects releases their hold on the respective fibers and both relieves and frees attention for other objects (*EA* 518). Variety actually helps the mind work more efficiently. In epistolary literature, even when there is essentially only one narrator, as in Graffigny's *Lettres d'une Péruvienne,* the letters themselves are of course still set at intervals. One narrative or sequence of events frequently interrupts another and in so doing gives pleasure to the reader, often at the expense of the fictional hero or heroine. But succession is a narratological as well as epistemological necessity. The literary characters can do without new disruptive experiences no more than anyone can learn without differentiating sensations and ideas. Differentiation necessitates feeling successive intervals, whether they occur between different

sensations or in the same sensation. To be understood in the Enlightenment idiolect, narratives and plot sequences in the text must, as must
words in speech, be articulated and interspaced.

In its sequential nature, eighteenth-century narrative often emphasizes, as does sensationist psychology, not the general, undifferentiated
mass of events and voices but the particular ones, which retain their
distinctiveness precisely because they are presented successively.[20] In
the hands of Voltaire in *Candide,* such a device facilitated the debunking
of the authoritative philosophical system of optimism and gave primacy
to the single individual as a legitimate source of truth.[21] The interpolated
narrative in *Candide* proves especially dynamic in educing a sense of
succession, as first one narrator then another alternately tells his or her
tale of woe. The resultant succession, like the number of tales told,
seems endless. Similarly, the discrete units of the age's many epistolary
novels with their separate and successive presentation of letters have a
kind of cumulative effect on the reader who ultimately feels over-
whelmed by the evidence presented throughout the work.[22] The reader's task consists in "unmixing" (*démêler* [*TSn* 136]) or decoding the
confusing perceptual world—one of the principal goals of the statue
and the characters in the period's literature.

Writers using a sensationist aesthetics should introduce their characters and readers alike to the same stimuli, namely, many different
sensations. As Helvétius puts it, "The reader would like every verse,
every line, every word to arouse a sensation in him (*DH* 2: 188 [F 691]).
In this context, Helvétius is referring explicitly to the sensations of the
reader, but as a sensationist, he cannot possibly dismiss the pedagogical
value of sensations for any learner: reader or character. Obviously, more

20. On the sequential character of narrative in general, see Robert E. Scholes and Robert
Kellogg, *The Nature of Narrative* (New York: Oxford University Press, 1966), p. 272.

21. I discuss this in "Interpolated Narrative in Voltaire's *Candide*," in *Approaches to
Teaching "Candide,"* ed. Renée Waldinger (New York: Modern Languages Association, 1987),
pp. 45–51. The individual also judges beauty. Diderot believed that beauty consisted in the
diversified "perception of relationships" and recognized the subjectivity of the individual
beholder in judging the beautiful. See "Recherches philosophiques sur l'origine et la nature
du beau," p. 435.

22. Because of its sequential features, eighteenth-century narrative has certain limits. Efforts
in the novel to produce multifarious sensations concurrently and to rid narrative of its
sequential limits would of course come later, especially in the *nouveau roman.* The representation of simultaneous aspects of human consciousness as it unfolds in modern novels such as
Robbe-Grillet's *La Jalousie* or Virginia Woolf's *To the Lighthouse* is virtually unknown to
authors of the eighteenth century, who preferred to deal with successive events in a rational
way to unearth the intricacies of human experience.

is at stake with readers than with fictional characters. When French Enlightenment authors want, however, to shape their readers' attitudes, they tend to do so by means of their characters, manipulating their sensations first. Fictional sensations affect the real ones of the reader, which ultimately take the form of ideas. In order to influence a person's mind, one must start with his or her sensations. I have suggested in the earlier sections of this chapter regarding some of the formal elements of literature that there is a certain complicity between the protagonist and the reader in that they are both learning. The acquisition of ideas in sensationist epistemology results from one's exposure to multiple sensations. The reader, although not subjected to actual sensations of pleasure and pain, can nonetheless learn from those of someone else in a fictional setting.[23] Readers can share the same surprises and interruptions as those experienced by protagonists in their lives. Indeed, their pleasure should exceed by far that of the characters who frequently endure painful experiences. Pleasure comes from novelty and fixes one's attention (*EA* 205). To increase the reader's attention, the author must increase the novelty of plots and narratives. As attention increases, so does mental activity with the result that learning proceeds rapidly. Although writers may use sensations as the means by which to increase their characters' and readers' attention, their goal lies in cultivating ideas from which, in conjunction with sensations, beauty ultimately springs.

Sensationist aesthetics closely interrelates sensations and ideas with beauty. Upon close examination, one can see that it indeed reduces the beautiful to the agreeable and the useful or their epistemological equivalents, sensations and ideas. In his definition of the beautiful, Bonnet writes: "From the *Variety* of *Relationships,* the *Unity* of *Action,* & the Usefulness of the *Goal,* the *Mind* deduces therefore the general *Notion* of the *Beautiful*" (*EA* 222). By now, it should be clear that by the terms "variety" and "relationships" the sensationists imply for the most part the results of experiences involving the senses, that is, sensations. These should not be too numerous or varied, especially if they have no goal (*EA* 223; *DH* 2: 198 [F 702]). Most, if not all, sensations produce ideas at some point, but they may not all be useful at once. The sensations that are gathered together must have as their common goal the production of a single idea. In this connotation,

---

23. Kavanagh, *Enlightenment and the Shadows of Chance,* p. 120. Kavanagh also points out the claim made by the novel of experience to be an actual story with "lessons equally as vivid and equally as valid as those the reader has learned from life itself."

sensations serve as a kind of ideological propaganda; they are directed solely toward forming useful ideas. In his remarks on the beautiful, Helvétius also tends to take a utilitarian approach to sensations and comes to speak of them practically as ideas: "the beauty of a Work is measured by the sensation it makes on us. The clearer and more distinct the sensation is, the more lively it is" (*DH* 2: 204 [F 708]). In point of fact, the two are indispensable to each other in achieving a sense of the beautiful in the reader. Sensations that are pleasant attract readers to ideas and persuade them of their validity and usefulness. To rephrase Bonnet, ideas represent the useful union of various sensations. From that union, we derive our notion of the beautiful. In the sensationist perspective, beauty thus arises from the birth of ideas, which depend upon sensations. The agreeable and the useful are naturally joined in the cognitive process itself.

Eighteenth-century authors have already aided their readers considerably by adopting a narrative form marked by division, succession, separation, and discontinuity. These characteristics of the period's narrative also point the way toward the process of a reasoning mind. When Condillac uses the expression *démêler,* as he does frequently (*TSn* 260–61 passim), he indicates the separation of sensations necessary to progress in one's knowledge. As the statue evolves, pleasure results from the statue's separation from itself which replaces its initial symbiotic and primary narcissistic attachment to itself. It moves, as does the ideal reader, from self to other, from a finite world to one with limitless possibilities, from naïveté to enlightened experience.

Condillac's *Traité des sensations,* supported as it is by Bonnet's and Helvétius's writings, thus furnishes a kind of sensationist aesthetics for the period that precedes its publication and for that which follows it. In it, Condillac demonstrates his singular ability not only to formulate the philosophical ideas that had currency at the time but also to generate a richly suggestive piece of writing for aesthetics. Through descriptions of the statue-man, the enumeration of its activities, and the way in which they took place, he gives us insight into the characters, plots, and narratives of the literature of the eighteenth century, showing who and what might best represent the contemporary world and how they would do so. The readers profit from an author's judicious use of character, plot, and narrative, growing wiser from their literary experience. This exercise, albeit one that remains at one remove from the actual world, will presumably prove useful to them in their own lives in the future by imparting to them an enhanced awareness of the way in which human beings encode and decode knowledge. Condillac's theory of the mind, which purports to trace a *universal* process, ironically succeeds best as a description of *contemporary* authors' concerns, which were at once epistemological and literary.

My interpretation of Condillac's work and that of his fellow sensationists as an indirect but formal aesthetic treatise of sorts contains of course an inherent contradiction. Empirical aesthetics by definition shunned rules. Yet my reading corroborates a view of Condillac as a rational sensationist, that is, a sensationist who could not avoid the lure of those qualities and activities that characterize reason and classical aesthetics, namely, clarity, precision, and particularly, I should add, rule-making.[24] Bonnet and Helvétius share this same tendency toward the classical. Nonetheless, Condillac and his contemporaries deserve not our condemnation for having mixed, as they did, classicism and empiricism but our praise for identifying, although perhaps unwittingly, the dualistic nature of human beings. The sensations and reason that guide and inform our lives enable us in part to experience what is highest and lowest in human existence. As the literature of the French Enlightenment abundantly illustrates, both faculties contribute to humanity's greatest triumphs as well as its sordid moments of degradation. For their crimes of inhumanity one cannot fault the sensual appetites of libertines any more than one can fault their finely tuned rational skills. The sensationists' inconsistent and failed method for separating sensation and reason demonstrates perhaps better than many a more coherent theory of the mind their profound inextricability.

24. Chouillet, *L'Esthétique des lumières,* p. 8; Knight, *The Geometric Spirit,* p. 16, 197; and Wojciechowska, "Le Sensualisme de Condillac," 314.

5

An Exemplary yet Divergent Text: Graffigny's *Lettres d'une Péruvienne*

F rançoise de Graffigny's *Lettres d'une Péruvienne* provides in many ways a textbook example of sensationist aesthetics. Her remarkably complex work contains several transitions, all of which stem, I believe, from such an aesthetics and which give it a multicolored texture not unlike that of the Peruvian *quipos* or knotted strings the heroine uses at first to weave her story.[1] This

---

1. Not all critics have fully taken into account the novel's complexity. In their edition of Graffigny's *Lettres d'une Péruvienne* (Paris: Flammarion, 1983), Bernard Bray and Isabelle Landy-Houillon state that this epistolary novel changes simply in its middle section from an "amusing and exotic fiction" to "the serious-minded critical panorama of contemporary mores" (p. 245). Such a judgment, however, does not adequately allow for the various intricacies of the novel. The full discussion of sensationist aesthetics in the previous chapter attempts to establish this as a major set of literary conventions for the period. That chapter derived sensationist aesthetics from the *Traité des sensations* and other sensationist sources. Although Condillac, Bonnet, and Helvétius themselves were probably not aware of the theory of aesthetics that arises from their thinking, authors both prior to and following publication of their work seem to share a view of novel-making that has its basis in the sensationism expounded by them. Far from diminishing the importance of Condillac and his fellow sensationists, such an interpretation attempts to show the profound level of support and understanding sensationism enjoyed in the eighteenth century. The present chapter refers primarily to the *Traité des sensations,* since it is most contemporary with Graffigny's novel. But it should be clear that Bonnet's and Helvétius's later works reinforce the aspects of a sensationist aesthetics that Condillac originally suggests in his writings.

Conversely, the period's literature also influenced or at least complemented the philosophy of the time. Such a reciprocal influence of philosophy on literature and of literature on

enormously popular eighteenth-century French epistolary novel about
the peripeties of a Peruvian princess abducted first by the Spanish then
captured by a Frenchman who takes her aboard his ship and ultimately
to Paris also serves to underline the interplay between sensationism and
the century's most persistent theme of sensibility. A close analysis of
this particular literary piece further indicates the ways in which a
work by a woman author can not only use but can subvert novelistic
conventions related to a sensationist aesthetics.[2] This theory will be
shown to generate contemporary subgenres (the *Bildungsroman,* the
critique of mores, the love novel, the novel of sensibility, and the novel
of seduction) as well as popular *topoi* (persecuted innocence, the
problem of evil, libertinism, exoticism, and cultural relativism). The
present chapter aims to illustrate both the way in which a sensationist
aesthetics is evidenced in Graffigny's piece and the way in which this
aesthetic theory promotes the rise and inconstant blending of some of
the most important subgenres and *topoi* in the eighteenth-century
French novel. The text ultimately reflects the inherent instability of
genre resulting from a sensationist aesthetics, an instability that profoundly characterizes this emerging literary form.

From the eighteenth century down to our own time, most critics
agree upon the mixture of topics treated in the *Lettres d'une Péruvienne,* although they express differing opinions about the success with
which Graffigny blends them. Readers in her day viewed it primarily as
a love novel with digressions on social criticism, whereas critics in this
century consider it a philosophical novel containing a love story. Still
others place emphasis on other aspects of the work, such as its so-called
socialism or its propagandizing for the constancy of a woman's (and not
a man's) love.[3] Yet the novel's sections on social criticism represent not

---

philosophy is evident in Graffigny's *Lettres d'une Péruvienne.* But it is perhaps most clearly at
work in Diderot's *Rêve de d'Alembert.* For a discussion of this work, see Chapter 8, esp. n. 34.

2. Janet Whatley has also noticed the rebellious nature of Graffigny's writings, calling her
"a conscious subverter" similar to Montesquieu. The present chapter shows exactly what
Graffigny is utilizing and subverting—nothing less than an entire aesthetics. See Whatley, "The
Eighteenth-Century Canon: Works Lost and Found," *French Review* 61 (1988), 419.

3. For a full exposition of the critical reception of Mme de Graffigny's work, see English
Showalter, Jr., "An Eighteenth-Century Best-Seller: *Les Lettres Péruviennes,*" diss., Yale University, 1964.

Showalter also calls attention to the moral formula that guided many writers in the period,
including Graffigny, at first to justify then actually to compose their works for their potential
moral utility to the reader (chap. 5). Showalter does point out, however, that Graffigny, like
many of the better writers, disregarded certain rules in the moral formula, such as the happy

mere digressions to break the monotony of a love story but natural extensions of a sensationist aesthetics.[4] I shall attempt to elicit the ways in which the novel reflects a *consistent* familiarity with sensationist aesthetics as the latter grew out of a shared world view in the eighteenth century. An underlying aesthetic unity governs Graffigny's composition of the seemingly disparate parts of her text and reveals much about the writing of novels in the eighteenth century. Whereas critics have generally found the philosophical character of the novel principally in its content, that is, the discussions of society, education, or religion, I am claiming that one philosophy in particular informs not so much the overall views expressed in the novel (several philosophies could be said to underlie Graffigny's often contradictory remarks) as the novel's very structure and form.[5]

In his *Traité des sensations,* Condillac, widely recognized as the sensationist thinkers' chief spokesman, indirectly provided an aesthetic treatise suggesting useful ways in which novelists before and after his time might develop or did indeed develop their works' formal elements. Employing the very epistemological and psychological principles inherent in sensationism, they conceived for their novels new characters, plots, and narratives and shaped the attitudes of their readers.[6] As a theory of the mind, sensationism provides a framework for explaining the origin of mental faculties through the body's senses alone. With his statue-man, which is at first limited alternately to one sense at a time

---

ending, for instance. Textual evidence suggests, however, that the moral formula directs this novel far less than does a philosophical one, namely, sensationism.

4. The apparent hodge-podge resulting from Graffigny's work, its combination of all the contemporary intellectual fashions, can be explained to some extent by Graffigny's character and the circumstances in which she wrote. She had to take into account suggestions from people in various quarters: "printers, censors, critics, and patrons, whose tendency is always to force the author toward a safe and commonplace middle ground." See Showalter, "A Woman of Letters in the French Enlightenment: Madame de Graffigny," *British Journal for Eighteenth-Century Studies* 1 (1978), 96.

5. Showalter comes closest to such a position when he lists the new "ideas" (exoticism, the epistolary novel, cultural criticism, and cultural relativism, etc.) that infused Graffigny's novel and that "became commonplaces" by the end of the century. In these ideas, he finds early signs of the romantic movement that was yet to come rather than outgrowths of a philosophy that was gaining force at the time. See "An Eighteenth-Century Best-Seller," pp. 280–81.

6. This new approach to eighteenth-century French literature is of course elaborated in the chapter on sensationist aesthetics. The first part of the analysis of *Lettres d'une Péruvienne* follows the same method used in the preceding chapter, studying by turns character, plot, narrative, and the shaping of the reader's attitude.

then exposed to several senses at once, Condillac devised a theory of cognition that both recognized the consequential obstacles in the learning process and postulated the centrality of sensation to it. Through sensations and only through sensations, especially those from touch, does the statue-man grasp any meaning of the world it inhabits. Like the literary characters in much eighteenth-century fiction, it displays above all traits such as confusion and egocentrism, in keeping with sensationism's firm belief in the difficult learning conditions of any individual. Its sense of self evolves gradually as the statue initially conflates its own being with the object at hand and the sensation it produces: the odor of a rose (*TSn* 15). Perhaps foremost among the traits for literary characters were their emotional sensitivity and a physical ability to react promptly through their senses to the slightest change in their environment, best resumed in the one word, *sensibility*.

For the eighteenth century, sensibility, which gave primacy to feeling or sentiment as a *modus operandi*, became closely associated with both living and learning, as Zilia, the female protagonist in Graffigny's *Lettres d'une Péruvienne*, constantly demonstrates. The work evidences the close connection between sensationism and sensibility. This latter behavioral characteristic, inextricably tied as it is to the senses and valued possibly more than any other in the century, is depicted as vital to one's physical presence in the world and to one's acquiring knowledge about that world. The heroine of Graffigny's novel defines her very existence in terms of her sensibility or tenderness, as she often calls it. The bloody spectacle of the Spanish soldiers leaving a path of destruction in the Peruvian temple of the sun takes from her everything except for her sentiment (*jusqu'au sentiment*).[7] Zilia's fear of being seen by "these barbarians" stops everything except for her breathing (*jusqu'à ma respiration*) in the following paragraph. It concludes in exactly the same place with the same *jusqu'au* construction. Feeling and breathing are placed in parallel positions to each other and are thus considered equally indispensable to her continued existence. External circumstances can remove or stop anything "up to but not including" (*jusqu'à* in its literal sense) sensibility. Even if one uncouples the parallelism created by *jusqu'à* in succeeding paragraphs and takes the expression

---

7. Françoise d'Issembourg d'Happoncourt, Mme de Graffigny, *Lettres d'une Péruvienne* (1747; definitive version, 1752), in *"Lettres portugaises," "Lettres d'une Péruvienne" et autres romans d'amour par lettres,* ed. Bernard Bray and Isabelle Landy-Houillon (Paris: Flammarion, 1983), p. 259. Subsequent page references are cited parenthetically in the text.

to mean "up to and including" or "and even," it is clear that without sensibility Zilia cannot report on her experience. Hence, her knowledge and narration stop with the loss of sensibility and resume with her regained consciousness: the words *jusqu'au sentiment* are followed by *Revenue à moi-même* when she "comes back" to herself, that is, her sensibility. It constitutes for Zilia, as for many eighteenth-century protagonists, a human being's very essence. "Nothing is mine," she says, "but my tenderness" (261). Déterville, the Frenchman who rescues Zilia from the Spaniards and becomes her admiring protector, confesses to having been "born tender," as he puts it (312). Sensibility represents in many ways for Zilia the *sine qua non* of her living state: "stripped of everything, dependent on everything, I possess only my tenderness" (309). Not surprisingly given the eighteenth-century view of women, authors in this period often chose female protagonists to represent the profoundly sensitive nature of the species.[8]

The tenderness displayed by these characters does not always apply, however, to all those living in their world. With the sacking of her city, Zilia experiences firsthand the carnage and horrors of war, and she has to confront the philosophical, but also very real, problem of evil. This popular *topos* or literary theme, along with its close counterpart, persecuted innocence, looms large in the first part of the *Lettres d'une Péruvienne*, which portrays the keen sensibility of its heroine. Zilia poses the pertinent rhetorical question: "what God persecutes in this way innocence and virtue?" (265). In the passage described in some detail above, Zilia actually swoons, as do many sensitive Enlightenment heroines in the face of similar scenes that overwhelm all human senses and sentiments.[9]

The sensibility of characters suggested by a sensationist aesthetics can also result, as it does in Graffigny's work, in a secondary generic division or subgenre of the period's literature beyond the general classification of a work as a novel or, in this case, an epistolary novel. Like Rousseau's Julie and Saint-Preux in *La Nouvelle Héloïse,* but

8. The appropriateness of heroines for the period's literature is discussed in both my review essay "Eighteenth-Century Female Protagonists and the Dialectics of Desire" and my chapter on sensationist aesthetics, pages 110–12.

9. In *Candide* (1759), Voltaire would give full treatment to the problem of evil, although the question had already been explored somewhat by Marivaux in *La Vie de Marianne,* Prévost in *Cleveland,* and others writing in the same vein about the misfortunes of an innocent protagonist in a libertine world. Cunégonde and the old woman in Voltaire's philosophical tale faint on numerous occasions when confronted with the so-called evil designs of others.

without their passionate attachment to each other, Zilia and Déterville are pitted against the European society in which they live. Déterville's mother, like the baron d'Etange, is a cold, unfeeling person who demonstrates a marked lack of affection for her own child and who remains unmoved by the supposedly genuine, authentic character of an outsider. The natural bonding between a mother and a son and a spontaneous, generous form of hospitality toward a guest have been displaced by the artificial charade of social customs.

Remarking upon the peculiar ways of the French from her privileged perspective as an ingénue and a foreigner, Zilia transforms her love letters into a critique of mores, a subgenre that particularly had attracted attention with the appearance of Montesquieu's *Lettres persanes* (1721) and that continued to appeal to the reading public throughout the eighteenth century. Differentiating the two works are the degree of sensibility of the protagonists and the facility with which each one moves or does not move back and forth among possible subgenres. The *Lettres persanes* presents a more classical text than does the *Lettres d'une Péruvienne* insofar as it maintains the style of a pure critique of mores. Its characters are indeed sensitive to what they observe around them, but their sensibility does not cause the work to give way, as it does in Graffigny's novel, to other subgenres like the *Bildungsroman* or the novel of sensibility. Graffigny's piece dramatically vacillates between several possible plots, as will be presently demonstrated. Although perhaps less pure, it possesses a broader popular appeal than Montesquieu's work.

Closely associated with the very notion of life in the eighteenth century, sensibility was also inextricably tied, as I have pointed out above, to the process of learning. Zilia can no more stop thinking than she can stop feeling. Her attempt to do so at one point early in the novel utterly fails. Zilia describes her experience as follows to Aza, the Peruvian prince and her fiancé, to whom she addresses most of her letters:

> Tired of the confusion of my ideas, disheartened by doubts that tear me apart, I had resolved not to think anymore; but how can one slow down the movement of a soul deprived of all communication, which acts only on itself, and which such great interests stimulate to reflection? I cannot, my dear Aza, I seek enlightenment with an agitation that devours me, and I find myself constantly in the deepest darkness. (279)

Feeling indeed leads to thinking, which ultimately after a long period of time results in knowledge. Frustrated by her attempts to learn quickly, Zilia comments frequently on her confusion and the difficulty of the learning process.

Writers embracing a sensationist aesthetics develop characters like the statue-man or Zilia, who are befuddled at first by the myriad undifferentiated sensations in their immediate environment but who ultimately reveal the painstaking difficulty of the learning process. Zilia explains her plight to Aza: "How can I remember ideas that are already confused at the moment I receive them, and that the time which has gone by in the meantime makes even less intelligible?" (265). Her exposure to a new language and culture puts her in a position analogous to the *tabula rasa* of Condillac's statue-man. Janet Altman has also independently recognized this similarity between the principal characters of Graffigny's and Condillac's work.[10] Altman further suggests that Condillac might have borrowed the narrative technique from Graffigny's 1747 novel for his *Traité des sensations* (1754). In composing his treatise, however, Condillac himself was unwittingly codifying a sensationist aesthetics that Graffigny and others before her had thoroughly absorbed in an intuitive way from Locke's philosophy and incorporated into the form of their novels.[11] The pervasive influence of the so-called Republic of Letters should not be underestimated here.[12] In Graffigny, the learning process is an extended and arduous one, especially for language: "these names mixed together, represent the sounds of words; but these names and sounds seem to me so indistinct from one another, that if I succeed one day in understanding them, I am quite certain that it will not be without many pains" (295). The word "pain" (*peine*)

10. Janet G. Altman, "Making Room for 'Peru': Graffigny's Novel Reconsidered," in *Dilemmes du roman: Essays in Honor of Georges May,* ed. Catherine Lafarge et al. (Saratoga, Calif.: Anma Libri, 1989), pp. 33–46.

In another article on this novel, Altman calls it "epistemological fiction," hinting at the connection between philosophy and literature that I am trying to make explicit here. See "Graffigny's Epistemology and the Emergence of Third-World Ideology," in *Writing the Female Voice: Essays on Epistolary Literature,* ed. Elizabeth C. Goldsmith (Boston: Northeastern University Press, 1989), p. 195.

11. Following Knight (*The Geometric Spirit,* p. 83), Altman reminds us in her own work of the currency of sensationist ideas in the eighteenth-century French intellectual world ("Making Room," p. 200, n. 13) but does not trace them to a specific aesthetics that Graffigny is at once using and subverting.

12. For a discussion of the Republic of Letters, see Dena Goodman, *The Republic of Letters: A Cultural History of the French Enlightenment* (Ithaca: Cornell University Press, 1994).

appears with some frequency in the novel. Indeed, the first two 1747 printings bore the imprint "A Peine," which the modern Flammarion volume editors question as a possible reference to Paris (243). It could also of course allude to the difficult (i.e., painful) life Graffigny had as a woman or, in the current context, to the rigorous learning process.[13]

Reflecting a sensationist aesthetics' implied directives for literary characters, Zilia also exhibits an egocentric attitude. Although she may not confuse herself with the odor of a rose, as does the statue-man, she does mistake her individual situation for a universal one. She describes the scene of violence in the opening pages as follows: "my senses, seized with a secret horror communicated to my soul nothing but the idea of all nature's destruction. I believed the peril to be universal" (266). Limited as they are by their senses, dependent upon their immediate environment, and possessing only a partial perspective, eighteenth-century protagonists often follow the same path as Condillac's statue, taking themselves for the entire world in which they live, the part for the whole. It is no wonder therefore, that Enlightenment authors chose synecdoche as one of the privileged figures for representing their times.[14]

Graffigny makes ample use of synecdoche, which constituted the major trope for sensationist aesthetics. Synecdoche evokes the inevitable naïveté of any learner who misapprehends in the beginning the part for the whole. The entire learning process that Zilia undergoes demonstrates, however, an increasing aptitude for recognizing the part as a part, for properly dividing undifferentiated sounds and articulating words, and ultimately for using synecdoche not in a naive but a sophisticated way. After sufficient intellectual development, one can indeed revert to a conflation of part and whole. Already by the time she reaches Paris, Zilia is properly using the term "throat" (*gorge* [292]), which along with the term "foot" (*pied*) was one of the century's well-known urbane euphemisms, referring not in actuality to the specific part of the body mentioned but delicately to the general erotic area. Likewise, she considers the city of Paris as the entire nation (337) but only the better to analyze the country's customs in a way befitting the most erudite *philosophe*.

---

13. On Graffigny's life, see Showalter's diss., "A Woman of Letters in the French Enlightenment."

14. For a discussion of the uses of synecdoche in *Candide*, see Frederick M. Keener, *The Chain of Becoming* (New York: Columbia University Press, 1983), pp. 203–5.

Now the plots suggested by a sensationist aesthetics inevitably entail movement, surprise, a process of decoding, and repetition.[15] The *Lettres d'une Péruvienne* recounts, as do many eighteenth-century stories, lengthy travels. In Zilia's case, these extend from Peru to France. The spatial displacement of characters was of course designed to underscore the diversity of human experience and the endless possibilities for learning. This diversity is apparent on a minute level to a sensitive individual such as Condillac's statue-man, who moves from one object to the next even within a very limited space. It becomes thrown into sharpest relief, however, when one travels from one country, indeed, one hemisphere, to another. Exoticism naturally serves as an ideal theme for the literature of these times. It provided a rich source of formal literary possibilities—foreign objects and lands that would attract the insatiable curiosity (268) of characters like Zilia. Through this behavior, Zilia favorably reflects a keen desire to learn as much as possible about her own world and that of others as well in order to become both enlightened and tolerant.

In describing what their characters do, Enlightenment authors frequently indicate their protagonists' sense of surprise and astonishment.[16] The Russian formalists termed such a technique of surprise "defamiliarization" and believed that it constituted the very foundation of novelistic art.[17] Zilia certainly does not count as an exception to this

15. See Chapter 4, pages 114f.; and Condillac's *Traité des sensations,* esp. pp. 109–13, 158–59.

16. See Chapter 4, pages 116–17. It will be recalled that the protagonists' movement from one place to another and from one feeling to another gave rise to this sense. Especially in real or imaginary travel literature, as Jay Caplan points out, "movement and being moved are mixed." See his *Framed Narratives: Diderot's Genealogy of the Beholder* (Minneapolis: University of Minnesota Press, 1985), pp. 76–77. Caplan also suggests the possibility of connecting "the pathos of discovery" with a large range of eighteenth-century discourses that he calls "the Novel."

The keen sensibility of many Enlightenment protagonists often prompted their own surprise and astonishment. There was also, however, a sympathetic reaction among those listening to or reading their tales, especially when these related the spectacle of a victimization. David Marshall describes the common assumption of sympathy in the period as follows: "Like other eighteenth-century observers of society and human nature, like other eighteenth-century theorists of an aesthetic of sentiment and sensibility, these authors [Marivaux, Dubos, Diderot, and Rousseau] often seem to depend on the powers of what many of their contemporaries assumed was an innate or natural sympathy. They seem to believe in both the need for and the possibility of a sympathetic transport that would allow readers and beholders of works of art or people in the world to exchange places, parts, and persons with the characters of others." See Marshall, *The Surprising Effects of Sympathy: Marivaux, Diderot, Rousseau, and Mary Shelley* (Chicago: University of Chicago Press, 1988), p. 179.

17. My thanks go to Peggy Kamuf for this observation. On the notion of defamiliarization,

norm intimated by sensationist aesthetics, which in giving primacy to the variety of experience also highlighted the sometimes spectacular differences between separate yet consecutive events. One of Zilia's first encounters with the wonders of the world occurs when she discovers that the "rocking house" in which the Spaniards are holding her captive is not attached to the earth (266). The changing of her captors—from the Spaniards to the French after a naval skirmish during which she remains unconscious—equally astonishes her. Given her enclosed environment, representative of everyone's initial dependence in the learning process on what lies immediately in one's perceptual field, she does not realize for days that she is at sea (273). She also marvels over a "pierced cane" (276), which the reader of course recognizes as a telescope used to sight the approaching land. Zilia confuses the sailors' joyous celebration over the imminent conclusion of their voyage for a sacrifice in honor of the Peruvian sun god. Everything she sees "strikes, surprises, [and] astonishes" her (279). Before realizing that she is gazing into a mirror for the first time, Zilia believes that she is looking at another Virgin of the Sun like herself (280). She resembles Condillac's statue in its perplexity upon opening its eyes for the first time, an action Michel Foucault finds as an appropriate myth or metaphor for much Enlightenment thought.[18]

These moments of a kind of primitive astonishment, however, soon allow for a full-fledged ongoing discussion of cultural relativism as one surprise leads to another. The sighting of land heralds in earnest its beginning. For Zilia, the European continent is the New World, a land of previously unseen phenomena that provoke constant observations about the diverse ways different people conduct themselves. The French behave religiously, according to Peruvian standards, in the midst of wholly secular, if not profane, activities. Zilia has difficulty at first understanding the reverence Déterville pays her as a woman, a demonstration of adoring words and gestures usually accorded in Peruvian

see Victor Shklovsky, "Art as Technique," in *Russian Formalist Criticism: Four Essays,* trans. and ed. Lee T. Lemon and Marion J. Reis (Lincoln: University of Nebraska Press, 1965), esp. p. 12, where Shklovsky writes: "The technique of art is to make objects 'unfamiliar,' to make forms difficult, to increase the difficulty and length of perception because the process of perception is an aesthetic end in itself and must be prolonged."

18. The two subjects Foucault finds especially apt to portray the eighteenth-century philosophical project are "the foreign spectator in an unknown country, and the man born blind restored to light." See *The Birth of the Clinic: An Archaeology of Medical Perception,* trans. A. M. Sheridan Smith (New York: Vintage, 1975), p. 65.

culture only to a divinity (278). She remarks upon the "continual agitation" of the French who would no doubt take the Peruvians' "serious and modest demeanor for stupidity" (282–83).

Cultural relativism can and often does constitute one of the principal *topoi* in the critique-of-mores subgenre. The seriousness and modesty prized by the Peruvians would, as Zilia notes, probably appear as ignorance to the French. Eighteenth-century authors of course often used cultural relativism as a way of showing the deficiencies of their own culture. The "other" culture tended to be one more closely aligned with nature and all the characteristics the period attributed to it: tranquility, simplicity, transparency, spontaneity, freedom, and so forth. Zilia's astonishment at the useless ornaments that adorn the dress of the French calls attention to their preoccupation with superfluous, unnatural objects. Moreover, the French make distractions of some of the earth's essential elements, water and fire, by creating lavish fountains and fireworks not to meet any urgent need but simply to amuse themselves (326–27). What is regarded as an element necessary to sustain life in one culture becomes mere entertainment in another.

In the plots derived from a sensationist aesthetics, the characters frequently become deeply involved in the process of decoding their world.[19] Like Condillac, Graffigny uses the word *démêler* (to untangle) in describing this activity that occupies a major portion of her heroine's time. The expression of course aptly evokes the state of confusion that besets everyone in the beginning as he or she tries to interpret the amorphous mass of sensations presented by the external world. Graffigny indicates Zilia's understanding or lack thereof with this particular term. In one instance, the Peruvian princess finally sees that her unusual clothes have become the object of surprise among the French (282). In another, she tries to determine whether the changing of meal times has a relationship to the planned change of lodging (285). Her own inner thoughts sometimes grow suddenly muddled and need a sorting out that is not always immediately possible (314). Little by little, Zilia's observations improve so that she ultimately can make insightful judgments about the foreign culture's "unbridled taste for the superfluous" which has led to the corruption of "their reason, heart, and mind" (328).

19. The twentieth-century term *decoding* may be used to denote one of the principal activities of the cognitive process. The linguistic usage of the term has of course come to obtain today. But it is no less appropriate for Enlightenment epistemology, concerned as it was with external signs or sense-data that in their turn need interpretation.

Zilia's enhanced understanding also enables her better to appreciate
Déterville's sensitive character (334).

Graffigny's *Lettres d'une Péruvienne* thus presents not just another
critique of mores but gives to this subgenre the additional texture of a
Bildungsroman, which itself also represents a logical outgrowth of a
sensationist aesthetics. This latter important eighteenth-century subgenre usually traced the maturation of a character from an attachment
to the senses to a higher level of understanding. In the process,
passionate desires or a preoccupation with the sensations often became
sublimated in the form of a reasoning mind. Graffigny's work charts in
this regard a full circle. The novel begins upon a note of confusion,
astonishment, and surprise because of Zilia's own lack of knowledge
and her saturated, overworked senses. Toward the end of the novel,
however, Zilia can comment upon her surprise over the ignorance of
those around her (343). Her astonishment, like her use of synecdoche,
develops from naïveté to sophistication.

The most impressive and noticeable progress Zilia makes comes
with her increasing knowledge of a foreign language, French. Indeed,
language can give one a new sense of freedom and can cultivate one's
reason, as it does eventually for Zilia. She states: "I understand that I
lack only the liberty to express myself in order to know from the
Cacique [Déterville] the reasons that make him keep me in his house"
(294). Language liberates her from slavish dependence upon her senses
and immediate environment. A new form of communication based on
the analytical powers of reason slowly comes to replace the former
language grounded in the senses; writing replaces a kind of weaving.

Zilia's shift from the *quipos* to the pen does not take place, however,
without a wistful glance backwards at what she is leaving behind. These
colored strings punctuated with intermittent knots have the distinct
advantage of "striking" the senses (270) and presenting the illusion of a
tangible language that gives one the impression of a close contact with
the reality of another person's thoughts. Sensationist psychology placed
high value on the evidence produced by perceptible phenomena of this
nature. Although this theory is not without its own illusions about the
reality of our sensations, it had to it a polemical thrust that explains
some of its excesses. Evolving as it did from British empiricism, sensationism aimed at locating the source of our knowledge and of even
abstract concepts less in the mind itself than in experience. (Locke
devoted, after all, a major portion of his *Essay* to debunking innate ideas
and principles.)

The Enlightenment's attitude toward so-called primitive peoples reinforced sensationism's insistence on concrete objects as the building blocks of experience and also helps one understand Zilia's knots as a kind of authentic language. This age mythologized to a large degree the noble savage's proximity to nature, which itself of course constituted for the period a primary basis of truth. The allure of primitives resided in their being presumably less alienated than Europeans, having less of a division, so to speak, between their actions or language and their thoughts. To complete the implications of this popular contemporary myth, their language could well be visible and, as such, readily understandable to others in the culture. The *quipos* thus approximate at a finite level the universal language of beneficent hearts, the language of sensibility itself, precisely because they directly transmit, according to this myth, a visual message, as do "eyes filled with goodness" and even tears (289–90).[20] The interior world of feeling becomes intelligible through palpable, exterior signs in the form of knots. With such a view of things, sensationist psychology mystifies somewhat the principal character and the reader even as it enlightens them. But in transcribing this theory into a narrative, Graffigny ultimately rejects confusion when its object is, as it is here, a woman. Instead, she chooses to educate her and, so, too, the reader.

The *quipos* represent, moreover, a kind of vital outlet for Zilia's sensibility, which as we have seen cannot be cut off, as it were. She calls them "the treasure of [her] tenderness" (271). Deprived of them, she is left with tears as her only form of expression. Graffigny's *Lettres d'une Péruvienne* follows to some extent the classical image of weaving, usually associated with domesticity and fidelity. Penelope weaves a shroud for her father-in-law Laertes in order to ward off the demands of her suitors and to allow her husband, Ulysses, enough time to return home.[21] In her knot-making, Zilia, too, presents an image of homespun loyalty to Aza. The act of weaving also sustains both women in their

20. For a different interpretation of the *quipos,* see Alice Charlotte Hogsett, "Graffigny and Riccoboni on the Language of the Woman Writer," in *Eighteenth-Century Women and the Arts,* ed. Frederick M. Keener and Susan E. Lorsch (Westport, Conn.: Greenwood Press, 1988), pp. 119–27. Hogsett finds in them "a language of the moment, a female language in its evanescence" marked by "impermanence and inadequacy" (p. 120). I concur with her reading insofar as it suggests for the *quipos* an immediacy of communication that was highly sought after in this age of sensibility.

21. In her correspondence, Graffigny actually calls the *Lettres d'une Péruvienne* "her Penelope work." See Showalter, *"Les Lettres d'une Péruvienne:* Composition, Publication, Suites," *Archives et Bibliothèques de Belgique* 54 (1983), 20.

respective lives but for different reasons. Whereas Penelope performs it
with an eye to the results it will produce (that is, the delay of any
marriage to one of her suitors), Zilia ties knots, and later writes,
increasingly for the process itself.[22] She composes her letters to Aza
undoubtedly more and more aware as her story progresses that he may
never receive them. Zilia does in fact ultimately send them to Aza but
not until Letter XXVI. The process of this special kind of weaving and
writing allows her to give expression to constant surges of the sensibility that defines her existence. "All that I have left," she writes, "is the
single and painful satisfaction of covering this paper with the expressions of my tenderness, since it [this paper] alone is the docile witness
of the feelings of my heart" (303). Zilia, like Scheherazade, tells her tale
to continue her life in a certain way but especially to make it worth
living. She informs Aza after dispatching the knots and letters that she
must continue to write: "How would I bear the length of your trip if I
deprived myself of the only means I have to converse with myself
about my joy, my transports, my happiness?" (321). Sensibility seeks a
necessary outlet in what is at once a creative and an educational
process, first in the *quipos* then in language. This progressive course of
action finally transforms Zilia from a domestic, dependent person into a
self-actualized, educated woman.

  Given the difficult path to the acquisition of knowledge, eighteenth-
century plots tended to emphasize the repetition that sensationism
acknowledged as fundamental to learning. Like Condillac's statue, Zilia
understands nothing of her new environment and describes her experience as "painful": "Everything around me is unknown and new to me,
everything interests my curiosity and nothing can satisfy it. In vain I pay
attention and use my efforts to understand, or be understood" (268).
Numerous errors seem continually to prevent Zilia from learning and
venturing any judgment (279). Convinced of the crucial importance of
language for teaching her the truth and calming her fears, she remarks

22. On the evolution of the female writing subject, see Peggy Kamuf's discussion of the
Portuguese Letters in her book, *Fictions of Feminine Desire: Disclosures of Heloise* (Lincoln:
University of Nebraska Press, 1982), esp. pp. 58–62. Kamuf stresses the tendency for women
writers to have their heroines regard the act of writing less as an enterprise with practical
implications for others than as a process leading to a woman's own self-actualization.
  Nancy K. Miller also stresses the solitude and self-containment of a woman writing for
herself, such as Zilia whose "subjectivity [is] constituted through the refusal of the love story
and retreat from its places." For a discussion of the notion of a private, female life of
subjectivity, see Miller, *Subject to Change: Reading Feminist Writing* (New York: Columbia
University Press, 1988), pp. 126, 133, 136, 144–46, 149, 151, 153, 157, and 160–61.

on the bothersome "length of time it will take her before being able to gain entirely a clear understanding" of her situation (281). She must perform the same tasks, linguistic or otherwise, time and again, step by step before gaining mastery of them.

As for the narratives that develop from a sensationist aesthetics, they accentuate particular voices and precisely that sequential procedure necessary to grow in one's worldliness. One learns a step at a time; two simultaneous sensations cannot receive full attention, as Zilia discovers. Equally preoccupied by the rapid speech and the ostentatious dress of the French, she finds herself unable to concentrate on either one: "my attention in listening to them keeps me from seeing them, and the attention I pay in looking at them keeps me from hearing them" (326–27). Visual and auditory stimuli must be sorted out separately. One cognitive act follows another in the same way Zilia's feelings do: "I pass successively from fear to joy, and from joy to uneasiness" (278–79).

Such a sequential approach to learning and feeling often gives the eighteenth-century novel the formal structure of letters expressing particular voices.[23] As an epistolary novel, the *Lettres d'une Péruvienne* furnishes an ordered, numbered sequence of letters that follow one another in a linear progression similar to the perceived operation of a reasoning mind. The first-person narrative, however, remains doggedly one woman's throughout the piece with the single, very minor exception of Déterville's short note, which is engulfed by Zilia's text. The consecutive nature of the letters themselves, combined with the mounting forcefulness and authority of the narrator's voice, produces an inescapable cumulative effect upon the reader. In a remarkably feminist gesture, Graffigny does not want her female protagonist to have either a narrative or an education that appears in any way, formally or substantively, as subordinate to that of even the most sensitive male character. These letters belong to Zilia and to no one else who might upstage her, expropriate her text, and divert attention away from the central subject of a woman's education.

A sensationist aesthetics finally shapes the reader's attitude even as it traces a plot of decoding for the main characters. Like the hero or heroine, the reader ideally untangles or unscrambles (*démêler*) the

---

23. Showalter finds in "particularity" the aesthetic principle that gives actual letters their attractiveness and interest for the eighteenth century. See "Authorial Self-Consciousness in the Familiar Letter: The Case of Madame de Graffigny," *Yale French Studies* 71 (1986), 123.

confusion of the world and proceeds from a finite to an unbounded view of things, from ignorance to sophistication. Perhaps because the voice does not change in Graffigny's work, the reader all the more easily apprehends the advances an individual makes toward an enlightened mind. Zilia herself may not immediately recognize the progress she has made and understandably bemoans her frequent state of mental obscurity. But by the end of the novel, her intellectual growth impresses the reader who in perusing this *Bildungsroman* has presumably developed a similar ability to distinguish clearly the perplexing external world and to progress from naïveté to enlightenment.

Graffigny's *Lettres d'une Péruvienne* thus exemplifies in many ways a sensationist aesthetics in its development of character, plot, and narrative, and the way it molds the reader's outlook. As did many eighteenth-century authors before and after her, Graffigny intuitively uses many of the literary conventions that stem indirectly from a theory of the mind and that by their *simultaneous* usage cause to diminish, if not efface, generic boundaries in the novel. Sensationist aesthetics thus tends to mix subgenres in an indeterminate way and to elide the differences between them.

Equally revealing for this aesthetics and Graffigny's novel are the ways this work does not conform to such an aesthetic theory. Graffigny rejects some of the frequent choices made by other authors who patterned their works on this aesthetics. She eschews libertinism as a *topos,* the novel of seduction as a subgenre, stereotypical male-female associations, and the traditional *Bildungsroman* plot. The present analysis supports a feminist interpretation insofar as it shows how Graffigny diverges from what a sensationist aesthetics normally requires for novelistic characters, plots, and narratives. But it ultimately finds Graffigny's work, especially in its combination of subgenres, to be as much a writing in keeping with the *Zeitgeist* as a reaction against it.[24] It recognizes the importance of both a woman's nature and her nurture for the content and form of a novel. Graffigny resists both more and less than others the century's literary and philosophical trends: more in her forceful feminist writing and less in the mixing of the genres. In her case, the path not taken in the variety of formal possibilities from a sensationist aesthetics available to an author provides an insightful glimpse into the workings of the eighteenth-century novel.

24. Feminist readings also acknowledge this other preoccupation of Graffigny with the ideas of her time. See Altman, "Making Room," p. 200, and Miller, *Subject to Change,* pp. 136, 159.

Although egocentric, her heroine does not display the eroticism directed towards self or others that distinguished numerous protagonists in the period's literature. The male myth of a woman capable of infinite desire simply has no embodiment in Graffigny's text. Nor does the heroine's vulnerability—a characteristic believed in sensationist psychology to define at least in part the human condition—receive undue attention. To be sure, Graffigny makes the obligatory reference to the problem of evil and persecuted innocence at the beginning of the novel in the context of Zilia's precarious situation as a woman faced by marauding Spanish conquistadors. But beyond these disingenuous, "realistic" passages, she does not dwell on her character's delicate female constitution, which might otherwise make Zilia the easy prey of rakish soldiers or Parisians and change the direction of the novel.

Graffigny also avoids associating woman with sensation and man with intellect, in contrast to sensationist psychology and much Enlightenment literature.[25] In the eighteenth century, female protagonists often served, and were indeed sacrificed to, the interests of a man's intellectual maturation.[26] Manon dies in Prévost's novel so that Des Grieux can return to the rational, patriarchal universe of the seminary. Perceived by the male imagination as a creature of sensation, a heroine ought in principle to remain at this level of understanding. At most she could exhibit the sensibility recognized as characteristically human but also intricately bound to the faculty of sensation.

To the contrary, Graffigny's novel presents a special kind of *Bildungsroman,* one for a woman. Like a character in this subgenre, Zilia advances towards reason. She receives an education that few women in the eighteenth century enjoyed. At first, she takes language lessons from her chambermaid whenever she can, then formally from a tutor Déterville provides for her in Paris. She repudiates the contemporary instruction of women that causes them generally to be scorned and often enclosed in convents (341–42). The *Lettres d'une Péruvienne* attempts in a small but significant way to rectify the lack of education women received—a gross injustice that kept them in a pitiful state of ignorance and an unfortunate narcissism (342). Zilia wonders how women can be expected to practice virtue when they are denied access to the means for learning about it (346). That a woman undergoes any

25. This gender bias was alluded to previously in Chapter 4, pages 110–12.
26. The following chapter (pages 159–63) will discuss the distorted use of the term *sacrifice* at the end of the century.

formal training at all goes against the accepted social practices of the time. Graffigny makes this palatable to her eighteenth-century audience, however, by limiting the instruction to language classes, which surely cannot be denied a hapless foreigner—even if she is a woman. These lessons represent a triumphant first step for women, who customarily benefited from little or no formal education.

But the rational world towards which the traditional, male-authored *Bildungsroman* and Condillac's *Traité des sensations* inexorably move does not ultimately represent the *telos* or end of Graffigny's work. At its conclusion, Zilia points out to Déterville that she "counts little on [her] reason" (360). Rather, she maintains sensibility as her guiding light because of the dangerous consequences of fully embracing the male-dominated world of reason for a woman. The growing awareness of one's reasoning abilities typically entailed a realignment from an acute, wholly absorbed sense of self—in the extreme, a primary narcissistic state in which one could even confuse oneself with an object like a rose in the outer environment—to an understanding of other things and people: a conversion from an intensely private world to a public one. Such a transformation was thought to be for the betterment of both the individual and the society in which he or she lived. Zilia, however, does not change course from her own self and what is like herself (i.e., Aza) to what is other than herself, namely, Déterville and the French. When asked by Déterville if she can love him, Zilia appears stunned: "How could that be? . . . You are not from my nation; far from your having chosen me for your wife, random chance alone brought us together" (312). Her decision to disregard Déterville's repeated amorous overtures and to reject his offer of love and presumably marriage in the end reflects a deviation in the well-known *Bildungsroman* plot. In this instance, otherness means not just that Déterville is not a Peruvian; it implies that he is not a woman and cannot entirely understand her particular circumstances. Zilia chooses a private, female life of subjectivity and sensibility over the other, public, rational domain which is male; friendship perseveres over love.[27]

27. In women's literature, Janet Todd has identified friendship between women as an alternative plot to the traditional heterosexual romance. See *Women's Friendship in Literature* (New York: Columbia University Press, 1980). Graffigny's novel offers of course a compromise with a friendship between a man and a woman. Zilia may have a library at her country estate and a certain desire to read all the books it contains (350). But the novel's concluding pages stress the complementarity of a man's and a woman's character that defines the friendship between Déterville and Zilia and that allows them to "economize the resources of [their]

Déterville's proposal then stands as a trap that would radically alter Graffigny's resolutely feminist plot by having it become simply another love novel (*roman d'amour*).[28] Graffigny will not sacrifice a Peruvian to the French, or another woman to the male order. Déterville reinforces Zilia's fears by speaking in terms of his "possession" of her heart (335). Well aware that "authority is entirely on the side of men" (345), Zilia does not want to relinquish what little power and freedom she has. Whereas in an uncorrupted society such as Peru's "the natural taste for property" urges one to love and marry another person, in France marriage leads to the woman's "annihilaton" (346). On all accounts, reason pushes Zilia into the arms of Déterville, especially after she learns of Aza's infidelity and his upcoming wedding in Spain. Yet it is her overriding, virtuous sensibility that keeps her forever loyal to Aza: "I cannot be admitted into so pure a society [Spanish society] without abandoning the motive that determines me, without giving up my tenderness, that is, without changing my existence" (356). Zilia may later recognize that her sorrows are due to her loss of reason, but she also recognizes the "impotence" of reason in the face of a "distressed soul" (359).

In the *Lettres d'une Péruvienne,* the novel of sensibility thus appears to triumph to a certain extent over the *Bildungsroman,* love novel, novel of seduction, and critique of mores. But as subgenres, the *Bildungsroman* and the love novel regain momentum in Zilia's last letter. After some brusk remarks to Déterville about his hopeless plans to chain her to a relationship based on love rather than friendship, Zilia proceeds to describe the nature of their future life together as she envisages it. She is to grow in her knowledge of the arts and sciences (no longer just in that of language), and he in virtue. The stimulating pursuit of knowledge—however slight it might be—of the universe, their environment, and their existence will give them more than enough to do in a lifetime (362). The dual project of living and learning reclaims the primacy it had earlier in the novel as a constant and necessary activity derived from a sensationist aesthetics. (The preceding letter

---

soul" (362). Déterville will teach her the arts and sciences, while she will enhance his moral qualities.

28. For lack of a better rubric, the editors of the Flammarion edition have chosen implicitly by their very title to call Graffigny's work a *roman d'amour.* I am arguing here that it is hardly just that. There is, moreover, a danger in such a "hierarchy of classifications," which, apart from being entirely inadequate in this case, can promote "invisibility for female authorship." See Nancy K. Miller, "Authorized Versions," *French Review* 61 (1988), 410.

had already noted Zilia's return to the "weakness of our first age" in which the senses, especially sight, operate in direct communication with the soul [359].) The tone shifts from that of a *Bildungsroman* about to begin anew, which Zilia's penultimate words foster, to that of a love novel with her concluding remarks to Déterville. Even while she sings the praises of friendship, Zilia invites Déterville to "come" (the word is repeated four times) to her in a way that hardly seems sanctimonious. Whether or not one can establish with certainty the sensual register this word might suggest, Zilia surely demonstrates with this litany an unquestionable anxiety about Déterville's absence and a pressing need for his physical presence at her side.

Although Graffigny does blend many of the *topoi* and subgenres that a sensationist aesthetics suggests, she gives an alternative interpretation of them. Her novel reveals an attempt to escape both the dialectics of desire that entraps women as sexual objects to be abused or possessed and the patriarchal maxims about male-female relationships.[29] That some readers criticized it severely for its so-called implausibility indicates their familiarity with conventional novelistic forms and their anxious expectations about seeing them realized in a work.[30] Graffigny does not accommodate the male reader by giving an anticipated,

29. Graffigny is apparently engaged in that very process of demaximizing plots that Nancy K. Miller describes in "Emphasis Added: Plots and Plausibilities in Women's Fiction," *PMLA* 96 (1981), 36–48. For a summary of the negative critical reaction to the novel, especially its unhappy ending, see Showalter's diss., chap. 6, "Ending the Novel," pp. 208–78.

Elizabeth MacArthur finds the lack of closure especially remarkable in the epistolary novel. I see no need, however, to restrict this observation to the epistolary novel alone. Works by Diderot such as *Jacques le fataliste, La Religieuse,* and *Les Bijoux indiscrets* would constitute notable examples of novels not cast in the epistolary form that nonetheless thwart attempts at closure. Pursuing an entirely different approach from that of MacArthur, I independently reached the same conclusion that she did about the open-ended nature of Graffigny's novel. See MacArthur, "Devious Narratives: Refusal of Closure in Two Eighteenth-Century Epistolary Novels," *Eighteenth-Century Studies* 21 (1987), 1–20.

30. Graffigny's novel violates at least two sets of noteworthy rules, what Peter Rabinowitz has called, for literature in general, rules of configuration and of coherence. Her plot moves from the sixteenth to the eighteenth century, thereby breaking the balance in action, a subdivision of the first set of rules. It also disrupts the conventional ending for a love novel by not having Zilia marry Déterville, thus creating what Rabinowitz would call a "deceptive cadence" in its coherence. Eighteenth-century readers noticed and took exception to the second violation much more than they did to the first. Graffigny of course employs a different conclusion to call into question the implications of the traditional love novel and to make her point about the constancy of a woman's love. See Rabinowitz, *Before Reading: Narrative Conventions and the Politics of Interpretation* (Ithaca: Cornell University Press, 1987), pp. 110–69.

predictable plot but explores new terrain within the same aesthetics. Her results illustrate the various outcomes of a sensationist theory of literature, which constantly informs the style if not always the content of this work, and the remarkable flexibility of the emerging novel as an art form because of this aesthetics. It may well be that the century's inchoate subgenres were in a state of flux as was the novel itself. But writers inspired by sensationist aesthetics promoted the further mixture of literary forms just as sensationist psychology did that of spiritual and corporeal substances.[31] By an inherent tendency to mix and combine as well as to "unmix" (*démêler*), sensationism, which permeates much of the thinking of eighteenth-century France, naturally had a corresponding effect on the period's literature. Graffigny's novel afforded contemporary readers a free flow back and forth between subgenres like the *Bildungsroman*, the critique of mores, the love novel, and the novel of sensibility.[32] Such a structure, which in its unusual combinations for those times "tests the limits," as Nancy Miller suggests, of "generic constraint," also serves to diminish the monotony of the love story and calls our modern critical attention to the highly problematic nature of genre.[33] Although Graffigny's novel may privilege only one gender's perspective in an almost revolutionary effort at demonstrating the feasibility and the necessity of a woman's education, it does so by weaving several different genres into its form. In the process, her work represents an almost inevitable tendency of the eighteenth-century novel towards openness, ambiguity, and the absence of any all-embracing coherence.

This complex novel, which makes several formal twists and turns, thus employs a variety of possibilities from a sensationist aesthetics. Graffigny manifests a serious and mature understanding of the period's philosophy, much more than the passing acquaintance with it for which

31. The sensationist tendency to mix soul and body is perhaps most evident in the work of Bonnet. See (*EP* 3 passim). Bonnet, it will be remembered, calls man a "mixed being."

32. On the instability of genres from a historical standpoint, see Alastair Fowler, *Kinds of Literature: An Introduction to the Theory of Genres and Modes* (Cambridge, Mass.: Harvard University Press, 1982), esp. pp. 45–48.

33. See Miller, *Subject to Change*, p. 136. Whereas Miller finds in the novel's so-called formal flexibility a sign of "what female Enlightenment might mean," I also find it a sign of what a sensationist aesthetics entails. Although the relatively short existence of the novel as a new literary form at the time might well have prevented it from having fixed generic categories, the day's reigning philosophy by its very nature aided and abetted these historical circumstances.

she is sometimes credited.[34] As I have tried to point out, a sensationist aesthetics unquestionably informs the *Lettres d'une Péruvienne* in many known ways and indeed in some new ones as well. The transitions in this novel from a sensationist realization of the senses' importance in the cognitive process to the ascendancy of reason and sensibility (and back again to a fundamentally sensationist outlook that Zilia resumes after her long "cruel experience" [359]) stress the vital tension between sensation and sentiment and the failure of any effort to dissociate them completely. Moreover, these transitions finally point to the ambivalent form of the novel and the world it represents, an instability that numerous authors throughout the eighteenth century would depict in ways as endlessly varied as sensory experience itself.

34. In her introduction to the Flammarion edition of *Lettres d'une Péruvienne,* Isabelle Landy-Houillon disparages the "reflection" Graffigny gives of contemporary philosophy, calling it "a bit affected" (p. 44). According to Showalter, Graffigny "had absorbed the liberal philosophy of the Enlightenment so thoroughly that when she read Locke in November 1738, to be ready for Cirey, she was astonished to discover that she had already thought everything he said." See Showalter, "The Beginnings of Madame de Graffigny's Literary Career: A Study in the Social History of Literature," in *Essays on the Age of Enlightenment in Honor of Ira O. Wade,* ed. Jean Macary (Geneva: Droz, 1977), p. 298.

6

The Perversion of Sensationism
in Laclos and Sade

As one of the major philoso-
phies for the French Enlightenment, sensationism had far-reaching
implications for almost every facet of life. Its major thrusts, however,
lay in education and sensibility, as its adherents wished to effect both
intellectual progress and a refinement in society's mores. Toward the
end of the century, though, many of the noble efforts by *philosophes* to
achieve a utopian world through sensationist principles had largely been
turned around. In literary works, the characteristics of Condillac's statue-
man, which as salutary, human traits were cultivated by his fellow sensationists Bonnet and Helvétius—characteristics such as the capacity for
curiosity, surprise, repetition, and movement—could cause the downfall,
not the salvation or mental edification, of protagonists in the hands of
lubricious, devious libertines. Repetition in particular, if associated in
the learning process with the imitation of a model, could lead to the
development of slavish, brutish characters rather than free, rational
ones. The precise, clear language that supposedly would emerge from
the systematic differentiation of sensations associated over time with
distinct words and concepts sometimes became hopelessly ironic.
Throughout the effort to heighten sensibility in order to increase the
chances for mental activity and moral education, sensationists reduced
to pleasure and pain the overall functioning of the organism. In the
process, however, sensibility itself could become crudely degraded to a

commodity in a heartless economy of desire. In literature produced during the last two decades of the century, a shift to a wholly secular world takes place. The notion of a sacrifice, which customarily referred to a sacred, religious rite and may also refer to the experience that sensationism considered as no less sacred, is ultimately "uncrowned," to use Bakhtin's term from the carnival world.[1] Finally, the very nature of the soul is grotesquely debased and brought into the material bodily lower stratum.[2] There results from such a "perversion" of sensationism both an inversion

1. Although a fictional woman may have been the object of a ritual sacrifice throughout the libertine literature of the century, the notion of a sacrifice is mocked in a particularly perverse way only in the late Enlightenment. See Pierre Fauchery, *La Destinée féminine dans le roman européen du dix-huitième siècle, 1713–1807: Essai de gynécomythie romanesque* (Paris: Colin, 1972).

On the carnivalesque, see Bakhtin, *Rabelais and His World,* trans. Hélène Iswolsky (Cambridge, Mass.: MIT Press, 1968), pp. 118–19. For a discussion of the theme of hierarchy inversion and the world turned upside down, see Peter Stallybrass and Allon White, *The Politics and Poetics of Transgression* (Ithaca: Cornell University Press, 1986). What I am generally describing in this chapter is very close to Bakhtin's depiction of the carnivalesque. Were it not for Sade's extreme monologism and the hierarchical order of the libertine world, the term *carnivalization* would indeed have been preferable to *perversion* for my purposes here. I have ultimately retained this latter term because of its more neutral political implications. Some mention of the carnivalesque was deemed appropriate, however, especially since I borrow some of its expressions.

In his widely read work on Rabelais, Bakhtin extends the notion of the carnivalesque beyond the Renaissance to the eighteenth century. Although it has lost much of its positive, regenerating sense of laughter and "gay relativity," the carnivalesque continues, Bakhtin believes, into these times. Infinitely and intentionally more disruptive than mere satire or the rococo's *insouciance,* this mode serves to stand a preexisting world on its head, to invert or deviate its order, and profoundly to transform its basic ways of thinking. For an account of the rococo, see Helmut Hatzfeld, *The Rococo: Eroticism, Wit, and Elegance in European Literature* (New York: Pegasus, 1972).

Terry Castle has also used Bakhtin's concept of carnivalization but applies it primarily to masquerade scenes in an attempt to show their centrality to eighteenth-century fiction. See Castle, "The Carnivalization of Eighteenth-Century Narrative," *PMLA* 99 (1984), 903–16.

Bakhtin's formulation of the carnivalesque, which reveals a world turned upside down in the Renaissance, achieves a kind of *brassage* or rough blending that yields a completely new synthesis. Although the different version of the carnivalesque suggested here may not cause the radical mixing of upper and lower classes in society, as Bakhtin suggests in his analysis of Renaissance culture, it does cause a significant mixing of upper and lower orders of perception in epistemology. What emerges from the Enlightenment as a result of the perversion of sensationism is no less radical a transformation than the carnivalization of *idées reçues* in the Renaissance described by Bakhtin. Whereas the latter witnessed the "birth of man" and premodern society, the end of the eighteenth century may be said to have witnessed the explosion of modernity in all its complexity and the "death" of the man of limitless possibilities first envisioned by sixteenth-century humanism.

2. Carnivalesque debasement, Bakhtin reminds us, originates from the region of the

and a deviation of the cognitive process.³ A different view of experience as well as a new relationship between the mind and body ultimately gave rise to a radical change in the perceptual order and societal expectations of it.

Laclos's *Les Liaisons dangereuses* and Sade's *La Philosophie dans le boudoir,* both of which present educational projects aimed at upsetting the existing norm, depict an inverted image of the statue-man's characteristics of curiosity, surprise, and movement.⁴ According to sensationist logic, these attributes generate more sensations and hence greater mental activity, resulting ultimately in more ideas and knowledge. Seen by sensationists not only as ideal but also as necessary parts of man's sensitive, psychological constitution for the acquisition of ideas, these characteristics can, however, be deviated from their utopian ends for

---

genitals and does not "besmirch with mud but with excrement and urine." See *Rabelais and His World,* p. 147.

3. Implicated with sensationism is the related philosophy of materialism, which is also perverted, although to a lesser degree. Materialism's extension of sensationist principles, the subject of a separate chapter, should not be confused with the perversion of sensationism.

4. These traits, which can be found in the description of the statue-man in Condillac's *Traité des sensations* and which are outlined in Chapter 4 of the present study, constitute, as it were, some of the factors contributing to knowledge as they appear in the writing of the sensationists. Bonnet and Helvétius follow Condillac in giving primacy to behavior characterized by these qualities. It is noteworthy that Laclos's libertines are quite aware of their educational project of composing a "catechism of debauchery." See Laclos, *Les Liaisons dangereuses,* in *Oeuvres complètes,* ed. Laurent Versini (Paris: Gallimard, 1979), 110: 256. This reference and all subsequent references to this text indicate first the number of the letter, then the page number in Gallimard's Pléiade edition; hereafter cited as, for example (*LD* 110: 256).

Sade's libertines also take their task as teachers seriously. The subtitle of the work by Sade used here, *Les Instituteurs immoraux,* makes their pedagogical responsibility explicit. Yet this does not keep the piece from having a tone of merry revelry. Bataille calls it a "humorous book connecting horror and jest." His interpretation echoes his attempt to link laughing to death and eroticism. See Georges Bataille, *Les Larmes d'Eros* (Paris: Pauvert, 1961 and 1971), pp. 75 and 115.

According to Jean Deprun, Sade exhibits full knowledge of the "sensationist vulgate," which he modifies at times with materialist qualifications denying the existence of a soul or God. See Deprun, "Sade philosophe," in Sade, *Oeuvres* ed. Michel Delon (Paris: Gallimard, 1990), 1: lxii–lxiii.

Both Laclos's and Sade's libertine characters generally use one of the century's prevailing philosophies to subvert its culture. "Not unlike Merteuil in the *Liaisons dangereuses,*" write Max Horkheimer and Theodor W. Adorno, "Juliette embodies (in psychological terms) neither unsublimated nor regressive libido, but intellectual pleasure in regression—*amor intellectualis diaboli,* the pleasure of attacking civilization with its own weapons." See Horkheimer and Adorno, *Dialectic of Enlightenment,* trans. John Cumming (New York: Herder and Herder, 1972), p. 94.

perverse educational purposes. Instead of cultivating the mind of their victims, libertines degrade it and elevate the body. Frequently, as in the case of the young Cécile Volanges, the victim shares the inexperienced situation of the statue-man, having neither really "seen" nor "known" anything, but endowed with innate curiosity (*LD* 3: 15; 4: 17). As masters of distraction, rakes entrap characters whose curiosity can indeed prove to be, in accordance with the popular proverb for their feline counterparts, lethal.[5] Valmont refers paternalistically to the Présidente de Tourvel as his "aimable curieuse," who can no more keep a secret than she can refrain from reading his letter of seduction (*LD* 23: 49; 34: 71). He smugly relies on her curiosity.

For their part, libertines find curiosity useful both in exploiting others' weaknesses and in rendering themselves invincible. Following sensationist principles, Merteuil recognizes its instructional utility but also realizes she must hide from those observing her the reaction she might have to the objects that her curiosity would normally lead her to seek (*LD* 81: 171). For the eighteenth-century ethos of sensibility based on uncontrolled curiosity *inter alia,* such a dominion over one's natural feelings requires an act of will so far superior to that of mere mortals as to border on the terrifyingly inhuman or the grotesquely monstrous. Beauty being determined, however, in the eye of the beholder, what sensitive eighteenth-century readers presumably consider as hideous becomes divine from the point of view of libertines who pride them-

5. Folklore also associates curiosity with death. See in particular the moral at the end of *Blue Beard,* in *Perrault's Fairy Tales,* trans. A. E. Johnson (New York: Dover, 1969), p. 43:

Ladies, you should never pry,—
You'll repent it by and by!
'Tis the silliest of sins;
Trouble in a trice begins.
There are, surely—more's the woe!
Lots of things you need not know.
Come, forswear it now and here—
Joy so brief, that costs so dear!

The French original retains the key word, "curiosity": "La curiosité malgré tous ses attraits, / Coûte souvent bien des regrets." See Perrault, *Contes,* ed. Jean-Pierre Collinet (Paris: Gallimard, 1981), p. 154.

The curiosity in Blue Beard's wives leads not only to the discovery of the forbidden chamber housing the bodies of his previous wives and to greater knowledge, but also to capital punishment. This folktale thus makes a further indirect connection between knowledge and crime, which becomes explicit in the works of Sade.

selves on their self-control, which allows them to dominate the minds of their victims. This is nonetheless significantly different from the healthy self-control recommended by Descartes in *Les Passions de l'âme*.

Curiosity and monstrosity are also paired in Sade's *La Philosophie dans le boudoir*. Radically different from either Condillac's or Bonnet's statue, interested as it was in the varying and often subtle degrees of olfactory distinctions among flowers, Dolmancé is attracted out of curiosity toward an enormous bodily part on Mirvel, a part whose very use is inverted in the act of sodomy.[6] In the process, Sade gives sensationism a cruel turnaround. Mocking the lofty intellectual value sensationists attribute to curiosity as the foreplay to ideas, Sade keeps it as an integral part of anyone's education but reduces its domain to genital organs or bizarre forms of orgasm.

The statue-man is also easily surprised by the number of new and different sensations in his environment. A constant state of surprise serves at first to underline one's acute sensibility but weakens over time as one's knowledge of diverse situations increases. Many eighteenth-century protagonists tend to replicate the initial, highly sensitive moments of the statue-man's existence, but they eventually progress towards reason or virtue. For their narrow purposes, libertines later in the century's literature maintain their victims in an early developmental state of pure sensation while they themselves, having reached the stage of rational premeditation, feign an innocent surprise. Their actions result in the regressive behavior, pain, and destruction of their victims and are devoid of any of the positive signs the sensationists found in surprise.

As one might expect, Laclos and Sade ridicule any otherwise beneficial effects of surprise. Representing the sensitive person *par excellence*, the Présidente "can neither dissimulate nor combat the impression [she] feels" and remarks on the state of "astonishment and confusion" in which she finds herself after Valmont's scheming (*LD* 26: 56). Merteuil, on the other hand, has mastered the art of dissimulation. She

---

6. Donatien-Alphonse-François, comte [marquis] de Sade, *La Philosophie dans le boudoir, ou Les Instituteurs immoraux*, ed. Yvon Belaval (Paris: Gallimard, 1976), p. 43; hereafer cited as (*PB*).

Pierre Klossowski also points out the derisiveness as well as the destructiveness of the act of sodomy, which at once apes and thwarts the process of reproduction necessary for the propagation of the species. See Klossowski, *Le Philosophe scélérat* (Paris: Editions du Seuil, 1947 and 1967), p. 32.

can make her eyes speak the "language of surprise" so that those who see her are duped into believing in her great sensibility, which is nothing more than a mask, albeit one that hides a diabolical laugh (*LD* 85: 186). Because of her sensitivity, the Présidente is doomed to remain surprised, merely reacting to planned schemes and never able to proceed to a rational level on which she could act freely and perform equally with Valmont. Merteuil, for her part, exploits sensory appearances to control others' thoughts. Contrary to the sensationist view of the cognitive process, sensibility here stands as an obstacle to freedom and reason. In a total turnaround, a catalyst has become an impediment, as the lower goal of the body is substituted for the higher one of the mind.[7]

Nor does the body of the victim experience any lasting pleasure, since Laclos and Sade generally associate surprise with pain. Such a rule applies to the victims as well as their families. Mme de Volanges writes to Mme de Rosemonde about her daughter's unhappy plight: "I stride, my dear friend, from one surprise to the next, and from one form of grief to another" (*LD* 170: 375). Sade's *Justine,* which appeared a few years before his *Philosophie dans le boudoir,* relates a seemingly endless list of perverse tortures and sexual acts that never cease to amaze the heroine without enlightening her.[8] Novelty of experience indeed yields surprise, as the sensationists had pointed out, but not necessarily pleasure or new ideas. Every libertine Justine encounters has some novel and surprising way of heightening his own pleasure at the expense of his victim's suffering. Moreover, the protagonist remains locked in a state of utter bewilderment, incapable of deriving any useful ideas from her numerous, painful experiences.

In perverse fashion, libertines undo the very creative potential for moments of surprise by frequently making them a prelude not to a new constructive order but to destruction. Laclos and Sade deliberately intend to break the icons of the Enlightenment—one of the most important of which was sensationism's mental construct of the statue— just as Rabelais overturns and degrades the Middle Ages' sacred image

7. Whereas the body enslaves the victims of libertines, it serves to liberate the libertines themselves. See Colette Cazenobe, *Le Système du libertinage de Crébillon à Laclos,* Studies on Voltaire and the Eighteenth Century, 282 (Oxford: Voltaire Foundation, 1991), p. 342.

8. See Sade, *Justine, ou Les Malheurs de la vertu,* in *Oeuvres,* ed. Michel Delon, vol. 2 (Paris: Gallimard, 1995), hereafter cited as (*J*). Although not the specific object of this chapter's scrutiny, *Justine* proves useful in the present analysis for the examples it provides that complement those from *La Philosophie dans le boudoir.*

of woman as an object of religious or courtly reverence. These authors tarnish the high intellectual standing of the sensationist statue in ways similar to those employed in *Pantagruel* by Rabelais, whose character Panurge causes a great lady to be followed by a large pack of dogs that urinate on her dress.[9] According to the reasoning implicit in the work of Laclos and Sade, the statue's surprise deserves not to be exalted but belittled and shown for what it really is, namely, nothing more than a sensationist mystification of knowledge. Our innate capacity for surprise does not help us build a greater stockpile of ideas, so to speak, or a better world. Instead, it reflects our ignorance and destroys what we may have previously created. Stagnation and destruction characterize the educational process in the literature of Laclos and Sade. If the literary characters make any progress at all, it has a distinctly libertine mark to it and redounds to the detriment, not the advancement, of society. Their denial of their own and others' existence—what Sade was to call "apathy"—allows them to commit untold destructive acts of cruelty.[10] Ultimately, they studiously unlearn what they already know, retaining only whatever helps them further their libertine goals. In order to do so, they must take new models to guide them.

The resulting educational process of repetition and imitation once again resembles that followed by the statue, but its ends if not its means differ radically from those of sensationism. Whereas this latter school of thought considers sensations as indispensable for the acquisition of ideas, Laclos and Sade consider them as ends in themselves. The means have become the end, as the body is substituted for the mind in the inverted educational hierarchy. The repetition of sensations therefore never takes on intellectual content, as it presumably does in the statue. If it has a pedagogical function at all, it serves to reinforce the desired goal of apathy in libertines themselves, desensitizing them to the sometimes terrible consequences of their actions. Eugénie thus comes to resemble Saint-Ange in her cold indifference to the suffering she causes. Libertines ensure the vacuity of the cognitive process for their victims, however, by giving themselves as models to be imitated. Repetition itself is subverted on the epistemological level not so much because the actions or sensations repeated are not one's own—most

9. For Bakhtin's treatment of this episode and the discussion of his Gallic attitude toward woman, see *Rabelais and His World*, pp. 229, 239–42.

10. See Maurice Blanchot, *Lautréamont et Sade* (Paris: Les Editions de Minuit, 1963), pp. 36–37, 45.

educational systems call for a tutor or model of some kind—but because the tutor here cultivates sensations gratuitously. Sensationism did assume the presence of the same sensitive being throughout different sensory experiences. But it especially saw in sensation much more than mere pleasure. The repetition of sensations served to differentiate them from others and to allow one to progress in one's own knowledge, whereas for the libertine it serves merely to prolong pleasure. As does any model for imitation, the libertine introduces a certain discontinuity in the learning process. A disruption occurs in the chain of events seen by sensationism as necessary for an individual's education. For the student's repetition or imitation, the libertine presents sensations, feelings, or ideas that do not belong to the novice. While assimilating a lesson, students normally reappropriate this intellectual baggage for themselves, modifying it to suit their own specific circumstances. It does not continue to remain the exclusive property of the tutor, as it were. The link previously opened in the cognitive chain closes, and the continuity as well as the integrity of the individual's education is reinstated. But libertines unrelentingly corrupt the process by encouraging a servile imitation and repetition of a lesson. They can justifiably speak of their empire over their victims, whose thoughts libertines actually control insofar as they continue to possess these thoughts. Once they possess another's sensations, feelings, and ideas, libertines in effect possess the whole person. Danceny notes this total dependence on the libertine model, whose welfare also involves his own safety: "In the matter of dangers, you alone must judge: I cannot plan anything, and I confine myself to beseeching you to look after your safety, because I cannot be calm when you are worried. For this purpose, it is not the two of us who are but one, it is you who are both of us" (*LD* 150: 344). Thus, the death of a libertine, as in Valmont's case, entails the death of one victim, the Présidente, and the living death in a convent of another, Cécile. Repetition in education does not automatically lead to the birth of ideas, as it does in sensationism, but at times to crime, monstrosity, or death.[11]

In this context, libertines can be said to have demonic or vampiric qualities. By achieving a definitive break in the so-called flow of knowl-

11. As Klossowski points out, "Reiteration is at first the desired condition for the monster to remain at the level of monstrosity." By repeating criminal acts in "absolute apathy," one stays in a "permanent state of transgression." See *Le Philosophe scélérat*, p. 39.

On the notion of monstrosity, see Marie-Hélène Huet, *Monstrous Imagination* (Cambridge, Mass.: Harvard University Press, 1993).

edge back to their victim's brains, libertines also realize a deviation in the flow of their hapless prey's blood. Justine learns that bleedings are commonplace events designed wholly for the satisfaction of rakes in their isolated retreats (*J* 290). Merteuil and Saint-Ange destroy individual thinking even as they substitute themselves for the victim's actual mother. Cécile and Eugénie lose both their minds and their hearts. Cécile delights in Merteuil's maternal affection for her without suspecting in the least its motivations (*LD* 29: 62). From the libertine's point of view, mothers stand in the way of unbridled pleasure and deserve ridicule if not actual punishment. As first a victim, then a pupil, Cécile becomes a willing accomplice of Valmont when he makes her laugh uncontrollably at her mother's ways (*LD* 109: 252). Dolmancé and Saint-Ange teach Eugénie that it is natural to hate one's mother, and they solicit with little resistance her active participation in her mother's rape and infection by a syphilitic valet (*PB* 64–65, 282–84). The late Enlightenment dashes the hopes of the *philosophes* for progress through positive repetition in the educational process, for this characteristic of the statue-man can be shown to produce insensitive, mechanical zombies. As their conscience or soul is constantly subjected to reiterated assaults, it deteriorates as a moral basis for action.[12]

Additionally, the related characteristic of movement in the statue-man becomes the object of outright scorn in the hands of Laclos and Sade. Moving physically from one object to the next and, by extension, from one sensation to another, the statue comes to know both itself and its environment better, as it learns to differentiate between itself and the appreciably diverse and different world it inhabits. Hence, the importance of travel in the period's literature. Laclos and Sade present an anti-*Bildungsroman* in their work. Their characters do not evolve toward some end desirable for society at large such as enhanced understanding or moral progress but stagnate in a circular pattern of repetition. Although a prodigy of personal development and growth, Merteuil contributes nothing to society and reflects the decadence of a libertine aristocracy. Even when libertines do travel, their trips are unproductive in a cognitive sense. Barthes makes such a point about Sade, but it could also be made for libertines in general, including

12. From the libertine perspective, such a development can be interpreted as a step forward in one's education, although not everyone may be capable of it. Certain innate qualities are required of the students whom the libertines are instructing. In this sense, the libertine code is antipopulist and aristocratic. See Julie C. Hayes, " 'Aristocrate ou démocrate? Vous me le direz': Sade's Political Pamphlets," *Eighteenth-Century Studies* 23 (1989), 24–41.

Laclos's: "Sadean roaming is *improper,* not because it is lascivious and criminal, but because it is dull and as though it were trivial, excluded from any transcendence, without any time limit: it does not reveal, transform, nurture, educate, sublimate, achieve, or regain anything, if not the present itself, cut off, dazzling, repeated. . . ."[13]

The libertine code, which as we have seen produces few positive results, is based to a large degree on movement or action, albeit in one place. Because of her desire to pull Danceny out of "his indolence, or to punish him for it," Merteuil cannot sleep one night (*LD* 63: 122). Valmont savors "les grands mouvements" for the particular delight they give him (*LD* 144: 333). Rakes fiendishly confuse movements of the mind and heart with those of the body and sensations. The ensuing mixture takes on grotesque proportions when the thin veils of *bienséance* or seemliness in *Les Liaisons dangereuses* are stripped away, as they are in Sade's writings. Sade crudely reduces the educational aspects of movement to that which gives pleasure. Any or all bodily parts of several people move according to the orchestrations of maestro Dolmancé in dizzying geometric and orgiastic configurations that defy the reader's imagination. Mocking the instructional value of movement, Sade transfers it totally from the mind to the body, whose genital organs seem to stay in a state of perpetual motion. Seen as the "first and most beautiful quality of nature," movement in the natural world extends of course in Sadean logic to the human body and is maintained by crime (*J* 190). The libertine imperative for movement thus explains not only the long list of perverse sexual acts but also the innumerable crimes of infanticide, matricide, rape, murder, and torture perpetrated by Sade's heroes. As an impetus for the century's major intellectual achievements, movement is thus ridiculed and shown to be capable of producing results diametrically opposed to those sought by the *philosophes.*

In the eighteenth century, the word *movement* had in addition to its usage for physical displacement an important metaphysical one and referred to the activity of the heart or soul. This can be seen, for instance, in the difference between the entry for *movement* in Antoine Furetière's *Dictionnaire universel,* which keeps a wholly figurative sense in psychological and spiritual matters, and in tome 10 of the *Encyclopédie* (1765), where the term begins to assume an increasingly physical sense in the same domains. Because the period took such a

---

13. Roland Barthes, *Sade, Fourier, Loyola* (Paris: Editions du Seuil, 1971), pp. 153–54.

vitalistic view of sensibility, the lack of movement in space or in one's inner being was associated with death. The prudish Présidente attempts to put herself out of reach of any danger by staying in one place during her husband's absence (*LD* 11: 33). Her geographical stability does not, however, ensure the immobility of her heart. She thus wrongly believes, as Valmont will soon show her, that one can immure oneself to the movements of the heart.[14] Letters suffice, as Danceny points out, to give a "portrait of the soul," and indeed, insofar as they communicate "all our movements" are preferable to physical portraits (*LD* 150: 345). As soon as the Présidente makes the fatal mistake of writing a letter to Valmont, she falls into his trap of exposing her soul to him. Movement of this kind becomes transformed into observable action only at the much later stage in the scene of seduction, which usually takes place on an ottoman in Laclos's novel. Although libertines often prefer actions to words, or doing to telling, they inevitably spend much of their time relating the movements leading up to their glorious moments of action. Moreover, the stories or harangues of Sade's characters function as a kind of creative verbal foreplay to subsequent erotic exercises. From a sensationist perspective, movements of the soul already constitute action inasmuch as sensibility entails the vibration of inner fibers, which may not be seen but which is nonetheless experienced.[15] Exteriorized and literalized in Sade as the body is turned inside out in a gyrating, pulsating mass, movements operate in Laclos on the subtle level of language. Not only can language reveal movements of the heart to the well-trained eye, but it can itself also serve to hide them and twist meaning.

In this latter function, libertine language becomes highly ironic and undermines the clear expression sought by sensationism. (Indeed, in his last work, *La Langue des calculs*, Condillac strove to create a language that would have the clarity of mathematics.) The irony in question, however, is one to which only the libertines and not their victims are privy. Through it, they indeed establish their mastery over their victims. *Double-entendre* and confusion triumph over one-sided readings and analytic reasoning. Valmont revels in his cruelly ironic letter to the Présidente, in which he manages to speak at once the devout language of sensibility and the shameless language of libertine

---

14. Diderot's *La Religieuse* also demonstrates the futility of this enterprise behind the walls of a convent.

15. See esp. Bonnet, *Essai analytique*, p. 152 passim.

desire. Writing from the bed and on the body of Emilie, one of his lovers, he can perfectly maintain both registers of discourse at the same time. "Never," he states "have I had so much pleasure in writing you . . . the very table on which I am writing you, consecrated for the first time to this use, becomes for me the sacred altar of love. . . ." (*LD* 48: 99). The words "table" and "altar" here each have two different referents that are inseparably fused so that any distinct notion of the words proves impossible. As in the carnival, what is elevated to the level of the sacred is also lowered to the profane and bodily realm. Consequently, any straightforward language becomes laughable or turned around. Merteuil uses the terms "most unpleasant, and impossible to foresee" to describe to Mme de Volanges the frolicsome and premeditated adventure she has just had with Prévan (*LD* 87: 194). The language employed is exactly opposed to the actual events or circumstances. In Sade, one is indeed prompted to laugh at the sound of the word "heart" in the mouth of Saint-Ange or Dolmancé as well as at references to temples of Venus (*PB* 49, 106; *J* 230).

Beyond their thorough perversion of the educational process as ideally perceived by sensationism, Laclos and Sade also sometimes took to task the sensibility that this philosophy always considered an innate part of our being. Sensibility is stripped of any redeeming moral qualities and coldly revealed as a mere capacity for pleasure or pain, which can be accounted for in quantitative terms. Hence, the so-called economy of desire that prevails in much eighteenth-century literature but that takes on particularly insensitive characteristics toward the end of the period. Simply put, pleasure has positive value. Pain, however, is more ambiguous. Endured when it possibly leads to pleasure or even valued when it increases pleasure, pain cannot always be avoided. Moreover, it represents a currency of sorts for libertines. Valmont speaks a thinly disguised commercial language in referring to the Présidente: "This woman is doubtlessly worth my giving myself so many cares; one day they will be my titles to her; and having, in a way, thus paid for her in advance, I shall have the right to do with her as I please, without having to reproach myself for my actions" (*LD* 21: 47).[16] The trouble Valmont

---

16. On the system of exchange in this novel, see Anne Deneys, "The Political Economy of the Body in the *Liaisons dangereuses* of Choderlos de Laclos," in *Eroticism and the Body Politic*, ed. Lynn Hunt (Baltimore: Johns Hopkins University Press, 1991), pp. 41–49.

goes to in pursuing the Présidente evidently causes him a certain amount of pain, which he will later use as his rightful and legitimate claim to have purchased her favors.[17] The period of three months he toils for the week or so of pure enjoyment shows an unquestionable sense of economy on his part: perseverance in pain, on the one hand, and deferment of pleasure, on the other (*LD* 133: 309). The vicious and fatal war game between Valmont and Merteuil begins largely as a question over personal worth in an economy of desire. Offended at the amount of time and effort Valmont has spent on the Présidente, Merteuil complains, "I am not worth your giving yourself so much pain" (*LD* 152: 349). For libertines of their ilk constantly preoccupied with the going rate of exchange for the desire they elicit, a battle for supremacy is sooner or later inevitable. The price demanded to avoid it in the form of a sacrifice appears too great to either one.

The very notion of sacrifice, a word used repeatedly in a voluntary or involuntary sense in *Les Liaisons dangereuses,* becomes twisted as Laclos mocks its traditional religious meanings as well as any positive value it may have had for the sensationists as a partial synonym for experience.[18] Although the term evokes the libertine jargon used throughout the century, it takes on a dark, sinister meaning and involves greater stakes in the late Enlightenment than it had previously. The will to power and domination by an entire subculture of libertines makes the sacrifices of their virtuous victims seem like a kind of immoral cleansing of society.[19] Bereft of any spiritual content, the sacrifices that take place in the works of Laclos and Sade have purely physical goals and do not bring enlightenment. Typically, the term applies in general to the amount of pain or absence of pleasure in the present endured for some ulterior pleasure. In religion, it has been shown to be the "ritual

17. He speaks of "cares and pains" in the same breath in a subsequent letter (110: 254), thereby reinforcing the association between the two words.

18. It bears pointing out here that sensationists view the entire learning process as long and difficult, although not entirely devoid of pleasurable moments. Its difficulty thus explains education's painful aspects, which give rise to the notion of the sacrifice required for the acquisition of knowledge.

19. The genocidal overtones of such a project, which is no longer an idle exercise in libertine banter and which takes on military proportions, become apparent only in the light of our century. Horkheimer and Adorno discern, as did many Jews, a "dialectical link between enlightenment and domination, and the dual relationship of progress to cruelty and liberation . . . in the great philosophers of the Enlightenment." See *Dialectic of Enlightenment,* p. 169 passim.

violation of a prohibiting order or decree" that allows those engaged in it to transcend the greatest possible anguish.[20] Although the general sense of the term holds for these works, one also detects a conscious transgression and a quasi-religious transcendence in the sacrifices described in them. Valmont speaks, for example, of the long days his aunt, Mme de Rosemonde, has asked him to sacrifice for her in the countryside by playing a card game with her, the local pastor, and the Présidente (LD 4: 17). Presumably, a stay in the tranquil countryside painfully keeps a libertine like Valmont from the lively cosmopolitan pleasures of the city. The three months—not all of which are without intermittent moments of pleasure—he ultimately spends pursuing the Présidente constitute more or less a voluntary sacrifice in this sense.

Although libertines do not mind sacrificing themselves by their own free will for their own purposes, they resent being sacrificed against their will for someone else's designs. This other sense of sacrifice, which is involuntary, moves them to anger and their victims to despair. Valmont is enraged at the thought of being "sacrificed" to Mme de Volanges, who is responsible for lowering his image in the Présidente's eyes and vows to punish her by corrupting her daughter (LD 44: 92). This sense of involuntary sacrifice humiliates a libertine of Valmont's stature, as the reader witnesses in Valmont's reaction to being sacrificed to Vressac by the viscountess de M . . . (LD 71: 140).

The victims of libertine excesses naturally share a certain amount of this other sense of involuntary sacrifice, however much they may participate willingly in their own ruin. It bespeaks the natural state of sensibility that all human beings presumably possess and into which we are born, according to Rousseau.[21] As Carol Blum has demonstrated, however, the involuntary feeling Rousseau has his characters trust as an innocent and good emanation of a virtuous heart can be exploited by libertines.[22] Their victims are convinced by them to give themselves over to these feelings but confuse in their minds heartfelt feelings and

20. Bataille, L'Erotisme (Paris: Les Editions de Minuit, 1957), pp. 29, 92, 98, 121. Bataille calls the sacred that element which is revealed in a victim's sacrificial death. He believes that it helps the participants witness a profound sense of the continuity of being they are ultimately seeking. See also René Girard, Violence and the Sacred, trans. Patrick Gregory (Baltimore: Johns Hopkins University Press, 1977).

21. Rousseau, Discours sur l'origine et les fondements de l'inégalité parmi les hommes, in Oeuvres complètes (Paris: Gallimard, 1964), 3: 125–26.

22. See Carol Blum, "Styles of Cognition as Moral Options in La Nouvelle Héloïse and Les Liaisons dangereuses," PMLA 88 (1973), 289–98.

sexual impulses. Consequently, their involuntary sacrifices take on a natural quality that justifies the reiteration of erotic behavior and ensures their downfall. In a remarkable feat of seduction, three different women, all of whom are intimate friends, and their lovers are almost simultaneously "sacrificed" to the rakish Prévan (*LD* 79: 162). Because of the brevity of this narrative episode, it is difficult to follow the transition from these victims' unconscious to their conscious sense of sacrifice. Clearly, though, they do not begin their dangerous liaison with Prévan as willing participants in their own degradation. Like them, the Présidente does not initially suspect the full extent of the sacrifice she must make for Valmont. Before she meets him, her sacrifices tend to follow those prescribed by the Church, involving restrained, pious behavior in this world so as to enjoy fully the next; spiritual concerns take precedence over physical ones. Such an order is totally reversed by the literature of Laclos and Sade in the late French Enlightenment. One follows step by step the Présidente's painful decline. She becomes increasingly aware of the exact nature of her sacrifice and does not hesitate to use the word to describe her experience. It indeed changes from an involuntary to a voluntary one.

Unlike the sacrifices a libertine may make, however, the victim's voluntary sacrifices typically ensure continued pain and self-destruction rather than pleasure and self-aggrandizement. Writing to Mme de Rose-monde about the painful distance she must keep from Valmont, the Présidente complains of the futility of her sacrifices: "Currently isolated in my painful solitude from everything that is dear to me, face to face with my misfortune, every moment of my sad existence is marked by tears, and nothing sweetens the bitterness of it, no consolation is mixed with my sacrifices: and those that I have made up until now only serve to make more painful for me those I still have to make" (*LD* 108: 250). The letter from Valmont that she mentions later in this same passage also represents another sacrifice. She is desperate to open it but knows she must not. In effect, these sacrifices slowly kill the Présidente, leaving her ultimately neither with any lasting pleasure nor with any eternal reward. With each sacrifice the Présidente makes for him, Valmont grows in power at her expense until at last he is the "possessor" or owner of her existence (*LD* 128: 299). While Valmont sacrifices himself for the Présidente and "buys" her, the Présidente sacrifices herself to him. Even in her prayers before her confessor in which she subjects herself to God's justice if He will pardon Valmont, the Présidente's final act is one of sacrifice. In a perverted version of religious sacrifice, most if not all of the characters in Laclos's novel are engaged in this ritualistic behavior.

Such behavior does not result in elevation of spirits and godliness, however, but in demonism and moral depravity. Sacrifices ironically raise libertines to divinities worshiped by those whom they have possessed, degraded, and compelled to voluntary sacrifices in their honor. The certain sign of the Présidente's depravity comes with her indignant response to being "sacrificed" to Valmont's courtesan friend Emilie, "a vile creature" not worthy of his time and effort (*LD* 135: 315; 149: 342). At this point her discourse begins to resemble that of Merteuil, for whom sacrifices represent matters of exchange in an economy of desire. For libertines—and by using the word "sacrifice" in this way the Présidente reveals that she has become one—they are acceptable only insofar as they remain voluntary.

As suggested earlier, Merteuil and Valmont declare a libertine's war on each other when neither one agrees fully to accept a sacrifice. In their case, the term takes on both meanings discussed above. In refusing a sacrifice for the other person, they both reject any voluntary or involuntary action of this sort. Responding to Valmont's proposal for the two of them to reunite in an amorous relationship, Merteuil writes a statement that makes the question of sacrifice a central issue for their ensuing letters: "I would demand sacrifices that surely you could not or would not make for me . . ." (*LD* 131: 307).

The novel's very *dénouement* hinges on the question of sacrifice between two powerful libertines. As this proves impossible, the stage is set for a battle of the titans. Merteuil makes a verbal stab at Valmont's libertine pride, based as it is on the dominance he maintains over his own and others' behavior, by claiming him incapable of sacrificing the Présidente to her. Moreover, knowing full well the pleasure Valmont derives from the Présidente and the ennui he feels with his young student, Merteuil rejects his offer of Cécile, whom he is willing to sacrifice, and demands that he stay with her. In a word, she twists the nature of the voluntary sacrifice with Cécile and calls for an involuntary sacrifice with the Présidente, both of which she knows would cause Valmont pain. The two-sided assault on his will forces him into the difficult position of keeping the person he wants to abandon and abandoning the person he wants to keep. When Valmont does superficially sacrifice the Présidente to her, Merteuil does not take his actions seriously and believes them to be prompted out of vanity rather than the total obedience she seeks: "Yes, viscount, you loved Madame de

Tourvel a lot, and you even love her still; you are madly in love with her: but because I enjoyed making you ashamed of it, you gallantly sacrificed her. You would have sacrificed a thousand of them, rather than suffer a joke" (*LD* 145: 333; see also 152: 350).

As his reward Valmont nonetheless seeks Danceny's sacrifice from Merteuil, without which he would feel duped. For Merteuil, any involuntary sacrifice is out of the question, for she claims to have her way always in the end. Moreover, she does not even want anyone to assume the right to complain about her free will, since as she says, "I wanted to deceive only for my pleasure, and not out of necessity" (*LD* 152: 348). Not only would she not accept any pain in the sacrifice of Danceny, but she refuses in this instance to give pleasure to Valmont, preferring to keep it entirely for herself. If Valmont is to enjoy any pleasure, he must pay for it with his own sacrifices, not hers. Referring to the trouble Valmont has taken to learn about Danceny's visits, Merteuil taunts her rival, "You gave yourself much pain to be informed about them, is it not true? Well! are you any further along in this matter for having done so? I hope you derived a lot of pleasure from your investigation; as for me, it did not harm my own" (*LD* 152: 349). Questioning the cognitive benefits of pain and sacrifice, Merteuil casts doubt on the entire sensationist project of acquiring knowledge. In a perversion of this philosophy's goals, pleasure alone emerges as the desired product of our daily toils. Nothing so grandiose as intellectual or spiritual enlightenment springs forth from the painful sacrifices of experience, no matter how finely tuned the libertine's or any other character's rational skills may be. Any vision of utopia consequently disappears. Sacrifices do not lift these characters up in either a mental or moral way but continually plunge them back into the world of sensation governed by pleasure and pain. The repeated sacrifices in Sade's works brutally reinforce the already dismal and circular sensory existence depicted by Laclos. Far from generating ideas or elevated states of the soul, experience is continually reduced to the body's sensations of pleasure and pain.

To the contrary, Laclos's and Sade's works from this period debase the very notion of the soul, with which sensibility was closely related, associating it more and more explicitly with the body and especially its lower parts. Over the century as increasing importance was attributed to physiology and clinical observations, the soul gradually becomes assimilated to the body.[23] To their own astonishment later, since Condil-

---

23. Little wonder then that one of the best collections of works in the United States on

lac was an abbot, the sensationists themselves started the process by introducing sensations—connected as they are to the physical world—as necessary elements for ideas. Respectful sensationists like Condillac and Bonnet referred most often to the conduit through which sensations passed as the *âme* or soul. Rarely did they refer to it as the mind, and practically never as the brain. As the materialistically oriented sensationist Helvétius discovered when his book *De l'esprit* was banned, one must be careful in the mid-eighteenth century not to overstep the limits imposed by the Church regarding the affinities between the soul and the brain. By the end of the century, however, scientific discoveries and the political atmosphere allowed writers to make such delicate connections more easily. The vague, delicious movements of the soul with which Danceny innocently is enraptured in Cécile's and Merteuil's letters are not far removed from those that constitute the former's "pleasure machine" and the latter's cold, mechanistic rationality (*LD* 106: 244; 150: 345). In short, the soul is shown to be a machine or an object inseparable from the body.

For the soul, traditionally viewed as the repository of such sacred faculties as conscience and understanding, any association with the body already represents a degradation. In Laclos's writings, the association between soul and body proves to be quite clear. Perhaps no image in the novel depicts this as poignantly as does that of Merteuil's face, which at the end has been hideously disfigured by a case of smallpox that has caused her to lose an eye. The inverted world is summed up by one observer: "The marquis de ***, who does not miss the chance to make a malicious remark, said yesterday, while speaking of her, that the illness had turned her inside out, and that now her soul was on her face. Unfortunately everyone found the expression to be accurate" (*LD* 175: 385). The self-righteous members of French society who jeer at Merteuil are no doubt justified in recognizing her monstrosity. But they fail to acknowledge that the transposition of the soul to the face, from the inside to the outside world—a substitution of the physical for the metaphysical—has already occurred in them, also. Too many other

---

sensationism and the related movements of materialism and *idéologie* is to be found at the National Library of Medicine in Bethesda, Md.

On the rise of modern medical science toward the end of the century, see David B. Morris, *The Culture of Pain* (Berkeley and Los Angeles: University of California Press, 1991), esp. his chap. "Sex, Pain, and the Marquis de Sade," pp. 224–43. "Medicine is foundational for Sade," states Morris, who also interprets Sadean pain as "the sign of a radically and wholly secular truth: the truth of the material body" (pp. 225, 233).

examples in the novel (Cécile, Danceny, the Présidente, not to mention Valmont, Merteuil, Prévan, and the members of the libertine milieu that dominates the novel's upside-down atmosphere) give the lie to any notion of the soul as existing anywhere other than in the physical, external world. It is not without importance that Laclos dramatically chooses the final pages of his novel to reveal the physicality of the soul, a characteristic that deprives it of any grandeur that ecclesiastics or sensationists would claim for it.

The humiliation that someone like Merteuil or one of Sade's characters feels at the association of soul and body becomes all the more apparent as the corporeal space in question coincides with areas for purely sexual behavior. In its exclusively physical aspects, the soul thus defined is concerned only with pleasure and pain. The raw, palpitating, fleshly mass that Sade serves the reader is all that remains of the soul. He has removed even the slightest pretensions of the soul to anything great or noble, pretensions that still exist at least on the surface in Laclos. There is no need to look within his characters' metaphysical souls, for they are completely empty of anything that sensationism or the ethos of sensibility tried to invest them with. No sublime ideas, no sentimental or beautiful feelings inhabit the Sadean soul. Saint-Ange locates the seat of "all women's sensibility" not in the heart or even the brain but in the clitoris and thereby demystifies in one reductive naming perhaps the most cherished human characteristic of the century (*PB* 61). Her language for sensibility belongs to the crass world of the marketplace and lowers it from the ethereal to the purely sexual. To understand the extent of this debasement, one must realize that although its sexual component was never completely denied, sensibility represented for the period one of humanity's greatest hopes for the progress and refinement of civilization. Identifying it with a specific sexual organ represents an immeasurable fall from grace, to say the least. Similarly, Sade calls the heart a "sacred organ," which in other contexts may not appear particularly shocking (*PB* 106). Alert to Sade's materialistic and perverse bent, the informed reader, however, quickly assimilates not only the corporeal but also the sexual connotation of the word "organ" in Sade. Like sensibility, with which it is often connected, the heart loses any figurative sense, as the writers at the end of the century degrade it through repeated associations with the physical and carnival world of the material bodily lower stratum.

However much libertines may reduce almost everything to physical enjoyment, the mind nevertheless continues to play an active role. Its activity focuses not on the acquisition of more ideas, as sensationism would have it, but on the sheer accumulation of pleasures. In an inversion of the sensationist formula, ideas serve sensations; reason and self-interest do not explain human behavior; and the mind justifies bodily delights.[24] As Saint-Ange counsels Eugénie, it takes only "a little bit of reflection" to rationalize a devil-may-care attitude toward public opinion of morality and a life of *fouterie* (*PB* 84). One must use one's wits (*esprit*) "to taste all pleasures" and show true genius, which will "break all the restraints of ignorance and stupidity" (*PB* 109). In addressing the question of genius, Sade strikes at the core of a central concern of the sensationists and *philosophes*. The words could easily be found in a number of passages from Helvétius's works. But in a complete turnaround, Sade substitutes ignorance in the ingenious means of obtaining physical pleasure for the ignorance and stupidity the *philosophes* associated with religious intolerance and all manner of prejudices. The intelligence derived from long experience with sensations promotes not a social or political agenda, as the sensationists might argue, but diversity of pleasurable occasions. Whether a man's fertile "seed" be considered his sperm, as Sade would have it, or, by extension, his ideas, it should, according to Sade, be "turned aside or deviated from the main path" that would produce anything constructive (*PB* 122–23).[25] His characters have no more use for babies than they do for utopian societies. Reason itself justifies infanticide and all forms of destruction, which is the law of nature, as these acts supposedly liberate men and women for the wanton pursuit of self-gratification.

In a step backward in the sensationist order of cognitive activities, ideas come to resemble sensations. When libertines have perfected their rational skills, they no longer need sensations to satisfy their sensual appetites. The celebrated lines from the free-thinking, "liber-

24. The "impoverished" conventional psychology to which Klossowski refers, without naming it, is of course sensationism, which indeed attempted to make self-interest the "motivation of human actions." Sade fiendishly insists on a certain perversion in human nature that is irreducible to the rational pursuit of self-interest. See Klossowski, *Sade mon prochain* (Paris: Editions du Seuil, 1947 and 1967), pp. 149–53. See also Bataille, *La Littérature et le mal* (Paris: Gallimard, 1957), p. 94. Bataille similarly states that the profound truth behind sexual pathology lies in desire, which is out of reach of any "reasoned enumeration" like that of Krafft-Ebing's *Psychopathia sexualis*.

25. Although unproductive for the generation of the species, Sadean sodomy can nonetheless also be interpreted as a positive radical gesture for revolutionary equality in society. See Lynn Hunt, *The Family Romance of the French Revolution* (Berkeley and Los Angeles: University of California Press, 1992), p. 146.

tine" *philosophe* Diderot take on a literal meaning: "My thoughts are my trollops."[26] Dolmancé admiringly calls Eugénie a libertine when she demonstrates a remarkable ability to "ejaculate in her mind without being touched" (*PB* 177).[27] One apparently earns fully the title only after gaining this ability. Merteuil has mastered the libertine art in this regard, having been seduced by Valmont's reputation before ever seeing him (*LD* 81: 176). A mental act stimulates her as would a visual and, one assumes, tactile encounter.

Unlike the mind, the heart or the feeling associated with it impedes the libertine accumulation of pleasures. Consequently, libertines suppress any movement from it and attempt to deny its very existence as anything other than a material organ. When they do let themselves be attracted by its charms, they pay for their mistakes with diminished mental abilities. Merteuil chides Valmont for allowing his heart to "abuse" his mind, which derives only "poor reasoning" from it (*LD* 134: 312). Dolmancé claims not even to know what the heart is and uses this term in similar fashion for "weaknesses of the mind" (*PB* 256). In libertine logic, it produces if nothing else only remorse, which makes one regret previous pleasures. Likewise in a parallel construction in the same passage, Dolmancé calls sensibility a "weakness of the soul," tightening not only the fairly obvious connection between the heart and sensibility but also that between the mind and the soul. The heart, the soul, and sensibility are thus all drawn into the increasingly limited domain of the physical mind and body, that is, the mind as part of the body, which itself is part of nature. Lest one doubt for a moment Sade's insistence on the physical basis for mental phenomena, one need only consult the following passage: "All intellectual ideas are so subordinated

26. Diderot, *Le Neveu de Rameau*, in *Oeuvres complètes*, ed. Herbert Dieckmann, Jacques Proust, and Jean Varloot (Paris: Hermann, 1989), 12: 70.

27. There is even a sense in which one can rightly view libertinism as a form of asceticism. See Anne Deneys, "The Political Economy of the Body in the *Liaisons dangereuses* of Choderlos de Laclos," pp. 49–56. But there are clearly limits to such an interpretation. Although libertines like Merteuil and Valmont may at times deny themselves carnal pleasures, they often do so for deferred gratification or for ever more exquisite pleasures of a mental *and* physical kind (i.e., head libertinism). Their activity, however, is far from being wholly intellectual, just as their fulfillment of any sort is not totally disembodied or cut off from previous sensory experience. Merteuil's disfigurement in *Les Liaisons dangereuses* serves as a harsh reminder on Laclos's part of the inability to separate the mind or soul from the body, as the novel's libertine protagonists had attempted to do in their exercises of mental eroticism. That not only the virtuous characters but also the libertines have to be reminded of this constitutes one of the novel's greatest ironies.

to the physics of nature that the comparisons furnished by agriculture will never deceive us in moral doctrine" (*PB* 243).

Left with an inversion of the physical over the mental, libertines quickly lose any remaining sense of traditional morals in their pursuits and thoroughly undermine sensibility. No longer do moral refinement and intellectual progress stand as goals in the topsy-turvy world of Laclos and Sade in the late Enlightenment, which collapses on itself. The well-nigh exclusive preoccupation with the physical subverts sensationism's plan for an exalted view of sensory experience leading to lofty ideas. An irrational, decadent ethos triumphs over the constructive attempts of the sensationists and *philosophes*. Sensibility does not necessarily produce salutary results but depends on myriad contingencies beyond human control, some of which inevitably entail dangerous liaisons. Rather than being uncritically considered as the most cherished human characteristic, sensibility takes on problematic if not terrifying proportions. Laclos suggests just such a radically different view of sensibility: "This sensibility which is so active is, no doubt, a laudable quality; but how much everything that we see every day teaches us to fear it!" (*LD* 165: 368). What formerly constituted one of humanity's most praiseworthy traits can become a potential source of evil.[28] The outcome of sensibility remains highly uncertain and inspires fear, as Laclos intimates in a plea for indulgence for those who hang in the balance: "Ah! to be indulgent, one need only reflect on how many circumstances independent of us, depends the frightening alternative between the delicacy or the depravity of our feelings" (*LD* 174: 384).

Having been praised for an entire century, sensibility becomes feared for the deviation it can take. Most characters in Sade's work have taken the other alternative leading to depravity and by their actions point either to the inevitability or, at a minimum, the constancy of evil. Only more sanguine than Sade by a slight difference of degree and not of kind, Laclos portrays the entrance onto the slippery slope of sensibility, whereas Sade shows its full decline. Both authors teach that our sensations can be controlled because of our omnipresent sensibility. We cannot help but react to what we see, feel, hear, taste, and smell. But the sensations one has when one does so (and one's resulting ideas) can be manipulated by someone like Merteuil or Valmont who gives

---

28. For an analysis of evil and determinism in Laclos's novel, see Suellen Diaconoff, *Eros and Power in "Les Liaisons dangereuses": A Study in Evil* (Geneva: Droz, 1979), esp. pp. 89–110.

false sensations or input known to produce a certain effect, thereby effecting a deviation of meaning. The source of sensations in the natural world has been contaminated by libertines' machinations, which stem sensations for their own purposes. Experience assumes a different meaning. It can no longer innocently come from or take nature as its pure source but must begin to account for the irrational, internal urges of desire. Libertines substitute artifice for nature as the cause of psychological activity. What one knows may still come from sensations, but the late Enlightenment gives a bitter lesson in the cruel deviation these sensations can take. Not always apprehended directly, experience may pass through the filter of libertines who deflect its message for their own ends.[29] They use sensationism against itself to suit a rakish world that has lost its natural innocence. Once deviated or perverted sensations have been introduced into the cognitive process, everyone must play the game of dissimulation or risk being victimized at the hands of cunning evil men and women.

By thoroughly confounding the means by which knowledge is acquired, Laclos and Sade invert the relationship of the mind to the body and reverse the century's thinking about progress. They do not merely extend sensationism's principles as do the materialists but deliberately pervert them.[30] Whereas materialism and sensationism both constitute positive, progressive theories, Laclos's and Sade's works point to dire, inescapable consequences. The two writers in general, and Sade in particular, present staunchly anti-Enlightenment visions of the world. No longer serving as mere conduits for ideas, as they were for the most part in sensationism, the senses become their own ends and drive the individual further into a hedonistic, narcissistic position. Such a view of experience represents of course a far cry from what the sensationists envisioned in their dreams for social and moral utopias. In a word, sensibility is problematic and unstable. It cannot be directed, any more than can plots generated by a sensationist aesthetics, toward a simple, univocal solution.[31] Laclos's and Sade's perversion of sensationism and sensibility reveals a modern, uncertain world whose character and complexity cannot be reduced to merely positive results. There will

29. The process for letters and fictional readers has been studied by Peter V. Conroy, Jr., *Intimate, Intrusive, and Triumphant: Readers in the "Liaisons dangereuses"* (Amsterdam: J. Benjamins, 1987), esp. pp. 35–48.
30. Materialism's extension of sensationist principles is the subject of Chapter 8.
31. In my chapter on Graffigny's epistolary novel, the instability of genre in eighteenth-century French literature is shown to have both historical and epistemological underpinnings.

always remain a certain amount of instability in sensibility, now pushing individuals to honorable ideas or actions, and then plunging them to degenerate deeds. If these two authors at the close of the eighteenth century insist as much as they do on the evil, destructive nature of humankind, it is to banish forever what they viewed as the unrealistic and impossible task the Enlightenment and its sensationist thinkers had given themselves to create a purely rational world. Human nature, understood as based on sensibility in the eighteenth-century outlook, has an irreducibly irrational side to it that history since those times has served to reconfirm in an almost vindictive way. By lowering their authorial gaze from the mind to the body and its sexual parts, these writers of the French *Spätaufklärung* lower our expectations of experience and shake us into a more realistic, somber perspective on human progress. That they largely succeeded in associating sensibility—a *sine qua non* of our existence—with evil leaves an indelibly deterministic mark on civilization's aspirations.

PART III

THE POLITICS OF SENSATIONISM

7

Cultivating Talent and Virtue

Interested in improving the lot of society, the major thinkers of the French Enlightenment often sought solutions in educational reforms and in the establishment of a system of legislation that encouraged the pursuit of the highest aspirations. In their concern for the way in which humans acquire knowledge, sensationists furnished a readily available and authoritative point of departure for accomplishing both ends. For their thinking was indeed, as one observer puts it, "a philosophy for progress."[1]

Two eighteenth-century writers, Helvétius and Rousseau, particularly stand out in the way they use sensationism in their pedagogical and legislative systems. However much they, along with the other *philosophes,* direct their common efforts toward making society better, they differ in their opinion of what constitutes a better society. Their views on progress in society become clear through a comparative study of the sometimes very similar, and at other times different, uses they make of sensationism. That they were influenced by this philosophy is either self-evident, as in the case of Helvétius, who himself fully subscribed to sensationist principles, or well documented.[2] Given little or no need to

1. See J. H. Brumfitt's chapter on "Sensationalism, Scientific Materialism, and Evolution," in *The French Enlightenment,* esp. pp. 99–107.
2. My chapter on Helvétius aims to show the depth of his sensationism. Scholars have studied the natural connection between his attachment to this school of thought and his pedagogical theory. See Mordecai Grossman, *The Philosophy of Helvétius,* and F. Mazzola, *La pedagogia di Helvétius* (Milan: Sandron, 1920). Whereas I emphasize the fundamental tenets

resolve the question of influence, I shall focus on the divergent results or consequences produced by each author's use of sensationism. These underline some of the important differences between the *philosophes* and Rousseau while at the same time emphasizing the powerful and pervasive influence of the same philosophy for sometimes competing ideals. Whereas Helvétius aims to cultivate talent and virtue, Rousseau has grave reservations over the pursuit of talent and is primarily interested in fostering virtuous behavior. Moreover, sensationism for Helvétius represents an instrument of control for society, whereas for Rousseau it liberates individuals.

As a *philosophe*, Helvétius wrote at great length about educational and legislative systems. Although Condillac outlined a formal education in his *Cours d'études pour l'instruction du prince de Parme* and Bonnet gave practical advice for a moral education in a number of his writings, neither one approaches the topic in as systematic a way as does Helvétius.[3] His work *De l'esprit* enumerates the different kinds of intellect and calls attention to the best ways of nurturing the mind, as does his later piece entitled *De l'homme, de ses facultés intellectuelles et de son éducation,* which echoes in its subtitle the instructional reforms to which he alluded earlier. Always informing his views is the sensationist concept of physical sensibility by which men and women, considered as relatively passive creatures, seek pleasure and avoid pain.[4] Such a reductive conception of humanity leads him to believe that

---

of sensationism as influences on Helvétius's thinking about education and legislation, Grossman works from a series of sensationist assumptions, some of which, notably that of the *tabula rasa,* are more implied than explicit. See esp. pp. 73–75, 116–17, 124.

Peter Jimack has conducted an excellent close reading of similar passages in Rousseau's *Emile* and in Condillac's writings. Except to say that sensationism's importance is "obvious" for education, Jimack does not, however, really point out the ramifications of Rousseau's considerable use of it, as I shall attempt to demonstrate here. See "Les Philosophes sensualistes: Condillac, Buffon, Helvétius," in *La Genèse et la rédaction de l'"Emile" de J.-J. Rousseau,* Studies on Voltaire and the Eighteenth Century, 13 (Geneva: Institut et Musée Voltaire, 1960), pp. 318–44. Jimack includes Buffon as a sensationist, but it seems more appropriate, given the vast scope of Buffon's *Histoire naturelle,* to consider him as one of the many eighteenth-century thinkers influenced by this philosophy.

3. Georges Bonnet groups Charles Bonnet's unpublished writings under several classifications, including ethics, pedagogy, aesthetics, and applied morality. See Bonnet, *Charles Bonnet (1720–1793),* pp. 18–19, 273–93. Oskar William Fritzsche devotes his monograph to the subject of Bonnet's pedagogical theory, finding some dozen works including the *Essai de psychologie* and the *Essai analytique* as evidence of it. See his *Die pädagogisch-didaktischen Theorien Charles Bonnets* (Langensalza: Beyer & Söhne, 1905), pp. 5–6.

4. See Chapter 3 for a full discussion of this concept.

educators and legislators can cultivate talent and virtue simply by controlling the environment in which people learn and act. Despite the noticeable inequality of different people's minds, everyone is equally susceptible to learning, since Helvétius maintains an essentially uniform opinion of human nature. Individual differences are accounted for by the varying circumstances in which random chance places people. Finally, Helvétius finds in the passions a major motivating force for effecting intelletual and moral improvement. For education and legislation, his use of sensationist precepts thus results in an egalitarian attitude toward human intellectual aptitude. It also points to the large degree of importance he attributed to chance and the passions, the latter of which are ultimately seen as omnipotent, as is education.

The equality of intellectual aptitude Helvétius perceives in humanity stems from his sensationist belief in its fundamental sameness. Surveying the entire world, one cannot but "agree that men all similar to one another, differ only by the diversity of their instruction; that in every country their organs are approximately the same, that they make roughly the same use of them" (*DH* 1: 212 [F 302]). Clearly, what makes people the world over act in the same way is their sensory apparatus endowing them with physical sensibility, to which Helvétius traces all behavior. They may of course act differently in specific ways, but generally they all seek pleasure and avoid pain.

Sensationism serves for Helvétius and for all sensationists as a methodology. Like Descartes's *Discours de la méthode*, it allows an investigator to reduce a question—in this case, "whether the mind should be considered as a gift of nature, or an effect of education" (*DE* 229)—to its simplest parts. From a sensationist perspective, those parts of course invariably consist of original components for our ideas, namely sensations. One cannot reiterate enough the important sensationist point, effectively used by Helvétius, that humanity's basic nature resides in its physical sensibility. He states this indirectly in the following passage: "it is necessary to reduce the question to simple points; to go back to the origin of our ideas, to the development of the mind; and to recall that man only feels, remembers, and observes similarities and differences" (*DE* 233). While not denying nature's capability to endow different people with more highly refined senses, memories, and abilities to pay attention, Helvétius nonetheless resists the larger claim that these faculties exhaust the explanations for the great diversity among minds.

In order to prove the equal intellectual aptitude of everyone, Helvétius must disprove claims for differences in diverse people's sensory acuity, memory, and attention affecting the overall accuracy of their minds.[5] Sensationism appears at first to be at odds with itself. If all of our ideas come from the senses, then it logically might follow that the person with the most finely tuned senses would have the clearest ideas. Helvétius takes considerable pains to disprove such a conclusion because it could weaken his argument for nurture or education over nature. To a sensationist, ascribing any qualities to nature was more or less tantamount to returning to the notion of innate ideas that Locke had devoted much of his *Essay* to debunking. The sensationists held that all knowledge arises from experience, viewed almost exclusively as external sensory experience. Only by reducing all operations of the mind to physical sensation does Helvétius, who goes beyond Locke in this regard, show that a mind's superiority results not from the different degrees of perfection of the senses (the effects of nature) but from the actual experience of the senses (the effects of education [*DH* 1: 76–80 or F 139–43]). Helvétius circumvents the potential pitfall to his case for the undisputed ascendancy of education as the determining factor of a mind by focusing not on the way people see a given object but on the relationships the object has with other objects (*DE* 234–35). True relationships between objects, such as greater or lesser height, brilliance, or color, remain the same despite differences in vision. People may perceive objects differently, but the objects keep the same relationships that they have with one another. The original, inborn perfection of any one sense leads not to mental superiority but to specific kinds of minds, like those of painters or botanists. Because of variations in sensory skills as well as in memory and attention, minds may be different, but they are not necessarily better.

By emphasizing the equal opportunity everyone has to develop his or her intellect, Helvétius aims not only to cultivate talent on a widespread basis but also to increase the chances of producing more geniuses for the benefit of all humanity. Recapitulating his thoughts, Helvétius states that "Nature has endowed all men who are commonly well constituted with the degree of attention necessary to raise themselves to the most elevated ideas" (*DE* 570, also 256). As long as one does not have serious mental handicaps, one can understand difficult concepts and attain truth. Genius, undoubtedly the surest indication of intellectual superiority, is "not a gift of Nature" but a product of rare

---

5. Helvétius discusses humanity's equal aptitude for mental operations in both of his major works. See *DE* 229–61 and *DH* 1: 76–215.

circumstances (*DE* 415–17). In other words, everyone has the aptitude to become a genius, but only a few are placed in the exact combination of situations to produce it. Random chance (*le hasard*) thus plays an important part in anyone's education.

In Helvétius's conception of learning, sensationism informs human beings' radical sameness as well as their radical differences, which arise from chance. At the same time, physical sensibility pushes all toward objects of pleasure and repels all from those that would do harm, just as it allows humans to experience a situation only from the perspective in which they happen to be at the time. Humans are at once fundamentally similar in what drives them and fundamentally different in what exactly they experience. A person may be equally as apt to learn something as someone else but may not enjoy the serendipitous opportunities to do so. These occur by pure chance, which overwhelmingly determines the greatest part of one's intellectual and moral education (*DE* 233, 527). To show the differences between people and to show that no one receives the same education, Helvétius traces the first instructions to those sensations an infant feels before and after birth: "In these moments what can be the true tutors of childhood? the various sensations it feels. These are so many instructions that it receives" (*DH* 1: 13 [F 57]). In accordance with the form of sensationism that emerged in eighteenth-century France, instructions here and at every subsequent stage of development consist in sensations. These change constantly, differing from one position and from one movement to the next. The more one attempts to make the education for two different people the same, the more apparent the task's impossibility becomes. Any attempt to reproduce exactly the same experience is doomed to failure, as Helvétius's examples make clear. The following example demonstrates admirably his point about perspectival relativism: "Take two children into a plain, a woods, a performance, an assembly, and finally into a store; these children, from their physical position alone, will be neither struck precisely by the same objects, nor as a result be affected by the same sensations" (*DH* 1: 16 [F 60–61]). The education one receives changes with exposure to different sensations, since all ideas in the sensationist view come from them. Simply put, two different individuals cannot possibly have the same sensations unless they are indeed the same person. With different sensations, they will have different ideas and ultimately different educations. One cannot thus control the majority of one's education, which is subject to chance. But one can do one's best to minimize the effects of chance. Helvétius's sensationist plan for education acknowledges the diversity of human minds while it impels them toward sameness. He summarizes the opposing forces in education as follows: "man's moral education is now almost entirely abandoned to chance. To perfect it, one would have to direct the plan according to public utility, found it on simple and unchanging principles. It is the only way to diminish the influence chance has on it" (*DH* 1: 32 [F 79]). That principle resides of course in physical sensibility, whose driving force comes for the most part from the passions.

For Helvétius, the passions serve as the primary means of cultivating talent and virtue. Although he recognizes the errors into which the passions can lead us by having us concentrate too much attention on a single aspect of an object, Helvétius hastens to point out that they also constitute "the source of our enlightenment" (*DE* 25–28). If properly directed, they can lead to great accomplishments; "great talents assume great passions" (*DE* 526). Without passions, one risks becoming mediocre. Helvétius seems prepared to accept the possible aberrations and mistakes attendant on great passions as long as a nation's idleness or laziness is avoided. But like the passions, laziness constitutes a deeply rooted part of our being and a continual obstacle to educational progress.

The same physical sensibility that makes human beings passionate by having them pursue pleasure, makes them lazy by having them avoid pain. Were it not for the counterbalancing forces of strong passions and the hatred of boredom, humanity would "gravitate unceasingly toward a state of rest," because any form of work calls for attention which is tiring and painful (*DE* 262). Given humanity's natural laziness, Helvétius anxiously nurtures the other side of our psychological being, namely, the passions. His educational writings emphasize the strength of the passions that alone counteracts the innate intertia in us and "endows us finally with that continuous attention concomitant to the superiority of talent" (*DE* 288). He associates idleness with vice, and movement with the passions and for the most part with virtue despite their potential for some harmful behavior (*DH* 2: 62 [F 529]; *DE* 268). Laziness results in stupidity, passions in wonderful inventions for the arts and sciences. Moralists have no right to condemn the passions indiscriminately, since "sublime virtue and enlightened wisdom are beautiful enough products of this folly to make it respectable" (*DE* 288).

As he depicts the force of passions in all matters, Helvétius comes to see their usefulness for pedagogical purposes. His historical examples demonstrate that "the pains and pleasures of the senses can inspire in us any kind of passion, feeling, and virtue" (*DE* 327). He cites, for instance, the Spartan practice of having seminude dancing girls insult the weaker warriors in public assemblies and praise the strong ones. To avoid future ignominy and possibly to gain a fair maiden's favors, soldiers will subsequently fight with redoubled courage for their country. A system of rewards and punishments reinforces virtuous behavior, seen here as the defense of one's country. Man's acts of virtue as well as of vice have a direct relationship with "the liveliness of passions, whose strength is measured by the degree of pleasure he finds in satisfying them" (*DE* 334).

The passions required for the cultivation of virtue also apply to that of talent, especially when that talent takes on the proportions of genius. In his chapter on genius, Helvétius points out that despite the preponderant role of chance in forming it, "genius must be driven by one of the passions," namely, ambition or "the keen desire for fame" (*DE* 423). Ambition, it will be recalled, anticipates early on a future pleasure and can thus tolerate in the short term painful hard work.[6] Genius indeed assumes great passions, without which it could never endure tiresome, long hours of thinking (*DE* 423, 540). Although he doubts that genius can ever be cultivated because of its dependence on circumstances over which humans have no control, Helvétius nonetheless suggests that talent requires far fewer exceptional conditions and remains an attainable goal for everyone. But like virtue, talent calls for "consideration and praise," for which most people have an irrepressible passion to some degree (*DH* 1: 246 [F 347]).

As emblematic of the passions, Helvétius revealingly chooses Samson's head of hair. This figure functions both metonymically and metaphorically. In its syntagmatic proximity to the brain, Samson's hair influences, as it were, his thoughts. By its paradigmatic resemblance to an erotic area, it has ramifications for his pleasure as well. Sensual delight is thus connected to intellectual and moral enlightenment, as Helvétius intimates in the following lines: "By destroying in a man the passion that animates him, you deprive him at the same time of all his knowledge; it seems that Samson's head of hair is, in this regard, the emblem of the passions: if this hair is cut off, Samson is no longer but an ordinary man" (*DE* 284).

This passage also insinuates a certain anticlericalism, particularly in

---

6. See Chapter 3, pages 90–91 for a discussion of this and the other passions.

view of the chapter heading, "One becomes stupid, as soon as one ceases being passionate." In the eighteenth century as in previous times, members of the clergy usually underwent a tonsuring at some point in their training.[7] Stripped of their hair or their passion, to use the metaphor employed here, they become stupid in Helvétius's opinion. For him, a physical emasculation of this kind, which on the semiotic level amounts to a castration, results ironically in not only an intellectual but also a moral degradation. Figuratively deprived of one of the primary instruments of desire itself, Samson and priests in general, following Helvétius's logic, lose their minds and hearts. The implications for priests, however, are less attenuated than they are for Samson, who falls merely to the state of an ordinary man. The unspoken others here clearly would drop to some subhuman form of brutishness. Although such a reading between the lines of a censored text may seem somewhat forced, it is unquestionably borne out in the unexpurgated *De l'homme*. The intellectual degradation Samson undergoes derives from the sensationist connection of ideas and sensations. The moral one, however, necessitates an understanding of Helvétius's conception of virtue.

The particular type of virtue Helvétius wishes to cultivate has public utility as its object. This notion constitutes a fundamental part of his educational philosophy and gives rise to his classification among utilitarian thinkers. Helvétius calls it "the principle of all human virtues, and the basis of all legislations" (*DE* 83). It serves to offset the strong urge people sometimes have to follow their own passions wantonly. As a check on vice, it thus brings personal interests into line with the general interest of all members of society in order to promote public happiness. Attention to public utility distinguishes the self-centered individual from the socially conscious community member and represents a new form of passion: "The first passion of the citizen should be that for Laws & the public good" (*DH* 1: 113 [F 183]).

In a chapter on virtue (*DH* 1: 262–66 [F 367–70]), Helvétius calls attention to the hypocrisy of the clergy who preach this quality. The word evokes by its Latin etymology an idea of strength and courage, while the trait itself can always be measured by publicly useful acts. The virtuous acts Helvétius typically cites throughout his works entail beneficial inventions of the defense of one's country. In both instances, the acts enhance the happiness of all by either increasing people's

---

7. For a contemporary discussion of this ancient practice of tonsure, see M. Boucher d'Argis's *Encyclopédie* article on the topic in 16: 413–14.

everyday pleasure or allowing them to continue enjoying it without fear of invasion by outside forces. Priests, who as Helvétius usually depicts them are only concerned with protecting their own narrow interests, cannot be virtuous in this sense of the word. Their intellectual and moral degradation or barrenness results hence from their thinking only of themselves, not of the public good, and from their perceived physical weakness and shortcomings, which cannot help their country in times of war. Bereft of any productive passions that might benefit the public at large, priests direct the passions they might have left only at themselves, and their actions have harmful effects on society. In Helvétius's eyes, they come to represent vice more than virtue.

One perhaps best discovers the kind of legislation Helvétius envisages for cultivating talent and virtue in his rejection of papal religion and his quasi approval of pagan practices. Underlying his esteem for paganism is its conformity to sensationist principles achieving public utility. "This Religion of the Senses," as he calls it, "was besides the most suitable for men, the most apt to produce those strong impressions, that it is sometimes necessary for the Legislator to be able to arouse in them" (*DH* 1: 57 [F 112]). Paganism recognizes the potential advantages of the passions and encourages them instead of repressing them. In a long passage, Helvétius describes its valuable contributions to society:

> Given this Religion, what was to be the most intense desire, the most powerful interest of Pagans? That of serving their Country with their talents, courage, integrity, generosity, and virtues. . . . Far from stifling the enthusiasm that a wise Legislation gives for virtue & talents, this religion stimulated it more. Convinced of the utility of passions, ancient Legislators did not at all propose to snuff them out. What can one find in a people without desire? Are they merchants, Captains, Soldiers, Men of Letters, clever Ministers? No: but Monks. (*DH* 1: 58 [F 113])

A healthy system of legislation rewards virtue and punishes vice. It alone can and should control them by creating awards and punishments for actions that are respectively useful or harmful to society (*DE* 365; *DH* 2: 95–96 [F 571]). Virtue promotes public utility, whereas vice undermines it. Likewise, a sound educational policy makes use of human susceptibility to physical sensibility and the passions in order to direct individual behavior as much as possible so that it redounds to the benefit of the public. In much the same way as enlightened legislators, wise educators should "place men in a position that forces them to acquire the talents and virtues desired in them" (*DH* 2: 336 [F 882]). In accordance with sensationist psychology, an ideal education should motivate a person by the allure of pleasure and fear of pain. Both a nation's strength and its law enforcement are supported by such an understanding of human proclivities (*DH* 2: 239, 353 [F 754, 906]). As long as legislators reward great talents and virtues on the one hand, and punish crimes injurious to public happiness on the other, the nation should not only prosper in the research and development of new ideas but through natural human inclinations also govern itself well at home and maintain a strong defense against potential aggressors. It may not be able to create geniuses, but by following a sensationist system of education and legislation, it could multiply them and "innoculate" the masses with good sense (*DH* 1: 221, 305 [F 315, 418]; *DH* 2: 347 [F 900]). Preferring poor and bellicose republics as the ones that best compensate talent and virtues, Helvétius apparently finds in the desire for money the only obstacle to implementing his plan of rewards and punishments (*DE* 371; *DH* 2: 103 [F 580]). But even this desire can be transformed into productive activity, and he dares not limit any passion that might prove useful to the fatherland.

Helvétius's educational and legislative theories thus have their foundation in his sensationist view of the passions, which themselves stem from physical sensibility. When he states rather categorically, "education can do anything" (*DH* 2: 332 [F 879]), Helvétius affirms his faith not just in the power of education but in the power of the passions that he strives to harness for intellectual and moral enlightenment. Readers of his works invariably and rightly call attention to this famous dictum. But they neglect to point out that he elsewhere claims the same abilities for the passions. They, too, "can do anything" (*DH* 1: 193 [F 276]). Their omnipotence in fact makes possible his suggestions for reforms in education and the law. Helvétius's forceful rhetoric about education and the passions underlines his own impassioned outlook on the basic nature of men and women as fundamentally sensitive beings, an outlook that informs not just his pedagogical theories but also the entirety of his work.

In his use of sensationism, Rousseau concentrates especially on inculcating in individuals the idea of freedom, for without it there can be no virtue. Freedom constitutes the requisite condition for cultivating virtue. Believing in the innate goodness of humanity, Rousseau envisages society as a pernicious force. Hence, his theory of education as presented in the *Emile* is a negative one in that it protects the young student against the perceived threat of society's corrupting and enslaving influence. Rousseau wants to preserve the presocial state of freedom as much as possible: "Before human prejudices and institutions altered our natural inclinations the happiness of children as well as of men consists in the use of their freedom."[8] Emile, the fictional young boy for whom Rousseau provides helpful guidance through an ever-present tutor, is never allowed to come into contact with society until a relatively advanced age, at which point his virtue is presumably ensured. He is, however, allowed to become acquainted with nature, for it represents freedom in one of its most positive manifestations.

Since according to sensationism all ideas come from sensations, if one wishes to encourage a particular idea, one creates a situation in which sensations of that idea are given full rein. Rousseau follows just such a sensationist rationale to reinforce not just any idea but one in particular—the idea of freedom, which in turn will allow men and women to exercise their innate goodness and act virtuously. He does so not only in the *Emile,* where a child's future is at stake, but also in his other writings for members of all ages in society. Taken together, the sensationist passages from his pedagogical, political, and other writings constitute nothing less than his *Morale sensitive, ou Le Matérialisme du sage.* In this work, mentioned briefly in *Les Confessions,* Rousseau wanted to create "an external systematic plan which adapted according to circumstances could put or maintain the soul in the most favorable state for virtue" (*OC* 1: 409). Although he never actually wrote this piece, Rousseau has it in mind throughout the composition of his *oeuvre.*[9] While focusing on some passages that have already attracted scholars' attention for their sensationist content, as well as on some new ones, I shall take a phenomenological approach to underline

8. Rousseau, *Emile,* in *Oeuvres complètes,* ed. Bernard Gagnebin and Marcel Raymond (Paris: Gallimard, 1969), 4: 310; hereafter cited parenthetically as (*Em*). I have used *OC,* followed by the volume number and page numbres, to refer to Gallimard's Pléiade edition (1959–95) of Rousseau's *Oeuvres complètes* in five volumes, of which the *Emile* is vol. 4. I have not followed Rousseau's particular system of capitalizing certain nouns. For Rousseau's own characterization of the first education as negative, see (*Em* 323).

9. Etienne Gilson has pointed out that despite the absence of any text entitled *La Morale sensitive,* scholars can reconstitute it by bringing together fragments of it. See *Les Idées et les lettres* (Paris: Vrin, 1932), cited in (*OC* 1: 1469). See also my *Seeing and Observing* for a discussion of the crucial importance of sensation for Rousseau's various modes of perception.

Rousseau's particular use of this philosophy.[10] Rousseau's use of sensationism ultimately leads not, as it does with Helvétius, to increased talent, which Rousseau views with suspicion, but to increased virtue through freedom. He cultivates in turn an idea of freedom by choosing sensations that are all especially characterized by their unimpeded or unobstructed nature, whether they relate to child-rearing, the countryside, fresh air, visual images, or public festivals.

In the *Emile,* practically every sensation to which the child is carefully introduced gives a feeling of freedom. Beginning even in infancy, this feeling should be repeated as often as possible and aroused in all five senses. In a sensationist vein, Rousseau writes: "Since everything that enters human understanding comes to it through the senses, man's first reason is a sensory one; it serves as a basis for intellectual reason: our first philosophy teachers are our feet, our hands, our eyes" (370). Perhaps the most striking example of the practice of fostering sensations (and hence ideas) of freedom in the *Emile* comes with the directive not to swaddle babies but to let them have full use of their arms and legs with loose-fitting garments (278). By wrapping the baby very tightly in its linens, the practitioners of swaddling confined appendages for fear that sudden, jerky movements might deform them. Throughout his discussion of this custom, Rousseau emphasizes at once the constraints of the old way he is combatting and the freedom of the new way he is proposing. Although his criticism of swaddling was by no means the first, it takes on almost archetypal importance within Rousseau's work, given his consistent assertion and protection of freedom.[11] It serves as an exemplary point of departure for setting the tone of his writing. In sensationist fashion, he mixes the physical with the psychological and intellectual. Physical sensations are clearly designed to foster ideas of freedom from the very earliest stages on. In Rousseau's *Emile,* one must read every line that gives a negative example of a child's upbringing as a positive recommendation for its opposite. Thus, when he writes about a confined and encumbered state, one must understand this both as a complaint and as an indication of the proper direction to take.

Rousseau's comparison of natural and unnatural states, of freedom and confinement, can sometimes assume exaggerated proportions. A

---

10. My approach to Rousseau here has been influenced by the work of Gaston Bachelard, esp. *The Poetics of Space,* trans. Maria Jolas (Boston: Beacon, 1969).

11. See the notes in (*OC* 4: 1305).

phenomenological consideration of the passages on postnatal child care in the *Emile* reveals some surprising details. In regard to the infant's early years, Rousseau states: "It was less cramped, less hampered, less tightly packed, in the amnion than in swaddling clothes. I do not see what it has gained from being born" (254). The severely limited space of the amnion inside the uterus is compared favorably to the disproportionate and limitless area outside of it. But the infant has little or no awareness of the world beyond the one that comes immediately into contact with itself. That world will remain unknown for some time to come. The infant only knows what it senses directly, what touches its skin. In the womb, it is in contact with a substance provided by nature. Once outside of it, the infant does not necessarily come into contact with unnatural substances. But man intervenes to ensure such conditions. In the case of swaddling, the linens wrapped around the infant give it one of its first experiences by shaping its future life. And that early experience produces not pleasure but pain, as Rousseau points out:

> Could such a cruel constraint not influence their mood as well as their temperament? Their first feeling is a feeling of grief and pain: they find only obstacles in all the movements they need to make. More miserable than a criminal in chains, they make vain efforts, they become annoyed, they scream. Their first voices, you say, are tears; and I believe it. You would impede them from their birth. The first gifts they receive from you are chains; the first treatments they feel are torments. Having nothing free but their voices, how could they not use it to complain? They are screaming about the harm you are doing them: tied up in this way, you would scream louder than they do. (254–55)

Rousseau starts this passage by making the sensationist connection between sensations and ideas, which remain in the infants' minds and ultimately inform their behavior. Helpless infants who have these painful sensations imposed on them will grow up to think of life itself as misery and of themselves as slaves to it.

The first wrong step in child-rearing, Rousseau suggests, consists in an outside intervention or an unnatural addition. Swaddling is not the only example Rousseau adduces in this context. He also mentions, albeit briefly, two other practices that similarly evoke an image of unnatural subjugation. Midwives commonly knead the newborn's head to give it a suitable shape, and braces hold the head in place so that it cannot move. It is as if whatever protrudes physically in the slightest suggestion of individual difference or freedom must be molded into a predetermined form or held immobile. As unnatural additions or changes, Rousseau also mentions the wine sometimes added to the water in which the baby is bathed after birth as well as the temperature of the water (277). He sees no need to alter the water's consistency or its temperature, since both modifications interfere with nature.

In ideal circumstances, absolutely nothing representing society and its artificial conventions should be allowed to affect the infant's senses. For in the eyes of Rousseau, who writes in this regard as a staunch sensationist, to *feel* nature is to *know* freedom. Only through such a view could the infant in its mother's womb be considered freer than the one after birth. In Rousseauian fashion, one might extrapolate his thought and say paradoxically that even in its cramped prenatal quarters the infant learns more about freedom than it does afterwards in the outside world. Only by crying can it act freely. Noteworthy about crying is the absence of any obtrusive barrier that might possibly block the infant's only expression of freedom. It is precisely such an absence that opens a natural space around the infant. That free space, devoid of any object encoded as part of society and its constraining influence, becomes for Rousseau the privileged place of learning. In his pedagogy, Rousseau in effect attempts to recreate in the outside world, subject to myriad social pressures, the natural inside world of the mother's womb. For him to do so, it is critical that the infant's senses be exposed to the *uninterrupted* contact of nature rather than to society. The air or space around the newborn infant replaces the amniotic fluid in which it previously bathed in total contact with nature. Rousseau expresses such a wish in a variety of ways, but foremost among them is his directive to raise the child in the country.

One cannot overestimate the importance of the countryside for Rousseau's pedagogical program; it affects all five senses in a positive way to reinforce the desired idea of freedom. The sights, sounds, tastes, smell, and feel of the countryside all produce salutary effects on the young Emile. Again, it is the uninterrupted quality of his interaction with nature that proves beneficial; the continuity of nature liberates him. In the country, his view of nature is unimpeded. Its sounds reach his ears without mingling with the voices of men and women. He cultivates his own garden and can enjoy the tasteful fruits of his own labors that come directly from it. He breathes the pure country air that he feels all around him.

Rousseau dwells on the natural element of air as a particularly important influence on the physical and moral well-being of a child. He writes about it in the following way that links mere passing sensations with something of a more lasting nature: "It is especially in the first years of life that air acts on the constitution of children. In a delicate and soft skin it penetrates through all the pores, it powerfully affects these newborn bodies, it leaves impressions on them that are not erased" (276). The remainder of this passage, which goes on to speak of the "good country air' and the "bad city air," makes clear that Rousseau is hinting at more than the physical influence air has on bodies. Having also moral and cognitive effects, air can result in lasting behavioral traits and permanent ideas. As long as it flows without encountering unnatural obstacles, it produces good, healthy, and free men. Once checked, however, by tortuous, man-made streets, air stagnates and causes sickness, vice, and death. Rousseau uses this section of the *Emile* to reinforce his point from the second *Discours* or *Discours sur l'origine et les fondements de l'inégalité parmi les hommes* (*OC* 3: esp. 146–47) that man originally lived in relative solitude: "Men are not made to be piled up in ant hills, but sparse on the earth which they are supposed to cultivate. The more they gather, the more corrupt they grow. The body's infirmities as well as the soul's vices are the unerring effect of this excessively numerous throng of people. . . . Man's breath is deadly to his fellow human beings: this is no less true in the literal than it is in the figurative sense" (*Em* 276–77). The stench created by close living quarters affects people's bodies and their souls. They cannot have sensations of putrefaction without feeling physically nauseous and morally degraded. Such an environment hems one in, diminishes one's sense of freedom, and gives rise to corruption.

Rousseau was not alone in deploring the unsanitary living conditions in cities, although he does emphasize more than others the psychological implications of these conditions. Contemporary descriptions of Paris streets hardly give a romantic image of them. Louis-Sébastien Mercier provides the following account:

> As soon as air no longer contributes to the preservation of health, it kills; but health is the possession about which man shows himself to be the most indifferent. Narrow and poorly con-

structed streets, houses that are too high & interrupt the free
circulation of air, butchers' shops, fish markets, sewers, cemeter-
ies, make the atmosphere polluted, weighed down with impure
particles, & makes this stale air grow heavy & have a malignant
influence. . . .

Houses raised on bridges, besides the hideous aspect they
present, prevent the airstream from crossing from one end of
town to the other, & carrying off along with the fumes of
the Seine all the polluted air from the streets that end up at
the quais.[12]

Even when Parisians travel to the country to enjoy its fresh air, they still
find the "loathsome odors" of the foul sludge that has been taken from
the supposedly lovely boulevards of the capital and dumped outside it
for up to a radius of a half-league.[13]

Like many of his fellow observers, Mercier suggests a need to provide
fresher sources of air in the twisted, narrow, medieval streets of Paris.
Their vision of a healthier and more windswept Paris would not be
realized on a grand scale until the Baron Haussmann's major opening of
wide avenues across the city in the following century. But already in
the eighteenth century with the plans for the Champs-Elysées, urban
designers and medical doctors alike were beginning to bring some of
the beneficial effects of the country to the city. For his part, however,
Rousseau adheres to his purist and sensationist approach of having a
child educated in the country, where there are no barriers to clean air
and, hence, no obstacles to acquiring a full idea of freedom and virtue.

Above all, the country provides for Rousseau socially unmediated
objects from nature. The child's constant exposure to so-called natural
objects maintains him or her as long as possible in an uncorrupted state,
even when these objects do not actively foster an idea of freedom. "The
dependence of things," Rousseau writes, "having no morality does not
harm freedom and does not engender vices" (*Em* 311). It is better for
people to depend on things rather than on other people who might
enslave them. Similarly, Rousseau favors, as a means of teaching students,
actual objects over human constructions such as words, which as
mere representations of content have neither the directness nor the

12. Louis-Sébastien Mercier, *Tableau de Paris* (1782–1788; rpt. Geneva: Slatkine, 1979),
1: 126–27.

13. Mercier, *Tableau de Paris,* 1: 127.

transparency of things at hand and can be used to hide shades of meaning.[14] In Rousseau's theory of education, things, detectable as they are through the senses, take precedence over words (*Em* 447). His student should never be shown anything that he cannot actually see (453). The young Emile's classroom is the great outdoors, which continues to furnish positive images of freedom while at the same time protecting him from vice.

Designed to promote freedom and virtue, the uninterrupted flow of sensations from nature in the learning process has corresponding equivalents in the ideal society Rousseau envisages. In *La Nouvelle Héloïse*, he depicts virtue in terms of unobstructed space. Wolmar's single rule of conduct at Clarens stresses openness: "Never do or say anything you do not want everyone to see or hear; and for myself, I have always regarded as the most estimable of men that Roman who wanted his house constructed in such a way that anything being done in it could be seen" (*OC* 2: 424). Noteworthy about this example is the homeowner's wish for others to be able to see him from all directions. Nothing or practically nothing would block their view. The unimpeded gazes of onlookers not only give them a heightened sense of freedom but also keep the man being perceived in a virtuous state. Rousseau's version of the Orwellian Big Brother has many sets of eyes that ensure virtue, but they belong to benign neighbors possibly in need of moral instruction, not to a threatening state that would control all behavior. There is always of course the danger that the state make spies of them. It bears pointing out, however, that the man living in such a glass house freely chooses to be seen. Rousseau does not emphasize the risk of denunciation in a kind of state-controlled panopticon for prisoners.[15] To the contrary, he uses the inverse of such a prison with the example of the virtuous man at the intersection of others' gazes to underscore the centrality of intimacy, freedom, and virtue in a community. Even such a public display of morality assumes intimate, private relations with neighbors, continuity with and not distance from them. Rousseau's utopian society actually combines both public and private forms of morality.[16] Aware of the sensationist possibilities for an education

14. For a discussion of Rousseau's predilection for transparency, see Jean Starobinski, *Jean-Jacques Rousseau: La Transparence et l'obstacle* (1957; rpt. Paris: Gallimard, 1976).

15. On the dynamics of eighteenth-century prisons and their fictional representations, see John Bender, *Imagining the Penitentiary: Fiction and the Architecture of Mind in Eighteenth-Century England* (Chicago: University of Chicago Press, 1989).

16. See the section "Morality in the Public and Private Society at Clarens," in my *Seeing and Observing*, pp. 19–31.

through the senses, Rousseau thus offers visual images to cultivate virtue.

In his political writings, Rousseau also uses visual images as instructional tools. Leaders should take advantage of public ceremonies to make lasting impressions on the people.[17] Sensations affect their hearts and minds, as Rousseau indicates in his *Considérations sur le gouvernement de Pologne:* "One could not possibly believe how much the people's heart follows its eyes" (*OC* 3: 964). It is important to make visual associations perfectly clear. To encourage freedom and virtue, one can give visually stunning parades of their opposites. Rousseau cites with approval the Romans' practice of displaying great luxury on their vanquished prisoners and kings bedecked with chains of gold and precious stones: "the more it glittered, the less it seduced" (*OC* 3: 964). Conversely, he proceeds to offer a more positive visual image of virtue for Poland's senate—two sheaves of wheat for the chamber in which its members convene. The contrast between the two images could hardly be more dramatic: superfluous, ornate objects, on the one hand, and necessary, simple ones, on the other. It also stresses Rousseau's preference for a self-sufficient, agrarian society over one based on artificial wealth and exterior commerce. Just as he wants to keep the young Emile in contact with nature, so, too, does he strive to maintain an entire society's proximity to the products harvested from it.

As a visual image, money represents values diametrically opposed to those evoked by nature's goods. It does not serve any immediate use but merely represents wealth arbitrarily.[18] Considering it more a sign of inequality and emptiness rather than true abundance, Rousseau suggests in his *Projet de constitution pour la Corse* that countries maintain their

---

17. Especially in its festivals, the French Revolution would make full use of sensationism's implication that visible objects can change people's ideas. For a study of these events in the Revolution, see Mona Ozouf, *Festivals and the French Revolution,* trans. Alan Sheridan (Cambridge, Mass.: Harvard University Press, 1988), esp. pp. 203f. Ozouf does not miss this point about sensationism: "the men of the Revolution—one has only to think of Mirabeau—had perfectly assimilated the empiricism of a century that had constantly eroded the independence that Locke still accorded human reflection. For them, reflection never freed itself from sensation; and man defined by his quality of being, a being of sense, is led not by principles but by objects, spectacles, images" (p. 203).

For an account of the French revolutionaries' interpretation of Rousseau's concept of virtue, see Carol Blum, *Rousseau and the Republic of Virtue: The Language of Politics in the French Revolution* (Ithaca: Cornell University Press, 1986).

18. For a full discussion of Rousseau's attitude toward money and wealth, see my "Rousseau's Theory of Wealth," *History of European Ideas* 7 (1986), 453–67.

healthy state of self-sufficiency if, like Corsica, they can survive without foreign trade (*OC* 3: 921). As he warns the Poles, the use of money remains hidden from view; it circulates secretly and can easily corrupt people (*OC* 3: 1005). Rousseau prefers tangible signs of abundance to the abstractness of money. In honoring virtuous Polish citizens, the nation should avoid monetary rewards for a variety of reasons in addition to their not being "public enough": they have a tendency "not to speak unceasingly to the eyes and hearts, to disappear as soon as they are awarded, and to leave no visible trace that might stimulate emulation by perpetuating the honor that is supposed to accompany them" (*OC* 3: 1007). In cultivating virtue, Rousseau insists repeatedly on the use of concrete objects perceived directly by the senses, which in turn convey information to the mind, where permanent memories or ideas can be stored. His sensationism even leads him to take a relatively indulgent view of property, which in its concreteness, has a less insidious effect on human beings than does money.[19]

Theater, another social convention, also presents a negative example of images in Rousseau's eyes. Because humans are sentient beings, they possess a sensibility that makes them particularly susceptible to feelings of pleasure and pain. Aiming to please more than to instruct, theater appeals to the senses or the body and not to the mind; reason, Rousseau believes, "is good for nothing on the stage."[20] Moreover, the theater moves yet another step away from nature or an original state by exhibiting actors, who make a living by representing someone else for public enjoyment. Their art consists precisely in deception, in having the spectators mistake mere sensory appearances for reality. The tears they shed on stage reflect not their own feelings but those of some other character. In selling their very souls, actors for Rousseau stand at or near the bottom of the ladder of alienated individuals: "I adjure any sincere man to say that he does not feel in the depths of his soul that in this traffic of one's self there is something servile and low" (*OC* 5: 73). Rousseau suggests that the actor approximates the alienated slave not only in a physical but also a psychological way. Not only does the actor give to someone else (alienate, in the eighteenth-century acceptance of the term) his or her own person for a price, but the individual becomes

19. Despite some of his more revolutionary positions, Rousseau believed, for instance, in defending property rights as "the most sacred of all the rights of citizens, and more important in certain respects than freedom itself" (*Economie politique,* in [*OC* 3: 263]).

20. Rousseau, *A M. d'Alembert* in *OC* 5, p. 17. Page references to Rousseau's *Lettre à d'Alembert,* as this work is generally known, are cited parenthetically in the text.

estranged or divided from himself or herself (alienated, in the modern sense). Such is not the case, Rousseau assures us, of the orator who does not become ensnared in the divisiveness representation requires, since the man and the character are one and the same being (*OC* 5: 74).

When Rousseau proceeds to give a positive example of theater, he not surprisingly prefers public festivals set in the fresh air outdoors. His remarks about theater resemble those he had against swaddling. In both cases, Rousseau opposes sensations of constraint to foster a sense of freedom:

> But let us not adopt these exclusive forms of entertainment that gloomily enclose a small number of people in a dark den; that keep them fearful and motionless in silence and inaction; that offer to the eyes only partitions, iron points, soldiers, distressing images of servitude and inequality. No, happy peoples, your festivals are not there! It is outside, under the sky that you must gather together and give yourselves over to the sweet feeling of your happiness. (*OC* 5: 114).

Consisting of light, fresh air, movement, and sounds, the positive images of freedom, which again are unimpeded, counter those of darkness, stagnant air, inaction, and silence.

By also having the spectators at public festivals become the actors themselves, Rousseau circumvents the alienation inherent in representation. They see one another without obstacles in much the same way as the neighbors of the virtuous Roman mentioned in *La Nouvelle Héloïse* see him in his house, which is open to public view. Such an exchange of unimpeded glances unites the people into a virtuous whole. As Rousseau sugests for the assembled members of the crowd, "give the spectators as a show; make them actors themselves; have each one see and love himself or herself in the others, so that all be better united" (*OC* 5: 115). The general will described in the *Contrat social* (*OC* 3: 371–74) results here from the fusing of individual wills united in a common interest. The process takes place first and foremost on a perceptual level. As an exemplary case, Rousseau cites the Genevans at a public festival of this nature and describes them as follows: "They are lively, cheerful, affectionate; their hearts then are in their eyes, as they are always on their lips; they seek to communicate their joy and their pleasures" (*OC* 5: 116). Nothing keeps one from seeing or hearing the hearts of these people. It is above all in the unobstructed communication between hearts that Rousseau hopes to build a free and virtuous society. And through his sensationist convictions, Rousseau attempts to achieve such communication by using the physical space all around us, by keeping it relatively free from unnatural objects that would interfere with our sensations and ideas of liberty and virtue.

In his attitude toward actors as well as toward all people, Rousseau privileges virtue over talent. Despite their impressive skills, actors fall prey to the corrupting tendency of their profession. Rousseau questions its moral validity for "women of breeding": "Does one even need to fight over the moral differences between the sexes, to feel how difficult it is for she who sells herself as a representation [in a performance on stage] not to sell herself soon in her very person, and never to let herself be tempted to satisfy desires she takes so much care in arousing?" (*OC* 5: 82). In the first *Discours* or *Discours sur les sciences et les arts*, Rousseau practically gives an apology of ignorance, so much does he fear the evil influence of pursuing talent. Statues and paintings, among other products of talent, give impressionable young children bad examples taken from mythology. Since children see them before they know how to read, according to sensationist theory they can acquire ideas that might lead them astray at an early age (*OC* 3: 25).

The display of talent leads not only to debauchery but also to inequality. For Rousseau, talent and virtue lie in an inverse relationship to each other. The more one seeks to distinguish oneself through talents, the less one pursues virtue: "Whence come all these abuses, if it is not from the harmful inequality introduced among men by the distinction of talents and the depreciation of virtues. That is the most obvious effect of all our studies, and the most dangerous of all their consequences. A man is no longer asked if he has probity, but if he has talents. . . . Awards are lavished upon the wit, and virtue remains without honors" (*OC* 3: 25). In the second *Discours*, Rousseau condemns the origin of the arts in the early stages of society as the first step toward inequality and vice (*OC* 3: 169–70). During outdoor gatherings that resemble the more sophisticated ones that will take place later indoors in society's theaters, an unhealthy exchange of glances occurs at the same time as does an insidious process of comparison. In these assemblies, everyone "began to look at others and to want to be looked at himself or herself, and public esteem had a price. The one who sang or danced the best; the most beautiful, the strongest, the most skillful or the most eloquent became the most highly respected, and that was the first step toward inequality, and toward vice at the same time" (*OC* 3: 169–70).

Although Rousseau uses sensationist tenets to cultivate virtue, he does not hold a wholly sensationist view of it. Politically and morally, virtue involves an active choice of good over evil. In Rousseau's opinion, human beings are not merely passive beings guided by sensations, as the sensationists would sometimes depict them, but active ones; thinking is acting (*Em* 573, 578).[21] Governed both by sensations and feelings, sentient beings have passive and active natures, respectively.[22] Moreover, in a sensationist pedagogy one uses external objects to develop ideas, whereas Rousseau, not disdaining the value of such teaching, locates virtue within us. Rousseau expresses the inner nature of virtue by way of a rhetorical question in the first *Discours*: "O Virtue! Sublime science of simple souls, are so many efforts and so much machinery necessary to know you? Are your principles not engraved in every heart, and does it not suffice for learning your Laws to go back into oneself and listen to the voice of one's conscience in the silence of passions?" (*OC* 3: 30). He echoes this passage in the "Profession de foi du vicaire savoyard" of the *Emile* as he counsels listening to inner feeling (579). Rousseau uses the sensationist principles that were coming to be widely held in his day not only because of the power of images or sensations in reinforcing ideas but also because he wants to counter the effects of society's negative influence. In Rousseau's pedagogical and legislative systems, his use of the theory thus serves as a counteractive force that might overcome the dominion of society and that might free humanity to look within itself for its virtue, which has always been there.

Helvétius's and Rousseau's uses of sensationism thus produce some distinctly different as well as similar results. Like most *philosophes*, Helvétius has in mind the mental and moral betterment of humanity when he uses sensationism. But Rousseau limits his use of it to forming virtuous citizens. However much the two may agree on the nature of humanity as primarily sensitive and hence capable of feeling pleasure or pain, they differ in their views of progress. Like his fellow optimistic

21. See the discussion of Rousseau's criticism of Helvétius above in Chapter 3, pages 86–87. Judging for Rousseau is not sensing, which is passive. My formulation of Rousseau's sensationism has been clarified here by a helpful discussion with Patrick Coleman and Gita May.

22. In his notes to the *Emile*, Pierre Burgelin suggests a crucial connection between the sensory and passivity, and between feeling and activity (1524). Burgelin's line of thought associates not only thinking but also feeling in its nonsensory meaning with acting. Any active faculty cannot be synonymous with sensation, which is passive. Feeling can, however, be influenced by sensation. See my definition of "seeing" as a combination of feeling and sensation in *Seeing and Observing*.

philosophes, Helvétius helps foster one of the great myths of the Enlightenment, namely, that improving people's education would necessarily improve their morality. They cultivate talent along with virtue, whereas Rousseau pessimistically separates them and points out the dangers of the blind pursuit of talent. In view of the woeful history of highly educated and civilized societies in our own century, the *antiphilosophe* clearly has been vindicated in some of his suspicions about the limits to cultivating talent and intellectual superiority. His own century, however, was to show those who survived to the end of it the excesses of virtue.

8

Materialism's Extension of Sensationist Principles

The history of materialism in eighteenth-century France parallels closely that of sensationism and in some respects antedates it, if one considers the anonymous manuscript *Ame matérielle*, written around the turn of the century, and Dr Maubec's *Principes physiques de la raison et des passions des hommes* (1709). Both philosophies have long histories dating back to the ancient Greeks. But it is La Mettrie's vision of man as a self-propelled machine in *L'Homme-machine* (1747), published two years after his *Histoire naturelle de l'âme* for whose materialist notions he had already been censured, that created a scandal and drew renewed attention to materialism at the same time sensationism was beginning to take hold in France. Around this period, Condillac brought out his *Essai sur l'origine des connaissances humaines* (1746), to be followed by other sensationist works by himself, Bonnet, and Helvétius. If one considers Condillac's *Traité des sensations* (1754) as the central statement on sensationism and d'Holbach's *Système de la nature* (1770) as the definitive expression of materialism, there are some sixteen years separating the two major works of each philosophy. These years indicate more than the obvious difficulties materialist thinkers encountered in having their increasingly audacious or, to use one of the watchwords of the period, hardy pronouncements accepted. These years also underscore materialism's gradual assimilation and extension of sensationist principles, which at the time carried considerable authority. (Indeed, this very process is already taking place on a subtle level within sensationism itself in Helvétius's *De l'esprit*.) Moreover, it seems plausible to assert that materialism in France reaches its purest form only after having thoroughly exploited the implications of sensationism.[1]

A number of important distinctions and similarities exist between the two philosophies. Whereas sensationism tends to trace everything in the human mental world, but especially ideas, to sensations, materialism traces absolutely everything in both the human and physical worlds to matter. This is not of course to say that sensations are ideas or matter but that sensationists and materialists derive their epistemological systems respectively from sensations and matter. Despite its efforts to show the continuity between mind and body, sensationism maintains a certain dualistic metaphysics significantly different from materialism's monism. Unlike materialists, sensationists either do not deny or actively assert the soul's existence. Although both theories posit movement as a constant force in our lives, the one explains it in terms of sensation, the other through matter. A chain of causes and effects also governs daily activities according to the assumptions of each school of thought. As for

---

1. Jacques Moutaux seems to confirm such a view by stating that in their approach to knowledge the materialists are "sensationists more than simply empiricists in the manner of Locke." In other words, sensationism was the contemporary philosophy that had the greatest effect on materialism. See Moutaux, "Matérialisme et lumières: Note sur l'intérêt des ouvrages de La Mettrie, Helvétius, et d'Holbach," *Corpus, Revue de Philosophie* 5/6 (1987), 5.

The transformation of sensationist principles into a materialism can be seen in La Mettrie's work. See Kathleen Wellman, *La Mettrie: Medicine, Philosophy, and Enlightenment* (Durham: Duke University Press, 1992), pp. 109–10, 122–25, 135–68. According to Wellman, La Mettrie uses Locke's and Boerhaave's sensationism to develop his own form of materialism. Wellman tends, however, to identify Locke totally with sensationism and to disregard the eighteenth-century discussion of this theory, especially that by Condillac, whose *Essai sur l'origine des connaissances humaines* was published only one year after La Mettrie's *Histoire naturelle de l'âme*. As this chapter suggests, we need not always look exclusively to Locke for an understanding of French philosophy in the Enlightenment. Although Lockean epistemology unquestionably had an important influence on eighteenth-century French philosophy, intellectuals in France developed their own responses to philosophical questions. These were worked out especially in the interaction of sensationism and materialism and in a French context for French men and women who did not benefit from the same liberties as those enjoyed by the English. Because of their less desirable circumstances, the French no doubt felt an urgent need to use philosophy for social reform.

Central to d'Holbach's work was the recurrent notion "that the only coherent deduction from a sensationistic epistemology was a rigorous materialism." See Alan Charles Kors, *D'Holbach's Coterie: An Enlightenment in Paris* (Princeton: Princeton University Press, 1976), p. 45.

the activities themselves, what for sensationism constitutes a more or less passive response to a stimulus becomes in the materialist view a mechanical one. Finally, the determinism implicit in sensationism becomes fully developed in materialism. In analyzing the transition from the ideas of the one philosophy to those of the other, one must therefore focus on questions of epistemology and of origin, the mind-body problem, the immateriality of the soul, movement, causality, passivity, and determinism. An examination of the interrelations between the two philosophies ultimately draws the lines between their adherents more clearly so as to promote a better understanding of both of them. It also helps highlight the eighteenth-century movement away from traditional metaphysics as well as focus the debate on a number of religious beliefs that are still fiercely defended and contested.

The so-called sensationist refrain that all of our ideas come through our senses takes a slightly different turn in materialist thought. From its standpoint, movement originates with matter itself; all matter is in movement. The sensations merely transmit to the brain the movement already inherent in matter. Materialists recognize the central role of the sensations in cognition, but they ultimately displace it somewhat. La Mettrie dedicates a long section in his *Histoire naturelle de l'âme* to several accounts confirming the importance of the senses in acquiring knowledge and concludes in sensationist fashion, "No senses, no ideas."[2] Although La Mettrie grants a major place to matter in the learning process, he does not take it quite as far as does d'Holbach, who wants to rid language of words without actual referents in the physical world. His goal of demystifying language of what he considers mere religious superstitions leads him, however, to adopt an epistemological system that derives thought from matter. What begins innocently in a sensationist vein becomes subtly turned around: "In fact it is never but through our senses that beings are known to us, or produce ideas in us; it is only as a result of movements imprinted on our body, that our brain is altered or our soul thinks, wills, & acts."[3] D'Holbach places these two statements parallel to each other. The first one takes a traditional, sensationist view, as the allusion to Aristotle makes clear in the lines

2. Julien Offray de La Mettrie, *Histoire naturelle de l'âme* (The Hague: Jean Neaulme, 1745), pp. 344–92; hereafter cited as (*HNA*); *L'Homme-machine,* ed. Francine Markovits, in La Mettrie, *Oeuvres philosophiques,* vol. 1 (Paris: Fayard, 1987); cited hereafter as (*HM*).

3. Paul-Henri Thiry, baron d'Holbach, *Système de la nature, ou Des lois du monde physique & du monde moral,* 2 vols. (1770; rpt. Geneva: Slatkine, 1973), 1: 165; hereafter cited as (*SN* 1) or (*SN* 2).

that follow it in the passage. But d'Holbach cites Aristotle only to use the inverse of his well-known axiom about the senses as the necessary conduit for whatever enters the mind. Whatever leaves the mind must correspond to some tangible object. He does not understand why Locke, who expounded on Aristotle's principle, failed to grasp this supposedly self-evident truth. The fact is that neither Aristotle nor Locke, as sensationists, ever intended the materialist interpretation d'Holbach gives to their thought. D'Holbach connects the senses to matter in such a way that the latter ultimately governs the former deterministically rather than interacts with them in a way that might lead one to believe that the senses can act independently. Naturally giving special prominence to the senses and sensations, sensationism takes a qualitatively different view of the relation between matter and ideas, between body and mind.

The sensationists prefer to consider the sentient individual as the independent initiator of the movements entailed in the dynamic cognitive process. From their perspective, an idea is possible in the first place because humanity is endowed with sensibility. Because of their sensitive nature, human beings receive and respond to the impressions left on them by objects. Bodies or objects do not move themselves; instead, humans must, according to Condillac, move about in order to establish their existence (*ER* 299). Even the anticlerical Helvétius reduces all mental operations to sensations, not matter (*DH* 1: 93, 111 [F 159, 179]). Ironically, it is the unorthodox, spiritualist Bonnet whose writings evoke an animated view of nature. In his hypothetical statue, he ties feeling to the vibration of the olfactory nerve, which receives its movement from the corpuscles emanating from a rose (*EA* 26, 32–33, 43).

Both sensationists and materialists place great stock, primarily for polemical reasons, in experience, which serves as a common thread interweaving their theories. They wanted to supplant preexisting paradigms for the mind, which they viewed not only as inadequate explanations but as serious obstacles to the variously progressive agendas they wished to implement. Locke first uses experience as an alternative explanation for the innatist theory of the origin of ideas. Previous thinkers had tried to explain ideas as already existing in the mind in some form at birth. Locke claims, however, that ideas originate in experience, which he successfully utilizes to debunk innate ideas. It then serves generally as a fundamental criterion for truth for his French sensationist disciples. Beginning with Condillac, they make systematic use of it as an intellectual tool to root out error and ignorance as well as to advance enlightenment, which in turn was to result in progressive gains for society. The falseness of superstition, received ideas, and metaphysical abstractions can be shown by resorting to concrete or real examples from experiences everyone has had. Men and women do not need to be told by authoritarian figures what is hot or cold, good or bad, beautiful or ugly when their everyday experience gives them a sense of this. Sensationism and materialism derived their tremendous explanatory power from the evidence of lived, irrefutable experiences. For society and culture, such teachings had widespread implications. If individuals could look only to themselves for truthful judgments about the moral and physical worlds, they did not need to rely on figures of authority like rulers, parents, and priests for validation of their actions. These philosophies were both intended to be ultimately liberating.

In the hands of the sensationists, experience appears at first rather innocent, since Condillac and Bonnet do not use it seriously to challenge the Church's dogmas. As an abbot in the Catholic Church, Condillac may have enjoyed some immunity from censorship. It must be said, though, that his writings do not openly attack the Church. Interested as he was in epistemological questions, Condillac no doubt considered himself more of an enlightened churchman and *philosophe* than a polemicist. He appeals to experience as a way of having his reader accept the truthfulness of his claims (*EOCH* 126, 159). Bonnet, for his part, goes to great efforts to reconcile some of his somewhat extraordinary views on future forms of life and the resurrection of the dead. For him, all theory comes from experience and observation (*EA* 302–3). Increasingly, however, experience comes to take on an authority of its own that Helvétius and the materialists certainly recognize and take advantage of in their battle against intolerance and fanaticism. The various uses of experience by sensationism and materialism reflect the extension of sensationism from its early metaphysical concerns with truth and analytic method in Condillac toward a growing preoccupation with practical matters in society and culture in Helvétius and the materialists.

Despite their recognition of the usefulness of experience, sensationists and materialists define it in slightly different terms. As one might expect, at the core of human existence for the one camp lie sensations, whereas matter constitutes the *sine qua non* in the existence of anything for the other group. For both, sensations and matter thus provide an original and common experience to all people everywhere. It bears pointing out that the very first experience of any kind for

Condillac's and Bonnet's statues is a sensation. All of the sensationists, including Helvétius, consider the sensations as an origin. Indeed, Helvétius traces everything back to physical sensibility. When they say, as they often do, that one must go back in time to the origin of anything *(remonter à l'origine)* to find an answer, that origin invariably consists of sensations. The sensationist genesis of ideas as well as of human existence repeatedly states quite literally that in the beginning there were sensations (*EOCH* 107; *TSn* 11; *EA* 13; *DE* 233, 289).

The materialists also grant the sensations an early, albeit not original, status in the composition of ideas. But they reduce the sensations themselves to matter, to mechanical parts of what we now call the nervous system. The sensationists, especially Bonnet, were already calling attention to the physiological mechanisms operative in the senses, yet they always relate these to the human individual. Sensationism acknowledges to some extent causation from object to perceiver and is associated somewhat with the system of physical influence as well as with occasionalism for other reasons.[4] In the subject-object dialectic, the sensationists emphasize, however, the subjective, conscious character of humanity, whereas the materialists tend to make mechanical automatons out of men and women—biological machines composed of nervous tissue and fibers whose reactions are purely physiological. Hence, the uproar over La Mettrie's *L'Homme-machine,* whose telling title seems to encapsulate materialist thought and to disenfranchise men and women of all that is human in them.[5] In its unabashed materialism, his work called unwanted attention to the atheistic implications of some of the writings of the *philosophes,* who were struggling at the same time to establish their own credibility in

4. In addition to the system of physical influence, the other contemporary competing systems for explaining the relation between the mind and body, namely, occasionalism and preestablished harmony, deny any such causation. They both attempt to maintain a causal role for a Supreme Being who either allows perception to take place on each occasion of sensation or who endows all human beings with perfect equipment for understanding their world. The system of physical influence was often linked with materialism. See Yolton, *Locke and French Materialism,* pp. 15–57 and p. 166.

5. See Ann Thomson, *Materialism and Society in the Mid-Eighteenth Century: La Mettrie's "Discours préliminaire"* (Geneva: Droz, 1981), pp. 33–58; and her "L'Homme machine, mythe ou métaphore?" *Dix-Huitième Siècle* 20 (1988), 367–76. Rejecting Vartanian's thesis about the mechanistic Cartesianism of La Mettrie, Thomson finds La Mettrie's materialism creative and dynamic. In her account of La Mettrie's materialism, which stresses the role of the imagination and his interest in psychological problems, the complexity of all mental processes can be explained by the organization of matter.

society and who wished to proceed more cautiously than La Mettrie. He invokes sensory experience itself—what we see—as sufficient proof of the overarching predominance of nature, which embraces all matter (*HM* 115). Matter defines the senses and precedes the sensations in the materialist epistemological chronology. Experience from the testimony of the senses helps sensationists and materialists alike avoid error and find truth. But materialists in general and d'Holbach in particular stop at nature and matter, which he equates with experience (*SN* 2: 171), as the only cause worthy of study. Moreover, he refuses to speculate about another origin for our existence (*SN* 2: 183).

Relying solely on experience, materialists indeed despair of finding an origin in anything other than matter. La Mettrie is indifferent to the very question of origins for a God or matter (*HM* 94). As a frequent proponent of materialism, Diderot flatly states in *Le Rêve de d'Alembert* through his spokesman, Dr Bordeu, that we are nothing in the beginning.[6] He does go on to add microscopic physiological parts to the incipient "imperceptible point," but all these parts serve simply to underscore the material quality of human existence. Diderot's writings about history treat it not so much as an artifact that originates in the past but as a constantly evolving process in the present.[7] When they do not profess outright atheism, materialists at best claim, as do sensationists, a certain agnosticism or skepticism. The origin of humanity, like that of nature, is unknowable (*SN* 1: 80, 88).

According to sensationists, humanity's original state is one of ignorance—in its etymological sense of simply not knowing. Before taking any position on humanity's innate goodness or evil, which they of course reject because of the *a priori* status it would have, sensationists ironically posit an epistemological void that is at the same time a beginning. As Helvétius puts it with a degree of wry humor in advocating the competent education of the masses: "Man is born ignorant [i.e., unaware]: he is not born stupid, & it is not even without any difficulty that he becomes so" (*DH* 1: 6 [F 49]). Condillac's and Bonnet's statues clearly have no knowledge of anything before their first sensations. Beyond that initial ignorance, however, Bonnet believes in no knowledge of "the *actual* Essence of Things (*EA* 168). He dismisses the

---

6. Diderot, *Le Rêve de d'Alembert,* in *Oeuvres philosophiques,* ed. Paul Vernière, p. 320; hereafter cited as (*RA*).

7. See Rosalina de la Carrera's discussion of Diderot's *Essai sur les règnes de Claude et de Néron,* in *Success in Circuit Lies: Diderot's Communicational Practices* (Stanford: Stanford University Press, 1991), pp. 93–123.

question of agency and concentrates only on the effects we see. Although the sensationists themselves do not deny an origin, they certainly allow for speculation in this regard. Materialists share the sensationist tendency to profess ignorance about the essence of matter and to focus only on what our senses reveal to us about its existence and appearances—that it appears to be colored and shaped, to be hard or soft, to move about or remain stationary. Such is La Mettrie's fundamentally sensationist position on the origin of knowledge (*HNA* 9), and d'Holbach holds to it as well (*SN* 1: 174). D'Holbach extends the ignorance of matter to all nature, with which it is synonymous in his way of thinking, but keeps alive the hope that we might one day more fully understand it (*SN* 1: 43). In the meantime, though, he encourages his reader not to cling to the superstitions of the past.

The ignorance that sensationists and materialists confess having about the essence of things leads them to different solutions of the mind-body problem, which is related in many ways to the question of origin. On the one hand, materialists make no distinction, as Descartes had, between the two substances. The soul or mind, being part of the body and not separate from it, takes on material qualities. La Mettrie sees no great difficulty in explaining the union of these substances and establishes a long list of ancients who do not distinguish between them (*HNA* 97, 331). Since the soul's faculties depend on the body, there is no reason, according to La Mettrie, to make two things out of one (*HNA* 170; *HM* 98, 103–4). D'Holbach, too, rejects the double nature of man as a pure and misleading invention designed to subject humanity to laws other than natural ones in the physical world (*SN* 1: 357, 360). Although not identical, body and soul are thus on the materialist account one substance with two kinds of properties.

On the other hand, sensationists do not go quite so far as materialists in fusing the mind, body, and soul. They maintain a respectful, if not pious, attitude toward them. Helvétius studiously avoids using the term *soul* in *De l'esprit* but identifies it with the faculty of feeling or sensibility in his posthumous work, *De l'homme* (*DH* 1: 86 [F 150]). By not making the mind entirely independent of the soul, he in fact makes it dependent on it, allowing him to "conclude that if the soul is not the mind, the mind is the effect of the soul or the faculty of feeling" (*DH* 1: 88–89 [F 153]). However intricately they may be connected in a physical way, the mind, body, and soul do not receive the designation of matter in sensationist epistemology. Dependence after all is not the same as identity. In playing on the difference between the two, sensationists can continue to make their epistemological claims without entering a polemical fray over religious beliefs, which Helvétius alone seems prepared to assault. Yet even he does not directly equate body and mind. Bonnet, to the contrary, intentionally keeps the body and soul separate as two completely different substances in one mixed being that is man (*EA* 3, 15). He considers his own position as a compromise between the radically materialist and spiritualist views of our being (*EP* 107). Condillac and Helvétius share Bonnet's spirit of compromise insofar as they all strive to highlight the interaction between the mind and body in the face of the tendency of the other theories to emphasize only one of these substances. By bringing together these two essential cognitive components, but maintaining their identity, the sensationists attempt to present a balanced view of human thought and behavior.

The difference of opinion between the sensationists and materialists on the nature of the soul is a subtle but important one.[8] Exactly how close a stance they take becomes clear with Helvétius's publication of *De l'esprit*, which the Church accused of antireligious, materialist views and which called into question some of the theretofore seemingly harmless sensationist beliefs of Condillac.[9] At stake in the question of the soul's nature, which was more than a theological debate at the time, is the legitimate authority of secular rule by kings. For their power was based on the notion of divine right. If the soul's immortality is doubted and divinity is questioned, so, too, is the power of monarchs. By making the soul a channel for sensations destined for the brain, sensationism effects a gradual rapprochement of the spiritual with the physical. Bonnet professes almost in vain the immateriality of the soul (*EA* xx), which the lion's share of his writing practically belies by elaborately mixing the body with the soul, itself changing and identifying as it does with each new sensation (*EA* 26, 80, 352). No one questioned the

---

8. For an excellent general discussion of the "materialization" of the soul in eighteenth-century France, see Vartanian, "Quelques réflexions sur le concept d'âme dans la littérature clandestine," in *Le Matérialisme du XVIIIe siècle et la littérature clandestine,* ed. Olivier Bloch (Paris: Vrin, 1982), pp. 149–65. Vartanian calls attention to the "functional nature of the soul," which La Mettrie, Diderot, and d'Holbach all tried to oppose to the notion of the soul as an immaterial substance. He also notes the physiological side of sensationism that lent support to the materialist belief in a mechanized soul. On "the progressive elimination of the soul as a philosophical entity from physiology," see Karl M. Figlio, "Theories of Perception and the Physiology of Mind in the Late Eighteenth Century," *History of Science* 12 (1975), 177–212. See also Kathleen Wellman, "Dilemma and Opportunity: The Physiology of the Soul," *Studies in Eighteenth-Century Culture* 22 (1992), 301–16.

9. Smith, *Helvétius*, pp. 103–4.

ability of the soul to feel, which on the surface at least appears to conform perfectly with Christian doctrine. One must be able to feel or know consciously the difference between good and evil in order to choose with one's free will the former over the latter. The slippage in the conception of the soul first occurs, however, with the ambiguity over feeling and sensing. Are feeling and sensing the activities of a conscious human being with a free will or are they merely the physiological responses (i.e., the action of nerves and muscles) of matter in motion determined by internal mechanisms and external stimuli? In the eighteenth century, one would indeed be at pains to deny the close interrelation of these terms as well as of the concepts of feeling and knowing, for whose virtual identification sensationism was in large part responsible. The sensationists and materialists responded in the affirmative respectively to these questions. According to sensationist theory, the ideas that constitute the bedrock of knowledge must come from the senses, our physical organs for feeling. As the soul is drawn ever more tightly to the sphere of the physical world of sensations, which in turn affects the mental world of ideas, it comes to take on a physical character itself *(le physique de l'âme)*. It is as if both the internal, physiological aspects of sensation coupled with the senses' necessary interaction with the external world "contaminate" the soul and give it an ineluctably physical side. Although this does not at first cause grave concern in the Church, it does begin to present a serious problem when materialists or sensationists like Helvétius with a marked materialist proclivity use it as a springboard for their arguments for the soul's materiality.[10]

Whereas for the sensationists the soul merely interacts with the senses and the physical world, for the materialists it is a part of the body itself. La Mettrie affirms the corporeal, material nature of the soul bluntly in *L'Homme-machine:* "the soul is but a principle of movement, or a material sensitive part of the brain, which one can, without fearing error, look upon as a mainspring of the entire machine, which has a visible influence on all others, and even appears to have been made first; in such a way that all others would only be an emanation of it" (*HM*

10. In an attempt to defuse the controversy surrounding the soul's materiality, several writers and reviewers of the period, including Voltaire and Diderot, followed Locke by disassociating immortality from immateriality. The soul could be material and remain immortal in accordance with Church dogma. See Yolton, *Locke and French Materialism,* pp. 68, 78, 80, 98, 296.

105). La Mettrie subordinates the soul to the brain, which itself is a physical part of the body. In the process, sensationism itself undergoes a similar transformation, as Aram Vartanian suggests: "it may be said that in the eighteenth century the man-machine theory involved the subordination of sensationism to a psychological method that was rooted not so much in sensory experience as in the facts of physiology."[11] The organic, mechanistic interpretation of human beings dominates, but does not exclude, the experiential one to which sensationism had given primary consideration.[12] La Mettrie's attempt to restore to the soul, given its lowered status from the spiritual to the material world, some of its former grandeur by making it a kind of king of all springs strikes one as a final mocking, if not humorous, gesture to the ecclesiastics. Basing his opinion upon experience, which "leaves no doubt about the connection of the functions of the soul with the state & organization of the body," Diderot tends to agree with La Peyronie in finding the center for the soul in the corpus callosum of the brain and considers the spirituality or immateriality of the soul a vain pursuit.[13] In *Le Rêve de d'Alembert*, Diderot substitutes sensibility for the soul, which he dismisses on physiological and psychological grounds.[14] D'Holbach resolves the question of the soul's material nature in a deceptively simple manner. Since "the soul is moved," he writes, "& is altered by material causes that act on it . . . we are authorized to conclude that all its operations & faculties prove that it is material" (*SN* 1: 117). Like his fellow materialists, d'Holbach uses the sensationist theorizing about the acquisition of ideas through the senses, which themselves are material, to reinforce his argument for the materiality of the soul (*SN* 1: 156). Material objects act upon material senses, which affect the soul. In turn, the soul must, as the materialist logic would have it, be material.[15]

11. Vartanian, *La Mettrie's "L'Homme machine": A Study in the Origins of an Idea* (Princeton: Princeton University Press, 1960), p. 121.

12. Vartanian, *La Mettrie's "L'Homme machine,"* p. 122.

13. See his addition to the article "Ame," in *Encyclopédie, ou Dictionnaire raisonné des sciences, des arts et des métiers* (Paris: Briasson, David, Le Breton, Durand, 1751), 1: 342. On the complex and uncertain relationship between the *Encyclopédie,* materialism, and Freemasonry, see Margaret C. Jacob, *The Radical Enlightenment: Pantheists, Freemasons, and Republicans* (London: George Allen and Unwin, 1981), pp. 256–66.

14. Vartanian, "Diderot, or, The Dualist in Spite of Himself," in *Diderot: Digression and Dispersion,* ed. Jack Undank and Herbert Josephs (Lexington, Ky: French Forum, 1984), pp. 250–68.

15. By more or less eliminating the soul as an independent, vital component of human behavior, the materialist account comes close to denying the existence of all conscious

By trying to find a role for the soul in acts of cognition or by not dismissing it altogether as the materialists tend to do, sensationists put themselves into a double bind. The role the soul takes as an instrument of feeling inevitably pulls it into the web of sensations and the physical, material sphere. Sensationism tends to preclude any absolute separation of mental from physical activity, of ideas from sensations. If the soul is to be involved at all in the acquisition of knowledge, it will be tainted by physical contact. The inclusion of the soul to maintain a certain spirituality and humanity for the species comes at the cost of allowing for the soul's materiality. The epistemological dilemma is further complicated by historical circumstances.

Benefiting from the increasing number of discoveries in anatomy at the time, sensationists attributed more and more aspects of the sensory process, which previously had been the somewhat mystical domain of the soul, to physical parts of the body.[16] As a scientist, Bonnet not surprisingly goes into great detail about nerve fibers and fluids, which, their spurious medical value today notwithstanding, indicate his general point about the physical causes of sensation (*EA* 445). While claiming sensation as a conscious process, the sensationists also partly make it, as the materialists do entirely, a bodily process. As the so-called anatomical parts of the soul come to the fore, so, too, does their material nature, for the body in its anatomy is composed of matter. In the process, the soul begins to lose its claim to immateriality. A chain reaction of imagined creations takes place in reverse; their credibility vanishes. Helvétius notes the illusory steps leading from the creation of souls to that of the country deemed worthy of their dwelling (*DH* 1: 176 [F 256]). Once the soul is no longer endowed with spiritual qualities, its final resting place is also thrown into question. Seen as pure creations of man's faculty of imagination, the immaterial soul, heaven, and God all ultimately fall together in the materialist cosmology, as does the divine right of kings. Especially for those in positions of power in the church and state, the specters of spiritual and secular anarchy seemed to be the only possible implications of materialism. Borrowing from sensationism, materialists demand that something have a material form before they can have an idea of it. Having no idea of God or any

---

processes. Such a position may be explained in part by materialism's radicalization of sensationist theory, which, it will be remembered, excluded to a large extent the active mental process of reflection from its explanation of the origin of ideas.

16. For a discussion of these discoveries, see François Duchesneau, *La Physiologie des lumières: Empirisme, modèles et théories* (The Hague: Nijhoff, 1982).

other spirit, La Mettrie cannot conceive how his soul is united to Him (*HNA* 226). The argument by design according to which nature's bounty and beauty prove the existence of God means nothing, as Diderot points out, to a blind man, who would need to touch God to believe in Him.[17] Since matter moves other forms of matter in the physical world, d'Holbach cannot reconcile a spiritual being with the creator and motive force of matter (*SN* 1: 26). He reduces the question of God's existence to a simple matter of vision, which either confirms or refutes an object's being: "everyone sees the sun, but no one sees God" (*SN* 2: 94). By adducing sensationist principles whose scope he has enlarged considerably, d'Holbach denies a divine presence that does not make even its outer shell or bark apparent to any sense. He replies to the spiritualists like Plato "that in order to believe a thing exists, one must at least have some idea of it; that this idea can come only through our senses, that everything our senses do not allow us to know is nothing for us" (*SN* 2: 122, 125). Epistemological arguments from sensationism for the basic ways by which we know anything serve here to reinforce materialist ontological claims about the nonexistence of a Supreme Being.

In the void left by the absence of an immaterial God, the materialists see nothing but matter. Its essential attributes, according to La Mettrie, consist in extension, motive power, and the physiological faculty of feeling or sensing (*HNA* 29–30, 37–38). Matter, all of which has an extended mass of some measurable proportions, can not only be moved but moves itself (*HNA* 29; *HM* 108).[18] La Mettrie does not rule out the eventuality that matter might indeed have the faculty of thought (*HM* 63).[19] Once one accepts the sensitive nature of matter, thinking matter becomes a distinct possibility in accordance with sensationist tenets about the natural dialectic between sensations and thought. Writing under the pseudonym of Dr Baumann, Maupertuis defended the concept of thinking matter and viewed the repugnant response to it as a result of people's misconception that the intelligence attributed to matter be the same as their own.[20] In his eyes, granting intelligence (i.e., mental processes) to all matter once rather than each time it occurs reflects a

17. Diderot, *Lettre sur les aveugles,* in *Oeuvres philosophiques,* pp. 118–19.

18. For the active and passive forms of matter, see below, pages 215f.

19. For a discussion of the reception in France of Locke's suggesion about thinking matter, see Yolton, *Locke and French Materialism.*

20. Pierre-Louis Moreau de Maupertuis, *Système de la nature,* ed. François Azouvi (Paris: Vrin, 1984), pp. 180–81.

"grand," "worthy," and ultimately efficient way for God to create the universe.[21] Diderot, as a materialist himself, hypocritically records his shock over the "terrible consequences" of Maupertuis's hypothesis and marvels over his reconciliation of "the most hardy philosophical ideas with the most profound respect for religion."[22] The following passage, however, clarifies Diderot's attitude about the physiological and affective sensibility of all matter: "From the elephant to the aphid . . . from the aphid to the sensitive, living molecule, the origin of everything, not one point in all of nature that does not suffer or enjoy pleasures" (*RA* 313). And once matter can feel, it can also think, for the *philosophes* of the French Enlightenment inextricably yoked sensibility and knowledge. Of the materialists, Diderot goes to the greatest effort to reconcile the paradoxical relation between active, conscious thought processes and passive, mechanical brain processes. The other materialists may not eliminate mental properties, but it is difficult to see how their materialist claims support them. A reductive explanation of consciousness in physical terms eludes them. D'Holbach defines matter in terms of extension, solidity, and distinct parts (*SN* 1: 90). He, too, affirms the necessity of movement for matter, making it an essential characteristic of matter for all eternity (*SN* 2: 132).

Of all the qualities the materialists discern in matter, they thus insist the most on movement, which is also recognized as crucial to cognition by the sensationists. Furthering their claim were advances in microscopes and telescopes, which "revealed that there could be no rest in nature."[23] In this regard, the French materialists were especially indebted to John Toland for having been "the first to have formulated the fundamental idea that movement is essential to matter," a tenet that became a basic part of their theory.[24] Although the sensationists fre-

---

21. Maupertuis, *Système de la nature,* pp. 183–84.

22. Diderot, *De l'Interprétation de la nature,* in *Oeuvres philosophiques,* pp. 226–29. Vernière notes that Diderot actually embraces these terrible consequences in *Le Rêve de d'Alembert* with his idea of a God-Universe in the form of a gigantic spider.

23. Barbara Maria Stafford, *Body Criticism: Imagining the Unseen in Enlightenment Art and Medicine* (Cambridge, Mass.: MIT Press, 1991), p. 348.

24. Pierre Lurbe, "Matière, nature, mouvement chez d'Holbach et Toland," *Dix-Huitième Siècle* 24 (1992), 54–56. Lurbe notes that "d'Holbach, following Toland, distinguishes 'a movement of mass by which an entire body is transferred from one place to another' and 'an internal and hidden movement, which depends on the energy that is characteristic of a body' " (55). Unlike Toland, however, who defines movement as the motive force of homogeneous matter, d'Holbach finds in movement "the dynamism . . . of a whole group of forces qualitatively distinct, heterogeneous and specific" (56).

quently emphasize movement in the cognitive process, they focus primarily on that which either leads to or arises from sensations themselves and not from matter. Condillac calls attention to the movement of bodily parts like the hand as indispensable in establishing the existence of exterior objects (*ER* 299). Bonnet does speak of the corpuscles emanating from a rose (*EA* 26, 43), but he expends his greatest effort tracing closely the movement communicated *within* component parts of the nervous system: its molecules, fibers, and fluids. For the interior world, Helvétius finds in sensibility the equivalent of movement for matter (*DE* 280). Sensibility represents a motive force for all humanity's inner workings just as movement creates all the various physical assemblages of matter. In a word, movement is in sensibility for the sensationists, whereas it is in matter for the materialists.

What each philosophy considers to be in movement serves to distinguish each one's respective utmost concern. The chief object of activity for sensationism lies primarily in human beings and only secondarily in what comes into contact with them. It is a man or a woman who is moved and who stands in the middle of things in the sensationist world view. Conversely, materialism concerns itself first and foremost with the movement of matter, of which human beings form only a minuscule part, and thereby dismisses sensationism's anthropocentricity. It reverses the at once passive but central role sensationism ascribes to men and women by making them mere parts, albeit active ones, in the greater whole of nature.

Despite their overall agreement about the essential character of movement in matter, materialists define that movement in various ways, most of which entail the use of metaphors. La Mettrie gives perhaps the most memorable description of it while speaking of the human body as "a machine that winds its own springs: a living image of perpetual movement" (*HM* 69). Seemingly confirming La Mettrie in his view of constant movement were a number of contemporary scientific experiments, among others, about the flesh of animals moving after death, the reviving of apparently motionless tissue by pricking or injections, and especially a living gelatinous substance found in fresh-water ponds and known as polyps, which the Swiss naturalist Trembley showed to possess several modes of self-propulsion and which when divided would reproduce as separate entities (*HM* 98–108). For his part, Diderot was convinced of the animated nature of all matter in the world, which he compared to a great bee hive in constant motion and in a state of

continuous flux (*RA* 291). In his dream, d'Alembert imagines bees
stinging one another in a hive. Such a scene represents the continual
action and reaction Diderot saw in matter.[25] D'Holbach uses the concept
of *nisus* or potential energy to explain the apparent rest of objects.
Presumably, immobile objects are exercising force or movement on
one another at all times. D'Holbach gives the following example to
demonstrate the materialist notion that everything, even what seems
motionless, is moving: "A five-hundred-pound stone appears at rest on
the earth, yet it does not for an instant stop weighing with force on this
earth which resists it or pushes it back in its turn" (*SN* 1: 18). In the
three reigns of nature, matter's molecules are continuously circulating
(*SN* 1: 33). Movement is, to use the deconstructionist expression,
always already there. Since the question of origin is dismissed out of
hand, materialists concern themselves only with what is moving and
continues to move, that is, with a series of actions and reactions.
Causality thus comes to have a particularly strong sense in materialism.

This strong sense of causality evolves to a certain degree in sensationism with the concept of succession. The mind reflects on its different
modifications successively and one at a time (*EOCH* 176), just as
Condillac's statue judges sensations and distinguishes them best when
they succeed one another (*TSn* 36). Bonnet analyzes the first two
sensations in his statue so as to pinpoint the chain or sequence of steps
in cognition. While viewing, as do the materialists, the entire world as
successive in nature—generations, forms, and movements all follow one
another—Bonnet attributes its first cause to an omnipotent, omniscient,
benevolent, and perfect God (*PP* 283–89; *EA* 175). Helvétius finds the
succession of desires necessary to our happiness (*DH* 1: 172 [F 252]).
All of the sensationists focus on succession, because they are interested
in showing the order of things. As Bonnet states, "All our Theories of
Causes & *Effects* are limited ultimately to knowing the *Order* in which
Things succeed one another" (*EA* 93). But it is above all order, and
specifically the order of thought processes, that concerns them. At the
bottom line of their theory, sensations *precede* ideas. Helvétius extends
the claims of sensationism to include human behavior and institutions.
But even he does not extrapolate the theory so as to embrace the

25. Diderot explicitly states his belief in matter's constant movement and heterogeneous
nature in *Principes philosophiques sur la matière et le mouvement*, in *Oeuvres philosophiques*, p. 398. According to Vernière in his introduction to this work (p. 390), Diderot formerly
did not believe movement to be essential to matter in his *Pensées philosophiques* and his
Encyclopédie article on Spinoza.

causality of the physical world, for sensationism represents a fundamentally humanistic tradition with man at its center and in bold relief. This tradition is perhaps best reflected in the theory's greater emphasis on mental faculties or thought processes like memory, judgment, and the imagination than on brain processes of a physiological nature.

To the contrary, materialism dwarfs the importance of humanity by subjecting it and everything else to the material world's laws of causality. Gradually stripped of all spirituality, humanity becomes but a small link in the Chain of Being, far removed from the elevated position Bonnet envisaged. Human beings simply act and react, as does all matter. From the materialist perspective, which is more or less egalitarian, there is no hierarchy that places one being over another. "Nature," states La Mettrie, "has used only one and the same dough, whose yeasts it has simply varied" (*HM* 90). Each and every being is subject to the causal laws of matter. La Mettrie praises his Dutch medical teacher Boerhaave for rejecting final metaphysical causes and being indifferent toward the first physical causes of the elements, seeds, and movement (*HNA* 247–49). D'Holbach defines causality in terms of movement: "A *Cause* is a being that puts another in movement or that produces some change in it. . . . Each being, as a result of its essence, is capable of producing, receiving & communicating various movements (*SN* 1: 13). As the interaction of moving, material objects changes the objects by either adding or taking away their properties, a tremendous chain reaction is formed: "from the dull oyster to active & thinking man, we see an uninterrupted progression, a perpetual chain of combinations & movements, from which there result beings, who differ among themselves only by the variety of their elementary substances, of combinations & proportions of these same elements" (*SN* 1: 39). D'Holbach explains the diversity of the human and physical worlds, both of which are viewed as material, through movement, which itself is viewed as inherent in matter. The organization of the two becomes clear through a series of causes and effects arising from their movement. D'Holbach stresses the interdependence of forces acting in nature; these are all tied together as small physical links in a great chain in such a way that one cannot isolate any exterior cause (*SN* 1: 51, 75, 163, 249; *SN* 2: 385). In doing so, he aims to demonstrate not only the material connectedness of everything but also the impossibility of isolated causes outside the system—such as the soul or God—capable of moving matter. Simply put, materialism does not allow for random chance *(le hasard)*.

Random chance constitutes in many ways a kind of litmus test for a thinker's materialism. If one includes it or any divinity as possible causes for explaining nature's phenomena, one cannot lay claim to a pure materialism. None of the sensationists, however, actively bars random chance from his theorizing, and Helvétius, who was suspected of materialism, makes of it a pivotal point in his educational proposals. In his eyes, it indeed represents the largest part in one's education and in the formation of one's mind (*DE* 233, 387–88). La Mettrie expresses a skeptical attitude about the creation of the universe, postulating possible hidden causes for it in nature: "destroying random chance does not prove the existence of a Supreme Being, since there can be something else which would be neither random chance, nor God, I mean Nature, whose study consequently can only make nonbelievers, as the way of thinking of its happiest scrutineers proves" (*HM* 96). By not substituting God for the absence of random chance as an operative force in the universe, La Mettrie professes a pure form of materialism. He criticizes Diderot, who in his early work *Pensées philosophiques* (1746) admits the existence of a God, for not being able to convince an atheist such as himself.[26] Later in his *Lettre sur les aveugles* (1749), for which he was imprisoned at the Château de Vincennes, Diderot would himself move to an increasingly materialist position with his account of the comments by the dying, blind English mathematician Saunderson on the existence of God and the creation.[27] Despite his movement away from deism, however, Diderot continued to grant central importance to random chance and gave it its fullest expression in *Jacques le fataliste*, which constitutes in many ways an apology of unpredictability.[28] Because of his equivocal attitude toward random chance and determinism, Diderot cannot therefore be considered a pure materialist. In this regard, d'Holbach provides the clearest example. Attributing nothing to chance, he finds the wish to do so a manifestation of our ignorance and blindness (*SN* 1: 65, 69–70). We substitute imaginary causes and beings for real ones whose existence we cannot explain. The word itself, like

26. See Diderot, *Pensées philosophiques,* in *Oeuvres philosophiques,* p. 21. For La Mettrie's criticism of Diderot, see (*HM* 95).

27. Diderot, *Lettre sur les aveugles,* esp. 118–24. See also M. L. Perkins, "The Crisis of Sensationalism in Diderot's *Lettre sur les aveugles,*" *Studies on Voltaire and the Eighteenth Century* 174 (1978), 167–68, esp. 168. For Perkins, Diderot "softens his stand at the end and leaves the door open for deism."

28. Vartanian, *"Jacques le fataliste:* A Journey into the Ramifications of a Dilemma," in *Essays on Diderot and the Enlightenment in Honor of Otis Fellows* (Geneva: Droz, 1974), pp. 325–47; and Huguette Cohen, "Galiani, Diderot, and Nature's Loaded Dice," *Studies on Voltaire and the Eighteenth Century* 311 (1993), 35–59.

that for God, is for d'Holbach an imagined one devoid of meaning in a world governed by no uncertain causes and rules: "Nature is not a blind cause; it does not act at random; everything it does would never be fortuitous for whoever might know its way of acting, its resources, & its course" (*SN* 1: 252; *SN* 2: 158–59, 163). In order to remain in conformity with d'Holbach's materialism, one must resist the urge to seek supernatural causes and look for actual material ones. Where Diderot discerns only loose connections between the phenomena of an infinitely varied nature, d'Holbach finds a highly deterministic system of nature that confirms his materialist ontology.[29]

Related to the question of causality in nature is that of human passivity, which sensationists and materialists alike acknowledge. Tracing as they do the sources of knowledge to sensation alone rather than to both sensation and reflection, as had Locke, the sensationists reduce severely the kind of mental activity in which human beings can engage. In their view, men and women simply react for the most part to their environment, as do Condillac's and Bonnet's statues to a rose. The sensation that results from the interaction of a sentient being with an object in the external world sets into motion a complex series of other reactions that ultimately gives rise to an idea. In the process, though, the individual remains more or less passive. Notwithstanding their sometimes eloquent arguments for freedom, the sensationists in their preoccupation with the very early stages of cognition tend to underscore human passivity. As sensationism comes to focus on the subsequent stages, it quickly emphasizes the individual's own activity. Condillac does distinguish between active and passive functions for his statue. Its activity arises from internal causes, primarily memory, whereas passivity characterizes it at the time of a sensation that comes from the external world (*TSn* 20). The statue functions as an active or passive being depending upon the location of any effect's cause within or without it respectively. Recalling sensations through memory, which is already present in it, the statue acts on itself, while with the assimilation of each new sensation from the outside world, it responds passively. Although Bonnet envisages the soul as passive after conception, he attributes to it at birth the quality of motive force, which causes the reproduction of ideas (*EP* 8, 75). Bonnet at once asserts an active role for the soul in perception and subordinates it to the body's passive

29. Günther Mensching, "La Nature et le premier principe de la métaphysique chez d'Holbach et Diderot," *Dix-Huitième Siècle* 24 (1992), 117–36.

process of sensibility.[30] For his part, Helvétius takes a stronger position than his fellow sensationists on the question of human passivity by equating what Condillac and Bonnet consider as the active faculty of judgment with feeling and sensation (*DE* 22, 24, 50). As he moves increasingly toward a materialist outlook, Helvétius views the soul as a passive mechanism, wholly indistinguishable from the faculty of feeling or sensing (*DH* 1: 86 [F 150–51]). The passivity of the body in receiving sensations has extended to the soul as the two become virtually synonymous in Helvétius's writings.

As one might expect from their emphasis on the material nature of all things, the materialists tighten the connection between the mind and body at the expense of the soul's activity. Like any force, the motive power that La Mettrie, following materialist philosophers, attributes to matter must come from movement and therefore exists only as a potential power for matter to move itself (*HNA* 11). In other words, once set into motion, matter moves itself. This is of course a somewhat subtle and restricted appraisal of matter's self-propulsion, but materialists cannot conceive of matter in the physical world that is not already in movement. Abstractly speaking, matter may be seen as not yet moving itself. But contingent circumstances always put matter in motion in a universe whose material parts were viewed, as they were by the materialists, as constantly acting and interacting with one another. Such a view naturally leads to a conception of matter as possessing both mechanical or passive and active properties, the latter having the most influence on nature (*HNA* 13–19). In materialism, it is matter rather than any faculty of a supposedly higher intellectual order that is per-forming any action. La Mettrie thus calls judgment a "passive acquies-cence" to the evidence provided by sensations, distinguishing it clearly from any action of the will, as Descartes would have it (*HNA* 309–10). Diderot again diverges here somewhat from mainstream materialist orthodoxy by depicting the mind as an extremely vibrant center of activity, subject less to laws of succession than to those of simultaneity. His belief in the possibility of simultaneous mental activities does not for that matter put him in agreement with the sensationists either, for they emphasized "serial analysis," linearity, and succession in their thinking.[31] The one-man orchestra depicted in *Le Neveu de Rameau*

---

30. See the chapter on Bonnet, pages 72–73.

31. Cf. Wilda Anderson, *Diderot's Dream* (Baltimore: Johns Hopkins University Press, 1990), pp. 19–20, 49. Anderson distinguishes Diderot from Condillac in this respect and is apparently alluding to the sensationists when she speaks of Diderot's "nonmaterialist predeces-

plays several instruments at once. Even this stunning image of the mind's flexibility and virtuosity in performing several diverse musical stunts at the same time does not, however, do justice to what is actually taking place in our brain. Elsewhere in an analysis of the order in which tenses and parts of speech in language occur, Diderot also paints an image of the body lumbering after an active mind. Language may necessitate the succession of words and ideas in order to make them comprehensible, but such an orderly exterior appearance should not be mistaken for the state of the soul. As Diderot writes, "sensation does not have this successive development of speech in the soul. . . . The formation of languages requires decomposition; but *seeing* an object, *judging* it beautiful, *feeling* a pleasant sensation, *desiring* possession, is the state of the soul at the very same moment, and what Greek and Latin render by a single word. . . . how cold a copy of what is happening in it is even the most lively diction."[32] Diderot's tendency to reduce human beings in the final analysis to sensibility rather than to matter brings to the fore his slight preference for vitalism over materialism.[33] He has Julie de Lespinasse describe herself as "a cluster of sensitive points" just as he has Bordeu extend sensibility to all parts of the body (*RA* 315, 322).[34] As a materialist, d'Holbach of course takes a radical attitude toward human passivity. Everything, even unto our dreams, proves the passivity of our soul (*SN* 1: 161, 358).

As it had for the sensationists, the materialist response to the question

---

sors" for whom "the problem of the time-linearity of sensation and thus of thought . . . had posed serious logical problems . . . in attempting to generate an explanation of the structure of consciousness" (p. 49).

32. Diderot, *Lettre sur les sourds et muets à l'usage de ceux qui entendent et qui parlent,* in *Oeuvres complètes,* vol. 4, ed. Herbert Dieckmann, Jacques Proust, and Jean Varloot (Paris: Hermann, 1978), 4: 158, 162.

33. The two outlooks remain paradoxically side by side in much of Diderot's writing, as Vartanian suggests. Diderot frequently creates "an adroit opposition between the vocabulary of feeling [i.e., sensibility and vitalism] and the rhetoric of mechanism [i.e., materialism]" (p. 393). Vartanian sees the two philosophies as "compatible" (p. 402) in Diderot's thought. See "Diderot's Rhetoric of Paradox, or, The Conscious Automaton Observed," *Eighteenth-Century Studies* 14 (1981), 379–405.

34. An exemplary text for the reciprocal influence of philosophy on literature and of literature on philosophy, Diderot's *Rêve de d'Alembert* not only incorporates philosophy into literature but also reinforces Diderot's philosophy through the work's literary form, the dialogue. By its diffusion of narrative voices, this form calls attention to the diffusion of sensibility in the body. According to Diderot, there is not one central point of sensibility, such as a soul located in one place, any more than there is one central narrative point of view that is all-encompassing. Mutiple narrators evoke both the multiple sensible points in the body and, above all, sensibility's movement from one point in the body to another.

218 The Politics of Sensationism

of the soul's passivity has further implications for free will. If one merely responds to material forces without any positive action of one's own, the terms will and freedom become meaningless. Sensationists, however, were more reluctant to abandon freedom than were the materialists. Human beings may operate in a passive way at the level of sensations, but they gain independence at a certain point. For Condillac, that point comes with the development of memory and the imagination: "As soon as the memory is formed, and the habit of the imagination is in our power, the signs recollected by the former, and the ideas revived by the latter, begin to free the soul from its dependence in regard to the objects by which it was surrounded" (*EOCH* 132). The active faculty of reflection, which stems from passive faculties generated by sensations, serves as a liberating force for the soul, making it free to choose. But much prior knowledge and experience are needed to allow one to act and choose freely. The process of choosing involves deliberation:

> If one does not deliberate, one does not choose: one merely follows the impressions of objects. In such a case freedom could not possibly take place.
> But, to deliberate, one must know the advantages and disadvantages of obeying one's desires or resisting them; and deliberation, as we have seen, assumes experience and knowledge. Freedom thus implies them equally. . . . Knowledge therefore relieves it [the statue] little by little from the slavery to which its needs appear at first to subject it: it breaks the chains holding it in the dependence of objects, and teaches it to abandon itself only by choice, and only as long as it believes to have found its happiness. (*DSL* 274–75)

Knowledge is power, in accordance with the popular saying. That power allows us to direct ourselves and not be driven by external circumstances. To express the control we must exercise over them, Condillac goes on to use the image of a knowledgeable pilot navigating his ship safely across the high seas. The waves, representing the action of objects on us through the senses, do not control the ship as long as the pilot has learned enough about navigation. Only tempests or the passions, to finish the allegory, can make us lose control of our free will. Otherwise, we govern ourselves instead of being governed by objects acting on our senses.

The point at which Bonnet finds his statue active, and hence sees the first exercise of will or freedom, comes with the act of preferring one sensation over another. One sensation may give more pleasure than another so that anyone will pay more attention to it and engage the motive force of the soul, which Bonnet defines as freedom (*EP* 157). A preference, however, is not a sensation but an action (*EA* 104–6). It necessitates the active use of attention. Freedom, which is the simple power of carrying out one's choice, and will, which acts on that power, thus start with the statue's second sensation (*EA* 114, 128, 285–86). The sensations may come about in a passive way, but the individual, by acting upon them, exercises his or her free will. Greater knowledge fosters an enlightened will that seeks truth, well-being, and perfection (*EA* 186). One gathers, however, that for Bonnet, this kind of will and freedom produces the most important benefits for the private individual rather than for society as a collective whole.[35]

Helvétius both reverses the sensationist proclivity toward assigning active faculties such as freedom and will to the soul and removes the ambiguity over our search for happiness. Not surprisingly, as he either avoids or abandons altogether the notion of a soul, he also drops some of the functions traditionally associated with it. As nothing more for Helvétius than the faculty of feeling or sensing, the soul "ought to be regarded as purely passive" (*DH* 1: 86 [F 151]). Consequently, external events shape the consciousness of men and women who do not play an active part in determining their own lives. Giving primacy as he does to physical sensibility as the determining factor in our minds and behavior, Helvétius takes sensationism to the extreme. It is not so much the case that we actively choose happiness as it is that the desire for happiness drives us.

For the sensationists, happiness constitutes an ambiguous concept. They relate it to a moral, abstract state as well as to a purely physical one. Its ambiguity no doubt stems from that ambiguity surrounding the faculty of feeling or sensibility, which at once applies to ephemeral

35. Such is indeed the Marxist criticism of eighteenth-century French metaphysics in general, both materialism and, indirectly, sensationism. Although French materialism may have been the historical precedent for dialectical materialism in the following century, by focusing as it did primarily on the single individual it did not presumably expand its scope far enough to include the entire human species. Moreover, Marxist historians claim, its emphasis on the study of "human nature" did not take into account other important factors such as human heredity, historical development, or evolution. See G. V. Plekhanov, *Essays in the History of Materialism,* trans. Ralph Fox (London: John Lane, 1934), esp. pp. 11–12, 74–75, 101–3.

feelings such as good or evil and to more concrete sense perceptions of pleasure or pain. Sensationists indeed tend to define good in terms of pleasure, and evil in terms of pain; the line of demarcation within each set of terms is never clear. Happiness consists in the pursuit of good, and pleasure in the avoidance of evil and pain. Whereas Condillac and Bonnet would have us choose with our free will happiness over misery, Helvétius, following the Stoics, views this choice as a predetermined one: "deliberation is thus always in us the necessary effect of our hatred of pain & our love of pleasure" (*DH* 2: 121 [F 603]). Necessity precludes any choice. Although supposedly speaking for the Stoics, Helvétius is also clearly speaking for himself when he states in a note to the passage quoted above: "Man is thus not free. His will is therefore as necessarily the effect of his ideas, in consequence of his sensations, as pain is the effect of a blow" (*DH* 2: 154 [F 645]). The connection Helvétius, like all sensationists, makes between sensations and ideas extends further here to the will. Once it does, sensations are perceived as the determinants of will. Helvétius does not take the last remaining step, which is but a short one, separating him from the pure materialists. But he certainly begs the question of the chief factors affecting the sensations, which in turn affect everything else. These the materialists find precisely and exclusively in matter in motion.

The materialists' attitude about material causality brings them ultimately to a deterministic outlook. La Mettrie reduces all intellectual faculties of the reasoning soul—perceptions, freedom, attention, reflection, the order or arrangement of ideas, examination, and judgment—to sensibility so that the reasoning soul acts only in a sensory way (*HNA* 288–317, esp. 303–5). As heralds of the first signs of freedom, sensations determine one's will by acting on the soul, which does not become involved in the deliberating process, because the same sensations start the process for it (*HNA* 292). There is no freedom or will without the faculty of feeling or sensing. Having reduced these faculties to sense perceptions, La Mettrie proceeds to dismantle the supposed immaterial, active source of them in the soul. In a very limited way, it may act on its own, but in so doing, it merely shares a quality common to all matter: "Let it suffice for us to notice that in attention, the Soul can act through its own force, I mean by its motive force, by that activity coessential to matter, & that almost all Philosophers, as has been said, have counted among the number of essential attributes of the sentient being, & in general of the substance of bodies" (*HNA* 294–95). Strategically, La Mettrie grants the soul movement and activity at the same time he associates it with the characteristics of all matter. The gain in the soul's activity comes both at the cost of its materiality and with the loss of its freedom and will. The mechanical man determined by material forces looms large in these pages, just as it does in d'Holbach's work.

In his determinism, d'Holbach traces everything to nature's law of necessity. Nothing happens by chance. By necessity, he means "the infallible and constant connection of causes with their effects" that allows one to conclude "that all phenomena are necessary, & that each of nature's beings in the given circumstances, & according to given properties, cannot act otherwise than it does" (*SN* 1: 50). Clearly, such an approach leaves little room to exercise one's will freely, as all actions take on a mechanical character. Man dupes himself into believing that he acts spontaneously and through his free will, whereas "he is continuously altered by causes which, in spite of himself, influence his machine, alter his being & regulate his behavior" (*SN* 1: 74). Among these causes, d'Holbach cites temperament, received ideas, true or false notions of happiness, and opinions that are reinforced by example, education, and daily experience (*SN* 1: 203). Lest there be any doubt about his position on human freedom, d'Holbach states unequivocally, "Man is thus free at no instant in his life" (*SN* 1: 203).

Such an absolute view of the ineluctable, necessary causality linking everything in the physical and psychological world is unquestionably fatalistic and, what is more, atheistic.[36] D'Holbach's definition of fatality indeed closely resembles that for necessity: "*Fatality* is the eternal, unchanging, necessary order established in nature, or the indispensable connection of causes that act with the effects they bring about" (*SN* 1: 220). It is nature's, and not God's, order or system that operates in the universe. At best, God is but another word for fatality, but even so He would be no freer than man (*SN* 2: 112). Rather than finding fatalism dangerous, d'Holbach points out its redeeming features that might help achieve a progressive and humane society. By indicating the true causes that govern people's wills, fatalism would help moralists and politicians while at the same time it would make people more tolerant and

---

36. In reinforcing the image of a predictable world without chance, materialism can also give rise to a rhetoric of domination, if not totalitarianism. See the remarks of Horkheimer and Adorno about the "great philosophers in the French Enlightenment" in their *Dialectic of Enlightenment*, p. 169 passim. See also Joan DeJean, *Literary Fortifications: Rousseau, Laclos, Sade* (Princeton: Princeton University Press, 1984). DeJean discerns a continuation of "the Classical concern for order and control" as well as for repression among several eighteenth-century literary writers (pp. 4, 18).

indulgent, since they presumably would understand that all is necessary (*SN* 1: 224, 241). In a radical departure from past practices, a secular elite of enlightened materialists might even replace priests and kings.[37] Insisting as they do on known, material, and tangible causes (*SN* 2: 95) in a manner not unlike that of the sensationists, materialists come to adopt atheism as their creed.[38] Departing from very similar premises and methodologies, the two theories arrive at significantly different conclusions about the existence of God and the place of humanity in the cosmos.

The radical extension of sensationist principles thus leads to a deterministic, fatalistic, and atheistic materialism. It was clearly not enough for some French Enlightenment thinkers to be concerned as was Condillac only at a metaphysical level with truth and analytic method while important practical social problems of intolerance and inequality remained unresolved. Materialists extended sensationist principles in part to achieve greater equality among the people in society and greater scientific objectivity in knowledge even at the possible cost of curtailing the freedom and humanity of individuals. In eighteenth-century France, philosophy came to be used less for abstract metaphysical goals than for paramount social and political reasons: namely, the restructuring of society. At the time, little did the sensationists suspect how far their connection of ideas with sensations would be taken. As one by one each active mental faculty is reduced to some form of sensibility, sensationism moves closer and closer to materialism. In allowing for a soul, Condillac and Bonnet stop short of making the mind a passive mecha-

---

37. The materialists' utopian goals, however, raise a number of questions. Were the materialists themselves or were the people the ultimate beneficiaries of the materialists' proposed policies? If the materialists were seizing power for themselves, they were simply substituting themselves, as masters of the people, for priests and kings. Or were the materialists sincere advocates of radical social change? Common wisdom and history support the view that too much power concentrated in the hands of any one person or group tends ultimately to corrupt.

On d'Holbach's political ideas, see Josiane Boulad-Ayoub, *Contre nous de la tyrannie: Des relations idéologiques entre lumières et révolution* (LaSalle, Québec: Editions Hurtubise, 1990). For a discussion of La Mettrie's ideas for improving society through political reform, see Wellman, *La Mettrie: Medicine, Philosophy, and Enlightenment.*

To reveal "a politically biased interpretive procedure," our late twentieth-century perspective has taught us to ask "for *what* political value, interest, or purpose has this procedure been developed?" See W. J. T. Mitchell, ed., *The Politics of Interpretation* (Chicago: University of Chicago Press, 1983), p. 4.

38. It should be emphasized, however, as Alan Kors has done, that atheism was not the sole interest, point of discussion, or religion of those who frequented d'Holbach's home. See Kors, *D'Holbach's Coterie: An Enlightenment in Paris,* pp. 41–81.

nism. Still embracing the concept of random chance, Helvétius's writings in their use of sensationism represent the last point to which the theory can expand without changing its fundamental character. Diderot, although basing much of his thinking on sensationist tenets, argues in many ways as an outspoken materialist but, like Helvétius, cannot dismiss chance as a factor in the organization of our being. La Mettrie and d'Holbach are, as it were, the hardy few. They give expression to the previously unmentionable possibility of a godless, wholly scientific world in which humanity is engulfed by the totality of nature. In the triumvirate of master themes for much eighteenth-century thought—humanity, God, and nature—only the latter remains in materialism; humanity and God have disappeared as primary concerns. By comparison with materialism, sensationism appears refreshingly humanistic. But one cannot help wondering if its concern with humanity is self-serving and self-deceiving, as the materialists would have us believe. However the case may be, it is still a matter of intense debate and interpretation whether important aspects of the orthodox, and even the unorthodox, religious humanism of the kind espoused respectively by sensationists like Condillac and Bonnet have any credibility today. In the face of the sheer number of mounting discoveries confirming causality in quantum physics, biology, neurology, and the other sciences, they appear to be losing ground to materialism. But as sensationists and materialists agreed in their skepticism, we do not know and may never know the order of all things. As long as we lack that total, encyclopedic understanding that Enlightenment thinkers strove to attain, controversial religious and difficult philosophical questions raised by them, such as the existence of God, the immortality of the soul, and the nature of that essential mental state known as consciousness, will remain open.

9

The Adoption and Critique of
Sensationism by the *Idéologues*

T he *philosophes'* dual project, on the one hand, of stamping out tyranny, intolerance, superstition, and error—perhaps best formulated in Voltaire's famous imperative *"Ecraser l'infâme!"*—and, on the other hand, of fostering a society that through enhanced knowledge could enjoy truth, virtue, and happiness, derived much of its support from sensationism. The developing philosophy's position against innate ideas also implied opposition to any form of prejudice. Although it could be used by others like Rousseau who did not share the positivist approach of thinkers within the mainstream of the Enlightenment, sensationism for the most part gave rise to theories of progress among its chief proponents as well as among those who were strongly influenced by it. It informed the progressive thinking of the century's most comprehensive project, the *Encyclopédie,* and that of most, if not all, major historical overviews of the human mind.[1]

It is not surprising then that at the very end of the eighteenth century

1. See Jean d'Alembert, *"Discours préliminaire des éditeurs,"* in *Encyclopédie, ou Diction-naire raisonné des sciences, des arts et des métiers,* 1: i–xlv; Anne-Robert-Jacques Turgot, *Tableau philosophique des progrès successifs de l'esprit humain,* in *Oeuvres de Turgot,* ed. Gustave Schelle, 5 vols. (Paris: Alcan, 1913), 1: 214–35; Turgot, *Plan de "Deux Discours sur l'histoire universel,"* in *Oeuvres,* 1: 275–323; and Jean-Antoine-Nicolas Caritat, marquis de Condorcet, *Esquisse d'un tableau historique des progrès de l'esprit humain,* ed. Alain Pons (Paris: Garnier-Flammarion, 1988).

and during the early years of the following century sensationism also played an important part in the formation of a new group of thinkers called the *idéologues*. Recognizing the key role of habit in forming human behavior and wishing to inculcate ideal values in the citizens of the young French Republic, these intellectuals gathered around the figure of Destutt de Tracy and included Cabanis and Maine de Biran among others.[2] The Auteuil salon of Mme Helvétius became an important center for the dissemination of *idéologue* thought. After the Terror in late 1795, the movement took hold as the new National Institute's class of moral and political sciences established a section for the analysis of sensations and ideas. For that class, Destutt de Tracy presented a series of memoirs expounding a sensationist viewpoint that was to form the basis of "ideology."[3] As an attempt to help avoid the errors of the past, the science of ideas or "ideology," putatively founded by Condillac,

2. For a discussion of the movement, see F. J. Picavet, *Les Idéologues: Essai sur l'histoire des idées et des théories scientifiques, philosophiques, religieuses, etc., en France depuis 1789* (Paris: Alcan, 1891). Picavet (pp. 101f.) divides the *idéologues* into three generations: those like Condorcet who died or gained their reputations before the turn of the century; those ordinarily called *idéologues* during the Directory or Consulate; and those who may have been known in the previous periods but whose work was consistent with the thinking of the latter part of the Empire or the Restoration. Picavet places all three of the major *idéologues* discussed here in the second generation.

An exhaustive analysis of *idéologie*, which is beyond the scope of the present study, can be found in Sergio Moravia, *Il pensiero degli idéologues: Scienza e filosofia in Francia (1780–1815)* (Florence: La Nuova Italia, 1974), esp. pp. 277–94, 332–36, 351–73, and 457–61. In this general treatment of the topic, Moravia also points out some of the similarities and differences between the *idéologues* and the sensationists, giving detailed discussions of Destutt de Tracy, Cabanis, and Maine de Biran.

Although Maine de Biran began to distinguish himself from the *idéologues* in 1804, he is still generally associated with this group. Tracy and Cabanis had a "profound" influence on his writings (Picavet, *Les Idéologues*, p. 477). Biran himself publicly acknowledged the work of Cabanis and Tracy as sources for many of his basic ideas. He frequented the Société d'Auteuil, which was led by these two thinkers who saw in Biran one of their own kind (Moravia, *Il Pensiero*, pp. 459–60).

For the members of this group of thinkers, whose concern with such arcane questions as the origin of ideas he disdained, Napoleon successfully substituted the pejorative term *idéologue* for *idéologiste*. See John Plamenatz, *Ideology* (New York: Praeger, 1970), p. 15. Our modern expression *ideology*, which comes from the writings of Karl Marx and of course carries a vastly different meaning, has its origin in this early movement led by Destutt de Tracy. Henceforth, I shall distinguish this theory from the modern term by enclosing it in quotation marks. I have borrowed this sensible convention from Emmet Kennedy, *A "Philosophe" in the Age of Revolution: Destutt de Tracy and the Origins of "Ideology"* (Philadelphia: American Philosophical Society, 1978).

3. Kennedy traces the origins of the movement and the name given its members in *A "Philosophe,"* pp. 38–74, 80.

aimed to show what we do when we think, speak, or judge. Tracy ultimately divided these related tasks respectively among the study of the formation of ideas or "ideology" proper, the expression of ideas or grammar, and the combination of ideas or logic.[4]

The *idéologues* not only used sensationism as a philosophy that was fundamentally compatible with their own views, but they also reacted critically to it.[5] Drawing them to the theory in the first place was a methodology that placed importance on an understanding of the nature of humanity before undertaking any intellectual project, on a movement back and forth between the general and the particular, and on an integrated view of all phenomena. They also adopted sensationism because it corroborated their attitude toward progress through education in a general way and through new ideas generated by language in a specific way. Reacting, however, to sensationism's exclusive focus on the sensations as the sole cause for ideas, the *idéologues* came to extend the notion of experience to embrace both external and internal phenomena. By taking into account internal operations, they circumvented the problematic passive nature sensationism attributed to human beings and restored somewhat the conception of a humanity composed of free, active agents. Their specific references to Condillac and the other disciples of Locke in the French Enlightenment further reveal their proximity to and differences from sensationism. While striving as did the sensationists to usher in an age of progress, the *idéologues* nonetheless began to rid themselves little by little of the traces of determinism associated with the earlier theory and thereby came to conceive of human beings as having more control of their own destiny. The history of "ideology" in fact reflects the changing attitudes of its proponents toward such active human components as the will and internal organs.[6] Although the *idéologues*, especially their leader, Destutt de Tracy, begin as almost pure disciples of the sensationists with

4. Antoine-Louis-Claude Destutt de Tracy, *Eléments d'idéologie,* 4 vols. (1801–15; rpt. Stuttgart-Bad Cannstatt: Frommann-Holzboog, 1977), 1: 18, 31, 93, 182, 195; 3: 520; hereafter cited as (*EI*). The work originally appeared in five parts. After the first three parts on ideology, grammar, and logic, respectively, Parts IV and V treat the effects of the will.

5. For another discussion of the sensationist background to "ideology," see Staum, *Cabanis,* pp. 34–48. Staum provides a useful précis of the works of Condillac, Bonnet, and Helvétius, whom he also sees as Locke's disciples and important influences on the *idéologues*.

6. In the period between his memoirs for the National Institute and the first part of his *Eléments d'idéologie,* Tracy, for instance, changes to a "voluntarist analysis of external reality." He acknowledges a will of sorts, but he immediately "merges" it with sensation. See Kennedy, *A "Philosophe,"* p. 115.

their conception of the commonality among all men and women, they eventually move toward a new vision of humankind and the politics of difference.

Like sensationism, "ideology" methodically starts with the beginning of human existence as a way to uncover truths in all areas of human endeavor. Understanding the basic nature of humanity presumably allows one to gain greater insight into the diversity of human activities. The simpler and the earlier the facts are about existence, the better they serve to explain it. Hence, sensationism's frequent directive "to go back to the origin" *(remonter à l'origine)* that "ideology" essentially follows.

At that origin both theories find sensibility, although Biran's development of "ideology" will also include other "primitive facts." There is no life without sensibility or the faculty of feeling and sensing. Destutt de Tracy attributes to Condillac alone "the honor of having discovered *that thinking is nothing but feeling, and that all ideas are only miscellaneous sensations whose combinations one simply has to sort out"* (*EI* 192). Cabanis clearly subscribes to the sensationist refrain *"that all ideas come through the senses, or are the product of sensations"*—which he terms a "fundamental axiom" and attributes somewhat generously to Locke as the first to have developed.[7] According to Cabanis, Helvétius later admirably summarizes Locke's thinking in this area, whereas Condillac—who himself is followed by his own disciples and reformers in Garat, Destutt de Tracy, Degérando, Laromiguière, Lancelin, Jacquemont, and Maine de Biran—perfects it (*RPM* 43–45).[8]

7. Pierre-Jean Georges Cabanis, *Rapports du physique et du moral de l'homme* (1844; rpt. Geneva: Slatkine, 1980), p. 44; hereafter cited as (*RPM*). *Les Rapports du physique et du moral de l'homme* was originally published in 1802. Other conventions used previously for the parenthetical insertion of page references in the text will also apply to Cabanis and later to Maine de Biran. Although similar thinkers in many respects, Cabanis and Tracy did have their differences of opinion. While they both recognized the importance of physiology in their new science of man, Tracy generally attributed more powers to internal sensations than did Cabanis, who held a strictly medical view of them. For this distinction and other nuances between Cabanis's and Tracy's thought, see Staum, *Cabanis,* pp. 237–43.

As Daniel Teysseire points out, Cabanis also recognized that the substance of the sensationist belief in the sensory origin of ideas can already be found in Hippocrates, whom Teysseire calls "a Monsieur Jourdan of analytic sensationism, who would have practiced this philosophy without having its actual name." See Teysseire, "Lien social et ordre politique chez Cabanis," *Studies on Voltaire and the Eighteenth Century* 267 (1989), 361–61.

8. Of the *idéologues* cited in this list as successors to Condillac, Cabanis singles out Destutt de Tracy as the only one fully to have explored "ideological" doctrine. In 1802, at the time Cabanis first published his work, Maine de Biran was still some ten years away from

For Cabanis, living itself is equated with feeling, as he states repeatedly (*RPM* 6, 78, 106, 399, 510). Although for his part Maine de Biran rejects sensationism's claim to reduce all intellectual faculties to some form of sensation, he nonetheless locates in sensibility a primitive fact of consciousness constitutive of the self's very existence. But it is an active, intimate or internal sense, as opposed to a passive sensory organ in communication with the external world, that allows one to feel oneself.[9]

Sensationists and *idéologues* alike insist on the importance of experience in their methods. Consisting of facts, experience presumably would provide each theory a verifiable basis for truth and consequently confer authority upon it. The theorists differ essentially in the way in which they interpret experience. Using Bacon's experimental method as a guide, sensationists base their thinking on the observations and experiences of the external world. So, too, do the *idéologues*, but they eventually broaden the foundation for his theory by including, as did Locke, reflection or internal mental operations with sensation as the sources of human understanding. Experience is seen by those of either persuasion primarily as the origin of human existence. Whenever one of them criticizes another group or school of thought, his criticism usually derives from the purported neglect of those first facts at the beginning of our existence that time and habit have all but erased from our memories.

Both theories under discussion make claims grounded in original experience or first facts. Destutt de Tracy can thus deprecate grammarians who "have never understood well the origin either of language or writing, for not having gone back to first facts" (*EI* 2: 448). Conducting himself as the medical doctor he was, Cabanis bases all his conclusions on physical facts and cites Hippocrates and Aristotle as his models for beginning with those facts (*RPM* 70–71, 74, 141, 219). Maine de Biran introduces a new kind of fact, but it is no less an integral part of experience. Clearly disturbed by the undue attention that sensation

---

completing his major philosophical statement about "ideology," the *Essai sur les fondements de la psychologie.*

   9. Marie-François-Pierre Gonthier de Biran [Maine de Biran], *Essai sur les fondements de la psychologie et sur ses rapports avec l'étude de la nature,* ed. Pierre Tisserand, in *Oeuvres complètes,* vols. 8 and 9 (Geneva: Slatkine, 1982), pp. 3, 26, 115, 345. This work, which is contained in one book with continuous pagination, is hereafter cited as (*EFP*). Biran's *Essai* represents a collection of his award-winning essays and other related writings first edited by Ernest Naville in 1859.

receives in the search for the origin of knowledge, he attempts to displace it with so-called primitive facts of our intimate sense *(faits primitifs du sens intime)*. Much of the venom with which he systematically attacks sensationism can be explained by his wish to create a new epistemological hierarchy at the top of which one no longer finds sensations. But like the sensationists, he, too, appeals to the authority of experience: "We could be blamed for establishing only on hypotheses the science of realities, whose principles we are seeking, and for having substituted abstractions, works of the mind, for real and primitive facts of thought, on which facts this science can be based. To dispel these reproaches, to remove any doubt that could remain about the nature of primitive facts, and to bring to the fore the laws of the faculty of reflection which alone is pertinent to them, I shall follow a method that is closer to experience" (*EFP* 476). His claims will also derive their veracity from experience, albeit an inner one that each individual must feel for himself or herself.

The methodology used by both "ideology" and sensationism derives much of its force from experience, which is seen as a seamless web of particular and general events. Both theories move back and forth between these events, although sensationism does sometimes have a marked tendency to proceed in linear fashion from the particular to the general. Conversely, "ideology" tends to move at times from the general to the particular. Such a tendency is explained by a split in the movement itself between a rationalist "ideology," practiced by Tracy, and a physiological "ideology," exemplified by Cabanis. The occasionally deductive method of the former contrasts with the inductive, empirical method of the latter, based as it is on observation. But both sensationism and "ideology" privilege the simple, elucidating truth of a first, primitive, or original moment in experience from which other more complex operations flow in an unbroken chain. Destutt de Tracy describes his method in contradistinction to that of sensationism, to which he alludes in the following passage:

> One must always take as one's point of departure that of the people to whom one is speaking, and the ideas that are most familiar to them. Yet it has been a long time since you have no longer had your first sensations, and a lasting habit has made you lose sight of the first judgments you came to regarding them. I must not then limit myself to tracing for you historically the relation of ideas of a man who starts with the most simple and

particular impression to arrive at the most compound and general idea. . . . It is thus in this state [of someone already with countless complex ideas] that you must be taken; these are the ideas that must be examined; and when, while still going back, we have arrived at the first one, everything will be untangled for you, the order and sequence of their formation will no longer escape you. (*EI* 1: 78–79)

As a point of departure, Tracy may indirectly belittle a statue reduced to one sensation such as those Condillac and Bonnet used, but he is no less interested than they in finding an origin for our ideas in our earliest experience. Although not the initial focus, the particular regains its ascendancy from Tracy's insistence on going back to an origin. Whether the method is inductive or deductive, the goal of an original, generative experience remains the same.

Cabanis, too, takes issue with sensationist reductionism but only in order to substitute for it a more broadly conceived origin that nonetheless has its roots in the particular. His allusion to the sensationists' method echoes that of Tracy:

We can thus conclude with every assurance, that the right form of analysis cannot isolate the operations of any sense in particular, from those of all the other senses; that they sometimes act necessarily, and almost always occasionally, together; that their functions remain constantly subject to the influence of different organs, or viscera; and that they are determined and directed by the even more direct and powerful action of the general systems, and notably of the cerebral center. (*RPM* 528–29)

As he goes on to say, Cabanis aims to provide a new *Traité des sensations*, showing "the sources from which the first determinations, ideas, and penchants arise, and the manner in which they are produced" (529). He calls attention to the newness of his project while at the same time he points out its derivative nature by citing Condillac and his major work by name. Working as he does with the relationships between the physical and psychological realms, Cabanis must show their interconnections rather than a one-sided stream of information. His preoccupation with physical influence, however, leads him to a new notion of the particular. Instead of limiting it to one sensation from one sense organ, as did the sensationists, he broadens it to embrace all physical operations in the body seen at any one time. By so doing, he tends to associate the particular with the physical and to envision a flow of influence back and forth between it and the psychological, which has in Cabanis's writings a decidedly more general character to it than does the physical side of human nature. Like Tracy, Cabanis seeks an origin for ideas in his contribution to the new science of "ideology." His association of the particular with physical facts, while allowing him to adopt a more fluid approach to general concepts than that of his contemporary, nonetheless keeps him close to the method of the sensationists.[10]

What distinguishes Maine de Biran's methodology perhaps the most from that of his fellow *idéologues* is his attempt to make of the psychological dimension of human beings a particular cause. The sensationists and, following them, Tracy and Cabanis, all lean heavily toward a view of human behavior as generally arising from particular physical laws. Cabanis of course tries to correct this view somewhat, but his efforts remain unbalanced and favor physical influence. In his endeavor to create the foundations of psychology, Biran alone sees the psychological, in the form of self-consciousness, as constitutive of an original experience from which numerous operations can be shown to arise. Although he understands the usefulness of analysis, of proceeding from the general to the particular, he no longer sees any purpose in analysis when one begins with the source itself, namely, the self (*EFP* 270). Biran attributes to the fact of consciousness the same certainty or *évidence* that the sensationists attributed to sensations. If one considers, as Helvétius does (*DH* 1: 213; *DH* 2: 281 [F 304, 809]), the Latin derivation of the word *évidence* from *video, videre* for the verb "to see," the concept calls for vision of some kind. In sensationist manner, Helvétius takes this to mean the assurance that comes from external sensory perception, whereas Biran looks within himself for the first form of certainty from which all others follow. The self that he sees in such an act of apperception does not result from sensations, as the sensationists would have us believe, but is always already there. In the concluding pages of the first part of his work, Biran summarizes his methodological position:

---

10. Teysseire, "Lien social et ordre politique chez Cabanis," 368–73. Following Cabanis's critique of Condillac, Teysseire notes that Condillac's sensationism is isolated from reality, whereas Cabanis attempts to account for the full complexity of human nature and sensibility in their totality.

The self that exists or apperceives inwardly as *one, simple, identical,* is not at all abstracted from sensations as what would be common or general in them, but it abstracts itself from them by itself through the act of internal apperception, which distinguishes and separates up to a certain point the individual or the *one* from the collective and the many; the acting force or cause, from the effect produced; action, from passion; in a word, the subject that is making an effort, from the term that is resisting and that suffers because of diverse alterations. The *self* is thus truly *abstrahens* in its reflexive action, and not *abstractus.*[11] (*EFP* 272)

In attributing to the self abstracting powers, Biran substitutes one particular for another. What formerly had been considered as original material for ideas, namely, particular sensible objects in the external world, loses ground to the particular inner experience of selfhood. The particular thus maintains for Biran, as it had for the sensationists, both a metaphysical and a methodological hegemony, but its content shifts from sensations to self-consciousness. In the process, Biran undermines the sensationists' origin for ideas and establishes another one in its stead. One might even say that he beats them at their own game by using their rules or methods to determine a more primitive origin than theirs.

Facilitating the *idéologues'* method of moving back and forth between the general and the particular is their integrated view of all human phenomena, which they share with the sensationists. When Tracy gives what amounts to a definition of "ideology," one cannot help noticing the interdependence of all domains of human activity:

We have indeed seen what the faculty of thinking consists of; what the elementary faculties are composing it; how they inform us about our existence, that of other beings, their properties, and the way to evaluate them; how these intellectual faculties are linked to other faculties resulting from our organization; how all of them depend on our faculty of will; how all are altered by the frequent repetition of their acts; how they are perfected in the individual and in the species; and finally what new changes the use of signs brings to them. (*EI* 1: 353)

11. It bears noting here that Biran's references to an "effort" imply primarily an act of the will or psychological self rather than merely a reaction to physical stimuli.

A kind of chain reaction occurs in the activities of men and women. The *idéologue* simply has to trace them up or down a continuous scale. Tracy regrets not having made more connections than he does with physiology but expects quite rightly to hear from his contemporary Cabanis on this subject.

Cabanis does not disappoint with his reply, which delineates in great detail the relationships between the physical and psychological. On two occasions he quotes Hippocrates' saying about the overall functioning of human beings, that for it *"everything converges, everything conspires, everything consents"* (*RPM* 131; *RPM* 341). All is "chained together," as it were, not unlike the ideas in Cabanis's work (*RPM* 590). The communication characteristic among the diverse parts of any one system, like that in the nervous system, applies to other systems as well so that all becomes related (*RPM* 504–5). Cabanis even extends this ordered view of human activities to the universe (*RPM* 577). The microcosm of man and macrocosm of the universe thereby reflect each other in their highly coordinated operations.

Maine de Biran links human phenomena together through the unity of the psychological self, which he opposes to the self that the sensationists envisaged from sensations alone. His claim for the unity of the self stresses both its psychological origin and its extensive purview: "Unity is absolute and indivisible in the *self,* which reproduces or apperceives itself constantly in any effort under the same form as *one.* In the *self* alone is the very first unity of substance, of cause or force, of existence ultimately" (*EFP* 243). The notion of a will, which plays a central role in Biran's conception of the self, cannot even be compared physiologically to sensibility (*EFP* 193). True to his somewhat polemical stance against what he feels to be the undue influence granted to sensations, Biran wants to separate as much as possible the psychological from the sensory or physical. Once he does so, however, and establishes the ascendancy of primitive facts of our intimate sense, which belong entirely to the psychological realm, he returns to a more orthodox "ideological" attitude about the interdependence of both realms. Biran comes in fact to speak of a double unity composed of the unity of resistance, "which is enveloped within the numerous and confused images that unceasingly besiege our mind," and that of the self (*EFP* 387). This double unity gives rise to all aspects of our existence as thinking beings. Like his fellow *idéologues* and the sensationists, although in a much more complex way than these latter, Biran espouses an integrated view of the human mind that reflects if not actual harmony then a certain sense of order or, at the very least, a lack of discontinuity in its operations. It is a view that suits well the reasoning of the thinkers of the French Enlightenment and their immediate successors, who saw limitless possibilities open to them if they could only work out the causal chain governing human thought.

Like sensationism, "ideology" aspired to progress through education. Destutt de Tracy wrote his *Eléments d'idéologie* for the central schools of the incipient French Republic. In showing young people what transpires when they think, he hoped to let them see ways of improving society. For he knew that the "gradual perfection of the individual and the species" owes much to the faculty of thinking (*EI* 1: 195–96). Adopting a position close to that of Helvétius regarding the overwhelming influence of environment on our moral and intellectual training, Tracy underscores the vast importance of acquiring a proper education and of making good judgments a matter of habit (*EI* 1: 233, 318). For his part, Helvétius places less emphasis on developing good habits than does either Tracy or Cabanis. He strives to maintain the same conditions of learning instead of expecting the individual to continue acting independently on his or her own, once a favorable environment has produced its desired effect. Such a nuance between them points out once again their different attitudes toward the active or passive nature of people.

Cabanis, too, calls attention to the significance of habit in education. Although he acknowledges the presence of certain characteristics in human beings already at birth, he sees no obstacle to changing them and thus engages, as do Tracy and the sensationists, in social engineering: "Nature produces man with well-defined organs and faculties, but art can increase these faculties, change or direct their use, create in a way new *organs*. That is the work of education, which is, strictly speaking, but the art of impressions and habits" (*RPM* 99). Cabanis divides education into physical and moral areas, speaking only of moral habits. But it quickly becomes clear that he also intends to establish good physical habits as well, since questions of hygiene or diet occupy a prominent part of his work. Needless to repeat, the two areas are closely interwoven. Cabanis even grants to the physical aspects of education—theretofore seen only as having a local, particular effect— overall importance: "it is necessary, in a word, that hygiene aspire to perfect human nature in general" (*RPM* 298).

When Maine de Biran speaks of progress, he typically casts it in the light of the progress an individual makes on the way to a psychological awareness of selfhood. Consciousness and thought separate us from animals. Education reflects the same kind of progress but on a different scale, applied as it was to society at large after the Revolution. Its methods should be nothing more than applications of psychological doctrines on the origin and formation of intellectual faculties (*EFP* 82). By becoming aware of his possession of a will, which definitively distinguishes him from the lower orders of creation, man becomes a fully human, thinking person (*EFP* 202, 308–10). An education that trains one to think, act, and exercise one's will by calling attention to the human ability to do so, as does psychology, would presumably lead sooner or later to progress. Biran's education is thus first and foremost psychological in nature.

From their interest in ideas, the *idéologues* naturally inquired into the origin of language, as had the sensationists. After all, language is often cited as the mother of thought, and much new thinking tends to generate progress. Tracy devotes an entire part of his *Eléments d'idéologie* to the study of grammar, whose importance has already been underlined in the first part of his work. Grammar is not just the science of signs but also of ideas, as he intimates in the first part and makes explicit in the second: "the science of ideas is very closely tied to that of words; because our compound ideas have no other support, no other bond uniting all their elements than the words that express them and fix them in our memory" (*EI* 1: 93, 99; *EI* 2: 1, 12–15, 421–22). "Ideology" is inseparable from grammar, just as logic is; one cannot speak of these as different sciences. They all show us how we come to know anything. Without language in the form of words or signs, men and women would lead a paltry existence and make little or no progress. Following Condillac, Tracy can go so far as to say that "languages are true analytic methods" (*EI* 1: 285–86). They facilitate analysis by allowing one to deal with far fewer data than one would have if faced with radically individualistic ideas.

The *idéologues* generally believe that by perfecting language, we would perfect our ideas. One of them, Laromiguière, fashioning his ideas after Condillac's *Langue des calculs,* aims to give language the same degree of reasoned accuracy as mathematics. He identifies analogy, simplicity, and "the rigorous determination of signs" as qualities that distinguish a perfected language of reason.[12] His addition of the last

12. Pierre Laromiguière, *Paradoxes de Condillac* (1805; rpt. Paris: Brunot-Labbé, 1825), p. 84.

quality to the two others underlines one of the problems any language can have, a problem of which Tracy was well aware. When the precision of a language suffers, so, too, does the progress that may come of it. In fact, it may even lead to error; signs thus have considerable advantages and disadvantages (*EI* 1: 313–16, 347). Recognizing the impossibility of a perfect universal language whose ideas one could never misunder- stand—since the value of any sign does not depend entirely on just its own nature but also on that of human beings' different intellectual capacities—Tracy nonetheless makes a number of practical suggestions for improving our everyday languages (*EI* 2: 394–420, 451–53). His primary concern is with sounds or spoken languages, because they have a more natural and spontaneous character than do the arbitrary signs of written languages. If thinking is feeling, as Tracy repeatedly states in sensationist manner, then language, which is intimately connected with thought, would reflect some of the same characteristics of simplicity and spontaneity that feeling has.

Cabanis echoes Tracy's remarks about the close connection between sensations, thought, and language. The signs of language serve to repre- sent and differentiate sensations, thereby allowing one to reason clearly and leading Condillac to claim "that one does not think without the help of languages, and that languages are analytic methods" (*RPM* 95). Cabanis more or less accepts Condillac's claim here but on condition that the term "language" be taken in its broadest sense as "the methodi- cal system of signs by which one fixes one's own sensations" (*RPM* 95). As one determines sensations and signs, one also establishes one's thoughts or ideas. For example, if I see a plot of grass and ascribe the word *green* to the visual sensation I have, this word helps me differenti- ate this color from that of, say, the sky. The word substitutes for the sensation and facilitates future mental comparisons of color. As other such substitutions of a similar nature occur, one can perform increas- ingly complex operations without referring to the original sensory phenomena. Progress is more readily and efficiently attained in the various sciences for the benefit of the whole society. Cabanis traces the propagation of this connection between language and ideas to Locke and Condillac: "Since Locke, the influence of languages on ideas had been suspected. Since Condillac, it is known that the progress of the human mind depends, in great part, on the perfection of the language appropriate to each science, and especially that which is common to an entire nation" (*RPM* 460–61).

Whereas Tracy and Cabanis assume the necessary existence of sensations before that of signs, Biran relates signs to psychological acts of the self. Contra Condillac and Tracy, he aims to demonstrate that "the large influence of signs on ideas is opposed to the principle of passive sensation" (*EFP* 93).[13] Although in the newborn child he does allow for instinctive screams or utterances that arise from the purely sensory level, Biran notes that those "spontaneous movements" or sensations become quickly "transformed by the infant itself into *voluntary signs,* which it will use to call for help" (*EFP* 201–2). Intent on excluding any constitutive role for passive sensation in the formation of signs for language, Biran has the will, that is, a psychological agency, generate speech. When he later resumes discussion of this critical first moment for the institution of signs, he bases it on immediate apperception: "Without the internal apperception of acts, or of the willed effort, there would be no signs instituted, and without instituted signs, no actual reflection, no ideas or distinct notions of our intellectual acts or their results, . . . finally no idea of a subject (a *self*) separate from its attributes and, consequently, no abstract, universal ideas" (*EFP* 491–93). Once again—this time regarding the connection of signs with ideas—Biran sets himself apart from the other *idéologues* and the sensationists. Where these thinkers see an indispensable role for sensations in the foundation of language and ideas, Biran sees at best only a secondary importance for them. In his view, it is the active nature of the will, not the passive character of sensibility, that gives rise to progressive knowledge through complex signs and thoughts. His seemingly sensationist identification of ideas with signs notwithstanding (*EFP* 636), Biran ultimately imputes to signs a primarily psychological content.

The similarities between the *idéologues* and the sensationists mask somewhat some of their fundamental differences.[14] I have already

13. According to Henri Gouhier, Biran particularly opposed Condillac's use of language to explain the higher faculties because it led Condillac to ignore or dismiss the active role of the will in human understanding. In Biran's opinion, Condillac paid too much attention to signs and consequently neglected the notion of volition. He believed Condillac's preoccupation with abstract mathematical language made him lose touch with physiological and psychological concerns. See Gouhier, *Les Conversions de Maine de Biran* (Paris: Vrin, 1947), pp. 78–83, 87–90, 106, 117, 136.

14. Some of the "disarray" among the *idéologues* and the "unravelling" of Condillac's legacy can be seen in the divergent answers given to the questions for the "prize contests on the Condillacian themes of language, habit, and decomposition of mental faculties." See Staum, " 'Analysis of Sensations and Ideas' in the French National Institute (1795–1803)," *Canadian Journal of History* 26 (1991), 393–413, esp. 400. Staum claims that Garat and Roederer accepted Condillac's tradition the most. While Laromiguière for his part pursued Condillac's

pointed out the importance of experience for both schools of thought, suggesting briefly their different interpretations of it. It will be recalled that the *idéologues* extend the notion of experience to include both external and internal phenomena. That they should do so indicates clearly their growing suspicion about the inadequacy of sensation as the sole principle for explaining our ideas. Although my previous discussion of the affinities between the two groups of thinkers may have already pointed in part to the solution the *idéologues* found to this problem, further analysis is still needed to make those differences explicit.

Despite their close adherence to many sensationist principles, the *idéologues* all differ from their predecessors insofar as they redefine the narrow epistemological focus on the sensations as a single, isolated category. In their scheme for cognition, they either add some other faculty to sensation, adapt its conditions, or, returning to a more Lockean perspective, include reflection with it. Thus, Tracy has the faculty of thinking or feeling "consist in feeling sensations, remembrances, relationships, and desires" (*EI* 1: 179). He may equate thinking with sensibility but insidiously adds to it three other elemental faculties (respectively, memory, judgment, and will), which Condillac sees as alterations or transformations of the one faculty of feeling (*EI* 1: 180, 321). Instead of making ideas or thought products of sensation alone, however, Tracy repeatedly lists the other faculties alongside it as causes (*EI* 1: 182, 188, 190–92). His position undeniably follows Condillac's very closely, but his is already breaking away from the rigid category of sensations. Whereas Condillac shows an evolution of sensation into other faculties, Tracy is "led to conclude that all our ideas are but diverse sensations and that thinking, feeling, and existing, are for us only one and the same thing" (*EI* 1: 191–92). At first, he may appear to be saying exactly what Condillac says, but Tracy is making a nuance here about "the four elemental faculties of thought not as transformed sensations, as had Condillac, but as sensation itself."[15] They do not represent an evolution of sensation but are already sensations. Tracy may perhaps be said to be more sensationist than Condillac himself, as he subsumes everything under sensation even in the face of mounting physiological evidence from Cabanis and psychological evidence from Biran for active internal operations.

----

ideal of the well-made language, he rejected, as did Degérando, the passivity inherent in his intellectual predecessor's notion of transformed sensations.

　15. Kennedy, *A "Philosophe,"* pp. 112–13.

Likewise, Cabanis at once embraces and corrects the sensationist view about the origin of ideas and human behavior in physical sensibility, citing Locke, Bonnet, Condillac, and Helvétius as those who have proven this view (*RPM* 103). Yet he questions the traditional formula given in philosophy books that derives all ideas from "the senses," as that word has too limited a connotation (*RPM* 105). His constant criticism of sensationism is that it takes only those exterior objects affecting the five sense organs as causes for ideas and feelings and that it overlooks the impressions from internal organs (*RPM* 7, 114–15, 270). Analytic philosophers, as the sensationists are sometimes called, concentrate their attention primarily on sensations coming to the body from without rather than on those within it. Both kinds of sensations are part of sensibility, but the two are not usually understood in the term "the senses." Cabanis attributes the neglect of internal impressions to the fact that they are not as distinct and easily classified as those from the senses, which distract us continually (*RPM* 134, 532). Ideas do originate in sensibility but not in mere externally received sensations. Cabanis thus expands the conditions of learning to include stimuli outside and inside the body, as he views external stimuli as not adequately corresponding to the notion of sensibility.

His other criticism of sensationism concerns the different influence of the various sensations and the interaction among them. Cabanis envisions his work as an added step to that of the sensationists: "It is a lot to have established that all ideas and psychological determinations are the result of impressions received through the different organs: it is taking, I believe, a step more, to have shown that these impressions offer quite obvious general differences, and that they can be distinguished by their center and the character of their products, even though meanwhile, once again, they act unceasingly on one another, because of the rapid and continual communication between the various parts of the sensory organ" (*RPM* 131). Cabanis in effect is refining with his work what is meant by sensation or sensibility. The sensationists indeed tend to have a monolithic view of it. This becomes apparent in the heuristic statues used by Condillac and Bonnet. These mental constructs assume that individual sense organs can act independently of any other corporal or psychological function. Cabanis of course wishes to accentuate the complex relationships operative in all areas of our existence. Hence, his insistence on "the positive impossibility for the individual organ of one sense to start acting in an isolated manner" and his criticism of Condillac's statue for its unrealistic appraisal of the intricate perceptual process, which typically involves several simultaneous sensations (*RPM* 32, 305–8, 524–29). By these latter sensations Cabanis refers not just to those of the five sense organs but also to other internal organs such as the stomach and reproductive organs, all of which work together and communicate with one another. The sensationists' statues also assume an equal necessity for sensations in the acquisition of ideas and in our very being, whereas Cabanis points out the varying degrees of necessity they have in our vital processes (*RPM* 179).

Of the *idéologues*, Maine de Biran distances himself the most from sensationism by giving renewed attention to reflection as one of the two sources, along with sensation, of our ideas. In fact, he accords it greater value than sensation by making it a primitive fact of our internal sense that is needed for consciousness. For Biran, psychology is above all a reflective science requiring an introspective method.[16] Sensation, at least that which Condillac and Bonnet have in mind for their statues, "is not yet a fact" (*EFP* 15). Hence, their statues have no sense of self or personal identity. Biran defines reflection, which alone can conceive facts of our intimate sense (*EFP* 75), as follows:

> That faculty by which the mind apperceives, in a group of sensations or in a combination of any phenomena, the shared relationships of all elements with a fundamental unity, as of several modes or qualities with the unity of resistance, of several diverse effects with one same cause, of variable alterations with the same *self,* a subject of inherence, and, above all, of repeated movements with the same productive force or the same will *I* [*moi*].
>
> Reflection has its origin in that internal apperception of effort or movements which the will determines; it begins with the first willed effort, that is with the primitive fact of consciousness. (*EFP* 476–77)

The importance Biran attributes to reflection as an inner sense makes him considerably more Lockean than his fellow *idéologues*. He would no doubt be taken for a pure disciple of Locke, were it not for the

16. In developing his new form of psychology, Biran repudiates the contemporary methods based on mathematical reasoning (Condillac's), inductive reasoning (Locke's or Bonnet's), and metaphysical reasoning (Descartes's) in favor of an introspective method based on reflection. See F. C. T. Moore, *The Psychology of Maine de Biran* (Oxford: Oxford University Press, 1970), pp. 9–76, esp. pp. 58, 75.

different way he develops the concept. In this regard, Biran's vision of the new science of psychology comes into play.

By basing psychology as he does on facts, Biran appears to follow the experimental method first proposed by Bacon. One observes and classifies facts in an attempt to find their source (*EFP* 32, 50–53). As the sensationists discovered, facts can be found outside ourselves in experience that we have through our sensations. Moreover, they can be found in experience within ourselves that we have through our intimate sense. It is this latter, interior experience that Biran believes not to have been sufficiently explored even by Locke, who at least recognized the importance of reflection for ideas, and that he takes as the object of psychology. Studying it will accomplish the major goals of "ideology" by allowing us to see how our ideas and faculties are formed. Psychology for Biran represents his own particular form of "ideology," in which sensation plays a vastly more reduced role than it does for Tracy and Cabanis. He criticizes sensationism as using an abstract point of departure in sensations: "Psychology relinquished its title, ignored its highest rights and functions, when it started with sensation as the origin of any faculty, and the only principle of all we are. Sensation is a fleeting mode that assumes a substance or a lasting being; it is a passing effect that assumes a permanent cause; and yet all metaphysics has been reduced to a game of sensations, separated from any idea of cause and substance" (*EFP* 600). In a word, sensations are not facts, whereas primitive facts of our consciousness apperceived by reflection are. Only they provide a solid basis for psychology by giving us an idea of the self as the cause of "intellectual acts" (*EFP* 67–68, 604).

The reactions of the *idéologues* to sensationism all ultimately serve to emphasize the active and complex nature of human beings, whose operations cannot be explained by supposedly simple, hypothetical statues. Without a doubt, they pinpoint some of the theory's weak areas. But they hardly give rise to its so-called bankruptcy.[17] Sensibility, which had been of utmost importance to the sensationists in their cognitive theory, remains central to the thinking of the *idéologues*. Yet it undergoes a certain transformation in the way in which it is conceived. Tracy may claim Condillac as the founder of "ideology" and himself as his successor (*EI* 1: 3, 4, 182), but he consistently adds to the notion of sensibility other

---

17. See Colin Smith, "Destutt de Tracy and the Bankruptcy of Sensationalism," in *Balzac and the Nineteenth Century: Studies in French Literature Presented to Herbert J. Hunt by His Pupils, Colleagues, and Friends,* ed. D. G. Charlton et al. (Leicester: Leicester University Press, 1972), pp. 195–207.

faculties, not the least of which is the will.[18] As he does so, it becomes increasingly difficult to associate sensibility with mere passive sensation. In his characteristic stubbornness, for which he earned the nickname "Têtu," Tracy at first resists any change to his purist approach to sensationism. But his fellow *idéologues* Cabanis and Biran give him reasons of a physiological and psychological nature not to see all faculties as mere sensation. His conception of sensibility, while expanding to include and account for other faculties and phenomena, finally reveals itself to be a dynamic one, as it is in Cabanis's interpretation of the mind and body. Cabanis shows that even in sleep the brain continues its activity and that as a "living machine" we all generally have a need to feel and act for our physical well-being and psychological happiness (*RPM* 155, 206). Breaking from Tracy's and Cabanis's form of "ideology" in 1804, Biran highlights activity on the psychological level, making the will a primitive fact from our intimate sense and a precondition of self-knowledge (*EFP* 26, 188). We must know that we are the ones who are willing an action in order to know ourselves. Consciousness arises from the apperception of activity within us that we have willed by our own effort.[19] He opposes the activity of the will to the passivity of sensibility. "The fundamental principle of sensationism," writes Gouhier, "does not change, but sensibility is enriched: this is why the *idéologues* do not consider themselves outside Condillac's school, although they do 'separate' from him. The same is true for Biran."[20]

The new view of humankind that emerges from the writings of the *idéologues* and their protégés thus calls attention to the complexity and interaction of all human operations. It endows men and women—as active, thinking individuals—with an enhanced sense of freedom and personal identity derived from within themselves. Insofar as they are

18. Condillac had explained our ability to acquire knowledge of objects in the external world through the sense of touch. But Tracy "corrected" Condillac by claiming such explanatory power not for the sense of touch but for voluntary mobility. It was precisely this latter notion that originally attracted Biran to this *idéologue*. Tracy would later modify his position in conformity to Condillac's theory of transformed sensations, much to Biran's dismay. See Gouhier, *Les Conversions de Maine de Biran,* pp. 138–41, 148, 169, 174–76.

19. There is, however, "a serious failing," as Moore points out, in Biran's not accounting for unconscious mental phenomena, which are not willed into existence. See *The Psychology of Maine de Biran,* pp. 112–13, 139. Similarly, but in an ironic philosophical dialogue worthy of Diderot, Taine criticizes Biran's exaggerated claims for reflective effort and his tendency to deny the utility of practical, tangible elements in our existence. He facetiously asks Biran to break up a mob of malcontents with three hundred soldiers—under the command of one captain—who all, stripped of their clothes, guns, ammunition, and bodies, have only their wills left. See Taine, *Les Philosophes français du XIXe siècle,* p. 67.

20. Gouhier, *Les Conversions de Maine de Biran,* p. 148.

free agents, they can to some extent determine their own existence and do not have to rely entirely on the vagaries of the environment. Climate and other similar external factors, however, will continue to exercise an influence on their lives as sentient beings. The *idéologues* obviously cannot dispel sensibility any more than can anyone else, but they can and do amplify its compass to include internal and external forces.

At stake in their interpretation and correction of sensationism is a desire to present, more so than had the sensationists, a complete and adequate view of human nature that might serve as a basis for improving society. In intellectual history, their achievements, however, tend to fly in the face of some of their premises. Whereas Tracy and Cabanis, unlike Condillac, purposefully avoid any assumption of a soul in a rational way, Biran affirms a will during a time of spiritual rebirth in France and thereby contributes to the spiritualists' message and the subsequent eclecticism of Victor Cousin. Despite their efforts to establish a new human or social science that might have "priority" over and unify all the other sciences, the *idéologues* find problems with applying quantitative methods to human behavior.[21] The more they try to render a unified picture of the human species, the more that coherent picture breaks down under the pressure of individual differences and complexities of both a physiological and psychological nature. Experience, which the sensationists originally had used to authorize a view outside the closed system of revealed religion and outside the self, receives with the *idéologues* a larger interpretation that condones, if not requires, an inward gaze. That gaze would now reveal a diversity of physical bodies and subjective wills. The inquiries performed by Cabanis, Tracy, and Biran into the individual physiological body and psychological self remove "ideology" from an exclusively sensationist standpoint, which even Tracy has to abandon. Groups of individuals with different wills, and not man in the abstract, become the object of study. The *idéologues'* call for humanistic study and rational examination thus ironically serves both the purposes of early nineteenth-century spiritualism and, at the same time, those of the emerging social sciences, which continue to posit not our sameness but our differences.

21. For a discussion of the priority of "ideology" over the other sciences and the emergence of social science as a new discipline whose goal was society's happiness, see Brian W. Head, *Politics and Philosophy in the Thought of Destutt de Tracy* (New York: Garland, 1987), pp. 88–100, 221–42.

Conclusion

$\mathbb{A}$s I have suggested in the preceding pages, sensationism constituted one of the most important ways of thinking for the French Enlightenment. Evidence indicates that it was indeed the most influential theory for the period, since it had, as we have seen, vast and far-reaching repercussions in philosophy, psychology, literature, education, and government. Should any thinker of the time want to confer authority on his or her argument, a sensationist rationale was almost *de rigueur.* Because of the broad range of subjects and authors for which sensationist principles had pertinence, the theory was put to varying and sometimes competing uses throughout the eighteenth century and into the next.

By focusing on the sensory origin of ideas and thereby narrowly interpreting Locke's empiricism, the French sensationists may well have been responding to political exigencies on the Continent. As depicted through the eyes of Voltaire, England was the land of freedom in the first part of the eighteenth century. French men and women did not enjoy the same degree of freedom that their English counterparts did. (The history of publishing and censorship during the century attests to the very different rights enjoyed on either side of the Channel.[1]) The need for progress was thus perceived as being greater in France than in

---

1. See Robert Darnton, *The Literary Underground of the Old Regime* (Cambridge, Mass.: Harvard University Press, 1982); and his *Edition et sédition: L'Univers de la littérature clandestine au XVIIIe siècle* (Paris: Gallimard, 1991).

England. In developing a theory based on sensations, which are linked to observable, external forces, French intellectuals probably felt that they could advance with greater certainty and speed than they could by basing their theory on reflection, which involved invisible, inner operations. Clearly, they wanted to banish innate ideas, which they saw as a source of error and obscurantism. As an indispensable part of sensationist methodology, the belief in the sensory origin of ideas served as a kind of battering ram against any unjust form of authority that derived its power from preexisting assumptions not verifiable by experience. Moreover, this sensationist tenet granted truth not to *ex cathedra* pronouncements about the nature of external objects but to the human relation to those objects. And these relations are of course determined to one degree or another by the sensations. Truth, and the progress that presumably was to come from attaining it, took on a decidedly relativistic character. Sensationism cannot therefore be disassociated from eighteenth-century relativism and its particular approach to progress.

The sensationists shared some basic beliefs and practices, as I indicated in the introduction, but they also had their differences. All of the major sensationists, Condillac, Bonnet, and Helvétius, reduced to a single principle—the senses—the origin of knowledge and the generation of the various mental faculties. Both Condillac and Bonnet used the mental construct of a statue-man to explain the genesis of our ideas. All of them used the soul to relate the mind to the body, although one suspects that Helvétius's use of the soul is mere expediency to avoid censorship. Despite their own vacillations on religious questions, Condillac and Bonnet do seem more sincere than Helvétius in their treatment of the soul. After all, Condillac did envisage a prelapsarian state in which the soul governed the senses before becoming dependent on them (*EOCH* 109). For his part, Bonnet attempted to justify metaphysically the resurrection of souls in an afterlife. There were then differences among the sensationists in their attitude toward the soul. It would be fair to say that these differences consist in what the sensationists add to or take away from, as it were, the soul. My order for the chapters in Part I—Condillac, Bonnet, Helvétius—reflects the increasing attention these sensationists paid to the physicality of the soul *(le physique de l'âme)*. Bonnet believed the seat of the soul had a preformed, material structure, and he differed markedly from Condillac in this regard. Helvétius denies any spirituality to the soul or is at best indifferent to its potential spirituality. As the soul takes on more physical qualities in the thinking of these writers, sensationism moves closer in its outlook to materialism.

In their divergent views of the soul, the sensationists also differ somewhat in their environmentalism. In principle, the more physical the soul, the more malleable and subject to external influence it becomes. For the most part, Condillac, Bonnet, and Helvétius all agree that human beings are profoundly shaped by their individual circumstances and experiences. In their appraisal of the learning process, everything appears at first blush to be acquired, and nothing is innate. The sensory origin of ideas was used by the sensationists precisely to combat innatism. Helvétius takes the most radical position on this subject by claiming that education can do everything and presents himself generally as a thoroughgoing behaviorist. Although conservative in his views on the physicality of the soul, Condillac, nonetheless also believes in the primacy of experience for any educational project. But by introducing the notion of specific fibers for specific functions, Bonnet takes a turn toward nativism.[2] For Bonnet, bodily constitution also plays a part in determining perceptions. Some fibers respond better to certain stimuli than do others. Although ideas according to Bonnet continue to derive from sensations from the external world, the responses of internal, physical structures add to the content of our perceptions. Bonnet's incipient nativism thus attenuates somewhat the environmentalism characteristic of sensationist theory.

As a theory that purports to be coherent, sensationism seems disturbingly to contain the very seeds of its opposition. It is, as I have shown on occasion, an unstable theory whose aesthetics gives rise to an inconstant blending of genres and *topoi.* In sensationist aesthetics, there is an uneasy combination of the classical—with its emphasis on the universal, the eternal, the agreeable, the useful, order, continuity, and closure—and the empirical, with its emphasis on the particular, the temporal, mixing, disorder, discontinuity, and open-endedness. Elements of both modes of writing are operative in sensationist aesthetics. The instability of sensationist theory undoubtedly arises from the instability of sensation itself, which belongs both to the realm of men and animals, to reason and brutishness. Sensations can trigger the rational (ideas) as well as the irrational (excessive sensibility, sexual abuses, violence). The theory itself seems to elicit now a vaulting optimism and

2. Modern neurological science tends to confirm the highly specific nature of parts of the human brain and nervous system for certain acts of perception. See, for example, Oliver W. Sacks, *The Man Who Mistook His Wife for a Hat and Other Clinical Tales* (New York: Harper and Row, 1970).

then a despondent fatalism. It is at once liberal, in indefatigably advancing the steady march of progress by challenging existing authority, and conservative, in maintaining its well-nigh sacred view of sensibility.

Additional work remains to be done on the ways in which the study of sensationism reveals the idealization as well as the destabilization of sensibility. It might, for instance, be productive to pursue the eighteenth-century sources of today's pro-life arguments. Although the sensationists were at best ambivalent in their attitude toward the established Church, they presented what is now regarded as a conservative view of human life. One might also explore further in the field of gender studies the instability of sensibility in light of the present analysis. Can the instability of sensibility, which has been shown here to be related to the instability of genre, be connected to the instability of gender as well? Does the instability of sensibility throw into question any notion of a clearly defined sexuality? Such studies would provide still other forceful examples of the complex politics surrounding any theory, demonstrating how the same theory can sometimes be put to contradictory or rival uses.

Because of the middle road it takes in assessing the relation of the mind to the body, sensationism can be shown, and was shown in the eighteenth century, to lead either to rationalism or its opposite. Viewing human nature as mixed, the sensationists never conceived of the mind without the body or the body without the mind. Not only do they not attempt to dismiss the body's senses as meaningless in the lofty operations of the mind, through their reductive analysis they make the senses the essential residue that is left after all other mental activities have been shown to derive from them. The sensationists of course try to reintegrate the residue or germ that is sensation, showing how it gives rise to ideas and reasons. But it also problematically gives rise to the chaos and disorder of brute nature. Humans cannot therefore simply choose the rational over the irrational but must take account of both impulses at once, always and already there beckoning in opposite directions that can never be wholly reconciled. Sensationism thus points as well as any theory to the profound duality of human nature.

Sensationism was not without its successes and its failures. One of its most brilliant successes lay in preparing the way for the establishment of a national system of education at the end of the century. Emphasizing as it did environmental influences on human beings, sensationism made it clear that education could succeed in improving the lot of all. Indeed, further research could also be done in studying the pedagogical writings of Condillac, Bonnet, and Helvétius and their influence upon the educational reforms that took place during the French Revolution. Sensationist theory also represented an important and necessary interim term between the spiritualistic rationalism of the seventeenth century and the incipient modern scientific inquiry of the eighteenth century. Its mixing of the mind and body in the concept of a soul, which partook of both spiritual and material realms, made palatable to cautious and reverent thinkers alike the emerging new view of the mind as a physical brain and the nervous system as a material substance. That view, which naturally was not recognized at the time for what it was, namely, a radical departure from the past, would slowly transform thinking about human anatomy and make possible some of the age's major medical discoveries. Sensationism thus stands at a critical turning point in the history of medicine.

For all of its successes, however, sensationism failed to explain convincingly any wholly active mechanism in human beings. It presented in the end a relatively static interpretation of human beings, who are in its view characterized sometimes as passive creatures largely unable to act on their own and subject to external circumstances. Accordingly, they merely react to these circumstances, seeking pleasure or avoiding pain. Diderot and Rousseau, among others, had criticized the sensationists for this limited view of human nature. But the *idéologues*, those who undestood and admired sensationism more than most eighteenth-century thinkers, were the very ones who carried out the most thorough and devastating critique of the theory.

Although sensationism recognized the centrality of sensibility to human existence, it also failed to take full measure of this human trait in all its specificity. The sensationists had without a doubt a clear understanding of the physical side of sensibility: to feel *(sentir)* is to sense. To feel, however, can also mean to feel with some faculty other than the senses. Moreover, individual experience, certainly as it was considered by the end of the century, was based on at least these two forms of feeling. The sensationists and those influenced by them formulated the sensorially oriented view of sensibility. But it was Rousseau who more than any other thinker in his time developed the sentimentally oriented view of sensibility.[3]

Together Rousseau *and* the sensationists justified the use of experi-

3. As a portion of Chapter 7 here and my earlier book on Rousseau point out, this thinker, too, was strongly influenced by sensationism. See my *Seeing and Observing*. For Rousseau as a sentimental writer, see Pierre Trahard, *Les Maîtres de la sensibilité française au XVIIIe siècle (1715–1789)*, 4 vols. (Paris: Boivin, 1931–33), esp. vol. 3.

On the sentimental current in eighteenth-century French literature, see the recent work by David J. Denby, *Sentimental Narrative and the Social Order in France, 1760–1820* (Cambridge: Cambridge University Press, 1994).

ence as a challenge to preordained statements about truth and contributed substantially to the loss of authority in the eighteenth century. Typically, Rousseau is seen as the precursor of romanticism and, by his detractors, as the cause of the radical, indeed harmful, individualism it left in its wake.[4] But Rousseau is far from being alone in claiming authority for individual experience. The sensationists and most of the *philosophes* themselves helped weaken enormously the base of authority by their definition of experience. Their definition, which assumed the notion of sensibility *qua* sensation, served as a powerful tool for eroding the authority of existing institutions. When joined with the Rousseauian notion of sensibility *qua* sentiment, the *philosophes'* progressive message indeed proved capable of revolutionary change. Experience, that master theme and guiding light in the eighteenth century, thus gains in force in everyday life as sensibility is understood at once as sensation and feeling: sensations provoked by internal and external stimuli and feelings drawn from within the self. Experience can only be amplified by the addition of internal impressions—whether they be feelings like those Rousseau evokes, the sensations from internal organs emphasized by Cabanis, the feelings of a primitive self as discussed by Maine de Biran, or impressions of phantom limbs described later by phenomenologists—to the sensory impressions from the external world.

As an ever-widening sense of individual experience increases, forms of authority begin to fall. What represents for an individual a normal process, represents for a culture a natural evolution. Just as the child becomes socialized and moves gradually away from parental figures of authority after having learned on its own and with others' help, so, too, does an entire civilization slowly distance itself from forms of authority that gave it strength and cohesion earlier. In the eighteenth century, what shook the authority figures of father, Church, and king, paradoxically giving respect for the first time to the child as a subject worthy of attention, was nothing less than the new view of experience, which itself was believed to be informed by the very shaking or vibration of fibers. Such an assessment of what we now call the nervous system may appear primitive to us. Yet as experience relocates authority in the self, it has the force, now as it did in the eighteenth century, to move not just individuals but entire institutions and societies.

---

4. Irving Babbitt, *Rousseau and Romanticism* (1919; rpt. Austin: University of Texas Press, 1977).

Bibliography

Works from the French Enlightenment, 1700–1815*

Biran, Marie-François-Pierre Gonthier de [Maine de Biran]. *Essai sur les fondements de la psychologie et sur ses rapports avec l'étude de la nature.* Ed. Pierre Tisserand. Vols. 8 and 9, in *Oeuvres complètes.* Geneva: Slatkine, 1982.

Bonnet, Charles. *Essai analytique sur les facultés de l'âme.* Copenhagen, 1760. Hildesheim: Olms, 1973.

————. *Essai de psychologie, ou Considérations sur les opérations de l'âme, sur l'habitude et sur l'éducation.* London, 1755. Hildesheim: Olms, 1978.

————. *Principes philosophiques sur la cause première et sur son effet.* London, 1755. Hildesheim: Olms, 1978.

Buffon, Georges-Louis Leclerc, comte de. *Histoire naturelle, générale et particulière.* Paris: Dufart, 1799–1808.

Cabanis, Pierre-Jean Georges. *Rapports du physique et du moral de l'homme.* [1802] 1844; rpt. Geneva: Slatkine, 1980.

Condillac, Etienne Bonnot de. *Essai sur l'origine des connaissances humaines.* Ed. Charles Porset. Paris: Editions Galilée, 1973.

————. *La Langue des calculs.* Ed. Anne-Marie Chouillet and Sylvain Auroux. Lille: Presses Universitaires de Lille, 1981.

————. *Oeuvres philosophiques de Condillac.* Ed. Georges Le Roy. 3 vols. Paris: Presses Universitaires de France, 1947–51.

————. *Traité des sensations. Traité des animaux.* Paris: Fayard, 1984.

————. *Traité des systêmes.* Ed. Francine Markovits and Michel Authier. Paris: Fayard, 1991.

Condorcet, Marie-Jean-Antoine-Nicolas Caritat, marquis de. *Esquisse d'un tableau historique des progrès de l'esprit humain.* Ed. Alain Pons. Paris: Garnier-Flammarion, 1988.

Diderot, Denis. *Oeuvres complètes.* Ed. Herbert Dieckmann, Jacques Proust, and Jean Varloot. 33 vols. projected. Paris: Hermann, 1975– .

————. *Oeuvres esthétiques.* Ed. Paul Vernière. Paris: Garnier, 1968.

————. *Oeuvres philosophiques.* Ed. Paul Vernière. Paris: Garnier, 1964.

Dubos, Jean-Baptiste, abbé. *Réflexions critiques sur la poésie et la peinture.* Geneva: Slatkine, 1967.

Encyclopédie, ou Dictionnaire raisonné des sciences, des arts et des métiers. Ed.

*See note 3 in the Introduction, page 4.

Denis Diderot and Jean Le Rond d'Alembert. 28 vols. Paris: Briasson, David, Le Breton, Durand, 1751–72.

Graffigny, Françoise d'Issembourg d'Happoncourt, Mme de. *Lettres d'une Péruvienne*. In *"Lettres portugaises," "Lettres d'une Péruvienne" et autres romans d'amour par lettres*. Ed. Bernard Bray and Isabelle Landy-Houillon. Paris: Flammarion, 1983.

Helvétius, Claude-Adrien. *De l'esprit*. Ed. Jacques Moutaux. Paris: Fayard, 1988.

———. *De l'homme, de ses facultés intellectuelles et de son éducation*. London: La Société Typographique, 1773.

———. *De l'homme, de ses facultés intellectuelles et de son éducation*. Ed. Geneviève and Jacques Moutaux. Paris: Fayard, 1989.

Holbach, Paul-Henri Thiry, baron d'. *Système de la nature, ou Des lois du monde physique & du monde moral*. 1770; rpt. Geneva: Slatkine, 1973.

Laclos, Pierre Choderlos de. *Oeuvres complètes*. Ed. Laurent Versini. Paris: Gallimard, 1979.

La Mettrie, Julien Offray de. *Histoire naturelle de l'âme*. The Hague: Neaulme, 1745.

———. *Oeuvres philosophiques*. Ed. Francine Markovits. 2 vols. Paris: Fayard, 1987.

Laromiguière, Pierre. *Paradoxes de Condillac*. 1805; rpt. Paris: Brunot-Labbé, 1825.

Marivaux, Pierre Carlet de Chamblain de. *La Vie de Marianne*. Ed. Frédéric Deloffre. Paris: Garnier, 1963.

Maubec, D^r, de la Faculté de Médecine de Montpellier. *Principes phisiques de la raison et des passions des hommes*. Paris: Girin, 1709.

Maupertuis, Pierre-Louis Moreau de. *Réflexions philosophiques sur l'origine des langues et la signification des mots*. Paris: n.p., 1748.

———. *Système de la nature*. Ed. François Azouvi. Paris: Vrin, 1984.

Mercier, Louis-Sébastien. *Tableau de Paris*. 1782–88; rpt. Geneva: Slatkine, 1979.

Montesquieu, Charles-Louis de Secondat, baron de. *Oeuvres complètes*. Ed. Roger Caillois. 2 vols. Paris: Gallimard, 1949–51.

Prévost, Antoine-François, abbé. *Oeuvres de Prévost*. Ed. Jean Sgard. 8 vols. Grenoble: Presses Universitaires de Grenoble, 1977–86.

Rousseau, Jean-Jacques. *Oeuvres complètes*. Ed. Bernard Gagnebin and Marcel Raymond. 5 vols. Paris: Gallimard, 1959–95.

Sade, Donatien-Alphonse-François, comte [marquis] de. *Oeuvres*. Ed. Michel Delon. 2 vols. Paris: Gallimard, 1990–95.

———. *La Philosophie dans le boudoir, ou Les Instituteurs immoraux*. Ed. Yvon Belaval. Paris: Gallimard, 1976.

Tracy, Antoine-Louis-Claude Destutt de. *Eléments d'idéologie*. 1801–15; rpt. Stuttgart-Bad Cannstatt: Frommann-Holzboog, 1977.

Turgot, Anne-Robert-Jacques. *Oeuvres de Turgot*. Ed. Gustave Schelle. 5 vols. Paris: Alcan, 1913.

Voltaire [François-Marie Arouet]. *Complete Works of Voltaire/Oeuvres complètes de Voltaire*. Ed. W. H. Barber and Ulla Kölving. 135 vols. projected. Banbury, Oxfordshire: Voltaire Foundation, 1968–.

———. *Essai sur les moeurs*. Ed. René Pomeau. 2 vols. Paris: Garnier, 1990.

Other Sources

Aarsleff, Hans. *From Locke to Saussure: Essays on the Study of Language and Intellectual History*. Minneapolis: University of Minnesota Press, 1982.

Altman, Janet G. "Graffigny's Epistemology and the Emergence of Third-World Ideology." In *Writing the Female Voice: Essays on Epistolary Literature*. Ed. Elizabeth C. Goldsmith. Boston: Northeastern University Press, 1989, pp. 172–202.

———. "Making Room for 'Peru': Graffigny's Novel Reconsidered." In *Dilemmes du roman*. Ed. Catherine Lafarge et al. Saratoga, Calif.: Anma Libri, 1990, pp. 33–46.

Anderson, Lorin. *Charles Bonnet and the Order of the Known*. Dordrecht: Reidel, 1982.

———. "Charles Bonnet's Taxonomy and Chain of Being." *Journal of the History of Ideas* 37 (1976), 45–58.

Anderson, Wilda. *Diderot's Dream*. Baltimore: Johns Hopkins University Press, 1990.

Andresen, Julie. "Langage naturel et artifice linguistique." In *Condillac et les problèmes du langage*. Ed. Jean Sgard. Geneva: Slatkine, 1982, pp. 275–88.

Aquinas, Thomas, Saint. *Summa Theologica*. Trans. Fathers of the English Dominican Province. 3 vols. New York: Benzinger, 1947–48.

Aristotle. *The Works of Aristotle Translated into English*. Ed. J. A. Smith and W. D. Ross. 12 vols. London: Oxford University Press, 1908–52.

Auerbach, Erich. *Mimesis: The Representation of Reality in Western Literature*. Trans. Willard R. Trask. 1953; rpt. Princeton: Princeton University Press, 1974.

Auroux, Sylvain. "Condillac, inventeur d'un nouveau matérialisme." *Dix-Huitième Siècle* 24 (1992), 153–63.

———. "Condillac, ou La Vertu des signes." In *Condillac, La Langue des calculs*. Ed. Anne-Marie Chouillet and Sylvain Auroux. Lille: Presses Universitaires de Lille, 1981.

———. "Empirisme et théorie linguistique chez Condillac." In *Condillac et les problèmes du langage*. Ed. Jean Sgard. Geneva: Slatkine, 1982, pp. 177–210.

———. "Le Rationalisme empiriste." *Dialogue* 13 (1974), 475–503.

Austin, J. L. *Sense and Sensibilia*. Ed. G. J. Warnock. London: Oxford University Press, 1962.

Babbitt, Irving. *Rousseau and Romanticism*. 1919; rpt. Austin: University of Texas Press, 1977.

Bachelard, Gaston. *The Poetics of Reverie: Childhood, Language, and the Cosmos*. Trans. Daniel Russell. Boston: Beacon, 1971.

———. *The Poetics of Space*. Trans. Maria Jolas. Boston: Beacon, 1969.

Bacon, Francis. *Novum Organum*. In *The Physical and Metaphysical Works of Lord Bacon*. Ed. Joseph Devey. London: Bell, 1911.

Bakhtin, Mikhail. "Epic and Novel: Toward a Methodology for the Study of the Novel." In *The Dialogic Imagination: Four Essays by M. M. Bakhtin*. Ed.

Michael Holquist; trans. Caryl Emerson and Holquist. Austin: University of Texas Press, 1981.

———. *Rabelais and His World.* Trans. Hélène Iswolsky. Cambridge, Mass.: MIT Press, 1968.

Barthes, Roland. *Sade, Fourier, Loyola.* Paris: Editions du Seuil, 1971.

Bataille, Georges. *L'Erotisme.* Paris: Les Editions de Minuit, 1957.

———. *Les Larmes d'Eros.* Paris: Pauvert, 1961 and 1971.

———. *La Littérature et le mal.* Paris: Gallimard, 1957.

Becq, Annie. *Genèse de l'esthétique française moderne: De la raison classique à l'imagination créatrice, 1680–1814.* 2 vols. Pisa: Pacini, 1984.

Bender, John. *Imagining the Penitentiary: Fiction and the Architecture of Mind in Eighteenth-Century England.* Chicago: Chicago University Press, 1989.

Berkeley, George. *The Works of George Berkeley, Bishop of Cloyne.* Ed. A. A. Luce and T. E. Jessop. 9 vols. New York: Nelson, 1948–57.

Bernstein, Michael Andre. "When the Carnival Turns Bitter: Preliminary Reflections Upon the Abject Hero." *Critical Inquiry* 10 (1983), 283–305.

Blanchot, Maurice. *Lautréamont et Sade.* Paris: Les Editions de Minuit, 1963.

Bloch, Olivier, and Charles Porset, eds. "Le Matérialisme des lumières." *Dix-Huitième Siècle* 24 (1992), 5–236.

Blum, Carol. *Rousseau and the Republic of Virtue: The Language of Politics in the French Revolution.* Ithaca: Cornell University Press, 1986.

———. "Styles of Cognition as Moral Options in *La Nouvelle Héloïse* and *Les Liaisons dangereuses.*" *PMLA* 88 (1973), 289–98.

Boileau, Nicolas. *L'Art poétique.* Ed. Guillaume Picot. Paris: Bordas, 1984.

Bonnet, Georges. *Charles Bonnet (1720–1793).* Paris: Lac, 1929.

Bonno, Gabriel. *La Culture et la civilisation britanniques devant l'opinion française de la paix d'Utrecht aux "Lettres philosophiques."* Philadelphia: American Philosophical Society, 1948.

———. "The Diffusion of Locke's *Essay Concerning Human Understanding* in France Before Voltaire's *Lettres Philosophiques.*" *Proceedings of the American Philosophical Society* 91 (1947), 421–25.

Boring, Edwin G. *Sensation and Perception in the History of Experimental Psychology.* New York: Appleton-Century-Crofts, 1942.

Boulad-Ayoub, Josiane. *Contre nous de la tyrannie: Des relations idéologiques entre lumières et révolution.* LaSalle, Québec: Editions Hurtubise, 1990.

———, ed. "Paul-Henri Thiry, Baron d'Holbach: Epistémologie et politique au XVIIIe siècle." *Corpus, Revue de Philosophie* 22/23 (1992).

Bréhier, Emile. *The History of Philosophy.* Trans. Joseph Thomas (vol. 1) and Wade Baskin (vols. 2–6). 6 vols. Chicago: University of Chicago Press, 1963–69.

Brooks, Peter. *The Novel of Worldliness: Crébillon, Marivaux, Laclos, Stendhal.* Princeton: Princeton University Press, 1969.

Brumfitt, J. H. *The French Enlightenment.* Cambridge, Mass.: Schenkman, 1973.

Caplan, Jay. *Framed Narratives: Diderot's Genealogy of the Beholder.* Minneapolis: University of Minnesota Press, 1985.

Carlson, Eric T., and Meribeth M. Simpson. "Models of the Nervous System in

Eighteenth-Century Psychiatry." *Bulletin of the History of Medicine* 43 (1969), 101–15.

Carré, R. "Sur la sensation condillacienne." In *Proceedings of the Tenth International Congress of Philosophy.* Vol. II. Amsterdam: North-Holland, 1949, pp. 1156–59.

Carrera, Rosalina, de la. *Success in Circuit Lies: Diderot's Communicational Practice.* Stanford, Calif.: Stanford University Press, 1991.

Cassirer, Ernst. *Language and Myth.* Trans. Suzanne K. Langer. New York: Harper, 1946.

———. *The Philosophy of the Enlightenment.* Trans. F. C. A. Koelln and J. P. Pettegrove. Princeton: Princeton University Press, 1951.

Castle, Terry. "The Carnivalization of Eighteenth-Century Narrative." *PMLA* 99 (1984), 903–16.

Cazenobe, Colette. *Le Système du libertinage de Crébillon à Laclos.* Studies on Voltaire and the Eighteenth Century, 282. Oxford: Voltaire Foundation, 1991.

Chomsky, Noam. "Recent Contributions to the Theory of Innate Ideas." In *Challenges to Empiricism.* Ed. Harold Morick. Indianapolis: Hackett, 1980, pp. 230–39.

———. "Some Empirical Assumptions in Modern Philosophy of Language." In *Challenges to Empiricism.* Ed. Harold Morick. Indianapolis: Hackett, 1980, pp. 287–318.

Chouillet, Jacques. *L'Esthétique des lumières.* Paris: Presses Universitaires de France, 1974.

Clifford, James. *The Predicament of Culture: Twentieth-Century Ethnography, Literature, and Art.* Cambridge, Mass.: Harvard University Press, 1988.

Cohen, Huguette. "Galiani, Diderot, and Nature's Loaded Dice." *Studies on Voltaire and the Eighteenth Century* 311 (1993), 39–59.

Coleman, Francis X. J. *The Aesthetic Thought of the French Enlightenment.* Pittsburgh: University of Pittsburgh Press, 1971.

Coleman, Patrick. *Rousseau's Political Imagination: Rule and Representation in the "Lettre à d'Alembert."* Geneva: Droz, 1984.

Comte-Sponville, André. "La Mettrie et le *Système d'Epicure.*" *Dix-Huitième Siècle* 24 (1992), 105–15.

Conroy, Peter V., Jr. *Intimate, Intrusive, and Triumphant: Readers in the "Liaisons dangereuses."* Amsterdam: Benjamins, 1987.

Corbin, Alain. *Le Miasme et la jonquille: L'Odorat et l'imaginaire social, XVIIIᵉ–XIXᵉ siècles.* Paris: Flammarion, 1986.

Cousin, Victor. *Philosophie sensualiste au dix-huitième siècle.* 3d ed. Paris: Librairie Nouvelle, 1856.

Cranefield, Paul F. "On the Origin of the Phrase *Nihil ist in intellectu quod non prius fuerit in sensu.*" *Journal of the History of Medicine and Allied Sciences* 25 (1970), 77–80.

Creech, James. *Diderot: Thresholds of Representation.* Columbus: Ohio State University Press, 1986.

Creighton, Douglas G. "Man and Mind in Diderot and Helvétius." *PMLA* 71 (1956), 705–24.

Crocker, Lester. *An Age of Crisis: Man and World in Eighteenth-Century French Thought.* Baltimore: Johns Hopkins University Press, 1959.

Cummings, Ian. *Helvétius: His Life and Place in the History of Educational Thought.* London: Routledge & Kegan Paul, 1955.

Darnton, Robert. *Edition et sédition: L'Univers de la littérature clandestine au XVIIIe siècle.* Paris: Gallimard, 1991.

———. *The Literary Underground of the Old Regime.* Cambridge, Mass.: Harvard University Press, 1982.

Dawson, Virginia P. *Nature's Enigma: The Problem of the Polyp in the Letters of Bonnet, Trembley, and Réaumur.* Philadelphia: American Philosophical Society, 1987.

DeJean, Joan. *Literary Fortifications: Rousseau, Laclos, Sade.* Princeton: Princeton University Press, 1984.

———. *Tender Geographies: Women and the Origins of the Novel in France.* New York: Columbia University Press, 1991.

Delbos, Victor. *La Philosophie française.* Paris: Plon, 1921.

Denby, David J. *Sentimental Narrative and the Social Order in France, 1760–1820.* Cambridge: Cambridge University Press, 1994.

———. "Transformations du discours sentimental autour de la révolution française." In *La Littérature et ses avatars: Discrédits, déformations et réhabilitations dans l'histoire de la littérature.* Ed. Y. Bellenger. Paris: Aux Amateurs de Livres, 1991, pp. 255–65.

Deneys, Anne. "The Political Economy of the Body in the *Liaisons dangereuses* of Choderlos de Laclos." In *Eroticism and the Body Politic.* Ed. Lynn Hunt. Baltimore: Johns Hopkins University Press, 1991, pp. 41–62.

Deneys, Henry, and Anne Deneys-Tunney, eds. "A. L. C. Destutt de Tracy et l'idéologie." *Corpus, Revue de Philosophie* 26/27 (1994).

Deneys-Tunney, Anne. *Ecritures du corps de Descartes à Laclos.* Paris: Presses Universitaires de France, 1992.

Deprun, Jean. "Sade philosophe." In Sade, *Oeuvres.* Ed. Michel Delon. Paris: Gallimard, 1990, 1: lix–lxix.

Derrida, Jacques. *L'Archéologie du frivole.* Paris: Denoël/Gonthier, 1976.

———. *De la grammatologie.* Paris: Editions de Minuit, 1967.

Descartes, René. *Oeuvres complètes.* Ed. Charles Adam and Paul Tannery. 13 vols. Paris: Vrin, 1964–.

Diaconoff, Suellen. *Eros and Power in "Les Liaisons dangereuses": A Study in Evil.* Geneva: Droz, 1979.

Dieckmann, Herbert. "Condillac's Philosophical Works." *Review of Metaphysics* 7 (1953–54), 255–61.

Du Bellay, Joachim. *La Deffense et illustration de la langue françoyse.* 1549; rpt. Geneva: Slatkine, 1972.

Duchesneau, François. "Condillac critique de Locke." *Studi internazionali di filosofia* 6 (1974), 77-98.

———. *La Physiologie des lumières: Empirisme, modèles et théories.* The Hague: Nijhoff, 1982.

The Encyclopedia of Philosophy. 8 vols. New York: Macmillan and the Free Press, 1967.

Fauchery, Pierre. *La Destinée féminine dans le roman européen du dix-huitième siècle, 1713–1807: Essai de gynécomythie romanesque.* Paris: Colin, 1972.

Figlio, Karl M. "Theories of Perception and the Physiology of Mind in the Late Eighteenth Century." *History of Science* 12 (1975), 177–212.

Fish, Stanley. *Is There a Text in This Class? The Authority of Interpretive Communities.* Cambridge, Mass.: Harvard University Press, 1980.

Folkierski, Wladyslaw. *Entre le classicisme et le romantisme: Etude sur l'esthétique et les esthéticiens du XVIIIe siècle.* Krakow, 1925; rpt. Paris: Champion, 1969.

Foucault, Michel. *The Birth of the Clinic: An Archaeology of Medical Perception.* Trans. A. M. Sheridan Smith. New York: Vintage, 1975.

———. *Les Mots et les choses: Une Archéologie des sciences humaines.* Paris: Gallimard, 1966.

Foulquié, Paul. *Dictionnaire de la langue philosophique.* Paris: Presses Universitaires de France, 1962.

Fowler, Alastair. *Kinds of Literature: An Introduction to the Theory of Genres and Modes.* Cambridge, Mass.: Harvard University Press, 1982.

Fox, Christopher, ed. *Psychology and Literature in the Eighteenth Century.* New York: AMS Press, 1987.

Fritzsche, Oskar William. *Die pädagogisch-didaktischen Theorien Charles Bonnets.* Langensalza: Beyer & Söhne, 1905.

Furetière, Antoine. *Dictionnaire universel.* The Hague, 1690; Paris: Le Robert, 1978.

Gardner, Elizabeth J. "The *Philosophes* and Women: Sensationalism and Sentiment." In *Woman and Society in Eighteenth-Century France: Essays in Honor of John Stephenson Spink.* London: Athlone, 1979.

Genette, Gérard. *Palimpsestes: La Littérature au second degré.* Paris: Editions du Seuil, 1982.

Gibson, J. J. *The Perception of the Visual World.* 1950; rpt. Westport, Conn.: Greenwood Press, 1975.

Gilot, Michel, and Jean Sgard. *Le Vocabulaire du sentiment dans l'oeuvre de J.-J. Rousseau.* Geneva: Slatkine, 1980.

Gilson, Etienne. *Les Idées et les lettres.* Paris: Vrin, 1932.

Girard, René. *Violence and the Sacred.* Trans. Patrick Gregory. Baltimore: Johns Hopkins University Press, 1977.

Goetz, Rose. *Destutt de Tracy: Philosophie du langage et science de l'homme.* Geneva: Droz, 1993.

Goldberg, Rita. *Sex and Enlightenment: Women in Richardson and Diderot.* Cambridge: Cambridge University Press, 1984.

Goodman, Dena. *The Republic of Letters: A Cultural History of the French Enlightenment.* Ithaca: Cornell University Press, 1994.

———. "Story-Telling in the Republic of Letters: The Rhetorical Context of Diderot's *La Religieuse." Nouvelles de la République des Lettres* 1 (1986), 51–70.

Gouhier, Henri. *Les Conversions de Maine de Biran.* Paris: Vrin, 1947.

Grimsley, Ronald. "Some Aspects of 'Nature' and 'Language' in the French Enlightenment." *Studies on Voltaire and the Eighteenth Century* 56 (1967), 659–77.

Grober, Max. "The Natural History of Heaven and the Historical Proofs of Christianity: *La Palingénésie philosophique* of Charles Bonnet." *Studies on Voltaire and the Eighteenth Century* 308 (1993), 233–55.

Grossman, Mordecai. *The Philosophy of Helvétius with Special Emphasis on the Educational Implications of Sensationalism.* 1926; New York: AMS Press, 1972.

Hagstrum, Jean H. *Sex and Sensibility: Ideal and Erotic Love from Milton to Mozart.* Chicago: University of Chicago Press, 1980.

———. *The Sister Arts: The Tradition of Literary Pictorialism and English Poetry from Dryden to Gray.* Chicago: University of Chicago Press, 1958.

Harnois, Guy. *Les Théories du langage en France de 1660 à 1821.* Paris: Les Belles Lettres, 1928.

Hartley, David. *Observations on Man, His Frame, His Duty and His Expectations.* Ed. Theodore L. Huguelet. 2 vols. Delmar, NY: Scholars' Facsimiles and Reprints, 1976.

Hasnaoui, Chantal. "Condillac, chemins du sensualisme." In *Langue et langage de Leibniz à l' "Encyclopédie."* Ed. Michèle Duchet and Michèle Jalley. Paris: Union Générale d'Editions, 1977, pp. 97–129.

Hatzfeld, Helmut. *The Rococo: Eroticism, Wit, and Elegance in European Literature.* New York: Pegasus, 1972.

Hayes, Julie C. " 'Aristocrate ou démocrate? Vous me le direz': Sade's Political Pamphlets." *Eighteenth-Century Studies* 23 (1989), 22–41.

Hazard, Paul. *The European Mind (1680–1715).* Trans. J. Lewis May. New York: New American Library, 1963.

———. *European Thought in the Eighteenth Century.* Trans. J. Lewis May. Harmondsworth: Penguin, 1965.

Head, Brian W. *Politics and Philosophy in the Thought of Destutt de Tracy.* New York: Garland, 1987.

Henschel, Bernhard. "Les Conceptions rationaliste et sensualiste du langage au siècle des lumières dans l'interprétation moderne." In *Actele celui de-al XII-lea congres internaţional de lingvistică şi filologie romanică.* Vol. I. Bucharest: Editura Academiei Republicii Socialiste România, 1970, pp. 913–18.

Hine, Ellen McNiven. "Condillac and the Problem of Language." *Studies on Voltaire and the Eighteenth Century* 106 (1973), 21–62.

Hobbes, Thomas. *The English Works of Thomas Hobbes of Malmesbury.* 11 vols. *Opera Philosophica* (Latin works). Ed. Sir William Molesworth. 5 vols. 1839–45; rpt. Aalen: Scientia, 1961–62.

Hogsett, Alice Charlotte. "Graffigny and Riccoboni on the Language of the Woman Writer." In *Eighteenth-Century Women and the Arts.* Ed. Frederick M. Keener and Susan E. Lorsch. New York, Westport, Conn.: Greenwood Press, 1988, pp. 119–27.

Holquist, Michael. *Dialogism: Bakhtin and His World.* London and New York: Routledge, 1990.

———, ed. *The Dialogic Imagination: Four Essays by M. M. Bakhtin.* Trans. Caryl Emerson and Michael Holquist. Austin: University of Texas Press, 1981.

Horkheimer, Max, and Theodor W. Adorno. *Dialectic of Enlightenment.* Trans. John Cumming. New York: Herder and Herder, 1972.

Horowitz, Irving Louis. *Claude Helvétius: Philosopher of Democracy and Enlightenment.* New York: Paine-Whitman, 1954.

Howe, Daniel W. "The Political Psychology of *The Federalist.*" *William and Mary Quarterly* 44 (1987), 485–509.

Huet, Marie-Hélène. *Monstrous Imagination.* Cambridge, Mass.: Harvard University Press, 1993.

Hume, David. *The Philosophical Works.* Ed. Thomas Hill Green and Thomas Hodge Grose. 4 vols. 1882; rpt. Aalen: Scientia, 1964.

Hunt, Lynn. *The Family Romance of the French Revolution.* Berkeley and Los Angeles: University of California Press, 1992.

———, ed. *Eroticism and the Body Politic.* Baltimore: Johns Hopkins University Press, 1991.

Jacob, Margaret C. *The Radical Enlightenment: Pantheists, Freemasons, and Republicans.* London: George Allen & Unwin, 1981.

Jimack, Peter. "Les Philosophes sensualistes: Condillac, Buffon, Helvétius." In *La Genèse et la rédaction de l' "Emile" de J.-J. Rousseau.* Studies on Voltaire and the Eighteenth Century, 13. Geneva: Institut et Musée Voltaire, 1960, pp. 318-44.

Johnson, A. E., trans. *Blue Beard.* In *Perrault's Fairy Tales.* New York: Dover, 1969.

Joly, Henri. "Condillac et la critique de l' 'Age de Raison.'" In *Condillac et les problèmes du langage.* Ed. Jean Sgard. Geneva: Slatkine, 1982, pp. 17–25.

Kamuf, Peggy. *Fictions of Feminine Desire: Disclosures of Heloise.* Lincoln: University of Nebraska Press, 1982.

Kassler, Jamie C. "Man—A Musical Instrument: Models of the Brain and Mental Functioning Before the Computer." *History of Science* 22 (1984), 59–92.

Kavanagh, Thomas M. *Enlightenment and the Shadows of Chance: The Novel and the Culture of Gambling in Eighteenth-Century France.* Baltimore: Johns Hopkins University Press, 1993.

Keener, Frederick M. *The Chain of Becoming.* New York: Columbia University Press, 1983.

Kennedy, Emmet. *A "Philosophe" in the Age of Revolution: Destutt de Tracy and the Origins of "Ideology."* Philadelphia: American Philosophical Society, 1978.

Kenshur, Oscar. *Dilemmas of Enlightenment: Studies in the Rhetoric and Logic of Ideology.* Berkeley and Los Angeles: University of California Press, 1993.

Kernan, Alvin. *The Death of Literature.* New Haven: Yale University Press, 1990.

Klossowski, Pierre. *Le Philosophe scélérat.* Paris: Editions du Seuil, 1947 and 1967.

———. *Sade mon prochain.* Paris: Editions du Seuil, 1947 and 1967.

Knight, Isabel F. *The Geometric Spirit: The Abbé de Condillac and the French Enlightenment.* New Haven: Yale University Press, 1968.

Kors, Alan Charles. *D'Holbach's Coterie: An Enlightenment in Paris.* Princeton: Princeton University Press, 1976.

Krafft-Ebing, Richard von. *Psychopathia sexualis.* New York: Physicians & Surgeons Book Company, 1965.

Krüger, Lorenz. "Empirismus und sensualismus: Ein Exkurs über Condillac." In *Der Begriff des Empirismus: Erkenntnistheoretische Studien am Beispiel John Lockes.* Berlin: De Gruyter, 1973, pp. 56–68.

Kundera, Milan. "Man Thinks, God Laughs." Trans. Linda Asher. *New York Review of Books,* June 13, 1985, pp. 11–12.

Lafarge, Catherine, et al., ed. *Dilemmes du roman: Essays in Honor of Georges May.* Saratoga, Calif.: Anma Libri, 1989.

Landy-Houillon, Isabelle. "Introduction." *"Lettres portugaises," "Lettres d'une Péruvienne" et autres romans d'amour par lettres.* Ed. Bernard Bray and Isabelle Landy-Houillon. Paris: Flammarion, 1983.

Lanson, Gustave. "Les Idées littéraires de Condillac." *Revue de Synthèse Historique* 21 (1910), 267–79.

Lasch, Christopher. *The Culture of Narcissism: American Life in an Age of Diminishing Expectations.* New York: Norton, 1978.

Lee, Rensselaer W. *Ut Pictura Poesis: The Humanistic Theory of Painting.* New York: Norton, 1967.

Lefèvre, Henri. "Hommage à Condillac." *Cahiers d'Histoire* 1 (1956), 349–64.

Lemoine, Albert. *Charles Bonnet de Genève: Philosophe et naturaliste.* Paris: Durand, 1850.

Le Roy, Georges. "Introduction à l'oeuvre philosophique de Condillac." In *Oeuvres philosophiques de Condillac.* Paris: Presses Universitaires de France, 1947, 1: vii–xxxv.

———. *La Psychologie de Condillac.* Paris: Boivin, 1937.

Lindenberger, Herbert. "Ideology and Innocence: On the Politics of Critical Language." *PMLA* 105 (1990), 398–408.

Locke, John. *An Essay Concerning Human Understanding.* Ed. Peter Nidditch. Oxford: Oxford University Press, 1975.

Lovejoy, Arthur O. *The Great Chain of Being: A Study of the History of an Idea.* 1936; rpt. Cambridge, Mass.: Harvard University Press, 1978.

Lurbe, Pierre. "Matière, nature, mouvement chez d'Holbach et Toland." *Dix-Huitième Siècle* 24 (1992), 53–62.

MacArthur, Elizabeth J. "Devious Narratives: Refusal of Closure in Two Eighteenth-Century Epistolary Novels." *Eighteenth-Century Studies* 21 (1987), 1–20.

Marshall, David. *The Surprising Effects of Sympathy: Marivaux, Diderot, Rousseau, and Mary Shelley.* Chicago: University of Chicago Press, 1988.

Mauzi, Robert. *L'Idée du bonheur au XVIIIe siècle.* Paris: Colin, 1960.

May, Georges. *Le Dilemme du roman au XVIIIe siècle: Etude sur les rapports du roman et de la critique, 1715–1761.* New Haven: Yale University Press, 1963.

Mazzola, Francesco. *La pedagogia di Helvétius.* Milan: Sandron, 1920.

Mensching, Günther. "La Nature et le premier principe de la métaphysique chez d'Holbach et Diderot." *Dix-Huitième Siècle* 24 (1992), 117–36.

Merleau-Ponty, Maurice. *La Phénoménologie de la perception.* 1945; rpt. Paris: Gallimard, 1976.

Miller, Nancy K. "Authorized Versions." *French Review* 61 (1988), 405–13.

———. "Emphasis Added: Plots and Plausibilities in Women's Fiction." *PMLA* 96 (1981), 36–48.

———. *The Heroine's Text: Readings in the French and English Novel, 1722–1782.* New York: Columbia University Press, 1977.

———. *Subject to Change: Reading Feminist Writing.* New York: Columbia University Press, 1988.

Mitchell, W. J. T. *Iconology: Image, Text, Ideology.* Chicago: University of Chicago Press, 1986.

———, ed. *The Language of Images.* Chicago: University of Chicago Press, 1980.

———, ed. *The Politics of Interpretation.* Chicago: University of Chicago Press, 1983.

Momdjian, K. *La Philosophie d'Helvétius.* Trans. M. Katsovitch. Moscow: Editions en Langues Etrangères, 1959.

Moore, F. C. T. *The Psychology of Maine de Biran.* Oxford: Oxford University Press, 1970.

Moravia, Sergio. *Il pensiero degli idéologues: Scienza e filosofia in Francia (1780–1815).* Florence: La Nuova Italia, 1974.

Morgan, Michael J. *Molyneux's Question: Vision, Touch, and the Philosophy of Perception.* Cambridge: Cambridge University Press, 1977.

Morick, Harold, ed. *Challenges to Empiricism.* Indianapolis: Hackett, 1980.

Morris, David B. *The Culture of Pain.* Berkeley and Los Angeles: University of California Press, 1991.

Morson, Gary Saul, and Caryl Emerson. *Rethinking Bakhtin: Extensions and Challenges.* Evanston: Northwestern University Press, 1989.

Moser, Walter J. "De la signification d'une poésie insignifiante: Examen de la poésie fugitive au XVIIIe siècle et de ses rapports avec la pensée sensualiste en France." *Studies on Voltaire and the Eighteenth Century* 94 (1972), 277–415.

Moutaux, Jacques. "Helvétius et l'idée de l'humanité." *Corpus, Revue de Philosophie* 7 (1988), 31–53.

———. "Matérialisme et lumières: Notes sur l'intérêt des ouvrages de La Mettrie, Helvétius et d'Holbach." *Corpus, Revue de Philosophie* 5/6 (1987), 3–13.

Niderst, Alain. "Esthétique et matérialisme à la fin du siècle." *Dix-Huitième Siècle* 24 (1992), 189–97.

Nietzsche, Friedrich. *The Birth of Tragedy.* Trans. Francis Golffing. New York: Doubleday, 1956.

Nisbet, Robert A. *History of the Idea of Progress.* New York: Basic Books, 1980.

Norris, Christopher. *Deconstruction: Theory and Practice.* London: Methuen, 1982.

O'Neal, John C. "Eighteenth-Century Female Protagonists and the Dialectics of Desire." *Eighteenth-Century Life* 10, n.s. 2 (May 1986), 87–97.

———. "Interpolated Narrative in Voltaire's *Candide.*" In *Approaches to Teaching "Candide."* Ed. Renée Waldinger. New York: Modern Language Association of America, 1987, pp. 45–51.

———. "Rousseau's Theory of Wealth." *History of European Ideas* 7 (1986), 453–67.

———. *Seeing and Observing: Rousseau's Rhetoric of Perception.* Stanford French and Italian Studies, 41. Saratoga, Calif.: Anma Libri, 1985.

Oxford English Dictionary. Prepared by J. A. Simpson and E. S. C. Weiner. 2d ed. 20 vols. Oxford: Oxford University Press, 1989.

Ozouf, Mona. *Festivals and the French Revolution.* Trans. Alan Sheridan. Cambridge, Mass.: Harvard University Press, 1988.

Paganini, Gianni. "Psychologie et physiologie de l'entendement chez Condillac." *Dix-Huitième Siècle* 24 (1992), 165–72.

Payne, Harry C. *The "Philosophes" and the People.* New Haven: Yale University Press, 1976.

Perkins, Jean A. *The Concept of the Self in the French Enlightenment.* Geneva: Droz, 1969.

Perkins, M. L. "The Crisis of Sensationalism in Diderot's *Lettre sur les aveugles.*" *Studies on Voltaire and the Eighteenth Century* 174 (1978), 167–88.

Perrault, Charles. *Contes.* Ed. Jean-Pierre Collinet. Paris: Gallimard, 1981.

Picavet, François. *Les Idéologues: Essai sur l'histoire des idées et des théories scientifiques, philosophiques, religieuses, etc. en France depuis 1789.* Paris: Alcan, 1891.

Plamenatz, John. *Ideology.* New York: Praeger, 1970.

Plato. *The Dialogues of Plato.* Trans. Benjamin Jowett. 4 vols. Oxford: Clarendon Press, 1953.

Plekhanov, G. V. *Essays in the History of Materialism.* Trans. Ralph Fox. London: Lane, 1934.

Poulet, Georges. *Etudes sur le temps humain,* vol. I. 1952; rpt. Paris: Editions du Rocher, 1976.

Praz, Mario. *The Romantic Agony.* Trans. Angus Davidson. Oxford: Oxford University Press, 1970.

Quemada, Bernard, ed. *Matériaux pour l'histoire du vocabulaire français: Datations et documents lexicographiques.* 2d ser. Vol. 22. Paris: Klincksieck, 1983.

Rabelais, François. *Oeuvres complètes.* Ed. Pierre Jourda. 2 vols. Paris: Garnier, 1962.

Rabinowitz, Peter J. *Before Reading: Narrative Conventions and the Politics of Interpretation.* Ithaca: Cornell University Press, 1987.

Rauch, André. "Le Souci du corps chez Condillac." *Stadion* 3 (1977), 60–89.

Ravven, Heidi M. "Spinoza's Materialist Ethics: The Education of Desire." *International Studies in Philosophy* 22 (1990), 59–78.

Ray, William. *Story and History: Narrative Authority and Social Identity in the Eighteenth-Century French and English Novel.* Cambridge, Mass.: Basil Blackwell, 1990.

Reeder, Claudia. "Paradoxe du (para)texte." *L'Esprit Créateur* 24, no. 2 (1984), 36–48.

Richard, Jean-Pierre. *Littérature et sensation.* 1954; rpt. Paris: Editions du Seuil, 1990.

Riffaterre, Michael. *Semiotics of Poetry.* Bloomington: Indiana University Press, 1978.

Robbe-Grillet, Alain. *La Jalousie.* Paris: Editions de Minuit, 1957.

Robins, R. H. "Condillac et l'origine du langage." In *Condillac et les problèmes du langage.* Ed. Jean Sgard. Geneva: Slatkine, 1982, pp. 95–101.

Rosbottom, Ronald C. *Choderlos de Laclos.* Boston: Twayne, 1978.

Rostand, Jean. "La Conception de l'homme selon Helvétius et selon Diderot." *Revue d'Histoire des Sciences et de leurs Applications* 4 (1951), 213–22.

Rousseau, G. S., ed. *The Languages of Psyche: Mind and Body in Enlightenment Thought.* Berkeley and Los Angeles: University of California Press, 1990.

Rousseau, Nicolas. *Connaissance et langage chez Condillac.* Geneva: Droz, 1986.

Russell, Bertrand. *Authority and the Individual.* New York: Simon and Schuster, 1949.

Sacks, Oliver W. *The Man Who Mistook His Wife for a Hat and Other Clinical Tales.* New York: Harper and Row, 1970.

Saint-Amand, Pierre. "Original Vengeance: Politics, Anthropology, and the French Enlightenment." *Eighteenth-Century Studies* 26 (1993), 399–417.

———. *Séduire, ou La Passion des Lumières.* Paris: Méridiens Klincksieck, 1987.

Saisselin, Rémy G. *Taste in Eighteenth-Century France.* Syracuse: Syracuse University Press, 1965.

Sayous, A. *Le Dix-Huitième Siècle à l'étranger: Histoire de la littérature française dans les divers pays de l'Europe depuis la mort de Louis XIV jusqu'à la Révolution française.* Vol. I. Paris: Amyot, 1861.

Scarry, Elaine. *The Body in Pain: The Making and Unmaking of the World.* New York: Oxford University Press, 1985.

———, ed. *Literature and the Body: Essays on Populations and Persons.* Baltimore: Johns Hopkins University Press, 1988.

Scholes, Robert E., and Robert Kellogg. *The Nature of Narrative.* New York: Oxford University Press, 1966.

Schøsler, Jørn. *La Bibliothèque raisonnée (1728–1753): Les Réactions d'un périodique français à la philosophie de Locke au XVIIIe siècle.* Odense: Odense University Press, 1985.

Searle, John R. *The Rediscovery of the Mind.* Cambridge, Mass.: MIT Press, 1992.

Sennett, Richard. *The Fall of Public Man.* New York: Vintage, 1978.

Serres, Michel. *Les Cinq sens.* Paris: Grasset, 1985.

Sgard, Jean, ed. *Condillac et les problèmes du langage.* Geneva: Slatkine, 1982.

———. *Corpus Condillac, 1714–1780.* Geneva: Slatkine, 1981.

Shklovsky, Victor, "Art as Technique." In *Russian Formalist Criticism: Four Essays.* Trans. and ed. Lee T. Lemon and Marion J. Reis. Lincoln: University of Nebraska Press, 1965.

Showalter, English, Jr. "Authorial Self-Consciousness in the Familiar Letter: The Case of Madame de Graffigny." *Yale French Studies* 71 (1986), 113–130.

———. "The Beginnings of Madame de Graffigny's Literary Career: A Study in the Social History of Literature." In *Essays on the Age of Enlightenment in Honor of Ira O. Wade.* Ed. Jean Macary. Geneva: Droz, 1977, pp. 293–304.

———. "An Eighteenth-Century Best-Seller: *Les Lettres Péruviennes.*" Diss. Yale University, 1964.

————. *The Evolution of the French Novel: 1641–1782.* Princeton: Princeton University Press, 1972.

————. *"Les Lettres d'une Péruvienne:* Composition, Publication, Suites." *Archives et Bibliothèques de Belgique* 54 (1983), 14–28.

————. "A Woman of Letters in the French Enlightenment: Madame de Graffigny." *British Journal for Eighteenth-Century Studies* 1 (1978), 89–104.

Singer, Alan. *The Subject as Action: Transformation and Totality in Narrative Aesthetics.* Ann Arbor: University of Michigan Press, 1993.

Smith, Colin. "Destutt de Tracy and the Bankruptcy of Sensationalism." In *Balzac and the Nineteenth Century: Studies in French Literature Presented to Herbert J. Hunt by His Pupils, Colleagues, and Friends.* Ed. D. G. Charlton et al. Leicester: Leicester University Press, 1972, pp. 195–207.

Smith, D. W. *Helvétius: A Study in Persecution.* 1965; rpt. Westport, Conn.: Greenwood Press, 1982.

Spencer, Samia I., ed. *French Women and the Age of Enlightenment.* Bloomington: Indiana University Press, 1984.

Stafford, Barbara Maria. *Body Criticism: Imagining the Unseen in Enlightenment Art and Medicine.* Cambridge, Mass.: MIT Press, 1991.

Stallybrass, Peter, and Allon White. *The Politics and Poetics of Transgression.* Ithaca: Cornell University Press, 1986.

Starobinski, Jean. *Jean-Jacques Rousseau: La Transparence et l'obstacle.* 1957; rpt. Paris: Gallimard, 1976.

Staum, Martin S. "Analysis of Ideas in the French National Institute (1795–1803)." *Canadian Journal of History* 26 (1991), 393-413.

————. *Cabanis: Enlightenment and Medical Philosophy in the French Revolution.* Princeton: Princeton University Press, 1980.

————. "The Legacy of Condillac in the Revolutionary Era." *Proceedings of the Annual Meeting of the Western Society for French History* 18 (1991), 207–17.

Stephanson, Raymond. "Richardson's 'Nerves': The Physiology of Sensibility in *Clarissa." Journal of the History of Ideas* 49 (1988), 267–85.

Taine, Hippolyte. *Les Philosophes français du XIXe siècle.* 2d ed. Paris: Hachette, 1860.

Temkin, Owsei. "Materialism in French and German Physiology of the Early Nineteenth Century." *Bulletin of the History of Medicine* 20 (1946), 322–27.

Terrasse, Jean, ed. *Rousseau et l'éducation: Etudes sur l' "Emile."* Sherbrooke, Quebec: Naaman, 1984.

Teysseire, Daniel. "Lien social et ordre politique chez Cabanis." *Studies on Voltaire and the Eighteenth Century* 267 (1989), 353–400.

Thomson, Ann. *"L'Homme-machine,* mythe ou métaphore?" *Dix-Huitième Siècle* 20 (1988), 367–76.

————. *Materialism and Society in the Mid-Eighteenth Century: La Mettrie's "Discours Préliminaire."* Geneva: Droz, 1981.

Todd, Janet. *Women's Friendship in Literature.* New York: Columbia University Press, 1980.

Trahard, Pierre. *Les Maîtres de la sensibilité française au XVIIIe siècle (1715–1789)*. 4 vols. Paris: Boivin, 1931–33.

Undank, Jack. "A Fly on His Hand: Interpreting Rousseau's 'Useless' Sensations." *French Review* 62 (1988), 259–74.

Undank, Jack, and Herbert Josephs, eds. *Diderot: Digression and Dispersion*. Lexington, Ky.: French Forum, 1984.

Van Sant, Ann Jessie. *Eighteenth-Century Sensibility and the Novel: The Senses in Social Context*. Cambridge: Cambridge University Press, 1993.

Vartanian, Aram. *Diderot and Descartes: A Study of Scientific Naturalism in the Enlightenment*. Princeton: Princeton University Press, 1953.

————. "Diderot, or, The Dualist in Spite of Himself." In *Diderot: Digression and Dispersion*. Ed. Jack Undank and Herbert Josephs. Lexington, Ky.: French Forum, 1984, pp. 250–68.

————. "Diderot's Rhetoric of Paradox, or, The Conscious Automaton Observed." *Eighteenth-Century Studies* 14 (1981), 379–405.

————. "*Jacques le fataliste*: A Journey into the Ramifications of a Dilemma." In *Essays on Diderot and the Enlightenment in Honor of Otis Fellows*. Geneva: Droz, 1974, pp. 325–47.

————. *La Mettrie's "L'Homme machine": A Study in the Origins of an Idea*. Princeton: Princeton University Press, 1960.

————. "Quelques réflexions sur le concept d'âme dans la littérature clandestine." In *Le Matérialisme du XVIIIe siècle et la littérature clandestine*. Ed. Olivier Bloch. Paris: Vrin, 1982, pp. 149–65.

Wade, Ira O. *The Intellectual Origins of the French Enlightenment*. Princeton: Princeton University Press, 1971.

————. *The Structure and Form of the French Enlightenment*. 2 vols. Princeton: Princeton University Press, 1977.

Wellman, Kathleen. "Dilemma and Opportunity: The Physiology of the Soul." *Studies in Eighteenth-Century Culture* 22 (1992), 301–16.

————. *La Mettrie: Medicine, Philosophy, and Enlightenment*. Durham: Duke University Press, 1992.

Wells, G. A. "Condillac, Rousseau and Herder on the Origin of Language." *Studies on Voltaire and the Eighteenth Century* 230 (1985), 233–46.

Werner, Stephen. "Indifferent Irony: A Reading of Sade's *Justine*." *Studies on Voltaire and the Eighteenth Century* 310 (1993), 1309–12.

Whatley, Janet. "The Eighteenth-Century Canon: Works Lost and Found." *French Review* 61 (1988), 414–20.

Wojciechowska, Wanda. "Le Sensualisme de Condillac." *Revue Philosophique de la France et de l'Étranger* 93, no. 3 (1968), 297–320.

Woolf, Virginia. *To the Lighthouse*. New York: Modern Library, 1937.

Yolton, John W. *Locke and French Materialism*. Oxford: Oxford University Press, 1991.

Index

Dieckmann, Herbert, 24 n. 25, 59 n. 67
diet, 235
differences, individual, 186, 244. *See also* diversity
differentiation, 118–20, 155
of sensations, 113, 131–32, 147, 154, 237
Directory, the, 226 n. 2
discontinuity, 116, 120, 123, 154, 235, 247
disorder, 247–48
dissimulation, 151, 157, 169, 189
diversity
of cultural practices, 95, 134
of experience, 133, 166, 175, 177, 228
of humanity, 213
of languages, 106
of minds, 175, 177–78
of physical world, 213, 244
of points of view, 99, 177, 244
of sensations, 177
divine right, 205, 208
dogmatism, 108
double-entendre, 157
dualism, 3, 198
duality of human nature, 119, 124, 248
Du Bellay, Joachim, 105
Dubos, Jean–Baptiste, abbé, 25, 106, 108, 133 n. 16
Duchesneau, François, 14–15 n. 3, 59 n. 66, 208 n. 16
duty, 8, 97

eclecticism, 244
economy
of desire, 148, 158–59, 162
of fibers, 68
of our being, 62, 64, 66–73, 76, 80, 82
education, 8, 57, 64, 84 n. 4, 88–89, 99, 101, 110–11, 113, 117, 127, 137–39, 141–42, 145, 147, 149, 149 n. 4, 150–51, 153–56, 158, 159 n. 18, 173–95, 203, 214, 221, 227, 235–36, 245, 247–48
effort, 233 n. 11, 238, 241, 243
egalitarianism, 111, 175–76, 213
egocentrism, 109, 113–14, 128, 132, 141, 180
empire or dominion, 154, 157, 159, 162
Empire, the, 226 n. 1
empiricism, 19, 34 n. 43, 58–59, 59 nn. 65 and 67, 91 n. 16, 105–6, 107 n. 8, 108,

108 n. 10, 124, 136, 190 n. 17, 230, 245, 247
Encyclopédie, 25, 106, 156, 180 n. 7, 207 n. 13, 212 n. 25, 225
Engels, Friedrich, 92 n. 17
England, 92 n. 17, 106, 245–46
enlightenment, 48, 56, 58, 84, 89, 96, 101, 110, 112, 123, 130, 132–33, 137, 140, 152, 159, 163, 178–79, 181–82, 201, 219, 222
Enlightenment, the, 3–5, 7–10, 14, 25, 35, 50, 57, 59, 97, 99, 105, 107, 110, 113–14, 119–22, 124, 129, 133–34, 137, 141, 148 n. 1, 152, 155, 159, 161, 168–70, 173, 195, 210, 222–23, 225, 227, 235, 245
enslavement, 118, 136, 147, 183, 185, 188, 191, 218
environment, 109, 115, 128, 131, 138, 142–43, 151, 155, 175, 215, 235, 248
as a check on reality, 50
dependence on, 110, 112, 117, 129, 132, 134, 136, 188, 218, 244
for language learning, 43, 47
learning, 84, 187
environmental
approach to education, 88
behaviorism, 84 n. 4, 100 n. 21, 247
environmentalism, 247
envy, 90
epistemology, 3, 6, 6 n. 12, 7–8, 42–43, 58, 61, 63, 65, 72, 82–84, 87 nn. 12 and 14, 88–89, 97, 101, 107, 113, 115, 119–20, 122, 124, 127, 131 n. 10, 135 n. 19, 148 n. 1, 153, 198–99, 201, 203–5, 208–9, 230, 239
equality, 89, 166 n. 25, 175, 222
eroticism, 116, 132, 141, 149 n. 4, 157, 161, 179
error(s), 3, 26–27, 29, 31, 34–35, 41, 48, 55–56, 98, 101, 138, 178, 200, 203, 206, 225–26, 237, 246
esprit, 166
essence of things, our ignorance of the, 203–4
euphemism, 132
evidence, 136, 201, 216
évidence, 32, 40, 232
evil, 8, 25–26, 41, 45–46, 97, 100, 168–70, 193–94, 203, 206, 220
problem of, 7–8, 126, 129, 141

evolution, evolutionism, 78 n. 15, 219 n. 35
existence, 29, 65, 67, 71, 86, 88, 100, 109,
    112–15, 119–20, 128, 138, 143, 151,
    153, 161, 163, 167, 170, 200–204, 209,
    211, 214, 228–29, 233–34, 236,
    239–40, 244, 249
exoticism, 7, 110, 126, 127 n. 5, 133
experience, 1–2, 2 n. 2, 4, 6 nn. 10 and 12,
    8–9, 14, 14 n. 2, 15 n. 3, 17–19, 22–25,
    25 n. 29, 26–27, 27 n. 31, 29–34, 36–37,
    38 n. 47, 39–46, 46 n. 56, 47–50, 53,
    57–59, 67, 70–71, 75, 82, 88, 97, 106,
    114–18, 120, 122–24, 129–30, 133–34,
    136–38, 146, 148–50, 152, 157, 159,
    161, 163, 166, 169–70, 176–77, 185,
    200–201, 203, 207, 218, 221, 227,
    229–32, 239, 242, 244, 246–47, 249–50
  beginning of, 16
  inner, 230, 233, 241–42
  novel of, 122 n. 23
  sensory, 18 n. 12, 23, 33 n. 38, 34–36, 38
    n. 47, 40, 42, 44–46, 48, 50, 53, 57–59,
    73, 82, 99, 105, 146, 154, 167 n. 27, 168,
    176, 203, 207
experimentation, 49–50, 118, 242
extension, 209–10
exteriority, 21 n. 18
external world, 21–22, 29, 80, 107 n. 5, 114,
    135, 140, 165, 185–86, 206, 215, 229,
    233, 243 n. 18, 247, 250

fables, as forms of instruction, 47
facts, 26–27, 32, 67, 72–73, 82, 228–29,
    241–42
  first, 229
  physical, 229, 232
faculties, 24–25, 30, 32–33, 36, 49–50, 62,
    65–66, 70, 74–75, 83, 85–86, 107, 124,
    141, 164, 175, 216, 218–20, 229–30,
    233, 235–36, 239, 241–43, 249. See also
    mind, the; soul, the
  of the mind, 17, 17 n. 11, 18 n. 12, 21 n.
    19, 23, 37, 52, 58, 74–75, 82, 84, 87,
    222, 246
faith, 15 n. 4
fanaticism, 97, 201
fatalism, 4, 83, 100, 221–22, 248
fatality, 221
fear, 29, 91, 97, 110, 112–13, 118, 128,
    138–39, 143, 168, 182, 192

feeling(s), 7–8, 29–30 n. 35, 58, 62, 67,
    69–71, 74, 77, 85–90, 92, 99, 106,
    114–16, 128, 130–31, 133 n. 16,
    137–39, 150, 154, 160, 165, 167, 175,
    179, 184–87, 191–92, 194, 200, 206,
    208–10, 216–17, 220, 229, 237,
    239–40, 243, 249–50
  faculty of, 65, 67, 71–72, 74, 88–90, 204,
    216, 219, 228
female qualities, imagined, 110, 112
fiber(s), 63, 65, 67–73, 76, 79, 120, 211, 247
  nerve, 27 n. 31, 115, 202, 208
  vibration of, 70–71, 74, 78, 118, 157, 200,
    250
fiction, 29, 109, 117, 122, 128, 183
Figlio, Karl M., 205 n. 8
figurative language, 45–47, 165
finger(s), for counting, 31–32, 53–54
flattery, 99
fluids, 208, 211
  nervous, 73
Folkierski, Wladyslaw, 106 n. 2
Foucault, Michel, 134, 134 n. 18
Fourier, F. M. Charles, 92 n. 17
France, the French, 5, 5 n. 5, 7, 15, 57, 96,
    100, 105–6, 120, 126, 130, 136, 139,
    142–43, 145, 198 n. 1, 222, 226, 235,
    245–46. See also Enlightenment, the
freedom, 65–66, 73–75, 118, 135–36, 143,
    147, 152, 182–90, 192–93, 215,
    218–22, 243–45
Freud, Sigmund, 119
friendship, 90–91, 142–44
Fritzsche, Oskar William, 174 n. 3
Furetière, Antoine, 156

Garat, Joseph, 228
Gardner, Elizabeth J., 110 n. 14, 111 n. 15
Gassendi, Pierre Gassend, abbé (known as),
    87
gender, 7, 110
  bias, 111, 141
  studies, 248
general, the, 3, 26, 106, 113, 121, 227, 230,
    232–33
generations, 212
genius, 87, 99, 166, 176–77, 179, 182
genre, 126, 145, 145 n. 32, 247
Gérando, Joseph-Marie de, 228, 239 n. 14
germ(s), 75–76, 81

self-
  absorption, 99
  actualization, 138
  awareness, 109, 123, 161
  consciousness, 232–33
  control, 151, 218
  discovery, 109
  gratification, 166
  interest, 3, 5, 8, 19, 46, 84, 91–97, 99, 113, 166, 181
  knowledge, 243
  love, 90–92
  preservation, 3, 71, 93, 109
  sufficiency, 190–91
selfhood, 233, 236
selfishness, 97
sensation(s), 1–2, 2 n. 2, 3, 7–9, 14–15 n. 3, 16–19, 22, 26–29, 30 n. 35, 31–33, 36, 38 n. 47, 40, 42–45, 48, 52–54, 58–59, 62, 65–69, 71–78, 83, 86, 88–90, 97–98, 106 n. 5, 109, 113–24, 128, 135–36, 139, 141, 146, 149, 151, 153–56, 163–64, 166, 168–69, 175–77, 183–85, 187, 189–90, 192–94, 198–203, 205–6, 208–9, 211–12, 215–20, 226–30, 232–34, 237–43, 246–47, 250
  transformed, 21 n. 19, 24 n. 26, 52, 239, 239 n. 14, 243 n. 18
sensationalism, 1 n. 1, 84 n. 4, 110 n. 14, 173 n. 1, 214 n. 27, 242 n. 17
sensationism, 1–9, 13, 15, 18–19, 24, 32 n. 37, 37–38 n. 47, 54, 62, 72, 77, 80, 82–84, 85 n. 5, 87–88, 101, 109–10, 113–14, 125 n. 1, 126–28, 136–38, 145, 148, 151–54, 157–58, 164 n. 23, 165–66, 168–69, 173–77, 182–84, 191, 194, 197–202, 205–9, 211–13, 215, 219, 223, 225–30, 235, 240–49
  logical, 4, 14, 59
  politics of, 4, 171–250
sensationist
  aesthetics, 7, 105–70, 169, 247
  approach, 42, 64, 67, 74, 96, 178, 188, 232, 237
  arguments or logic, 1, 79, 94, 149, 165, 183–84, 199, 202, 245
  method, 35, 124, 246. *See also* method
  perspective or viewpoint, 32, 34, 34 n. 40, 58, 61, 64, 77, 78 n. 16, 100, 123, 146, 157, 175, 244

philosophy, 107
position or view(s), 8, 69, 72, 75, 78, 81, 88, 112, 120, 152, 182, 193–94, 199, 204–5, 211, 226, 240
precepts or ideas, 2 n. 2, 101
principle(s), 55, 84, 87 n. 14, 147, 150, 174–75, 181, 194, 197, 209, 222, 239, 245
project, 163
psychology, 111, 113, 116 n. 17, 117, 121, 136–37, 141, 145, 166 n. 24, 182
refrain, 2 n. 2, 50, 74, 199, 228
tendency, 219
tenet(s), 9, 78, 87, 209, 223, 246
theory, 2, 5, 7–8, 19, 47, 88, 118, 193–94, 206, 249
vulgate, 149 n. 4
sensationist(s), 2 n. 2, 3–6, 8, 15, 26, 38, 42, 46, 50, 72, 74, 77, 80, 83–84, 86, 97, 108, 115–17, 119, 121, 124, 127, 147, 149, 151–52, 159, 164–66, 168, 170, 173, 175–76, 186, 194, 198, 198 n. 1, 200–206, 208, 210–12, 214–20, 222–23, 226 n. 2, 227, 229–36, 238, 240–42, 244, 246–50
sensationniste, 1 n. 1
sense
  of hearing, 22, 44
  organs, 19 n. 13, 20, 231, 240–41
  of smell, 62, 66
  of touch, 21–22, 106–7, 107 n. 5, 109, 114, 128, 243 n. 18
senses, the, 2, 8, 15–16, 18–20, 21 n. 19, 22, 26, 30–32, 37, 39, 42–45, 47–53, 58, 62, 64–65, 68, 70, 74–75, 77–89, 106–8, 122, 127–29, 132, 136, 144, 146, 168–69, 175–76, 179, 184, 186, 189–91, 199–200, 202–4, 206–7, 209, 218, 228, 231, 240, 246, 248–49
  moving away from, 23. *See also* abstraction
sensibility, 3, 7–9, 31, 47, 65, 67, 72, 74–75, 77 n. 14, 79–81, 88–90, 107 n. 5, 109–10, 112, 115, 118, 126, 128–30, 137–38, 141–43, 146–47, 150–52, 157–58, 160, 163, 165, 167–70, 191, 200, 204, 207, 210–11, 216–17, 219–20, 222, 228–29, 234, 238–40, 242–44, 247–50
  physical, 4–5, 83–86, 89–95, 97, 99–101, 113, 174–75, 177–78, 182, 202, 219, 240